GCSE
ECONOMICS

Keith West
Matthew Humberstone School
Cleethorpes

EDUCATIONAL

First published 1985
Second edition 1987
Revised 1990
Reprinted 1992, 1993

Text: © Keith West 1984
Design and illustrations: © BPP (Letts Educational) Ltd 1984

Letts Educational
Aldine House
Aldine Place
London W12 8AW

British Library Cataloguing in Publication Data
A CIP record for this book is available from the British Library.

ISBN 1 85758 304 3

Acknowledgements

The author and publishers are grateful to the following organizations for permission to reprint material to which they hold copyright:

BBC p.181; *The Financial Times* p.171; HMSO p.180; *The Independent* p.181; Pedigree Petfoods p.183; *The Star,* Sheffield pp.192–4; *Walton and Weybridge Informer* p.182.
  Also to be thanked are the following Examination Groups for their permission to use examination questions:
London East Anglian Group
Midland Examining Group
Northern Examining Association
Northern Ireland Schools Examinations Council
Scottish Examination Board
Southern Examining Group

Printed in Great Britain by Staples Printers St Albans Ltd

Letts Educational is the trading name of BPP (Letts Educational) Ltd

PREFACE

This book has been written primarily to prepare candidates for GCSE Economics. It should also prove useful as a preparation for AS-level Economics, first year A-level Economics where students have no economics background, and certain business studies and professional examinations which contain economics content.

As an experienced teacher, moderator and examiner at 16+ I have prepared the units to show students the standards and skills required at this level. In addition, specialist advice has been sought from three additional economics teachers in different parts of Britain.

The book is made up of units which cover the main topics studied at GCSE, and units which offer advice about the nature of the examination e.g. the *types* of examination question and compulsory *coursework*. As a *revision guide* the book contains details of the *skills needed* for answering examination questions well, and *actual* GCSE examination questions with suggested answers.

An important feature of the book is the *summaries*. Each unit ends with a summary which outlines the key ideas, trends and issues in the topic covered.

I wish to express my special thanks to David Sowden for his work in the first book, suggested amendments to the second and the excellent summaries in Units 1–10. Roger Mallows has also contributed to this book, through the provision of stimulating data response material, recommended improvements and the perceptive summaries of Units 11–20. In addition, the book received a thorough vetting at the hands of Bill McFarlane, my Scottish consultant, who has improved the final version through his demanding questioning and helpful suggestions. The coursework section owes much to Gerry Gorman, whose ideas and approach I have largely utilized.

Less significant but nevertheless useful assistance has been provided by my eldest son, Malcolm (as a student user), my daughter, Nyree (as an artist), and two of my students, Andrew Jackson and Philip Rogers, who obtained updated information for me via Prestel.

However, most of all I am very grateful to my wife, Chris, for her interest, consideration and accurate typing to deadlines.

The shortcomings, which I expect fellow teachers (and some students) to identify, are now entirely my own.

K. C. West

CONTENTS

INTRODUCTION

Organization of the book

This book has been designed for GCSE and SCE level candidates. It is not a substitute for a textbook, but a comprehensive revision guide, based on examination experience. Each part in the book has a clear and specific function. The most important part is **Core Units** 1–20.

The main syllabus topics, which are given for each board in the syllabus analysis on pp. xii–xiv form chapters called **'Units'**. Within each unit there is a subdivision into **Sections** representing the most important areas of knowledge and understanding.

Throughout each unit **Mnemonics** are used to aid memory. For instance in Unit 5, external economies of scale can be remembered by **'LICE'** which stands for **L**abour, **I**nformation, **C**oncentration and **E**ducation.

Within each section the main points are in **bold type** for emphasis. This is done particularly where there is an introduction, e.g. 5.1, in which the key points of 'productive', 'paid employment' and 'indirect' have been emphasized in this way. At the end of each unit, there is a **summary** of the main points which have been covered.

THE STRUCTURED APPROACH

Research on cognition by Reed shows that information is better recalled if it is presented in an **organizational framework**. A framework makes retrieval systematic.

This book contains 20 **Core Units** (Units 1–20), containing the necessary information relating to GCSE Economics. Unit 22, **Sample questions and answers**, gives examples of recent examination-board questions for students to attempt and provides guidelines to the answers.

In the **Core Units 1–20**, which are the bulk of the book, the **same structure** is repeated across units. This shows you the way in which information needs to be stored and retrieved. The different details in each unit are designed to make the material as different as possible. This should encourage separate stores of information to be developed.

Evidence shows that pupils learn hierarchical information quickly and have considerable difficulty in learning the same information when it is presented in a random manner. Thus a **hierarchical** structure, as in this book, enables the search of memory to be structured and material to be recalled more efficiently.

The study of how people retrieve information reveals that they are likely to group from **two to five items together**. Groups of this size form a hierarchy. This has been borne in mind in the organization of material under headings.

There are usually three or four subheadings within each section. Most of the mnemonics feature four or five ideas within a subheading. There are often several key words, which are emphasized, within a mnemonic.

For instance, **Unit 5.6 Large-scale production** is structured as follows:

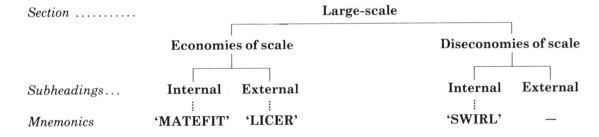

Section	Large-scale			
	Economies of scale		Diseconomies of scale	
Subheadings...	Internal	External	Internal	External
Mnemonics	'MATEFIT'	'LICER'	'SWIRL'	—

Learning and remembering

When we **learn** we use our senses in the following proportions:

75% sight
13% hearing } relevant to this subject

6% touch
3% smell } irrelevant to this subject
3% taste

Thus, seeing the printed page and hearing about the subject are vitally important.

It is also reckoned, by the British Audio-Visual Association, that we **remember**—

80% of what we say
50% of what we see and hear
30% of what we see
20% of what we hear
10% of what we read

Clearly, reading information **on its own** is a poor way to remember. However, combined with **saying** the information, it is very effective.

You should try to **read** and **say aloud** what you revise. You therefore need to study in isolation. You are likely to distract or annoy other people if you study with them around. Also, by being on your own, you are less likely to be interrupted, and more likely to learn effectively.

Revision

Revision is an important part of effective studying. As GCSE examinations are the culmination of two years' school work there is plenty of information which needs to be learnt. This makes thorough and well-organized revision most important. I would recommend a **minimum of 15 hours** revision in the period before your Economics examination. This should enable you to cover sufficient syllabus topics to give you a fair choice of questions on the normal essay-dominated examination paper.

A **programme** of revision is thus clearly needed. It is usually advisable to have a schedule of revision covering **all** of your examinations. Once you know the dates of your examinations you should work out when you are going to revise for each one, bearing in mind the **quantity of revision** needed. For some subjects, such as English Language, a lot of revision is not required, whilst for others, such as Economics, it is! You should have a rough idea of how much revision is needed for each subject and the total amount of time available for revision. Build a couple of blank days into your schedule for emergencies. By **Easter** you should have all this information and be able to devise your programme of revision.

The length of your revision programme depends partly on when your examinations are timetabled. You should start at least two weeks before your first examination. If most of your exams are bunched together at the start of the examination period then more time (say three weeks) will be needed for revision before the start. In general, the period of **intensive** revision and examinations will be about one **month**.

You need to ask yourself 'Is it **worth** devoting one month out of a lifetime to revision in order to obtain "good" exam results?' If you are not sure that the answer is **'Yes'** then bear in mind the following:

1 A month is just $\frac{1}{900}$th of a lifetime. It is not much to give up, as there is a lot at stake.
2 You will undoubtedly gain higher grades by revising than by not revising and thus better qualifications. In the long run those with better qualifications earn more and have a more satisfying life!
3 You will gain respect from friends and teachers.
4 You may well prove certain teachers wrong—there's an incentive!
5 You will prove to yourself that you have self-discipline, i.e. you can make sacrifices.
6 A proper revision schedule allows some relaxation anyway.

The **order** in which you revise is important. Try to arrange your revision schedule so that you revise for a subject in the last few days before you take that examination. If that is not possible, and you have two subjects being examined on the same day, then make your least familiar subject the last one you revise. Similarly, the order in which you revise the topics of a subject is important. Topics with which you are least familiar/happy should be revised towards the end of your schedule and quickly reviewed right at the end of your revision programme.

The **use** made of revision time is important. It is not a case of just sitting down and reading a book for two hours! Your revision timetable needs structuring. Effective revision requires:

Organization and planning

We have already outlined the pre-study planning needed and the priorities which need to be set. In addition, you should plan how to use your revision time. Psychologists reckon that **30-minute revision**, followed by a **10-minute break**, up to a maximum of **2 hours at a time**, is the most effective. This should be done in a quiet place at home or school (e.g. library).

Maintaining motivation

A revision schedule should have clear **objectives** and immediate built-in **rewards**, as well as the long-term prospects of better examination results. For instance, you should set yourself a target, e.g. learn Unit 5 in a two-hour revision session and get a good mark in its sample GCSE question. If this is achieved, reward yourself, e.g. listen to your favourite LP for 20 minutes.

Motivation can be maintained by using techniques to stop mind-wandering. For instance, occasional **physical movement** such as getting up and pacing the room and talking aloud often break the monotony of continued study. Many experts suggest revisions at **different times of day** each day and frequent **change of subject**, as well as targets and rewards to stimulate interest and prevent boredom.

Learning the notes

There are several possible methods of learning which could be employed. There is no one definitive method, but some are more accredited than others. You could:

1 Make notes from a unit and then read and re-read the notes.
2 Learn key words and sentences/definitions off by heart.
3 Read a unit several times and then test yourself by writing out/saying out loud the main points.

Whichever method is used, the memory needs to be trained and you should make the best use of the resources at your disposal. This book should be a most useful resource!

A simple memory-training technique, which has been referred to already, is the **'work-test-rest'** routine. The test element is particularly important because it tells you how effective your revising has been. If, after a period of learning, you can write out the main points from memory accurately (when checked against the book or notes), both immediately and days later, then you have developed an effective technique. Another aid to memory is the **mnemonic**. These have been used extensively in this book as a type of shorthand to help remember several main points.

THE P.Q. 4R METHOD

This study method incorporates many of the general points made above. It was developed by E. L. Thomas and H. A. Robinson in 1972. It has been loosely used by the author in the preparation of this book and can be applied to revising from this book as follows:

P = Preview

You should survey the syllabus analysis on pages xii-xiv to discover which units you need to cover for your examination, because the syllabuses vary between examination boards. Then, in each unit, you should see which topics are covered.

Q = Questions

This method advises asking yourself questions about the sections. This may involve transforming the subheadings into questions. For instance 5.4. What is the Division of labour? What are its advantages/disadvantages?

4R = READ, REFLECT, RECITE, REVIEW

Read

Read through the text answering the questions to yourself as you go along.

Reflect

This means try to understand the text and think of examples (in this book plenty are given). You should also relate the material learned to other knowledge. In each chapter you will find cross references to other units of the book.

Recite

Try to recall what you have read (and spoken—see above, **Learning and remembering**). If you cannot recall the information, re-read the text.

Review

Go through the unit again, after a break. In the review you should recall the main points and answer the questions. At this stage you could answer the units sample GCSE question.

Revision also involves **examination preparation generally**. Probably your teacher will have organized revision tests during the year, a mock examination, and a review of major topics. Although many frown upon 'question spotting', certain topics are fairly predictable and your teacher should have made you wise to them. He/she may even have several **'bankers'** for you to concentrate upon. However, do not rely on just such topics, although obviously devote time to them.

In your revision at school, you will probably have practised writing 'against the clock', i.e. **test essays**. If not, you should do so as part of your revision. This book can help. After learning a unit, you could tackle its GCSE question for half an hour; then read the answer section where the main points which were needed in the answer are outlined. If you are genuinely pleased with the answer which you have written then pass on to another unit. Be particularly careful to 'know' your **examples**. You do not want to have to think them up during the actual examination.

The final general aspect to revision is **coping with stress**. You need to be able to manage stress. For some casual people it is less of a problem. For most students a properly devised revision schedule should help allay stress somewhat. It should **balance study** and **other activities**. Thus, if you divide your daily revision time into four two-hour periods, then leave one of these periods free. This can be used for thorough relaxation, going out, or watching television—i.e. a break from studying. Furthermore, if you are getting behind with a unit you could push over into one of these free periods if it means you take pressure off yourself and become less worried about completing all of the necessary revision. If, generally, you are finding that units are taking longer to revise than expected, adjust your revision programme. In devising a programme of revision, at the start of this section, I suggested allowing a couple of blank days for an emergency—getting behind is one such emergency!

In your periods of relaxation it might occasionally be worth meeting friends who are doing similar revision. Discussion with them can be reassuring and common problems can be examined, even if they are not resolved. Whatever you do, do **not** give up.

To pass examinations you need to be:

1 **Honest**—i.e. don't kid yourself when you sit reading that you are learning.
2 **Realistic**—i.e. don't skimp through a topic in 10 minutes, looking at the headings—and hope to remember it.
3 **Self-disciplined**—i.e. don't shelve your revision work because a friend calls or television looks interesting or you fancy a walk in the sun!

Syllabus analysis

This is difficult with the GCSE examinations because of the differing approaches to syllabus presentation by the Boards. Content topics have been clustered under broad headings and the groupings vary enormously. Where a grouping is based on content mainly, it often corresponds with the layout illustrated in this book.

However, there are many places where a theme or skill is identified as a syllabus sub-heading and sections are taken from various traditional syllabus areas, e.g. London East Anglian Group section 5 is called 'the role of financial institutions and their importance for the economy'. It covers the functions of money (Unit 8 in this book), financial institutions amongst the money and capital markets (Units 10 and 11), and finance for business (Unit 3).

In contrast, the NEA syllabus A is organized around three key decision-making groups within the economy, i.e. households, firms and the public sector. It is thus constructed in an unconventional form.

The approach in this book follows the most likely schemes of work for actual teaching and thus is organized to complement a student's notes.

Another problem for the analysis is that variable amounts of detail are given by the different Boards. This is not surprising given the GCSE accent on skills and concepts, rather than the recall of learned knowledge. Some syllabuses lack specificity, although the Northern Ireland SEC laudably give detailed notes for guidance.

Candidates studying with the Southern Board need to be aware of the options available. Each candidate studies the core and either the Social Economics or the Economic Principles option. There are certain specialist topics within each option, which also gives a different perspective on some of the core content.

A standardized classification has been attempted, but is hampered by the lack of detail in some syllabuses. The assessment objectives are not always specified for the component papers, and in some cases only minimum and maximum percentage values are given.

The Northern Ireland scheme is the only one with differentiated papers. Paper 2 and coursework are compulsory to all candidates with Paper 1 being designed for C–G range candidates and Paper 3 prepared for A–E range candidates.

Analysis Table

	Southern			Northern		London East Anglian	Midland	Northern Ireland	Wales	Scotland
	Core	Social economics	Economic principles	Sylla-bus A	Sylla-bus B					
1 Economic ideas										
Roles	●	●		●						
Concepts	●			●	●	●	●	●	●	●
Economic problem	●			●	●	●	●	●	●	●
2 Economic systems										
Capitalist	●			●		●	●	●	●	
Collectivist	●			●		●	●	●	●	
Mixed	●			●		●	●	●	●	●
Subsistence								●		
3 Business units										
Public and private			●		●	●	●	●	●	●
Public corporations			●		●	●	●	●	●	●
Companies			●			●	●	●	●	●
Partnerships			●			●	●	●	●	●
Sole traders			●			●	●	●	●	●
Cooperatives			●			●	●	●	●	●
Finance			●	●		●	●	●	●	
Shares			●	●		●	●		●	●
4 Demand and supply										
Demand	●			●	●	●	●	●	●	
Supply	●			●	●	●	●	●	●	
Price	●			●	●	●	●	●	●	●
Elasticity	●			●	●	●	●	●	●	
5 Production										
Types	●			●	●	●	●	●	●	●
Factors			●	●	●	●	●	●	●	●
Division of labour	●			●	●	●	●	●	●	●
Costs			●	●	●	●	●	●	●	●
Large scale			●	●	●	●	●	●	●	
Growth of firms			●		●	●	●	●	●	
Small firms			●		●	●	●	●	●	
6 Location of industry										
Factors			●			●	●	●	●	●
Regional problems			●		●	●	●	●	●	●
Regional policies			●		●	●	●	●	●	●
7 Markets										
Introduction	●			●	●		●	●	●	●
Perfect competition	●			●	●		●		●	●
Monopoly	●			●	●		●	●	●	●
Government and monopoly	●			●	●		●	●		
Imperfect competition	●				●				●	
8 Money										
Definition	●			●	●	●	●	●	●	●
Functions	●			●	●	●	●	●	●	●
Qualities	●			●		●	●	●	●	●
History						●				●
Measurement	●		●			●	●		●	
9 Inflation										
Definition	●				●	●	●	●	●	●
Types	●				●	●	●	●	●	●

	Southern			Northern		London East Anglian	Midland	Northern Ireland	Wales	Scotland
	Core	Social economics	Economic principles	Sylla-bus A	Sylla-bus B					
Measurement					●	●	●		●	●
Method of calculation					●		●	●	●	●
Effects	●				●		●	●	●	●
Causes	●				●		●	●	●	●
Control and policies	●				●		●	●	●	●
10 Banking										
Types		●		●		●	●	●	●	●
Commercial banks		●	●	●		●	●	●	●	●
Balance sheet								●		●
Credit creation		●	●	●				●	●	●
Money market			●			●				●
Bank of England		●	●	●		●	●	●	●	●
Monetary control	●		●							●
11 Saving										
Borrowers		●		●		●	●		●	●
Savings institutions		●		●		●	●		●	●
Stock Exchange		●		●		●	●	●	●	●
Personal savings		●		●			●	●	●	
12 Population										
Growth						●	●	●	●	●
Size						●	●	●	●	●
Structure						●	●	●	●	●
Mobility						●	●	●	●	●
World population							●	●		
13 Wages and trade unions										
Means of payment		●		●	●		●	●	●	
Demand for labour				●	●				●	
Supply of labour				●	●					
Wage differentials		●		●	●		●		●	
TU—aims, functions		●				●	●	●	●	●
TU—organization		●		●		●	●	●	●	●
Government		●				●	●	●	●	●
TUC and CBI		●				●	●			●
14 National income										
Circular flow			●	●	●	●	●	●	●	●
Measurement			●	●		●	●	●	●	●
Statistics			●	●	●	●	●	●	●	●
Economic growth			●	●	●	●	●	●	●	●
Wealth distribution				●			●	●		
15 Public finance										
Public expenditure	●			●	●	●	●	●	●	
Taxation—aims	●	●		●	●	●	●	●	●	
Taxation—types	●	●	●	●	●	●	●	●	●	
Taxes	●			●	●	●	●	●	●	
Incidence	●		●	●	●					
Budget and PSBR	●			●	●	●	●		●	
National Debt	●			●	●	●				
16 Unemployment										
Characteristics	●			●	●	●	●	●	●	●
Costs	●			●	●	●	●			●

	Southern			Northern		London East Anglian	Midland	Northern Ireland	Wales	Scotland
	Core	Social economics	Economic principles	Sylla-bus A	Sylla-bus B					
Measurement	●			●	●	●	●	●		●
Types	●			●	●	●	●	●	●	●
Causes	●			●	●	●	●	●	●	●
Policies	●			●	●	●	●	●	●	●
17 Trade										
Advantages	●			●		●	●	●	●	●
UK patterns	●			●		●	●	●	●	●
Terms of Trade								●		
Government control		●		●		●	●	●	●	●
Protection		●		●	●	●	●	●	●	●
Internal organizations	●	●				●		●		
EEC	●	●			●	●		●	●	●
18 Balance of payments										
Accounts	●		●	●	●	●	●	●	●	●
Problems	●		●	●	●	●	●	●	●	●
Policies	●		●	●	●	●	●	●	●	●
Exchange rates	●		●	●	●	●	●	●	●	
IMF			●			●		●		●
19 Government policy										
Objectives	●		●	●	●	●	●	●	●	●
Limitations	●		●	●	●	●	●	●	●	●
Methods	●		●	●	●	●	●	●	●	●
Problems and policies	●		●	●	●	●	●	●	●	●
Local government			●		●	●			●	
20 Consumption and distribution										
Distribution		●				●		●	●	●
Wholesalers		●				●			●	●
Retailers		●				●		●	●	●
Advertising		●					●			●
Marketing		●								●
Consumer protection		●							●	
Credit		●							●	

Assessment patterns and weightings

Southern	**Paper 1**	**Paper 2**		**Paper 3**
Weighting	30%	50%		20%
Marks	40	100		40
Features	Objective test Thirty multiple choice questions	Written paper Two data questions One structured essay from three choices	} Part I	Coursework Two assignments of 750–1000 words
		One data question One structured essay from three choices for your chosen syllabus option	} Part II	
Time	1 hour	2 hours		Submit by 30 April

Skills					*Total*
Knowledge and understanding	19	16		3	38
Application of knowledge	6	11		5	22
Analysis	5	11		6	22
Evaluation and judgement	0	12		6	18

Northern – Syllabus A	**Examination paper**		**Coursework**
Weighting	70%		30%
Marks			40
Features	Section A Thirty short-answer questions Compulsory	Section B Seven structured essays including data Compulsory	One, two or three projects up to 3000 words
Time	2½ hours		

Skills				*Total*
Knowledge	Not specified		0	40 max
Application	Not specified		11.25	60
Analysis	Not specified		11.25	minimum
Judgement	Not specified		7.50	

Northern – Syllabus B	**Paper 1**	**Paper 2**	**Coursework**
Weighting A-G candidates	40%	40%	20%
C-G candidates	80%	N/A	20%
Features	Five compulsory questions each including data	One compulsory data question One essay from a choice of three	Three projects between 500-750 words each
Time	2 hours	1 hour	

Skills				*Total*
Knowledge	30-36		4	34-40
Application	20-22		4	
Analysis	14-16		4	60-66
Judgement	10-12		8	

London East Anglian	**Paper 1**	**Paper 2**
Weighting	75%	25%
Features	Written paper Section A 15% short-answer questions B 20% data questions C 40% choice of three from seven questions	Coursework Three assignments of 1000 words
Time	2½ hours	

Skills				*Total (reweighted)*
Recall and use of knowledge	28	10		40
Application and analysis	19	10		30
Judgement	28	5		30
	—	—		
	75	25		100

Midland	Paper 1	Paper 2	Paper 3	Coursework
Weighting	25%	50%	(25%) *or*	25%
Marks	40	80	100	120
Features	Objective	Written	External enquiry	Coursework
	Forty multiple choice questions	One data economics-comprehension question Two essays from five choices		Three assignments of 1000 words
Time	1 hour	2 hours	—	Submit by 30 April

Skills					Total
Recall and use of knowledge	11.25%	7.50	(9.375)	9.3	28
Explain terms and concepts	6.25	18.75		0	25
Select, analyse, apply	7.50	17.50	(9.375)	0	25
Reasoned judgements	0	6.25	(6.25)	15.7	22
	25%	50%	(25%)	25%	

Northern Ireland	Paper 1	Paper 2	Paper 3	Coursework
Weighting	40%	40%	40%	20%
Marks	40	60	60	20
Features	Short-answer questions	Structured including two data questions	One compulsory data question Two structured questions from choice of four	2000 word (max) report on specified topic
	Compulsory	Compulsory		
Time	1½ hours	2 hours	1½ hours	

Skills					Maximum
Knowledge and understanding	24	8	14	8	30–40
Application, analysis and judgement	16	32	26	12	70–60

Papers 1, 2 and Coursework will be taken by candidates in likely C–G range.
Papers 2, 3 and Coursework will be taken by candidates in likely A–E range.

Wales	Paper 1	Paper 2 (Coursework)
Weighting	80%	20%
Features	Written paper	Internally assessed coursework
	Section	
	A Twelve short-answer questions (24%)	Fieldwork *or* two assignments totalling 1000–3000 words
	B Two data questions (24%)	
	C Two structured essays from choice of six (32%)	
Time	2½ hours	

Skills			Maximum
Knowledge and understanding	34	5	40
Application, analysis and judgement	46	15	Minimum
			60

Scotland (Ordinary grade)

	Paper 1	Paper 2
Weighting	40%	60%
Marks	40	60
Features	Forty multiple choice questions	Three essays
Time	1 hour	1¾ hours

Examination Boards: Addresses

Northern Examining Association

JMB　　　Joint Matriculation Board
　　　　　Devas Street, Manchester M15 6EU

ALSEB　　Associated Lancashire Schools Examining Board
　　　　　12 Harter Street, Manchester M1 6HL

NREB　　Northern Regional Examinations Board
　　　　　Wheatfield Road, Westerhope, Newcastle upon Tyne NE5 5JZ

NWREB　North-West Regional Examinations Board
　　　　　Orbit House, Albert Street, Eccles, Manchester M30 0WL

YHREB　Yorkshire and Humberside Regional Examinations Board
　　　　　Harrogate Office – 31-33 Springfield Avenue, Harrogate HG1 2HW
　　　　　Sheffield Office – Scarsdale House, 136 Derbyshire Lane, Sheffield S8 8SE

Midland Examining Group

Cambridge　University of Cambridge Local Examinations Syndicate
　　　　　Syndicate Buildings, 1 Hills Road, Cambridge CB1 2EU

O & C　　Oxford and Cambridge Schools Examinations Board
　　　　　10 Trumpington Street, Cambridge CB2 1QB, and Elsfield Way, Oxford OX2 8EP

SUJB　　Southern Universities Joint Board for School Examinations
　　　　　Cotham Road, Bristol BS6 6DD

WMEB　West Midlands Examinations Board
　　　　　Norfolk House, Smallbrook Queensway, Birmingham B5 4NJ

EMREB　East Midland Regional Examinations Board
　　　　　Robins Wood House, Robins Wood Road, Aspley, Nottingham NG8 3NR

London East Anglian Group

London　University of London School Examinations Board
　　　　　Stewart House, 32 Russell Square, London WC1B 5DN

LREB　　London Regional Examining Board
　　　　　Lyon House, 104 Wandsworth High Street, London SW18 4LF

EAEB　　East Anglian Examinations Board
　　　　　The Lindens, Lexden Road, Colchester CO3 3RL

Southern Examining Group

AEB　　The Associated Examining Board
　　　　　Stag Hill House, Guildford GU2 5XJ

Oxford　Oxford Delegacy of Local Examinations
　　　　　Ewert Place, Summertown, Oxford OX2 7BZ

SREB　　Southern Regional Examinations Board
　　　　　Eastleigh House, Market Street, Eastleigh, Southampton SO5 4SW

SEREB　South-East Regional Examinations Board
　　　　　Beloe House, 2-10 Mount Ephraim Road, Tunbridge Wells TN1 1EU

SWEB　　South-Western Examinations Board
　　　　　23-29 Marsh Street, Bristol BS1 4BP

Wales

WJEC　　Welsh Joint Education Committee
　　　　　245 Western Avenue, Cardiff CF5 2YX

Northern Ireland

NISEC　Northern Ireland Schools Examinations Council
　　　　　Beechill House, 42 Beechill Road, Belfast BT8 4RS

Scotland

SEB　　Scottish Examination Board
　　　　　Ironmills Road, Dalkeith, Midlothian EH22 1LE

THE GCSE

Changes in the exam system

GCSE was first assessed in 1988. *National Criteria* have been established and published. All syllabuses must conform to them. It was decided that any course in GCSE Economics should have general and specific aims.

GENERAL AIMS

1 To provide students with a sound knowledge of economic principles and elementary economic theory and to develop those economics skills and concepts which will enable them to understand better the world in which they live.
2 To develop an initial and yet critical understanding of the more important economic forces and institutions with which they will come into contact and of the interdependence and dynamics of economic actions.
3 To prepare students to participate more fully in decision-making processes as consumers, producers and citizens.
4 To develop the ability to use language and number accurately and effectively and also to develop diagrammatic and graphical applications, where applicable, to assist in communicating their knowledge and ideas.

To this end it is important to develop an understanding of basic economic principles and of the economic relationships and conflicts which exist in an economy, with particular reference to the United Kingdom.

While a course may be in part at a descriptive level, students should be introduced to those elementary economic concepts and theories which are necessary for the purpose of understanding particular economic problems.

SPECIFIC AIMS

The specific aims of a course are to enable students to:

1 understand the basic economic problem of allocating scarce resources and ways in which it may be resolved;
2 develop a knowledge and understanding of the main aspects of the British economy with reference to individuals, groups and organizations within the local, national and international community;
3 develop an awareness of major issues of economic policy within the United Kingdom;
4 develop an understanding of basic economic terminology and elementary theory and the ability to use the tools of economic analysis and the ability to use and apply them correctly in particular situations;
5 develop a basic economic numeracy and literacy and the ability to handle simple data;
6 develop the ability to identify and discriminate amongst differing sources of information;
7 acquire and develop the ability to distinguish between facts and value judgements in economic issues.

Assessment

ASSESSMENT OBJECTIVES

The National Criteria lay down that the following objectives must be assessed in all syllabuses in Economics.

Candidates will be expected to:

1 demonstrate recall of knowledge in relation to a specified syllabus content;
2 demonstrate an ability to use this knowledge in verbal, numerical, diagrammatic, pictorial and graphical form;

3 demonstrate an ability to explain and apply appropriate terminology, concepts and elementary theories;

4 select, analyse, interpret and apply data;

5 distinguish between evidence and opinion, make reasoned judgements and communicate them in an accurate and logical manner.

These Assessment Objectives are weighted in specific syllabuses differently (see syllabus analysis) but they must conform to two underlying stipulations. The weight given to recall of knowledge and understanding should not exceed 40 per cent of total, whilst the weight attached to application, analysis and judgement should not fall below 60 per cent.

ASSESSMENT TECHNIQUES

Four techniques are recommended for GCSE Economics examinations and all schemes must include a variety of them.

1 **Objective questions.** These have been used for many years now and rarely account for more than 25 per cent of the total mark allocation.

2 **Data response questions.** The National Criteria specify that a minimum of 20 per cent of the assessment must be by this means.

3 **Essays.** These are now to be less open and more structured than at O level.

4 **Coursework projects.** The National Criteria specify that at least 20 per cent of the assessment shall be by coursework, internally assessed. In most schemes of assessment the coursework will take the form of a project. An alternative method is to require up to three (shorter) assignments, based on the same investigatory techniques.

These techniques are illustrated in more detail in Unit 21.

Differentiation has become an important issue with GCSE syllabuses and thus examinations must be able to show the varying achievements of different-ability candidates. All exams need to be able to show what a candidate knows, understands and can do. Thus in most Economics syllabuses projects (or assignments) are required and some exam questions are structured on an incline of difficulty (i.e. the parts of the question get progressively harder).

GRADE DESCRIPTIONS

The National Criteria specify the likely standards of achievement of candidates in certain key grades.

Grade C

Candidates will normally be expected to have shown a higher level of attainment in the areas expected of Grade F candidates and, in addition:

1 an ability to use and comment on information which is presented in non-verbal as well as verbal forms;

2 an ability to select, analyse, interpret and organize more complex information;

3 an ability to evaluate and make reasoned judgements.

Grade F

Candidates will normally be expected to have shown:

1 some ability to recall knowledge in relation to the specific aims and content of the syllabus;

2 some facility with data in its various forms;

3 a familiarity with the most central of the concepts and ideas; an ability to organize data in a rudimentary way and an ability to engage in simple interpretation.

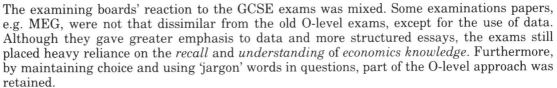# The 1988 GCSE Exams

The examining boards' reaction to the GCSE exams was mixed. Some examinations papers, e.g. MEG, were not that dissimilar from the old O-level exams, except for the use of data. Although they gave greater emphasis to data and more structured essays, the exams still placed heavy reliance on the *recall* and *understanding* of *economics knowledge*. Furthermore, by maintaining choice and using 'jargon' words in questions, part of the O-level approach was retained.

In contrast, some other papers were significantly different from those set in the past. For instance, the NEA syllabus A examinations provided a wide variety of stimulus material which (some) students found interesting, and questions were asked which directly sought *use* and *understanding of the data*. This exam, by offering no choice, was actually fairer to candidates in that all pupils had to answer the same questions. One of the problems of choice is that it is almost impossible to test the same skills with different questions, and inevitably some questions prove harder than others. This introduces an element of luck into a candidates performance because his/her marks partly depends upon what sort of questions are available and which questions he/she chooses.

However, the most popular examinations in terms of exam entries were undoubtedly those of the Southern Examining Group. Its syllabus and exams retained *choice* through a core and two options (Economics Principles or Social Economics) approach. Although many of its questions included data, the emphasis was still on the recall and understanding of knowledge.

As chief examiner for NEA syllabus A, I can report that these examinations did reward *positive achievement* as the GCSE was intended to do. For instance, in the examinations, 95 per cent of the candidates scored at least 40 out of 140 marks. Also over 70 per cent of the candidates obtained more than half marks. Thus the exams did seem to enable candidates to show what they knew, understood and could do.

1 ECONOMICS IDEAS AND CONCEPTS

In this Unit, many economics terms are used. It is assumed that you know what they mean from your study so far.

1.1 Introduction

Economics is about making the best use of 'things'. These things are usually referred to as 'resources' which may be human, natural or man-made. For instance, the **Population** of a region (see Unit 12) is one major resource. These resources are used to make goods and provide services in order to satisfy people's needs and wants. **Thus Economics is about the creation and distribution of wealth**.

Goods and services are produced, distributed and consumed in various ways which differ between **economic systems**. These systems are examined in Unit 2, and the main aspects of **production** are outlined in Unit 5. The specific features of the British mixed economy which students need to know are in **Business units** (Unit 3). GCSE Economics syllabuses concentrate on production and consumption in the main, whereas Commerce examines distribution and the aids to trade in detail. However, the elements of **distribution** which most touch on economics, and are questioned by some boards, are considered in Unit 20.

Resources, goods and services usually have a price which is determined by **market forces** (see Unit 7). The goods which are sold in markets are valued using **money**, which is featured in Unit 8. Changes in the value of money are examined in Unit 9 under the heading of **Inflation**. Some products and services are freely available, e.g. wild raspberries, a walk on the moors. In order to pay for goods and services and to utilize free amenities, decisions have to be made involving utility, choice, income and wealth.

The usefulness and satisfaction gained from a good or service needs to be assessed. This is its utility. The more useful a good is, the higher the **demand** for it is likely to be. The concept of demand is examined in Unit 4. However, we cannot do and have everything we want because we lack time and money. This **scarcity** means that we have to make choices between alternatives. The cost of an alternative which is given up in order to gain the utility of the chosen good is known as **opportunity cost**. These concepts are further considered in Unit 1.3.

1.2 Roles

The use made of resources may vary, from different viewpoints. People have roles in society as consumers, producers and citizens.

All people are **consumers**—they buy goods and services and they make economic decisions. They choose how to allocate their resources of time and money in order to maximize satisfaction. Their decisions affect other people in society.

Most people act as **producers**. They contribute their labour to the production of goods and services when they are employed. A person's capacity to produce depends on his skills, abilities and interests. The income received enables money to be spent on consumption.

All members of society are **citizens**. Although their involvement in political decision-making varies enormously, people have certain economic rights which politicians can influence. For instance, increased taxation reduces an individual's ability to spend his income as he likes. The economic environment is determined by decisions made by elected politicians, e.g. the laws on consumer protection, the spending plans of nationalized industries.

1.3 Underlying economic concepts

These main concepts are summarized below. The 14–16 Economics Education Project identified them as crucial to the understanding of economics at this level. They can be remembered by the word **'SCOCIE'**, based on the initials of the concepts.

Scarcity and choice

Scarcity arises because of *unlimited wants* and *limited resources* with which to make the wanted goods. Wants result from human greed and thus are never totally satisfied. These unlimited wants apply to rich and poor alike. Thus, as **resources are scarce, choices** are continually being made. Consumers choose which wants to satisfy, producers choose which resource combinations to use and citizens choose (indirectly) how they want society to develop. (See Unit 1.4.)

Opportunity cost

When **choices** are made, **alternatives are given up**. Consumers forgo certain wants, producers relinquish other methods of production, and citizens (in a democracy) accept policies with which they disagree. Thus the opportunity cost of spending £3 to watch a football match is anything else that could be done with £3 during the period of time involved. Governments, as well as individuals, are always involved in opportunity-cost decisions because their funds are so extensive and their responsibilities are so wide.

Opportunity cost does not necessarily involve money as the alternatives may be free. For instance, **time** could be spent sunbathing or weeding, neither of which costs money to do. Generally, the opportunity cost of a decision is the alternative wants which remain unsatisfied.

Interdependence

In modern economies people **specialize** in education, training and employment. This enables increased total production and more for each person. This system forces dependence on others, e.g. a school teacher needs to buy the goods from a grocer and the services of a plumber because he cannot provide them for himself. Thus he earns the income to pay for them by his specialization.

International trade (Unit 17) increases interdependence between economies and the **Balance of payments** (Unit 18) indicates the extent of the dependence.

Efficiency

When making decisions consumers, producers and citizens are interested in obtaining the most effective resource utilization to lessen the scarcity problem. However, their interests differ, as a benefit to one group may be a cost to another, e.g. price controls imposed by a government may benefit consumers (through lower prices) but appal producers (who, for example, cannot raise prices to maintain profits).

There are various types of efficiency in Economics. At GCSE we are concerned with **technical efficiency**; which means that organizations should try to produce at their **lowest costs of production** in order to be termed 'efficient'. It is not the same as profit!

Costs and benefits

Most economic decisions are analysed with regard to the costs and benefits of the decision. These costs and benefits can be either **private** or **social**. Private costs and benefits are internal to the firm or individual whilst social costs and benefits are external to the firm/individual and are experienced by society as a whole.

Usually, if the **private benefits** of a possible decision outweigh the **private costs** then the decision goes ahead. For instance, if the forecasted future revenue for a factory exceeds the costs of creation, production, maintenance, etc, then the factory is likely to be built.

Most private decisions have social effects. However, it is very difficult to calculate the **social costs** and **benefits** of a decision because it often involves intangible things such as extra noise, loss of rural amenities and so on. For example, whilst a new factory may be desirable from a private cost benefit point of view, its social costs may be greater than its social benefit. Sometimes, governments intervene for social reasons and make attempts to stop private decisions from going ahead. The frequency and the extent of government interference with private decision making reflects the nature of the economic system (Unit 2).

1.4 The economic problem

In theory the basic economic problem is how to use the available resources in a community to meet the existing needs of society. The **resources** are usually **limited** (or finite). All countries have land, raw materials, people and capital but their quality and quantity vary significantly. For instance, Britain has insufficient land (245,000 sq km) to meet its food needs but a large and enterprising population (56 million). In contrast Tanzania has a plentiful supply of land (945,000 sq km) but a relatively small population (16 million). However, Tanzania's average income per head is £155 and Britain's is £5520.

On the other hand, **needs and wants are infinite** (unlimited). The basic needs of food, clothing and shelter are fulfilled for most people living in the developed countries of the world. With the improvements in the standard of living people's demands and expectations have accelerated, e.g. families want two of most luxuries (colour TV) instead of one, so wants are outstripping needs.

In **underdeveloped** countries basic needs are often rarely met, although occasionally the luxurious wants of the rich few are satisfied, e.g. expensive racehorse purchases of Arab oil sheiks. The GDP per capita of Tanzania indicates that its capacity to produce goods and services is very restricted and thus the average standard of living is low.

As all wants cannot be met, choices have to be made in allocating the resources. In making these choices, decisions about production have to be made:

1 For whom to produce?
2 What to produce?
3 Where to produce?
4 How to produce?

For whom to produce?

This depends on the type of economic system (see Unit 2). The type of economic system used in allocation of resources will be determined by the **political structure** of the society. For instance, the USSR, which is a communist state, has a centrally planned economy in which the government decides the purpose of production. In theory, production is organized for the equal benefit of all society, rather than for a particularly privileged or wealthy group.

What to produce?

The goods and services produced will be dependent on the first decision. For instance, in 1929 in the USSR, Stalin decided that production should be concentrated on **capital** goods to further future economic development and national defence. This meant that the consumer goods section was neglected. Thus the people's immediate needs were partly sacrificed for the overall benefit of society and the indirect benefit of future generations.

In a market economy, those with most income and wealth will usually heavily influence what is produced. For instance, in the USA ostentatious luxury services, such as doggie funerals, abound because the rich are prepared to pay for them. Thus income and prices determine what is produced.

Where to produce?

In theory, goods and services are produced where the **average cost** of production per unit is lowest. The factors influencing location are outlined in Unit 6. In a command economy the State dictates where goods are made and what services are provided. However, in a mixed economy, the 'best' location is not always chosen, because of government policies, government regulations and inefficient decisions made by firms.

How to produce?

The factors of production need to be combined in the most **efficient** way to produce lowest average cost. The quantities of labour and capital will vary between products, e.g. oil production is capital intensive whereas the postal service is labour intensive. Mechanization will be introduced, in theory, if the average cost of production can be lowered as a result.

In the real world, economic decision-making may mean that some resources are not used, or are underutilized. For instance, the factor labour may be left unemployed in market and mixed economies whereas in a centrally planned economy labour is sometimes employed without regard to its output.

PRODUCTION POSSIBILITIES

The basic concepts (1.3) all feature in the economic problem. The problem of 'what to produce' and also 'how much to produce' can be illustrated through a production possibility curve. This curve, shown in Fig. 1.1, indicates the possible combinations of goods which can be produced if resources are fully utilized.

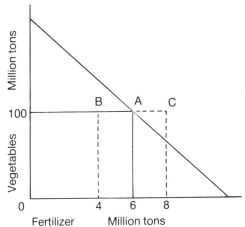

Fig. 1.1 Production possibility curve

In Fig. 1.1 we assume a simple peace-loving economy with no trade and the potential to produce just two goods. Vegetables represent a consumer good and fertilizers represent a capital good.

At point A, 100 million tons of vegetables and 6 million tons of fertilizer are produced. Above A on the curve, more vegetables can be produced but at the expense of fewer fertilizers. Thus the **opportunity cost** of more vegetables is less fertilizer. Conversely, below A on the curve more fertilizer will be combined with fewer vegetables.

However, the combination of 8 million tons of fertilizer and 100 million tons of vegetables (Point C) cannot be reached as there are insufficient resources. This **scarcity** means that a **choice** has to be made between the quantity of each product required. Point C can only be achieved by economic growth, which makes more resources available.

If production is at B on the curve, it indicates **inefficiency**, i.e. the existing resources are not being fully utilized. Fewer fertilizers (4 million tons) are being produced at B than at A, although the volume of vegetables is maintained (100 million tons).

1.5 Summary

Economics is concerned with the creation and distribution of wealth in which people have roles as both producers and consumers. As resources are scarce and our wants are unlimited choices have to be made. The alternatives forgone in these choices are known as opportunity costs. In order to make the most efficient use of scarce resources various production decisions have to be made, such as what, where, how and for whom to produce.

In solving these problems specialization and exchange by both individuals and countries are involved. Effective resource utilization means interdependence and shows efficiency.

2 ECONOMIC SYSTEMS

2.1 Introduction

Economic systems are divided into three main types—capitalist, collective and mixed. A fourth category, subsistence, which does not apply in the modern world, is also included. In addition the term **'black economy'** has been developed for illegal activity in both collectivist and mixed economies. This **unofficial trading** occurs in order to satisfy the consumer and the producer and avoid payment to the government. It takes the form of:

1 **Payments in kind**—one man mends another's plumbing leak in return for having his lawnmower repaired. Neither man records the income (and this avoids paying VAT if they are self-employed).
2 **'Barrow jobs'**—these are jobs done at cheap prices with no documents involved so that expenditure tax (VAT) is not declared and the income is not officially recorded. This saves the producer paying extra income tax. A good example is hairdressing. It has been estimated that the value of the 'black economy' in Britain is £15 billion per year.

The main types of economic system are differentiated by **who allocates** the resources (see Unit 1.4). In the capitalist system resources are owned by private individuals who decide their usage; whereas in the collective system the resources are commanded by the state. Private individuals and the government control resource use in a mixed economy.

The advantages and disadvantages of the **different economic systems** depend to some extent on a person's **viewpoint**. It is worth bearing in mind that political and economic ideas intermingle. For instance, a Socialist would see an uneven distribution of wealth as a disadvantage whereas a Conservative might not. Also, the economic performance of a system may be measured in many ways, i.e. per capita income, volume of output, environmental conservation, the 'quality of life'. The measure chosen will probably indicate a personal value judgement.

2.2 Capitalist

Also known as **Free Market**

Features

In this type of economy there is **no government interference** in economic activity. Resources are allocated on the basis of price. The **private individuals** who own resources sell them to the **highest bidders** who organize production to make **maximum profits**. The goods and services produced are sold to consumers at market prices which are determined by demand and supply.

This is known as the **price mechanism**.

The sellers of successful products make a profit and the buyers are satisfied. Rising demand for a good leads to increased output by the supplier in order to gain higher profits. This increases the demand for land, labour and capital resources. It assumes they are **adaptable** and **perfectly mobile** in their use. Conversely, unprofitable goods are no longer produced, as resources are transferred into profitable ventures. In addition, this system assumes that consumers have **perfect knowledge** of the goods and services on the market. This helps to make the consumer sovereign—**he** decides what is supplied, by his spending.

Advantages

Efficiency. As unsuccessful producers go out of business, it is argued that they must cut every corner and employ every cost-cutting device in order to sell at the lowest possible price. Such cut-throat **competition** keeps producers on their toes and stimulates **innovation** in selling and production techniques. These new ideas make such an economy **dynamic**.

Economic freedom. For the individual this is maximized; he can dispose of his income how he wishes without having to pay taxes to the government. He can sell his labour/skills to any employer and buy whatever goods and services he wants. He is not restricted by government regulations.

Incentives. Employers and employees have the incentive of the possibility of unlimited wealth if they work hard.

Disadvantages

Excessive luxuries. Production may be organized to meet the needs of those with plenty of money, as producers can probably make larger profits from the manufacture of luxury products. As a consequence basic services may be neglected.

Externalities. Pollution, for example, may occur because producers in maximizing profits only consider their own private costs and not the social costs of their activity.

Public goods. These may not be produced. Certain public services such as defence are only effectively provided on a national basis and so without a government they would not be operated. Instead private armies might be developed and political factors would override economic ones. The price mechanism is not well equipped to provide certain goods whose benefits cannot be attributed to individual users.

Wealth distribution. As political power is dependent on income and wealth in this system, an uneven distribution of resources is particularly unfair. The rich have more economic freedom than the poor and more 'votes' (money) in how the system develops.

Social hardship. During times of rapid change, many people will suffer as demand for their labour falls. This may have social and political effects, such as **poverty** and **militancy** respectively. The lack of government involvement means that the relief of poverty is only done voluntarily by charities. Furthermore as there is no government to set basic standards, consumers may be **exploited** through unsafe, unhealthy and misleading trading.

Wasteful competition. This may arise when firms strive to increase sales against their rivals, e.g. the early British railway companies often duplicated services between towns, which wasted resources from the point of view of national interest. Alternatively, monopolies and cartels may replace competition thereby leading to higher prices and poorer-quality goods as well as unethical trading. (See Unit 7.)

Britain during the **Industrial Revolution** was a clear example of these features. Those with wealth and education (which had to be bought), who were the landowners and merchants, developed the nation's resources and utilized new inventions, such as the steam engine. Costs were cut through the development of the factory system and gigantic profits were made. British trade expanded and economic society changed dramatically. However, because there was little government involvement, the consequences for many were undesirable— unemployment, particularly for agricultural labourers, slum housing, lack of sanitation for city dwellers, appalling working conditions and exploitation for many factory labourers. Reformers such as Shaftesbury and Chadwick and voluntary charities tried to fill the gap which was later occupied by the government. The initial government response to stay outside the market place was known as a *laissez-faire* approach. It could be argued that the few profited at the expense of the many.

The **USA** is usually given as an example of modern capitalist society. However, in practice the State and Federal Governments do get involved in providing some basic services. Nevertheless, the extremes of poverty and wealth indicate that there is little redistribution of income by the government. In reality, the USA is a mixed economy with a larger percentage of the private sector than most economies.

2.3 Collectivist

Also known as **Planned**. Sometimes termed **Command** when referring to practice in modern world.

Features

In this economy, **everything** is decided by the **government**. All the basic production questions (see Unit 1) are made by the central government as it **controls the resources** on behalf of the people. The politics of the society have determined its economic system. Communist political theory requires state control.

Thus land is used as the government decides and workers are allocated to jobs most suited to their skills. Labour tends to be very **specialized** and geographically mobile, for instance 60 per cent of all doctors in the USSR are women who have been selected on ability from an early age and not allowed to fritter their skills away. Production schedules are devised in the light of **long-term** plans. These plans are based on the government's assessment of the consumers' needs. There is little scope for individualism. **Prices are fixed** by the government. In theory, profits are returned to the people indirectly through lower prices, better services and investment in social capital. The resource of labour is paid **almost equally**.

Less international trading takes place than in capitalist economies, mainly for political reasons. The command economies prefer to be fairly **self-sufficient**, fearing infiltration and foreign economic pressure. However, in recent years, China has opened up itself to Western goods, e.g. Cherry Valley of Lincolnshire sell Peking ducks in Peking! Similarly, the USSR has become increasingly dependent on USA grain and surplus EEC agricultural produce.

Advantages

Economies of scale. These can be acquired by this organization of production (see Unit 5.6). Wasteful competition will be eliminated and natural monopolies (see Unit 3.2) placed under state control.

Basic needs. For most of the population basic needs can be met, rather than production being geared to the demands of the rich few.

Full utilization of resources is obtained by state control and planning. Full employment is maintained and economic growth can be planned, as resources can be allocated towards capital goods and away from current consumption.

Less inequality in incomes and wealth.

Disadvantages

Lack of personal freedom. People do not get the chance to choose their career but have to accept the job which the government allocates to them.

A large bureaucracy. Many planners and administrators are needed to operate the system. Production and consumption are matched through government planning machinery, but **choice** is limited to the production which the government authorizes. Bureaucrats who are publicly responsible make decisions but they do not take risks as entrepreneurs do. It can be argued that there is **inefficient** use of resources when price does not determine their allocation.

Few incentives. In the production process there are few incentives because people are directed into jobs and prices are fixed. This might mean that production per head is not as high as it might be. In addition, actual demand may be different from planned demand leading to shortages and surpluses. This reduces consumer satisfaction and leads to a 'black economy'.

In practice, the **USSR**, which is usually given as the best example of a planned economy, operates a mixed economy. Ninety-five per cent of activity is state controlled but there is a developing private sector. People are allowed to own their own property, such as holiday homes, but the private ownership of the **means of production**, including land, is forbidden by law. These assets and savings could be passed on. Thus a large gap between rich and poor has developed. The tax rate is not very progressive, so a well-off factory manager earning £400 a month maintains his differential over the factory worker on a minimum wage of £45. The result is that a **privileged élite** of about 250,000, composed of party officials, diplomats, armed services personnel and professional people have a much higher standard of living than the majority of the population. In addition, the élite have many **perks** such as special shops selling cheap imported luxuries, holiday villas, 'the thirteenth month' salary.

2.4 Mixed

As the name suggests this economy is a mixture of capitalist and collectivist.

Features

There is a **public sector** controlled by the government which provides many public and merit goods and a **private sector**, in which individuals risk capital in producing goods and commercial services. In the public sector, **profit** is not the main motive, unlike the **private sector**. The amount of mixture of public and private is determined by the **government**. Thus it varies between countries and within one country over time. For instance in Britain, Labour Party governments prefer a large public sector whereas Conservative Party governments **denationalize** and privatize to reduce the size of the public sector. In a mixed economy the public sector usually provides:

Public goods and services. These give benefits which everybody obtains but which cannot be charged for on an individual basis because of their indivisibility, e.g. national defence. No entrepreneur would provide them because consumers could refuse to pay their share and yet still benefit. Instead the government collects the money through taxes and pays for the services provided.

Merit goods. These are deemed to be worthwhile for everyone by the government and they are 'free' on the basis of need, e.g. education is 'zero priced' in the state sector.

Uneconomic goods and services. The private sector is unwilling to supply these, e.g. coal, railways. When these goods and services make a loss, this is made up by government **subsidies**. In a capitalist system all 'loss-makers' would go out of business to the detriment of many consumers.

Transfer payments. For example, these can be income for certain non-earners, such as grants for students and pensions for widows. The money to pay for these incomes comes out of taxation revenue.

In addition, the government also **regulates the private sector** directly and indirectly, through legislation, fiscal policy and monetary policy. Occasionally there are **mixed enterprises** in a mixed economy. In these enterprises the public and private sectors join together to form companies for trading purposes, e.g. Gas Corporation and Amoco to obtain gas from oilfields.

Both the USA and the USSR appear to be becoming **more mixed** and less rigid. In Britain the non-market sector of the economy accounts for 40 per cent of GDP and 30 per cent of employment.

Advantages

It is usually argued that this system obtains the **best of both worlds**. Necessary public services are provided and most goods are competitively marketed. Producers have the incentive to work and save, even though the government intervenes through fiscal policy to change income levels. Consumers receive basic services, a large measure of economic freedom and plenty of choice. Citizens have some influence over the use of national resources. (See Unit 2.2 advantages of capitalist system, and Unit 2.3 advantages of collectivist system.)

Disadvantages

Again the disadvantages of the capitalist (Unit 2.2) and collectivist systems (Unit 2.3) may be said to apply in certain circumstances. For instance, the removal of the profit motive from some industries, such as steel, which are taken into public ownership, might mean **lower efficiency** and less innovation. However, alternatively, the existence of government control in other industries, e.g. British aircraft production with its Concorde, may lead to **greater innovation** and higher efficiency.

2.5 Subsistence

Features

This old system of economic organization does **not apply** to economic systems today, although some small groups of people and individuals may practise a subsistence 'way of life'. **Before trade** took place, some communities were organized to meet just their **own basic needs**. Each person performed a task, or tasks, of benefit to the community and the produce of their labours was **pooled**, so there was enough for everybody. The group was often based on a tribe. The system required trust and co-operation. Often money was not used. Production was just enough to meet consumption. For instance, people planted seeds to grow food to give them energy to plant seeds, and so on. They did not create a surplus—they were trapped in subsistence.

With improvements in world communications, these communities became less isolated, and trade began. In order to trade they needed to produce a surplus, which they did by specialization; in this way, they escaped from the subsistence trap.

Advantages

The people fulfilled their basic consumption needs and lived a simple, uncomplicated life. It was free from the competitiveness of modern living.

Disadvantages

These heavily outweighed the advantages and led to the decline of the subsistence economy. In this economy, there was **little choice** and little progress. Economic activity was irregular and resources tended to be underutilized, e.g. if a person took two hours to perform his/her job, then he/she might use the remainder of the time in leisure. Thus, the economy tended to **stagnate**. In addition, the growth of the population made the organization of work and distribution of produce **complicated**.

2.6 Summary

Modern economic systems can be divided into three main types: Capitalist, Collective and Mixed. Each differs in resource allocation and political style.

In a capitalist economy there is no government interference, resources are privately owned and are allocated by price in pursuit of maximum profit. Nineteenth-century Britain and 20th-century USA are often given as examples of such an economy. Conversely, in the USSR which demonstrates a collective economy, the production questions are answered by the state controlling the resources on behalf of the people. As with capitalist economies in practice there is some degree of mixing.

Mixed economies feature both public and private sectors. It is often said this system as used in Britain combines the best of both worlds, however, possibly it could represent the worst of both worlds. Also we can identify subsistence economies which can be found in parts of the Third World today where only basic needs are satisfied leaving no surplus to trade with.

3 BUSINESS UNITS

3.1 Private and public sector

The public sector refers to business organizations which are set up and controlled by **central government** and **local government**. The largest and best-known type are the public corporations, which are popularly called 'nationalized industries', e.g. British Rail.

The private sector is made up of business units set up by **individuals** and **groups** of people. There are a variety of types—sole traders, partnerships, companies and co-operatives. They are subject to various laws laid down by governments. However, the distinction between the public and private sectors is not clear at all. British governments have bought shares (equity) in the private sector companies, and made loans to them to maintain their viability, e.g. British Leyland. Such organizations have been termed **'mixed enterprises'**.

The Industrial Re-organization Corporation 1966–70 and National Enterprise Board 1974–79 sponsored **state involvement** in the private sector under successive Labour governments, e.g. IRC created ICL (International Computers Ltd.). In contrast, Conservative governments have sold off parts of the public sector, e.g. British Rail sold off Thomas Cook to the Midland Bank. Also they have reduced their holdings in mixed enterprises, e.g. British Petroleum went from 49 per cent to 33 per cent under government control by the sale of shares to the private sector. This policy of **privatization** aims to increase the size of private sector and encourage individual economic activity.

Between 1979 and 1985 the Conservative government extended privatization, notably by selling off **British Telecom for £4 billion in 1984/85**.

Different types of privatization

1 Selling off organizations supervised by the state, e.g. British Telecom.
2 Tendering for external services, e.g. hospital laundry.
3 Deregulation (allowing free competition), e.g. long-distance coach travel in 1980.

Reasons for privatization

1 To provide funds for the government so that it can meet its PSBR targets (Unit 15.6).
2 To reduce the need for state finance (taxes) to pay for losses incurred by nationalized industries, or for new investment.
3 To encourage wider share ownership.
4 To increase efficiency, as the privatized operation will have to respond to market forces.
5 To encourage competition in some sectors where at present there is a monopoly, e.g. British Telecom.
6 To reduce trade union power—private firms are less likely to give in to industrial action seeking big pay increases.

Arguments against privatization

1 Many privatized assets have been sold off too cheaply. Thus the tax payer has suffered. For instance, the sale of Rover to British Aerospace.
2 Some nationalized industries have been changed from a state monopoly to a private monopoly. This means that competition has not been increased e.g. British Gas.
3 Services may decline, as the accent is now on making a profit. For example, there have been complaints about British Telecom since its privatization.
4 There is no evidence that privatized firms perform any better in the private sector, according to a London Business School report.
5 Danger of lower wages and worse working conditions for the work force.
6 Overseas buyers of the shares reap profits which go abroad, thus adding to Balance of Payments debits.
7 The attempts to make profits often result in higher prices, and so consumers suffer.

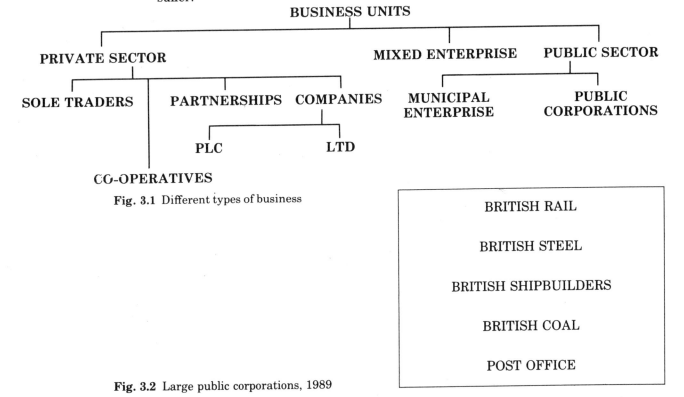

Fig. 3.1 Different types of business

Fig. 3.2 Large public corporations, 1989

3.2 Public corporations and nationalized industries

Public corporations and nationalized industries are not exactly the same. Some public corporations, such as the Bank of England and regional water authorities, are not classed as nationalized industries because:

1 They do not sell goods and services.
2 They do not derive their revenue directly from their consumers.

However, the major nationalized industries which are also **public corporations** have the following characteristics:

1 They were created by **Act of Parliament** with specific organization and functions.
2 General public control is under a **Minister** responsible to Parliament.
3 Assets are **publicly** owned.
4 Daily management is by a **Board**, appointed by a Secretary of State (Minister) and under a limited degree of government control.
5 They are not required to make a **profit**.

Reasons for public corporations   'WEE' and 'SUDS'

Natural monopolies should be controlled by the state to:

1 Avoid **Wasteful** duplication—for example, more resources would be used if two postmen from rival organizations competed to deliver the post. It would be unlikely that the service would be any better and the price any cheaper. In the past, rival railway companies provided alternative services to many towns. Since nationalization, this no longer occurs and there is less duplication.
2 Achieve **Economies** of scale—for example, British Steel's huge complexes enable most of the technical benefits of large-scale production to be achieved. This tends to lower costs per unit than would otherwise be the case.
3 Prevent consumer **Exploitation**—for example, nearly all houses require electricity. If this service were not provided by the Electricity Council and publicly controlled, very high prices could be charged to consumers who would have no option but to pay.

Part of the private sector has been nationalized in order to:

4 Provide **Sufficient** capital for large-scale development, e.g. Concorde would not have been developed if British Aerospace had not been created and government money had not been available.
5 Provide an **Uneconomic** service, e.g. British Rail operates trains on routes on which it makes a loss; but it provides a necessary service for many small towns and villages.
6 Prolong the life of a **Declining** industry in order to protect employment—in the shipbuilding industry uneconomic and inefficient yards have been kept open in order to maintain employment in already depressed areas and to minimize social misery.
7 Control industries of **Strategic** importance, e.g. atomic power is in public ownership. Nuclear weapons are in the hands of the government rather than ordinary individuals!

These are the main **economic** arguments for public corporations. There is also the political argument that 'ownership of the means of production and distribution' is power and this should be under state control. Some in the Labour Party take this view, although a majority support the mixed economy and thus favour a larger public sector than the Conservative Party wants.

Disadvantages of public corporations   'DIPPI'

1 **Diseconomies** of scale may occur in large units. For instance, some industries are difficult to control as they have many plants across the country. This produces long lines of communication and often little check over output.
2 Lack of competition may lead to **Inefficiency**. This occurs because nationalized industries as monopolies can usually still sell their product or service when prices rise. This may mean that costs are not as closely controlled as in industries where firms face competitive rivals. However, some nationalized industries do face

competition; (a) from other nationalized industries, e.g. coal versus gas, electric, oil in domestic fuel supply, **(b)** from imports, e.g. steel from Japan and West Germany. This competition may be unfair if trading rivals are subsidized.

3 Little **Public** control either through Minister, Parliament or Consultative Committee, all of whom supposedly represent the consumers' interests (see next section).

4 **Political Interference** may occur. As nationalized industries contribute over 10 per cent of GDP, governments have tried to extend their political policies through nationalized industries. Price increases by British Steel have been stopped and investment spending by gas authorities has been hindered in order to set an example on inflation and public spending respectively. By such actions the government hoped that private enterprise might follow suit. Thus long-term planning by nationalized industries has been disrupted as governments seek to meet short-term political objectives.

Control over public corporations

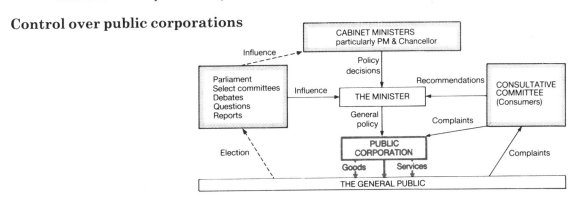

Fig. 3.3   Control of public corporations

The Cabinet—the Cabinet as a whole may decide policy regarding a public corporation. This will bind the particular Minister who is responsible, whether he agrees or not. Thus, for example, uneconomic coal pits were at one time kept open against the Minister's and Board's advice (this policy was later changed).

The Minister—each public corporation is under the general supervision of a Government Minister, who may appoint the Chairman of the Board and other members. For instance in 1983 Norman Siddall's contract as Chairman of NCB ended and the Conservative Government then appointed Ian McGregor, former Chairman of British Steel (he has since retired). The Minister may give the board guidance on general policy. However, the board is responsible for daily matters and internal policy.

The Minister also negotiates on behalf of his industry with the Chancellor of the Exchequer when seeking finance for development. On other occasions he may defend the industry in answer to MPs' questions and during debates.

MPs—MPs, as individuals, can obtain information and exert a little indirect influence over the policies of public corporations. A group of MPs in a Select Committee may pry deeply into an industry's affairs, and through their criticisms bring about changes.

Consultative Committees—these semi-official public bodies collect complaints from the general public who use the goods and services produced by public corporations. They also suggest improvements.

Finance for public corporations

The income to meet current expenditure usually comes from the sale of goods/services and from government subsidies.

The income for capital is borrowed from the Treasury, which lays down a **rate** of **return** which should be obtained. Each year the total amount borrowed from the Treasury is calculated—this is known as the **external financing limit**. A public corporation should not exceed its target.

Municipal enterprise

District and County Councils provide goods and services for public consumption in local communities. For instance, local transport is mainly provided by municipal authorities and is usually **subsidized**. Some councils have diversified into the building sector and other trades and actually compete with the private sector.

The control of municipal enterprise by the public is again very indirect. However, it is less complicated with councillors on committees taking the responsibility for decisions and being made accountable at local elections.

3.3 Companies

CHARACTERISTICS

Limited liability. Before 1862, few companies were formed because the risks of loss were too great. Unlimited liability meant that people starting up a business might lose all their personal assets if the business failed. Nowadays, a shareholder's liability in a business is limited to the amount of his original share subscription. Unfortunately, this law is often used unscrupulously.

Legal entity. A company is a separate 'being' in law. It is distinct from its shareholders. As such, a company can sue, be sued, enter into legal contracts, own property and continue its separate existence, unaffected, for example, by such events as the death of any of its shareholders.

Registration and submission of documents. A company has to register with the Department of Trade and supply.

> 1 **Memorandum of Association.** This outlines important information for **outsiders** such as the title of the company, its registered address, the amount of authorized capital and the type of trade which it is in.
> 2 **Articles of Association.** This document lays down the rules and regulations governing the **internal** organization of the company, e.g. powers of directors.

In addition a company needs to keep proper books of account by law. These may be inspected by the Inland Revenue and Customs and Excise department.

Directors elected by shareholders at AGM. The Board of Directors decide company policy and the Managing Director is there to carry it out. The Annual General Meeting declares the **dividend** for ordinary shareholders, outlines the company **performance** over the last year and presents the **Balance Sheet**.

Directors usually control elections, from which their powers are derived, when no large shareholder dominates. Usually meetings support the **existing management** while the company is profitable and often the AGM lasts half an hour. Vacancies on the Board are often filled by **nominees of the Board** and ratified at AGM. Shareholders have very little power in practice, although in theory they can change the Articles of Association, sanction dividends and confirm the choice of auditors.

Shareholders. Two minimum, no maximum.

1980 COMPANIES ACT

The Act amended company law and distinguished two main types of company: public limited companies (PLC) and limited companies (Ltd. Co.) There are two major differences:

> 1 **PLC.** This suffix must follow the title of a company whose shares are quoted on the Stock Exchange. This covers the companies previously called public limited company.
> 2 **Ltd. Co.** This suffix is used with companies whose shares are not freely transferable on the Stock Exchange. These companies were formerly known as 'private limited companies'.

The main similarity is **two shareholders minimum and no maximum**.

Advantages of PLC

PLC such as Bass-Charrington, Watneys have advantages which can be remembered by the word **'ALES'**.

> 1 **Access** to capital through the Stock Exchange (rights issues) and the Money Market makes expansion easy. In addition, shareholders can easily sell shares without depriving companies of long-term capital.
> 2 **Limited** liability increases risk-taking and enterprise. It also makes people more willing to buy shares.
> 3 **Economies** of scale can be obtained, leading to lower costs per unit.
> 4 **Specialists** can be employed. The suppliers of capital (shareholders) are separated from the managers of capital. Thus, people can invest in chemicals without knowing about them and trust the experts to use their capital wisely.

Disadvantages of PLC

These can be remembered by mnemonic: **'DISAD'** appropriately for disadvantages.

> 1 **Diseconomies** of scale may occur—see Unit 5.
> 2 **Interests** of the management may be different from those of the shareholders.

In most PLC there are thousands of shareholders who are not united and only meet at the AGM. Thus the management's aims usually prevail. For instance, the management may want maximum sales/bigger market share, whilst the owners want a large return on their investment. However, increasingly, **directors hold shares** in the companies which they manage and this may make their interests closer to the interests of shareholders.

3 **Small** groups of shareholders may dominate a company. Often the **institutional investors**, such as insurance companies and pension funds, may wield great influence over company policy, e.g. West Midlands County Council own 1 million out of 364 million shares in BAT. Clearly, shareholders with just small holdings lack the influence and expertise to have much effect. However, occasionally an AGM hits the headlines—in 1982 a few shareholders, critical of Rio Tinto Zinc's operations in Namibia and Australia, disrupted the meeting and the police were called! Usually, though, the Chairman rushes through the formalities and the AGM is a public relations exercise in keeping shareholders happy.

4 **Accounts** have to be submitted annually to the Department of Trade—however, companies are often years behind!

5 **Documentation** is expensive and extensive. Since 1980, all companies except those trading under the name of the owner, need to disclose their identity on their stationery and in their business premises. Companies no longer provide a cloak of anonymity.

LIMITED COMPANIES (private limited company)

These are generally smaller in size, but more numerous. They are not quoted on the Stock Exchange, but they must file annual accounts with the Registrar of Companies. They are usually family businesses which have been made into companies to gain the advantages of limited liability. The best example is Littlewoods—the retail variety chain store.

Advantages of limited company

1 Some privacy retained in a family organization.
2 Limited liability.
3 Continuity maintained.
4 General benefits, such as flexibility, specialization, which accrue to small firms. See Units 5.7 and 5.8.

Disadvantages of limited company

1 Limited amount of capital.
2 Transfer of shares not easy as the consent of other shareholders is needed and private buyers need to be found, and the Stock Exchange cannot be used.
3 Vulnerable to changes in demand, as often specialist companies.

3.4 Partnerships

CHARACTERISTICS

The main headings can be remembered by the word **'DUO'**.

Deed of partnership is signed by the partners. The decision of one partner then binds the other partners. The **partnership deed** (agreement) usually gives details of:

Amount of capital contributed by each partner,
Share of profits/losses to each partner,
Salary to each partner,
Type of trade engaged in,
Arrangements for dissolution of partnership,
Number of partners and name of partnership.

If no written agreement is made, the 1890 Partnership Act has laid down the following **guidelines**:

Loans to receive 5 per cent interest,
Equal division of profits,
No salary for partners,
No interest on capital.

So the **DUO** includes **AS STAN** and **LENN**.

Unlimited liability. This means that the partner's own personal assets may have to be used to pay any debts. However, the **1907 Act allowed limited** partnerships. In these the general partners have unlimited liability and sleeping partners have limited liability. General partners usually receive fees whereas sleeping partners get a return from the profits.

Ownership. Between two and twenty people may create, own and control a partnership, e.g. estate agents. In the cases of solicitors and accountants, more than twenty partners are allowed.

Advantages of partnerships

1 Easy and cheap to set up.
2 More capital available than sole trader, as more providers.
3 Specialization among partners, e.g. solicitors specialize in divorce, conveyancing, wills.
4 Small enough to maintain good employer–employee relations and good consumer–producer relations.
5 Worries shared between partners eases the mental load.
6 Trust is encouraged.

Disadvantages of partnerships

1 Unlimited liability for some/all partners.
2 Size may be limited by lack of capital.
3 Personal differences can cause problems in the running of the business. Partners need to agree and trust each other, otherwise management becomes difficult.
4 Dissolution of the partnership, when one partner dies, may cause loss of goodwill, reputation and contacts.

3.5 Sole traders

There are nearly **3 million** self-employed people in Britain. They mainly provide **specialist** services and crafts, e.g. plumbing, printing, hairdressing, window cleaning. These people may work entirely on their own or employ a few workers. In either case, they are **totally responsible** for all decisions made, they control their own business and they have unlimited liability. The sole proprietor takes all the risks and receives all the profits.

Advantages

1 Flexible and efficient because of personal control.
2 Good relations with employees as frequent contact and working together.
3 Easy and cheap to set up—no documentation needed except VAT registration if turnover exceeds £18,700.
4 The owner is his own boss and thus has considerable freedom in his work. He also has the incentive to succeed as all profits accrue to him.

Disadvantages

1 Very risky, because of unlimited liability.
2 Lack of continuity—holidays, illness and death may mean that the business ceases to operate. Temporary closures may lead to a loss of trade and stability.
3 Shortage of capital which may inhibit expansion. Borrowing is often difficult and expensive because of the individual's lack of contacts, assets and reputation.

3.6 Co-operatives

The aim of the other private sector organizations is to make a profit for the owner/shareholders. However, the initial aim of the original co-ops in Britain was to break even and **return any profits** back to the customers. There are two types of co-operative:

Producer co-operatives. These are groups of workers who provide the capital and jointly run the business of making goods. Only a few workers' co-operatives have been set up in Britain and these have been mainly **'buy-outs'** by workers. For instance, when the Meridan Motorcycle Co. went into receivership, most of the workers used their redundancy pay to buy the company's assets and reestablish the business—this venture eventually failed. In Israel, the **kibbutzim** (collective farms) are very numerous and economically successful. Most producer co-operatives operate through committees of workers and **elected** managers who make decisions.

Consumer co-operatives. The best-known co-operatives of consumers are the **Co-op Retail Societies** (CRS). They originated in 1844 with the **Rochdale Pioneers**. This group of 28 weavers put their money together to open a retail store, because they disliked being exploited by existing shops which sold poor-quality goods and charged expensive credit. They bought goods from their own shop and distributed the profits according to how much they had spent. This method of redistribution through a **dividend** per £1 spent was a basic principle of the Co-operative movement up to the 1960s.

Co-operative Wholesale Society (CWS)

This was set up in 1863 to buy in bulk for the CRS. It provides **70 per cent** of their needs such as packaged food, household goods and electrical equipment. It owns **133 factories** which produce for CRS and other retailers. In addition, it is the nation's biggest **farmer**, producing one-third of all liquid milk, biggest **undertaker** and biggest **transport fleet** manager. The sales of £2 billion in 1982 also made it the biggest wholesaler in Europe. It now has a substantial number of shops and has moved away from failing retail societies, especially in London and Scotland.

Decline of Co-op Retail Societies

Between 1950 and 1975, CRS share of the grocery market fell from 20 per cent to 13 per cent, although it has slightly recovered since (to 15 per cent). The reasons for their decline were:

1 Heavy dependence on **food sales** (75 per cent of total, compared to 60 per cent in Tesco) where the profit margins are low and the sales fairly stable.
2 **Small-sized stores** giving little scope for expansion.
3 **Location of shops in decaying urban areas** and underpopulated rural areas.
4 **Lack of centralization**, as most coops value their local status and independence, there was little bulk buying to gain economies of scale.

This decline began with the development of **supermarkets** and **family motoring**. The result has been many closures and society amalgamations, as well as the ending of dividend payments. The number of cooperatives has fallen from 932 in 1958 to 95 in 1986. The existing CRS are mainly in the **North of England** and they sell **15 per cent of food** bought in Britain. Their market share has recovered a little because mergers have taken place to create a viable size of shop and a new go-ahead **image** has been presented.

However, in many **rural areas**, uneconomic co-ops still operate and provide a service to the community. They are **subsidized**: often CWS does not charge transport costs of delivery to CRS in outlying areas. Falling profits have meant no dividends, less capital and less incentive for people to buy from co-operatives.

Common characteristics

Ownership. Co-ops are owned by their shareholders. Any purchaser can become a **shareholder for £1 minimum**. The shares receive a fixed rate of interest, which is usually low.
Aims. Co-ops have **broader objectives** than most businesses and have diversified into many areas. The Co-op movement has a bank, insurance society and has MPs who represent its interests. It is not narrowly profit-orientated but has political and social aims.
Control. CRS are run by **Boards of Management**, which are **elected**. Every shareholder has one vote, irrespective of the amount of shares he/she holds. Thus a £1 shareholder has the same power as a £1000 shareholder. This is very different from public companies—see Unit 3.3. Interestingly the CWS is controlled by the CRS on the basis of their purchases rather than one vote per member!
Capital. The deposits of members, which receive interest, can be used to finance expansion. In addition, co-ops borrow like public companies from the banking sector.

Advantages of co-ops 'CELT'

1 **Customers** get profits
2 **Economies** of scale through bulk buying from CWS
3 **Limited** liability
4 **Tax** on profits is lower because co-ops are classed as friendly societies.

Disadvantages 'BON'

1 **Board** of management is part-time—the members are chosen on the basis of popularity rather than business expertise
2 **Old-fashioned**, low-quality image
3 **Not unified**—individual societies may plan their own purchases and prices, but an overall marketing strategy can be difficult to achieve.

3.7 Finance

Sources of finance for **Sole Traders** and **Partnerships**

1 Personal **savings** and loans from friends/relations.
2 **Bank loans** and overdrafts. Loan guarantee scheme. (Unit 5.8.)
3 **Trade credit**, i.e. receiving goods ready to sell before paying for them, usually one month.
4 **Hire purchase**, capital assets such as machines can be bought in this way.
5 **Leasing**, use of equipment/vehicles without having to pay the capital cost but there is a rental charge.
6 **Profits** ploughed back into the business.
For **private companies** (Ltd.) (1 → 6 +).
7 **Shares** sold privately.
For **public limited companies** (PLC) (1 → 7 +).
8 **Shares** sold to general public through merchant banks and stock exchange (see Units 10 and 11).
9 **Investors in industry.** This body is independent of the Government, being funded by the clearing banks (85 per cent) and Bank of England (15 per cent). It is subdivided into: **(a) Industrial and Commercial Finance Corporation** which provide **long-term** finance for **small- to medium-sized firms**; they give between £5000 and £3 million per firm. By 1983, 4000 firms had received £480 million between them. This sort of finance enabled the development of the hovercraft. **(b) Head Office Division** (formerly the bulk of Finance Corporation for Industry) provides **medium-term** finance for **larger** firms. In 1980, 45 companies received £300 million between them. It provides loan finance up to £35 million and equity capital up to £5 million. **(c) Shipping and Energy Division**. In shipping they provide finance for the purchase and leasing of ships whilst in energy they have provided equity and loan finance for UK oil exploration and production. In these two areas it has invested £175 million.
10 **Government bodies. (a)** National Enterprise Board 1974 set up by the Labour Government to provide loans and equity capital for British firms. The NEB was an expanded version of 1967 Industrial Re-organization Corporation, which promoted restructuring of industries. In 1979 it was put under the British Technology Group, run by the Department of Trade, and parts were sold back to the private sector. **(b)** Welsh Development Agency, similar to NEB. **(c)** Scottish Development Agency, similar to NEB. **(d)** The Rural Development Commission (RDC) also gives money to firms in rural areas for development.
11 **Government grants.** Certain firms may be given specific amounts in rare circumstances, e.g. Rolls-Royce 1971; ICL 1982.

3.8 Shares

A shareholder **owns** part of a company. He takes a **risk** in putting up his capital but he does have **limited liability**.

Nominal and market value

The nominal value of a share is the price paid when it was **first issued**. The market value is the price which can be obtained when the share is **sold**, usually on the Stock Exchange. Large companies will have thousands of individual shareholders, e.g. ICI has 500,000 shareholders with the largest being the Prudential Assurance Co., with just 3 per cent of total shares.

Ordinary (equity) shares

These shares pay a **dividend**, twice yearly. The dividend received **varies** from year to year, and is decided by the board of directors in the light of profits made. The owner of equity shares has **voting rights** at the AGM; thus he can influence how the company is run.

Anyone owning more than **4.9 per cent** of a company's equity has to inform the Department of Trade. To avoid this, shareholders not wishing to reveal their influence often 'warehouse' their shares with relatives, so that their influence does not become apparent.

The Diamond Commission on the distribution of income and wealth in the UK showed the pattern of ordinary share ownership (Fig. 3.4).

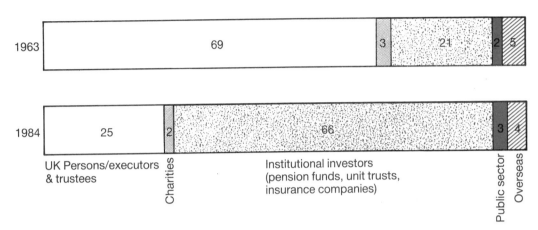

Fig. 3.4 Ordinary share ownership in the UK

Preference shares

These shares give the holders first call on the company profits. The shareholders receive a dividend which is a **fixed** percentage of the **nominal** value of the share. Preference shareholders have no rights in the control of the company's activities.

Some issues are **cumulative**. If the dividend is not paid in one year because of low profits or losses, then the amount owed is carried forward to the next year. It will be paid (hopefully) when the company is more successful.

Debentures

These are not shares. They are **loans**, for which the holders receive a **fixed** rate of interest. This is paid **before** the profits are calculated. If a company fails to pay interest on debentures, the debenture holders can force it into bankruptcy. Thus, debenture holders get paid before shareholders. They do not have any voting rights.

Authorized, issued and fully paid capital

A company's share capital is not all raised at once. There are three stages:

1 **Authorized share capital: total** share capital of company laid down in its Articles of Association, e.g. 200,000 × £1 shares.

2 **Issued**, the amount that shareholders have subscribed so far, e.g. 50,000 × £1 shares.

3 **Fully paid**, all the current issue has been paid, e.g. all 50,000 have been paid.

New issues

A company may issue some new shares in order to raise more capital, e.g. 1983 Tottenham FC (Spurs) raised £2.9 million. Although existing shares are bought and sold in the Stock Exchange, new issues are sold by Issuing Houses (merchant banks) who often underwrite the amount, i.e. promise to buy any shares not taken up. (See Unit 11.2.)

3.9 Summary

Production in Britain is organized in a number of ways. The public sector involves public corporations and municipal enterprises, which operate on a large scale but under political control. The Conservative government believes that the disadvantages outweigh the advantages and thus has pursued a programme of privatization.

In the private sector there are sole traders, partnerships, limited companies (Ltd) and public limited companies (plc) which are highly profit motivated and producer and consumer cooperatives which tend to be more consumer orientated. The finance for private sector companies may be obtained from many sources including share issues, banks, other financial institutions, the government and independent bodies.

4 DEMAND AND SUPPLY

4.1 Introduction

In Unit 2 we noted how scarce resources are allocated by **The Price Mechanism** in a free market. It is therefore of vital importance for economists to be able to explain how prices are determined.

'Market prices are determined by the interaction of Supply and Demand.'

Throughout this unit relationships have been simplified. The reader must remember that in the real world economic relationships are generally much more complicated.

4.2 Demand

Definition: 'The amount consumers are willing and able to purchase at a given price per period of time.'

Demand needs to be **'effective'**, i.e. backed by necessary money. The **individual** demands of people are added together to form the **market** demand. This is illustrated in Fig. 4.1.

The demand schedule for LPs per week (millions)

Price £	Quantity demanded
2	12
3	10
4	8
5	6
6	4
7	2

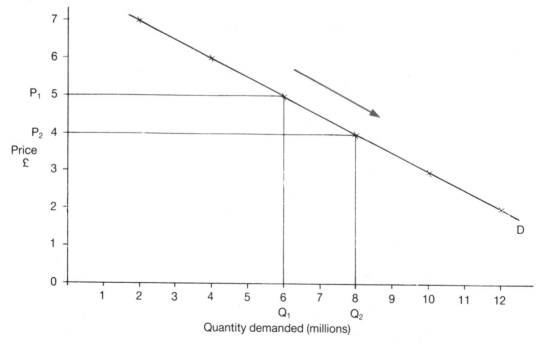

Fig. 4.1 Extension of demand

The Demand Curve shows the same information as the Demand Schedule but in a graphic form. As the price of LPs rises the 'amount consumers are willing and able to purchase' falls. For instance, at £6, 4 million LPs are bought but at £3, 10 million LPs are bought. Thus there is an inverse relationship between **Price** and **Quantity Demanded** for most normal goods.

Contractions and extensions of demand

Extensions and contractions of demand result from **Price** changes only. It is **assumed** that other things, such as conditions of demand below, are held constant. As we can see in Fig. 4.1, when price falls from P_1 to P_2 the quantity demand rises from Q_1 to Q_2. This is an extension of demand. Conversely when price rises from P_2 to P_1 the quantity demanded falls from Q_2 to Q_1. This is a contraction of demand.

Change in the conditions of demand

It is clear that demand depends upon many factors—not merely price. These are known as the underlying conditions of demand. They can be remembered by the word '**CIST**'.

Complements. Many goods are in joint demand, e.g. cars and petrol. It is clear that changes in the price of cars will affect not only the demand for cars but also the demand for petrol, as the two go together. Generally, if the price of a complementary good increases then the demand for the jointly demanded good is likely to fall. Thus if the price of petrol rises, demand for cars is likely to fall.

Income. If you were to receive an increase in income (e.g. from a Saturday job) you would be in a position to increase your demand for LPs even if the price remained unaltered. It is clear that changes in the level of income are likely to have a considerable impact on demand. Furthermore changes in the distribution of income will also affect market, though not individual, demand. For example, if income tax becomes more progressive (see Unit 15.3) the demand for luxuries may fall and the demand for normal goods may increase.

Substitutes. Many products have a number of close substitutes or goods which may be consumed instead. For example, many people would be largely indifferent as to whether they eat cabbage or cauliflower for dinner. Hence if the price of cauliflower suddenly rose, consumers are very likely to buy cabbage instead. Thus when the price of a substitute good rises, demand for the original good increases too.

Tastes and fashions. This will obviously be a major factor affecting the demand for certain products. Many people would not be 'seen dead' in last year's style of clothes no matter how cheap they are now. Tastes can be influenced by advertising. Thus over the past decade demand for lager has risen while the demand for bitter has fallen. The health food mood has led to more demand for brown bread and vegetable oil margarine and less for white bread and butter.

Graphic representation of changes in the conditions of demand

A demand curve shows only the effects on quantity demanded of changes in price. To demonstrate the effects of changes in the conditions of demand it is necessary to shift the entire demand curve. A new demand schedule has occurred.

Price £	Quantity demanded (D_2)
2	14
3	12
4	10
5	8
6	6
7	4

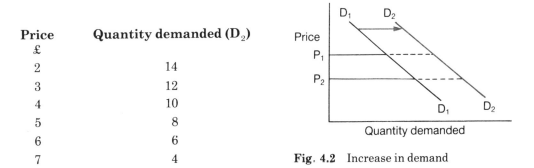

Fig. 4.2 Increase in demand

An increase in demand means that **more** of a good is demanded at **each** price than before, and thus results in a completely new Demand Curve.

After an increase in income existing consumers will be able to afford more LPs and new customers will enter the market. Hence at each price the quantity demanded has risen (e.g. at £6, 6 million LPs are bought now instead of 4 million). A new curve (D_2) is thus parallel and to the right of the original curve. Always remember to include an arrow showing the direction of change.

A decrease in demand may have been caused by:

1 An increase in the price of **Complements**.
2 A reduction in the level of **Income** perhaps caused by a lower level of taxation or increased wages or both.
3 A reduction in the price of **Substitute** goods.
4 An adverse change in **Taste or fashion**.

These can be remembered by '**CIST**'.

4.3 Supply

Definition: 'The amount producers are willing to offer for sale at any given price.'
As with demand, price is a major influence on quantity supplied. As price rises so does profit, therefore, new suppliers are attracted into the market and existing firms are tempted to increase production.

Supply Schedule
— LPs per week (millions)

Price £	Quantity supplied
2	2
3	4
4	6
5	8
6	10
7	12

This market supply schedule is a combination of the supplies offered onto the market by all the individual producers.

In Fig. 4.3 as price rises from P_1 to P_2 so Quantity Supplied rises from Q_1 to Q_2. Vice versa when price falls.

Contractions/extensions of supply

Figure 4.3 shows the extension of supply. This occurs when producers increase supply as the **price** rises. It shows a movement **along** a curve and it assumes that conditions of supply remain unchanged.

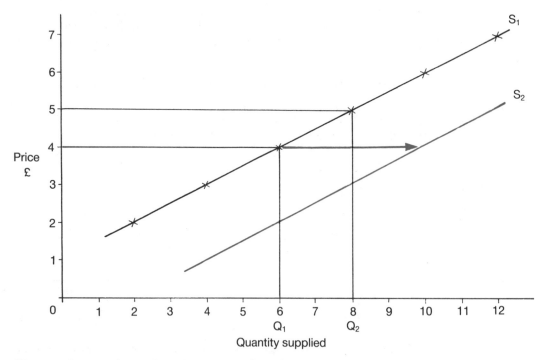

Fig. 4.3   Increase in supply and extension of supply

Conditions of supply

Basically anything that influences profit will affect the conditions of supply. There are a number of conditions of supply which may change and produce a new supply curve. These can be remembered by the word **'COPING'**.

Costs. This item refers to the cost to the firm of paying the Factors of Production (see Unit 5.5). If a firm has to pay more for its raw materials, etc., it will require a higher selling price in order to maintain its normal profit at existing output levels. An increase in costs will lead to a decrease in profit and therefore a reduction in supply.

Other prices. The impact of other prices depends on the relationship between the good being supplied and other goods.

1 **Unrelated goods.** If the price of ice cream rises it will not induce BL to switch its Longbridge lines to the production of Raspberry Ripple!

2 **Goods in competitive supply.** However, many firms are capable of switching production at relatively short notice and will do so if higher profits can be obtained. For instance, a market gardener of peas is likely to react to high carrot prices by planting more carrots and fewer peas next season.

3 **Goods in joint supply.** The production of one good leads to production of another, e.g. if farmers raise more cows, this will increase the output of leather even though its price has remained unchanged.

Innovations. We live in an age where rapid technological change is the norm. Thus firms are often able to use technological change to produce goods much more cheaply, e.g. the use of robots and computers.

Government policy. Here we are particularly concerned with the effects of **Indirect taxation** and **Subsidies** upon the supply curve. For instance, an increase in VAT means that suppliers will wish to sell the same quantity at higher prices and so the supply curve will shift to the left. When a tax is imposed the producer receives the selling price less the tax—this reduces profit and therefore decreases supply. Vice versa for a subsidy.

Graphic representation of changes in the conditions of supply

As with demand, the supply curve shows only the effects on changes in price upon quantity supplied. To demonstrate the effects of changes in the conditions of supply it is necessary to shift the entire supply curve. (See Fig. 4.3.)

An increase in Supply shifts the Supply to the right. This may have been caused by 'COPING':

1 A reduction in Factor Cost
2 A fall in the price of other related goods
3 A technological breakthrough
4 A government subsidy.

4.4 Price

Definition: 'Price is determined by the interaction of Supply and Demand.'

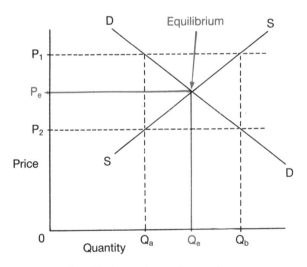

Fig. 4.4 Equilibrium price and quantity

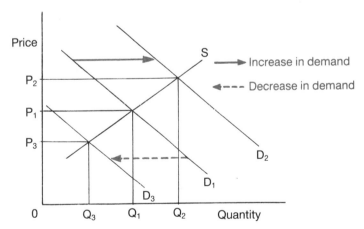

Fig. 4.5 The effects of changes in the conditions of demand

Equilibrium is defined as: 'The position from which there is no tendency to change.'

In Fig. 4.4 at Price P_1, Demand is OQa while Supply is OQb thus indicating an **Excess supply**. In this situation suppliers, as in the January or Summer Sales, will lower their prices to eliminate this excess supply. Thus at all prices above P_e there will be excess supply and a tendency for price to fall, until demand and supply are equal at the equilibrium price.

At P_2 there is clearly an **Excess demand** thus at all prices below P_e buyers will bid up prices in order to obtain goods which are in short supply, e.g. sugar. At P_e there is neither a tendency for price to rise nor to fall, thus P_e represents equilibrium price.

The effect of a change in conditions of demand: in Fig. 4.5 we can see that following an increase in demand ($D_1 \rightarrow D_2$) both equilibrium price ($P_1 \rightarrow P_2$) and quantity ($Q_1 \rightarrow Q_2$) will rise. Conversely when demand falls ($D_1 \rightarrow D_3$) so too will equilibrium price ($P_1 \rightarrow P_3$) and quantity ($Q_1 \rightarrow Q_3$).

Effects of a change in conditions of supply

In Fig. 4.6 as supply increases $(S_1 \rightarrow S_2)$ equilibrium price falls $(P_1 \rightarrow P_2)$ but equilibrium quantity rises $(Q_1 \rightarrow Q_2)$. Similarly when supply falls $(S_1 \rightarrow S_3)$ equilibrium price rises $(P_1 \rightarrow P_3)$ but equilibrium quantity falls $(Q_1 \rightarrow Q_3)$.

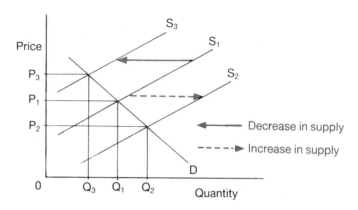

Fig. 4.6 The effects of changes in the conditions of supply

4.5 Elasticity

The **shape** of a demand curve is known as its elasticity. It tells us 'by how much demand will change in response to price changes'.

Definition: Elasticity is defined as: 'The responsiveness of supply/demand to a given change in price.'

Measurement of price elasticity of demand

Elasticity is measured by the **Coefficient of elasticity $\Sigma D/\Sigma S$**

$$\Sigma D = \frac{\% \, QD}{\% \, P} = \frac{\text{percentage change in quantity demanded of the good}}{\text{percentage change in price of the good}}$$

Calculation can be: (a) over a range of prices, **(b)** at one point on a curve, or **(c)** over the whole curve. It is normally calculated between two prices.

Examples. If a **price increase** from £5 to £6 brings about a fall from 6 million to 4 million LPs demanded per week, then $\Sigma D = \dfrac{-33\frac{1}{3}}{+20} = -1\frac{2}{3}$.

Note that the same data give a different result if a **price fall** is considered.

Then $\Sigma D = \dfrac{+50\%}{-16\frac{2}{3}} = -3.$

In calculating Σd the minus symbol is usually ignored.

In these two cases the D curve is **relatively elastic**, indicating that demand is very responsive to price changes. The Σd formula gives a value between 1 and ∞ (infinity).

Conversely, the quantity demanded may be very **unresponsive** to price changes. For instance, when price of LPs fell from £3 to £2 quantity demand increased from 10 million to 12 million.

$$\Sigma D = \frac{\% \, QD}{\% \, P} = \frac{+20}{-33\frac{1}{3}} = 0.6$$

In this latter case ΣD is less than 1 which indicates relatively inelastic demand. Elasticities between 0 and 1 show **relatively** inelastic demand.

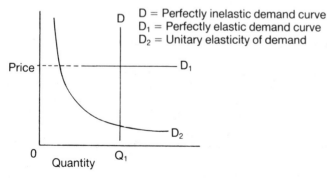

D = Perfectly inelastic demand curve
D_1 = Perfectly elastic demand curve
D_2 = Unitary elasticity of demand

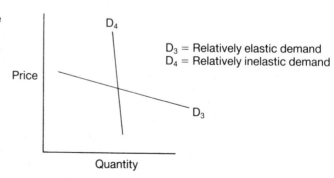

D_3 = Relatively elastic demand
D_4 = Relatively inelastic demand

Fig. 4.7 Examples of perfect demand curve elasticities

Fig. 4.8 Examples of relative demand curve elasticities

Perfectly inelastic demand occurs when demand remains constant at Q irrespective of price. In this case $\Sigma D = 0$ and demand is said to be perfectly inelastic.

Perfectly elastic demand is represented in Fig. 4.7 by curve D_1 as at any price above P_1 demand falls to zero hence $\Sigma D = \alpha$ and demand is said to be perfectly elastic.

Unitary elasticity is a special case where $\% \Delta QD = \% \Delta P$ at all price/output levels along D_2 hence $\Sigma D = 1$ and demand is said to have unit elasticity. In this situation Total Revenue $[P \times Q]$ will be unchanged following a price change. A demand curve with a constant unit elasticity is called a **rectangular hyperbola**.

These curves are all theoretical special cases and we should expect to find most cases where demand is either **relatively elastic** (D_3) **or relatively inelastic** (D_4).

Straight-line demand curves

It is important to note that elasticity will vary along the length of any straight line demand curve. As the quantity demanded increases, the curve becomes more inelastic. See Fig. 4.9.

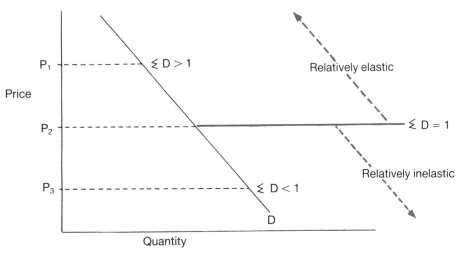

Fig. 4.9   A demand curve of varying elasticity

Factors influencing (price) elasticity of demand

These can be remembered by the word **'THIS'**.

Time. In the short term consumers may not fully appreciate possible alternatives and thus continue to purchase certain goods following a price rise. However, in the longer period they will become more aware of other possibilities. Therefore, *ceteris paribus*, demand is more elastic in the long run.

Habit. Quite often we purchase goods automatically without, perhaps, being fully aware of the price which we are paying, e.g. newspapers, milk. Thus goods which are habitually bought are more likely to be in inelastic demand. Furthermore some products have an **addictive** effect, e.g. cigarettes. The nicotine addict will continue to burn away his/her money almost regardless of price.

Income. Some goods constitute only a small proportion of consumers' income, e.g. matches. In this case even a 100 per cent rise in the price of matches can be quite easily absorbed since most consumers spend only a tiny fraction of their income upon matches. Demand is thus likely to be inelastic. Compare this with how you think consumers would react to a doubling of car prices.

Substitutes. Possibly the single most important factor is the closeness and availability of substitutes. For example, petrol has no genuinely effective freely available substitutes. Thus motorists have little option but to keep on buying it. However, faced with a rise in the price of cabbage the consumer has a wide range of more or less acceptable substitutes to choose from. Thus the demand for petrol is inelastic while the demand for cabbage tends to be elastic. In general the more substitutes and the closer the substitutes the more elastic the demand.

The **width of definition** is also significant. The demand for food generally is inelastic but the demand for specific foods, e.g. sprouts, will be more elastic.

Measurement of elasticity of supply

The co-efficient of elasticity of supply is defined as

$$\Sigma S = \frac{\% \, QS}{\% \, P} = \frac{\text{proportionate change in quantity supplied of the good}}{\text{proportionate change in price of the good}}$$

When **(a)** $\Sigma S > 1$ Supply is said to be Elastic, **(b)** $\Sigma S < 1$ Supply is said to be Inelastic, and **(c)** $\Sigma S = 1$ Supply is said to have Unit elasticity.

A **Perfectly Inelastic Supply Curve** has $\Sigma S = 0$ and is illustrated in Fig. 4.10. Supply does not respond to price changes at all. Unlike perfectly inelastic demand, $\Sigma S = 0$ may be observed in many real-world cases during the **short run**. Consider a farmer, once he/she has planted the seed the eventual harvest will depend upon climatic conditions and changes in price will have no effect at all upon supply. In the long run, however, we would expect farmers to adjust the pattern of their crops in the light of price fluctuations.

Perfectly Elastic Supply is shown by S_2 in Fig. 4.10 its $\Sigma S = \alpha$, i.e. if price falls below P_2 then producers will be willing to offer nothing for sale at all. Unlike perfectly inelastic supply, $\Sigma S = \alpha$ is a purely theoretical concept.

We can see that any straight-line Supply Curve through the origin will have a constant ΣS of 1.

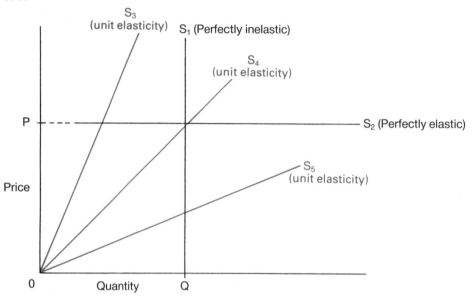

Fig. 4.10 Different supply curves

Factors affecting elasticity of supply

Time. In most manufacturing industry production plans can be altered relatively quickly, bearing in mind that contracts for purchases of raw materials, etc., are often binding for around six months. However, in agriculture the eventual size of the harvest, once the seeds are planted, depends upon climatic conditions. Current market prices will have no effect upon crop yields at all. It takes seven years for a newly planted rubber tree to yield its sap, hence we can see that in many cases supply is likely to be more inelastic in the short run. Generally, the elasticity of supply increases over time.

Factors of production. Manufacturers can only respond to increased prices if the extra factors of production are freely available. If, however, the factors of production are unavailable or available only at an increased cost, then firms may be less inclined to respond to rising prices by increasing output. Thus supply will tend to be more inelastic.

USES OF ELASTICITY

A knowledge of real-world elasticities will be vitally important to both **government and industry**. The former is able to raise revenue by taxing goods with an inelastic demand (see Unit 15). The latter will use their market research to enable them to evaluate the likely effects of any changes in the price of their products. Thus helping them to maximize their profits.

Income elasticity of demand

This concept shows the responsiveness of demand to changes in income. It is calculated by

$$\frac{\text{percentage change in demand}}{\text{percentage change in income}}.$$

For example, if income increased by 10 per cent and demand for LPs grew by 8 per cent then

$$Y.\Sigma d \text{ (income elasticity of demand)} = \frac{+8}{10} = \frac{+4}{5}.$$

As the $Y.\Sigma d$ is between 0 and 1 the good would be considered as normal.

In cases where demand increases more than income, the $Y.\Sigma d$ will exceed 1. This would indicate a **luxury** such as expensive consumer durables, or meals out. Conversely, the demand for **inferior** goods will tend to fall as income rises. Thus $Y.\Sigma d$ will be a minus value for wash leathers as better-off people will pay for window cleaners' services.

4.6 Summary

Price is determined by the interaction of supply and demand. When price changes demand/supply will extend or contract. When the conditions of demand/supply change the entry curves will shift to the left or right as appropriate. For instance, changes in the price of complements, the price of substitutes, the level of income and taste influence the demand curve.

The shape of the demand/supply curve is known as its elasticity which measures the responsiveness to price changes. Elasticity is measured by an elasticity co-efficient $\Sigma D/\Sigma S$. Where $\Sigma D/\Sigma S > 1$, demand/supply is said to be elastic, where $\Sigma D/\Sigma S < 1$, demand/supply is said to be inelastic. Many factors influence the price elasticity of demand and supply. For instance, supply elasticity is influenced by time and the price and availability of factors of production.

Income elasticity of demand measures the responsiveness of demand to changes in income.

5 PRODUCTION

5.1 Introduction

The making of goods and the providing of services is known as production. Today a decreasing number of people actually create/manufacture articles and more are employed in the service sector. Those providing services ensure that wants are met and goods are sold in the form, at the time, and when and where they are required. A dentist is just as **'productive'** in economic terms as a farmer, as both fulfil needs and get paid for doing so (see Fig. 5.1). Thus **any paid employment** which arises from the supply of raw materials to the consumption of a good/service may be considered as 'productive': e.g. professional golfer = productive; amateur golfer = non-productive.

Direct production refers to a worker supplying his own needs, i.e. self-sufficiency, subsistence farming. In modern society nearly all production is **indirect** with people producing goods and services for others.

5.2 Types of production

There are three types of production. The percentage of the working population employed in each type is shown in Fig. 5.1.

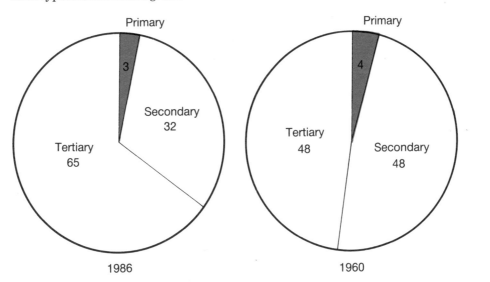

Fig. 5.1 Percentages of working population in different types of production

Primary

Extraction of raw materials from the earth's surface, e.g. coal-mining. This sector is providing less employment because machinery is replacing manpower. Traditional British industries such as **fishing** are declining because of increased competition, although **North Sea oil** and **gas** are providing new jobs.

Secondary

Conversion of raw materials **into finished products**, e.g. manufacturing **tweed skirts**. Again, British manufacturing now employs fewer people. This is because capital is substituted for labour, and Japanese, American and European competition is taking away some traditional British trade. See De-industrialization below.

Tertiary

Provision of services for people. These services are essentially of two types:

1 **Commercial services.** A charge is made and the provider of the service seeks to make a **profit**, e.g. an estate agent charges a fee for selling a house, a car mechanic mends a vehicle. This type of service is **increasing** as people have more leisure time and their standard of living is improving. Thus **luxury services**, such as eating out at restaurants and playing golf, are becoming more numerous.

2 **Social Services.** These services are provided **free** or subsidized at a **cheap rate**, because the government thinks it is desirable. They are not given in order to make a profit, but in order to meet a need. Examples are dental treatment, provided free to people under 16 and subsidized for adults, and the work of **school teachers**. Services such as these have increased because the government wants certain minimum standards to be met and the public are demanding that much more should be provided. For instance, an ageing population produces a need for more social services, such as meals on wheels.

Before the Industrial Revolution, most of Britain's population was employed in agriculture (primary production). As Britain has become wealthier through the growth of the economy, the structure of industry and commercial life has changed. Then, in each sector, more jobs involve **brain power** and fewer need muscle power. For instance, in the steel industry between 1950 and 1970 total employment increased but the number of process (manual) workers was nearly halved.

Many secondary industries have declined whilst tertiary production has increased.

De-industrialization

This term refers generally to the **fall in manufacturing output** and the consequent closure of factories. The decline in British manufacturing has occurred since 1950, when manufacturing produced 37 per cent of national income, and it has intensified since 1979.

Trade in British manufactured goods moved into deficit in 1982 as exports fell and import penetration increased. Foreign control of the market in motor vehicles exceeds 40 per cent and in chemicals 35 per cent. These factors together with the growth of oil and gas production mean that manufacturing's share of national income had fallen to 23 per cent in 1985.

This decline in manufacturing has been marked by large falls in employment and smaller falls in output. These combined have led to **increased productivity**. This means more output per head, whereas increased production means more total output. For instance, from 1975 to 1982 manufacturing employment fell by 19 per cent, output by 10 per cent **but** labour productivity increased by 11 per cent. Thus total production (output) fell, but productivity increased.

5.3 Factors of production

All productive processes require factors of production in varying proportions. The factors are land, labour, capital and enterprise.

Land

A **natural** resource covering all 'free gifts of nature', e.g. earth, trees, flat land, sea, rivers, etc. Land can be bought or rented, but it is necessary before production can be started. The owners of land receive **rent** for its use.

Labour

A **human** resource—workers of every type in every kind of activity from surgeons to shop assistants. Different jobs require **different qualities** of strength, skill, education and responsibility. The bigger the organization then usually the wider is the variety of human work required. Labour is 'owned' by individuals who sell it to firms, and receive wages/salaries in return.

Factor of production	Examples: Farmer	Engineering Co.	Dentist
LAND	Fields	Factory site	Surgery premises
LABOUR	Farm labourer	Different types of worker	Receptionist
CAPITAL	Tractor	Machinery	Chair and equipment
ENTERPRISE	Planning crop rotation	Organizing production and selling	Choosing place to set up

Fig. 5.2 Examples of factors of production

Capital

Capital is a **man-made** resource, e.g. machinery, a lorry or a robot. It is used to **make consumer goods** and services. Without capital, there would be no production. Usually capital and labour are combined. Capital **lasts a long time** but eventually needs replacing. When its value declines with age, it is said to be 'depreciating'. Some industries are labelled as 'capital-intensive' in that they have few labour costs and rely heavily on automated machinery, e.g. the chemical industry. The money borrowed to provide capital is paid **interest**.

Enterprise

Another **human** resource. This factor refers to the organizing, planning and risk-taking by the owner of a business. He receives **profit** for his work, and is called the **entrepreneur**. However, in modern economies large businesses are seldom owned by one person; instead they are owned by many shareholders and controlled by a Board of Directors (see Unit 3.3).

Not all enterprises aim to make a profit. Charities such as Oxfam aim to cover their basic costs and give the surplus away. Also some nationalized industries operate in order to provide a service rather than to make a profit.

5.4 Division of labour/specialization

Even in a subsistence economy (see Unit 2) people specialized. For instance, one person farmed while another collected wood, and so on. This specialization was **by product**. As the scale of production expanded the division of labour occurred on a finer scale. People specialize **by process**, i.e. they make part of a product—e.g. fish is caught, filleted, packed and sold by different people. Today most **consumer durables** are produced on a large scale by the joint efforts of thousands of workers.

Specialization occurs at various levels in a modern society—individual, factory, firm, industry. **All workers are specialists**.

For instance, the individual may have a specialized job, e.g. paint spraying in a factory which concentrates on one aspect of production such as car-body assembly. This factory may be part of a large firm which sells different makes of car in the vehicle industry. The vehicle industry includes the production of bicycles, motor bikes, buses, lorries and vans as well as cars. Throughout this industry the division of labour operates with different workers working separately and each producing something which contributes to the production of the final product.

Advantages to a firm of the division of labour   'POST ME'

1 **Practice makes perfect**, the repetition of a task improves worker expertise.
2 **Output increases** as more is produced per man.
3 **Savings in training** and time occur because workers need less instruction if they are only performing part of a job or operating just one machine.
4 **Tools/equipment**, each worker does not need a complete set of tools because he is only performing part of the output, unlike a traditional craftsman.
5 **Machinery** can be used more often. Such mechanization leads to faster and cheaper output.
6 **Efficiency** will probably be increased if piece rate can be used to reward individual workers. The use of piecework is facilitated by mass production and specialization.

Disadvantages to a firm 'DIMS'

1 **Dislocation of production** can easily occur because of the interdependence of the specialists. One problem, such as absence, faulty workmanship or a strike, may stop the whole production process.
2 **Industrial action** is more likely.
3 **Motivation** of workforce may be reduced when individuals perform a single monotonous task. They may become dissatisfied with their jobs and alienated from their employers.
4 **Size of market** limits the division of labour. If the market is small then there is less scope for specialization.

Advantages to individuals

The increased production and reduced cost per unit have led to a general improvement in the standard of living. Individual workers can concentrate on the jobs for which they are best suited. Thus a man interested in motor repairs may become a mechanic and not worry about food, clothing and housing production as these jobs are performed by others.

Disadvantages to individuals as consumers

Standardized products are made, leading to less choice. Loss of individual craftsmanship may lead to lower quality products being made, e.g. machine-knitted not hand-knitted jumpers.

5.5 Costs of production

Fixed and variable costs

Fixed costs are costs which **do not change with the level of production**, e.g. the rent of premises is paid usually months in advance whether a dentist treats 1 patient a day or 50 a day.

Variable costs **change with** the amount of **production**, e.g. the amount of filling used by a dentist is dependent on the number and type of patients treated.

In Economics, the definition of the **short run** is determined by fixed costs. The short run is defined as a period of **time in which at least one cost of production is fixed**. Thus, the short run varies between firms and industries, e.g. in manufacturing it is probably about nine months (the period of time needed to change the use of a piece of land) which is the most immobile factor of production. A decision in principle would be followed by drawings, planning applications and buildings before the new use could be operational. In the **long run all costs** are considered to be **variable**.

Average and marginal cost

1 **Total** cost = all current costs of production (fixed and variable) added together.
2 **Average** cost = total cost divided by total number of units of output.
3 **Marginal** cost = extra cost of increasing output by **one** unit.

Average costs often fall as production increases, because fixed costs are spread over more units of output. The point of **lowest average cost** is called the **Optimum** output. This is the point of **maximum efficiency**. The average cost curve is normally U-shaped in the short run because beyond the optimum cost diminishing returns set in.

Marginal cost falls faster than average cost and **rises faster than average cost**. The marginal cost curve crosses the average cost curve at the lowest point of average cost (see Fig. 5.3).

Output	Fixed costs	Variable costs	Total cost	Average cost	Marginal cost
5	30	10	40	8	8
10	30	40	70	7	6
15	30	60	90	6	4
20	30	70	100	5	2
25	30	120	150	6	10
30	30	180	210	7	12

The marginal cost is calculated by dividing the increase in output into the increase in total cost at each level.

Average and marginal revenue

In practice a firm's **total revenue** is its income over a period of time. It is usually composed of sales but may also include government grants and subsidies.

Note

1 Average cost falling;
   marginal cost is less.
2 Average cost at minimum;
   marginal cost is equal.
3 Average cost is rising;
   marginal cost is greater.

In economic theory, we assume that total revenue is just from **sales** and that all **goods are sold at the same price**. (Later we shall see that this is not true for a monopoly (Unit 7.3).)
Thus total
revenue = sales × price.
Average revenue = total revenue divided by number of units sold.
Marginal revenue = extra revenue obtained from the sale of one more unit.

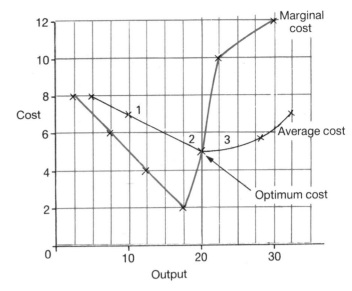

Fig. 5.3 Cost schedule and cost curves

Profit

Generally, and simply, a profit arises when **total revenue exceeds total costs**. Alternatively, if total costs are greater than total revenue a loss occurs.

Normal profit

Total costs include normal profit which is considered as a **cost** of production. In theory, this is the amount of profit which an entrepreneur needs, to stay in a particular industry. Normal profit is the **least profit** which an entrepreneur is prepared to make and **stay** in that industry.

Normal profit is the reward for organization and risk-taking earned by the factor 'enterprise'. Any profits earned above normal profit are an extra reward for the entrepreneur's success in an industry and they are termed **'abnormal profit'**.

In practice, there is usually not just one profit from the sale of a good, but several. By the time a consumer buys a product from a shop, profits may have been made by the manufacturer, distributor and seller. All these entrepreneurs calculate **profit margins**, i.e. they add a percentage to purchase price which they have paid, before they resell the good.

Profit maximization

In Economics it is assumed that firms seek maximum profit or minimum loss. The position of maximum profit is where **marginal cost equals marginal revenue with marginal cost rising**, i.e. the extra cost of producing one more unit equals the extra revenue received from selling it.

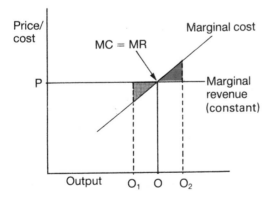

Fig. 5.4 Profit maximization

This situation is true when the firm can sell as much as it produces at the market price. This is valid only in a competitive market (see Unit 7.3).

In Fig. 5.4, MC = MR at price P and output O. If one less unit is produced, O_1, then some profit is being given up (the black shaded area). Alternatively, if O_2 is produced then a loss is incurred on the output of that unit (red area) as marginal cost is greater than marginal revenue.

Often a business will remain in operation for a short time even if making a loss. It might consider the loss to be temporary and be prepared to sustain the loss. If it is a public company it might maintain its dividend by using profits retained from earlier years.

If a firm's **losses** are **less** than its **fixed costs** then it is better to continue production, because the financial sacrifice is lower. This is illustrated in Fig. 5.5 when total revenue changes with the fluctuations in price of a product.

Total revenue £	21 million	26 million	19 million
Fixed costs	2 million	2 million	2 million
Variable costs	20 million	20 million	20 million
Total cost	22 million	22 million	22 million
Profit + Loss −	−1 million	+4 million	−3 million
Production decision	Continue as loss less than fixed cost	Continue as profit	Possibly cease as loss greater than fixed costs

Fig. 5.5 Profit/loss and production decisions in the short run

5.6 Large-scale production

In the past, before the Industrial Revolution, production was on a small scale. As **transport was undeveloped, markets** were **local** and not very large. Each village had its own specialist craftsmen and goods were often custom built. The main traders in villages and towns were **sole traders** and **partnerships**. The population of the UK was fairly small.

The development of the **factory** system requiring water, and later steam power, led to manufacturing on a larger scale. Even then the manager was usually the owner **(entrepreneur)** and knew all his employees. As transport became more rapid and communications improved, **markets** became **larger** and firms grew in size. In addition, the advances made in agriculture and health led to a rapid increase in population size which also extended the size of the market. As large factories could produce much more at lower average cost than individual craftsmen, small enterprises either went out of business or were swallowed up by large firms. This process of **merger**, or conglomeration, has speeded up in the twentieth century and now many companies are **international**, e.g. Royal Dutch Shell. Consequently, the average size of firm has increased considerably. Ninety-three of the biggest 100 American firms have investments in Britain.

Output	Total cost	Average cost
0	200	0
1	300	300
2	320	160
3	333	111
4	340	85
5	345	69
50	400	8
51	510	10
52	572	11
60	840	14

Fig. 5.6 Costs and scale of production

Large-scale production occurs when all factor inputs are increased. This cannot happen in the short run.

Operating on a large scale has many **advantages**. These are known as **economies of scale**. By producing large quantities, firms are able to reduce the cost per unit. The fixed costs are spread over a greater quantity of units and so average cost falls—Fig. 5.6, output 1 to 50. Thus, it costs £8 each to make 50, but £111 each to produce 3 units. However, after 50 units, average cost begins to rise. Thus beyond 50 units **diseconomies of scale** operate. There are certain handicaps which occur and raise the costs of production when a firm expands beyond a certain size.

Economies and diseconomies are of two types—internal and external:
Internal—**specific advantages to one firm** which arise because of the way it operates.
External—general advantages to **all firms** in an industry.

Internal economies of scale

These can be remembered by the mnemonic **'MATE FIT'**

Managerial. In most firms, as production increases, management and supervision do not need to increase at the same rate. Thus one managing director can probably control a company with 100 employees as easily as 400. Furthermore, a large firm can use many specialists, whereas in a small firm people have to be more general, undertaking several tasks. The manager of a small firm might actually work on the machines, deal with complaints, solve industrial disputes and carry out the paperwork. He may be a 'jack of all trades' and master of none. However, in many cases, the owner-manager may be a successful and efficient co-ordinator. In the large firm the use of specialists brings about the advantages of the **division of labour** (see Unit 5.4).

Technical. Larger-scale operations may make use of **advanced machinery**. Some machines are only worth using at a **minimum level of output** which may be beyond the capacity of a small firm, e.g. it is no good using a computer to calculate the wages of three employees but for 1000 it becomes viable. Also, resources can be used for **research and development** in large organizations because the cost is easily absorbed as a small part of the total cost. Such research may bring about improved processes and development of **new products**, e.g. plastics from chemicals.

Large-scale production enables **full utilization of capital** equipment and **lower average cost**. For instance, a small furniture store may use its delivery van only two days per week whereas a large departmental store has its delivery van operating every day.

The production line of a mass-produced consumer durable, such as a TV set or motor car, is the epitome of internal technical economy. It enables **time** and **cost savings**.

Financial. Large organizations are usually well known and this often makes it easier for them to **borrow** money from commercial banks than businesses such as Fred's Café. A large company may also obtain a **preferential rate of interest** (lower) on its borrowing, because it has many valuable assets and a **reputation** for reliability.

Trading. These advantages cover several areas:

1 **Purchasing.** Large organizations often gain discounts for bulk buying, e.g. large regular order may gain 25 per cent off price, thereby reducing unit cost. Occasionally, the bulk buyer can dictate type of product and quality to be supplied. Marks & Spencer do this with their suppliers. One large order is more convenient and less costly in administration for the supplier than several small ones.

2 **Selling.** Large firms can spread advertising and other marketing costs over a large number of units, e.g. in winter 1983 Tottenham FC spent £100,000 on a series of **adverts** to attract families to watch football. The **cost of this spread over** their average 30,000 attendance was little per head. However, Halifax Town could not have afforded such advertising with just 2000 spectators normally.

3 **Diversifying.** Instead of selling just one product, large firms may produce **several products for different markets**. Thus, if one product makes a loss, the profits on others will carry it. When Shell had a tough time selling petrol and other oil products in America it diversified into growing carrots, oranges and lemons! The extent of ICI's diversification is shown in Fig. 5.7.

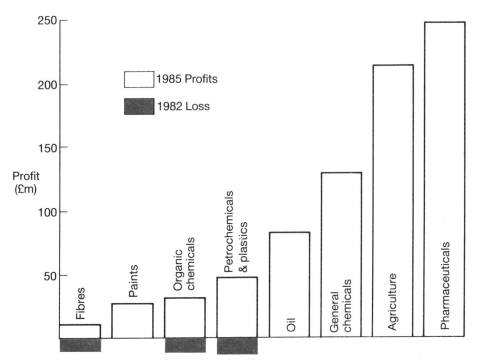

Fig. 5.7 ICI trading profits by product (1985)

External economies of scale 'LICER'

Labour. A pool of skilled labour may develop in an area where many firms are concentrated (e.g. white-collar computer workers in Silicon Glen, Scotland). This helps to reduce a firm's training costs and probably makes recruitment easier.

Information. This may be shared by firms in an industry, particularly against foreign competition. They may combine resources into research facilities or use computers on a time-sharing basis.

Concentration. Often the firms in an industry are localized in a region. A concentrated industry may benefit by attracting specialist suppliers of raw materials, components and services. BL cars at Solihull rely on local suppliers of radiators, petrol tanks, door hinges, hand brakes and so on, within a 50-mile radius. As these suppliers have a regular local bulk buyer they too can benefit from internal economies of scale.

Education and training. Specialist facilities are provided within most industries to develop the knowledge and skills of the manpower. Industrial Training Boards provide many general needs, although small firms receive a better return because of their smaller outlay. Specialized requirements may be met locally, e.g. Grimsby Technical College refrigeration technology is specifically geared to frozen fish and food industry.

Reputation. An area may develop a reputation for successful production, which will benefit the firms there, e.g. computers and electronics in Silicon Glen between Glasgow and Edinburgh.

Internal diseconomies of scale 'SWIRLL'

Standardization of product. This often results with the mass production technique being used. This **lack of individualism** may reduce customer choice and increase customer neglect. Each item may not be as well made as the equivalent would be by an individual craftsman, e.g. pottery. Furthermore, standardized products on production lines may **not** be **able** to adapt to **changing trends** very quickly.

Waste. Unless there is thorough supervision (which is costly) waste may remain undetected. Materials may be **misused**, **lost** or **stolen** or machinery may be underutilized; all of which increase the costs of production. Manpower may be wasted too. A firm may be overmanned, employing staff who are not really needed. As a result some of the advantages of large-scale production may be lost.

Impersonal behaviour. The lack of a **personal touch** may lose sales for a big firm. In addition, it may be difficult in a large hierarchy to **get hold** of the people responsible for decisions.

Red tape. Memos from one department to several may be needed to explain any decision made. This involves **people, time and cost** in perhaps unnecessary communication rather than production. Co-ordination may be complicated. For instance, the accountant may want to cut costs but the marketing executive may seek increased advertising expenditure in order to raise sales.

Labour relations. In large organizations labour relations tend to be more difficult to manage, particularly if several trade unions are involved. Trade unions may be well **organized** and more **militant**, thus industrial **unrest** may result.

Large units of capital often require special facilities, e.g. large blast furnaces have to be lined with expensive heat-resistant material.

External diseconomies of scale

The main external diseconomy to firms in an industry arises out of **shortages** which may occur. Scarcity of labour or resources may lead to competition by firms which will up the **costs** of production, e.g. high fees paid to qualified divers by North Sea oil companies.

There may be diseconomies to a local community where firms are concentrated. Land prices may escalate, pollution may arise and traffic problems may occur. However, these **social costs** do not directly affect the firm, although they may indirectly suffer through inability to attract workers, and bad publicity. The **decline** of a heavily concentrated industry will affect the whole economy of the area, e.g. north-east depression in 1980 as coal, steel and shipbuilding all declined, giving much higher than average unemployment.

The diseconomies of scale may outweigh the economies of scale. For instance, Watney became the second biggest brewer in Britain in the 1960s through takeovers but in 1972 it was taken over by Grand Metropolitan Hotels. However, in 1976, it was broken up into regional companies because of its decline in performance over 15 years.

5.7 Growth of firms

In the private sector, most firms start from small beginnings. Some expand and swallow up other small firms whilst others continue to remain small. Firms grow through internal expansion and integration.

INTERNAL EXPANSION

A firm may expand from within by producing and selling more of its existing products or by extending its product range. These moves may result from:

1 Growing market, e.g. jeans.
2 New markets, e.g. video machines.
3 Technical improvements, e.g. automatic washer.

Successful firms usually feature **enterprising management**, a devoted **workforce**, available **finance** and **unused capacity** in the growth period. The rate of growth is usually limited by the speed with which research and development, management and selling teams can be developed.

INTEGRATION

This is the process of **firms joining together** through either:

1 **Merger.** The amalgamation of two or more firms to form one organization, e.g. Cadbury–Schweppes. Usually the shareholders in the old firms got shares in the new firm in agreed proportions. The Monopolies Commission vets large mergers (over £15 million).
2 **Takeover.** The acquisition of shares in one company by another. The takeover price is usually in excess of the market price of the shares. It is financed by cash, or shares in the company which is taking over, or both. It is different from a merger in that the directors of the target company may oppose the bid and there may be strong objections and conflict.

TYPES OF INTEGRATION

Horizontal

Firms join together in **same industry** and at **same stage** of production, e.g. National Westminster formed from the Westminster and the National Provincial banks. Thus a good is produced by one large company rather than two. For example, in Fig. 5.8, the Four Fish Finger producer takes over another firm making fish fingers, the Five Fish Finger factory.

Reasons/advantages

1 Larger production unit leads to **economies of scale**.
2 Reduced competition leads to more control over market and **greater market share**. The integration may be defensive against imports.

This type of integration accounted for most of 19th-century mergers. It is most common today at the **retail stage**, e.g. W. H. Smith. Occasionally, **demergers** occur when part of a large company is sold off, e.g. House of Fraser do not wish to sell off Harrods, the largest of its 100-plus department stores, although this has been demanded by prominent shareholders.

Vertical

One firm **controls different stages** of production, which might otherwise be independent. Thus in Fig. 5.8 if the Four Fish Finger producer buys out a trawler owner it will have its own source of raw materials, rather than having to buy them from a supplier. It may of course still buy from other suppliers, e.g. Ross Group have their own fleet of trawlers.

This type of integration may be:

1 **Backwards** when the producer purchases stages of production **towards the source of raw materials**, e.g. above.
2 **Forwards** when the producer purchases stages **towards the market**, e.g. in Fig. 5.8 the Four Fish Finger company has acquired a shop through which it can sell its goods.

Reasons

1 **Increased efficiency** and lower costs between various stages of production by eliminating delivery costs and middlemen profits.
2 **Safeguard sources of supply/outlets**—control of own sources probably enables more flexible production.
3 **Increase barriers to entry**, thereby making it more difficult for competitors.
4 **Improve research by co-ordination** between stages of production.
5 **Better access** to markets.

6 **Full use of by-products**, e.g. ammonia and slag from blast furnaces enabled diversification by British Steel.

A nationalized industry, such as British Coal, is a good example of total vertical integration. British Leyland can be given as an example of failed integration, maybe.

Lateral/conglomerate/diversified

The expansion of an existing firm into an **unrelated industry** with which it was previously not connected, e.g. BP into eel farming. The integration may occur as a result of research findings.

Reasons

1 **To increase profits in the long run.** If a firm is in a declining industry it may seek profits elsewhere as a precaution, e.g. British Match Corporation made 75 per cent of all matches in Britain but diversified into packaging and printing. This enabled risks to be spread and a wider range of products to be sold.
2 **To make better use of assets/resources.** Economies in common activities such as accounting, outlets and exporting could be achieved. For instance, the Cadbury–Schweppes merger enabled chocolate and soft drinks to be sold through the same retail shops, thereby reducing distribution and selling costs.

The **failure** of lateral integration indicates **diseconomies of scale**. This sometimes occurs through management loyalty to former companies, and squabbles, in the new set up.

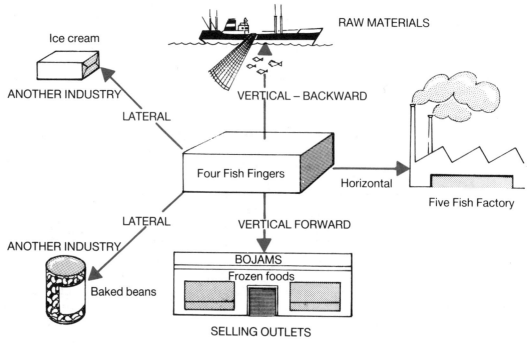

Fig. 5.8 Different types of integration

5.8 Small firms

Definition: This varies considerably. The 1971 Bolton Committee laid down a variety of cut-off levels, based on **employment** and for **turnover**. It restricted its analysis to firms **run by owners** and having **miniscule market share**. For example: 200 employees in manufacturing and £50,000 turnover in retailing (£200,000 at today's prices) were maximum limits for 'small'. Thus most **hotels, pubs** and **farms** are small firms: as are hauliers with less than five lorries. If the **self-employed** are included, then there are about 3 million small firms in Britain.

Development. There are fewer small firms in Britain than in most other countries. Up to 1979, they were a declining breed. However, since 1979 their numbers have increased dramatically. There is now a high **birth rate** and high **death rate**.

Strengths 'FIT'

Flexibility. Small firms, particularly self-employed, can adapt readily to **customers' needs**, e.g. working unsociable hours in order to fulfil a contract; designing products to meet individual requirements. They provide a **personal service** and often fulfil needs which large firms neglect.

Industrial relations. The boss of a small firm tends to have a wide **general knowledge** of his good/service and through working with his few employees he may have a **friendly** relationship with them. This should make morale high and industrial action low.

Transport costs. Usually small firms have a local market, thus transport costs are fairly low. Furthermore in remote areas, the high transport costs to larger firms reduce their interest in the market and perhaps guarantee a local monopoly for a small firm.

Weaknesses 'STEAM'

These weaknesses cause 2000 liquidations per year:

Susceptibility. If a single product supplier, a sharp change in demand may spell disaster, e.g. Rolls-Royce 1971 collapse at Derby had ripple effects throughout local economy as local firms, such as window cleaners, were heavily dependent on one big contract and they 'went bust'.

Taxation. High **income tax** rates are a disincentive to effort while tax reliefs on pensions, national savings, etc., channel funds to institutions who are less able/interested in the small firm sector. However, many **tax reliefs**, such as three-year start-up losses being offset against previous tax payments, can be claimed (assuming the small-firm owner uses an accountant!)

Expensive finance. Small businessmen face a tougher life than large companies' directors because **loans are more expensive** and security requirements are higher. Furthermore, they are less well informed and lack the **prestige and status** of their corporate rivals. However, in recent years the major clearing banks have started small business advisory services which may have helped a little.

Administration. Accounting, disclosure of information and **filling forms** weigh relatively more heavily on the owner-manager. For instance, the introduction of VAT created a major problem for many small businesses as more extensive records needed to be kept. Similarly, the Employment Protection Acts have increased government regulation of their activities.

Management defects. Often there is little forward **planning**, no **budgeting** and nepotism (promotion of relatives) which make the business unstable. Many have new ideas but lack capital.

Limitations on small firms growth

These may **'SAP'** its strength.

Size of market. This keeps many small firms small. A market can be limited by:

1 Supply of raw materials, e.g. a diamond cutter.
2 Demand, e.g. valet usually employed by high-income groups.
3 Transport costs, e.g. small-scale caterers.
4 Perishable product, e.g. flower sellers.

Available capital. Small businesses rely heavily, especially when opening, on loans from family and friends and their own savings. These sources are known as borrowing from **'Aunt Agatha'** and they have become more difficult to get in recent years. A lack of finance can also limit expansion (see Unit 3.7). The main sources of finance for small firms are compared with those available to big public companies in Fig. 5.9. Undistributed profits dominate in both.

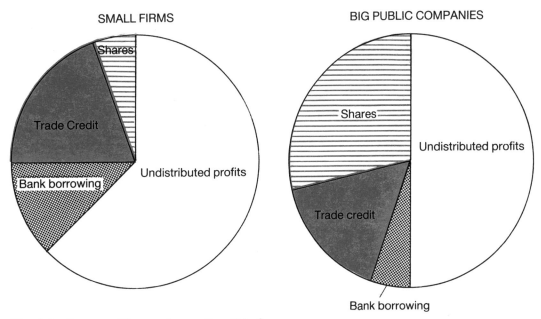

Fig. 5.9 Sources of finance for small and big firms

Personal preference. The owners of small firms often do not want the headaches and problems of expansion, and so choose not to expand.

Government help—Since 1981 Budget

This introduced several new schemes to aid small firms in overcoming basic weaknesses.

Business Start Up Scheme. To encourage outside investors to provide equity capital of between £1000 and £20,000 in a new firm for up to five years. In return, the government gives the investor his marginal rate of income tax in tax relief.

Loan Guarantee Scheme. The government guarantees to financial institutions 70 per cent of loan on new loans up to £75,000.

Preferential Corporation Tax. Small firms pay 29 per cent (as opposed to 52 per cent) with profits of less than £100,000. This reduces the tax burden and leaves more undistributed profit for expansion.

Inheritance Tax. Increased exemptions and the raising of threshold to £71,000 has made it easier for people to pass their businesses on intact to their children.

1980 Employment Act. This made small firms exempt from certain requirements, e.g. maternity reinstatement, uniform dismissal procedures.

Enterprise Allowance Scheme. See Unit 16.7.

Value of small firms   'ICEES'

Innovation. Small firms seem more likely to develop new techniques than bigger firms.

Competition. The existence of many firms in an industry may lead to more competition and lower prices. This is particularly the case in retailing.

Employment. Jobs are created by small firms as they tend to be labour-intensive.

Efficiency. As small firms seem to have better labour relations and exercise closer supervision over their employees, it is often argued that they are more efficient than larger enterprises.

'Seedbed' function. Small firms, like seeds, may develop into industrial giants, e.g. a man selling hot dogs in street gradually builds food chain empire.

5.9 Summary

The making and providing of goods and services is known as production, which can be divided into three sectors: Primary, Secondary, Tertiary. Since 1950 Britain has suffered extensive de-industrialization with output and employment in the secondary sector following.

There are four factors of production: land, labour, capital and enterprise. These factors will be specialized, particularly labour, in modern society in order to lower the costs of production. These costs can be divided into fixed and variable. Maximum efficiency occurs when average costs are minimized. The difference between total costs and total revenue is profit and firms are assumed to pursue maximum profit which occurs when marginal costs equal marginal revenue (and marginal cost is rising).

Producing on a large scale has many advantages known as Economies of Scale. These may be internal and external to a firm. Diseconomies of scale may also arise. Firms may grow through both internal and external expansion, the latter being known as integration.

Despite the advantages of large-scale production most firms remain small and perform valuable functions in the economy. The Conservative government has successfully increased the number of small firms in Britain since 1980 through various schemes, acts and tax concessions.

6 LOCATION OF INDUSTRY

6.1 Background

The location of industry really refers to the location of **factories and offices** rather than whole industries. Whole industries do not suddenly start, but individual firms do. We are mainly concerned with the location of the **firms** which compose an industry. Even within firms though, there may be factories and offices around the country for different reasons, e.g. Laporte Industries main plant is on the Humber, most of its subsidiary factories are near the coast, but its head office is in London. However, often a **large proportion of an industry** is concentrated in one geographical **area**, e.g. car-making in West Midlands, whisky distilling in southern Scotland.

The individual location decisions will generally be determined by **profit** calculations in the private sector. Alternatively, a public corporation may locate a new plant in an area of high unemployment for **political** and **social** reasons.

The factors determining location **vary between industries and sectors**. For instance, new firms providing a service usually begin in the area where the owner lives, to have access to customers. New branches of existing firms often radiate out into other nearby towns in the region to make control easier. The final location decision will in theory be based on the least cost.

The employment trend towards the Tertiary Sector and the decline of primary and secondary production (see Unit 5.2) have dramatically changed the importance of various location factors. In the past, **geographical factors**, such as available supplies of water, determined where some firms would site. Entrepreneurs often had no **choice**.

However, modern industry is footloose (not tied to a certain location by dependence on one source of power), as the sources of power are more varied and widely available. The costs of several available sites may be similar so a modern firm may be able to choose from several possible locations. These two trends have meant that modern industries are **more dispersed** and **less concentrated** than in the past. Highly concentrated industries derived peculiar advantages from locating in specific areas, e.g. water supplies for Lancashire textiles, and were manufacturers in the main. The new dispersed industries relate to the service sector and require large populations to provide a market.

6.2 Factors influencing location   'PANTS GLEEM'

Power

Access to power was influential during the Industrial Revolution when steam power was needed. **Steam** was generated from **coal** and so many firms were located near coal mines. As coal was bulky and costly to move, it was more economical to locate near the source of power than to transport the coal to a factory. This factor was crucial in iron and steel production. However, as **electricity and gas** have been developed, **nationwide supplies** have been created through national grids. Thus power as a locating influence has declined, as shown by the many abandoned water mills and the fact that coal is now imported.

Natural advantages

In each case below there is a natural advantage, followed by an industry to which it applies and an example.

1 Soil—agriculture, e.g. Lincolnshire.
2 Deep-water harbour—shipbuilding, e.g. Tyneside.
3 Sea—fishing, e.g. Aberdeen.
4 Climate—cotton, e.g. Lancashire—damp climate.
5 Rock structure—oil, e.g. Wytch Farm, Dorset.
6 Forest—timber, e.g. Kielder Forest.
7 Tidal estuary—chemicals waste disposal, e.g. Humber.
8 Water—nuclear power, e.g. Windscale, Cumbria.
9 Water—brewing, e.g. Burton upon Trent.
10 Flat land—motor vehicle assembly, e.g. Midlands.

Transport/communications

Transport takes many forms and each can be a crucial cost as shown below.

Road. Access to motorways is increasingly important. Industrial estates have developed alongside motorway interchanges.

Rail. More important in the past when rail was the main means of freight transport. With the reduction in rail network and increased cost, it has declined as a locating factor. However, many large companies such as Fords, Dagenham, have their own lines, sidings and stock.

Sea. Firms relying on imported raw materials are often located near deep-water ports, e.g. oil refining at Immingham.

Air. Speed is essential for fashion goods such as Dior dresses. Generally, a good transport system increases the attractiveness of an area as it enables **speedy delivery** of raw materials and finished products. Firms have moved out of city centres to the suburbs and **outlying districts** to avoid the congestion which may develop. In addition, the land for factory building may be cheaper outside towns.

Supplies of raw materials, components and water

Access to raw materials was vital to the old extractive industries, e.g. quarrying next to a quarry! This was so that impure waste was not transported, being quickly and easily dumped. Today, fish products are made by firms located at fishing ports so that the offal can be disposed of locally, without undue cost.

Generally, if the essential raw materials are bulky and costly to move and involve a lot of waste, firms are attracted to the source of the raw materials, e.g. canned peas alongside farming areas. In contrast, if **weight is gained** in production then firms will tend to **locate near its market**, e.g. lemonade near towns/cities.

Many consumer durables are dependent on component parts, which have to be **assembled**. The suppliers of components tend to be found near the car makers. Thus, a new car plant might need to be located in the same area to take advantage of this.

A large supply of **water** is needed in the production of goods such as steel and chemicals. Thus, the raw material may influence where a factory is sited.

The **pull of raw materials has declined** with improvements in transport. The extension of the motorway system and competitive haulage industry have reduced transport costs as a percentage of total cost. Figure 6.1 shows the importance of raw materials, transport, water and power to aluminium smelting at Lynemouth.

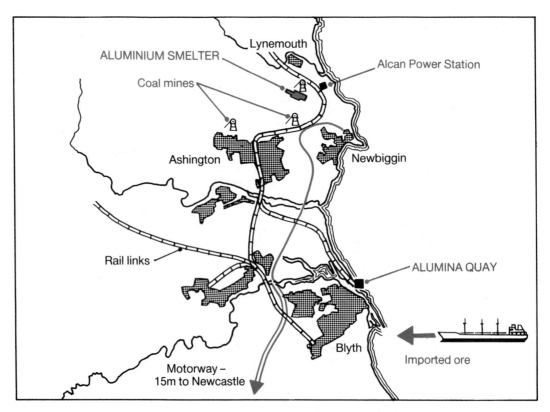

Fig. 6.1 Pull of raw materials and power in manufacturing

Government policy

Since the 1930s, successive governments have tried to influence the location of firms. They have occasionally interfered for non-economic reasons, but **supplied economic incentives** such as rent-free buildings and grants. The aluminium smelter in Fig. 6.1 attracted a 40 per cent grant being in a development area. Also, by using the coal from local coalfields, it kept pits open which otherwise might have been closed. This slowed down **unemployment** in the area. Such policies artificially distort costs, and may persuade firms to locate in a place which otherwise might not be economic.

The government has set **examples** by locating some of its offices in seemingly uneconomic locations, e.g. Giro centre at Bootle, DVLC at Swansea. In 1982, the government refused extra funds to ICL unless it located the next part of its development programme in mid-Wales. In 1986–7 the government spent **£600 million on regional aid**. In addition, it has created Special Development Areas and Enterprise Zones to attract firms to areas of high unemployment and banned location in areas of natural beauty and historic significance.

Labour

Available and appropriately skilled labour is necessary for all firms. As labour is not very mobile, quantities of labour with certain characteristics often occur in certain areas, e.g. textile workers in Nottingham, blast furnacemen in South Yorkshire. **Cheap**, often **female, labour may attract** firms to areas of high unemployment, e.g. clothing manufacturing.

Conversely, certain types of labour may be a **disincentive** to prospective employers. The **absenteeism** and **strike** records on Merseyside have been cited as reasons why some firms have been reluctant to establish themselves there despite government grants. The lack of an **assembly line tradition** led to increased labour costs/unit at Bathgate.

External economies

When the firms of an industry are concentrated in one area, the area tends to adapt to its special needs, as explained in Unit 5.6. These economies of **concentration** give a cost advantage to a firm setting up and so pull firms to certain locations, e.g. prestige of Sheffield Steel and the specialist training facilities encourage cutlery firms to locate there.

Markets

The products of many **new industries** (e.g. cookers) and the **service sector** (e.g. hairdressing, insurance brokers) need access to their customers. Thus, they seek locations near centres of population, which the producers of perishables and retailers have always sought.

Similarly, where the **cost of transporting the finished product is high**, a firm will tend to locate near its market, e.g. bread and lemonade. As London and the South-East is the biggest market in the UK, it pulls new firms into its region. This is despite government attempts to hinder the pull because of the congestion and overcrowding which it partly causes.

6.3 Regional problems

Different regions of the UK suffer from contrasting problems.

High unemployment, e.g. Northern Ireland and Scotland. Figure 6.2 shows that there has been little change in the **traditional pattern**, whereby unemployment rates in Scotland and the North are well above the national average while in the South-East and East Anglia are well below it. However, the West Midlands, which is normally below average, rose above the national average partly as a result of the decline of engineering and motor-car production in 1980s.

The staple industries such as **coal and shipbuilding** which were flourishing in the 19th and

Region	Year percentage unemployed			
	1971	*1981*	*1986*	*1988*
North	5.7	15.3	17.9	11.5
Yorks/Humberside	3.8	12.3	14.5	9.3
East Midlands	2.9	10.2	12.3	7.2
East Anglia	3.2	9.2	10.5	4.8
South East	2.0	8.1	9.7	5.1
South West	3.3	10.0	11.8	6.2
West Midlands	2.9	13.7	14.9	8.5
North West	3.9	13.9	15.6	10.5
Wales	4.4	14.8	16.2	10.3
Scotland	5.8	13.8	14.9	11.0
Northern Ireland	7.9	18.4	21.3	16.2
UK Average	**3.5**	**11.4**	**13.0**	**7.9**

Fig. 6.2 Unemployment rates by standard region 1971–88

early 20th centuries have **declined** and not been replaced by modern growth sectors which are attracted by markets. Their decline has created localized unemployment, e.g. specific towns with over 20 per cent unemployment for years. Such unemployment is a waste of resources. Also it creates income inequalities between regions with certain areas being less prosperous.

Congestion and overcrowding, e.g. London and the South-East. The pull of the market has worsened these problems by creating miles of urban sprawl and inadequate recreational space. The problems cause economic inefficiency as time and money are added to journeys by traffic holdups. Public facilities are overstretched and social problems created.

In contrast in the areas of falling population, social services, transport and other local facilities may be **under-utilized**. Thus, the best use of resources is not achieved.

Inner city decay, e.g. London, Birmingham, Manchester. In many large cities, such as these, there are areas containing run-down housing, disused industrial property, empty shops and boarded-up houses. The problems created are **social**, but they have **economic side effects**, e.g. increased **vandalism** raises insurance premiums on the shops of remaining traders, whilst the need for public expenditure on policing and renewal may raise rates.

Since 1945 **'the regional problem'** has been focused on trying to narrow the unemployment difference between regions. The regional problem has been seen in terms of an **imbalance** between the standard regions. This imbalance has been in terms not only of unemployment, but also of earnings and social capital. In 1975, the government began to take a broader perspective and devised a more general industrial policy (see Unit 19).

6.4 Regional policies

Alternative approaches

Free market. In which firms make their own decisions on the choice of location, **without government guidance**. In theory they might take advantage of high unemployment in order to reduce wage rates and thereby lower costs relative to other potential sites. However, in practice, national collective bargaining prevents this, whilst unemployment benefit may act as a deterrent to unskilled unemployed seeking lower-paid jobs. It also assumes that firms seek **lowest cost location**, which many do not.

This approach only looks at private costs and benefits (i.e. to the firm). The social costs of high unemployment, reflected in such things as juvenile delinquency, increased crime and depression, are neglected. They clearly have an economic dimension, e.g. cost of control, detection, cure, etc.

The defenders of the free market argue that restrictions on location may deter firms from building at all. Furthermore, governments give **benefits** which are **short term** and so in the long term some sites become uneconomic, if they are chosen for short-term reasons, then in the long term the resources may be wasted.

Government intervention. Government tries to influence location policies of firms. It has concentrated on attempts to reduce unemployment differences. A few measures have been introduced to combat congestion. Since 1979, regional aid has been reduced because the Conservative government believe in less government interference in economic decision-making, and more cost effective use of public funds.

1 Move work to the workers—capital mobility.
2 Move workers to the work—labour mobility.

In summary, it is clear that in practice, the debate centres around the **extent of intervention** rather than 'to intervene or not to intervene'.

Government policies

Regional unemployment

Capital mobility. Over the years the government has created Assisted Areas, which are currently of two types.

1 **Development Areas.** Large areas of high unemployment with declining basic industries.
2 **Intermediate Areas.** Areas where unemployment is increasing and there is little prospect of economic growth.

Firms setting up in these areas receive **incentives** such as:

1 Grants towards cost of machinery, buildings, factories.
2 Factory rents on favourable terms.
3 Grants and subsidies towards employing/training workers.
4 Tax allowances on plant and machinery.

As an example, the 1986 rates of grant are given in Fig. 6.4.

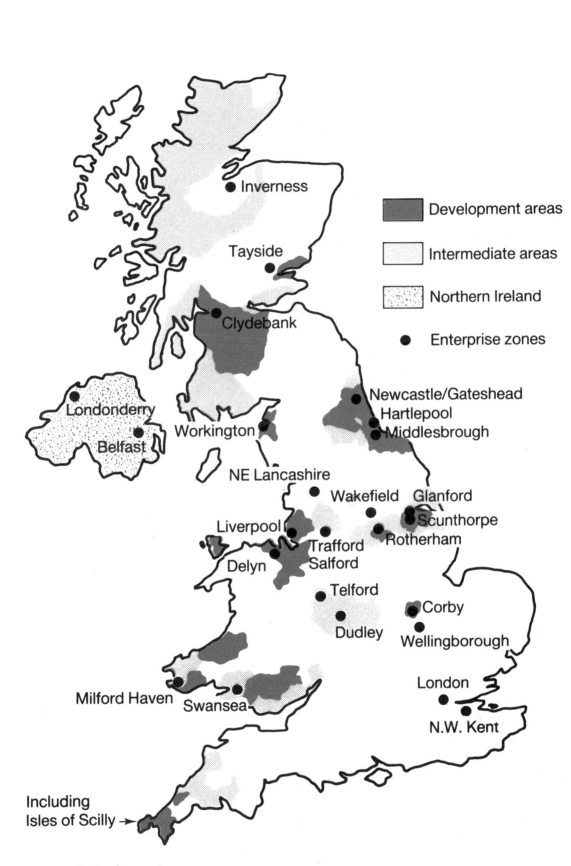

Fig. 6.3 Assisted areas

Automatic assistance	15 per cent capital grant on new buildings and machinery	or	£3000 per new full-time job created	Whichever is the greater

100 per cent tax allowance on new plant
75 per cent tax allowance on building costs

Discretionary assistance	40 per cent grant towards training costs
	Negotiable grants/loans/rents

Fig. 6.4   Development area assistance 1986

The incentives cost about £750 million annually. They act as **external economies** to an area. Furthermore, the extension of the motorway system has improved the facilities which some areas can offer. Many local authorities were given money by central government to improve their areas by making them look more attractive, e.g. clearance of derelict land, landscaping slag heaps and building industrial estates.

The government has also tried to **deter** movement to prosperous areas. **Industrial Development Certificates** (IDC) were needed before certain buildings could be erected, as well as normal planning permission. These certificates were **not** needed in Development Areas in order to encourage expanding firms to locate there. Similarly, between 1965 and 1979 Office Development Permits were required in the South-East and Midlands. However, IDCs are not needed anywhere now.

Labour mobility. The encouraging of workers to move from areas of high unemployment to areas of low unemployment received little financial support. **Grants of £600** were given to workers who moved and **council housing** was made easily available. If this geographical mobility had been successful, it would have made congestion worse, and turned depressed areas into ghost towns.

Generally, **occupational** rather than geographical mobility (see Unit 12) has been encouraged by generous payments to workers who retrain on government schemes at government centres. Government policies have been classed into **'sticks'** and **'carrots'**; sticks being deterrents such as IDCs, and carrots being incentives such as grants.

Congestion

New towns. Since 1946, more than 30 new towns have been established in Britain. They were set up to attract people out of overcrowded old towns into newly created ones. Towns such as Washington (near Newcastle), Skelmersdale (Liverpool) and Milton Keynes (serving London) were planned to contain **housing and work** thereby stimulating growth.

Urban decay

Enterprise zones. Created 1981 to encourage business development and selected run-down inner city areas. Enterprise zones would be a focal point for growth. The advantages given were, **(a)** free rates, **(b)** no industrial training board payments, **(c)** 100 per cent tax allowance on building costs, and **(d)** simplified planning and VAT procedures. Local authorities have also spent funds on attracting industry and by setting up **Enterprise Boards**.

By the end of 1984, 48,000 jobs had been created in Enterprise Zones (EZ) at a cost of £250 million in lost taxes and rates.

EZ criticisms:

1 Only one genuine new firm for every five located there.
2 Property values in EZ increased in value whilst those outside fell.
3 Firms relocate within a region to benefit from EZ concessions; little national mobility.

The results of regional policy

Assessment of regional policy is difficult because:

1 We cannot tell what would have happened without the policies.
2 Not all the jobs created were 'new', many being perhaps diverted from other areas where firms might have been located. Department of Trade research suggests an average of 30,000 new jobs per year were created as a result of regional policy, 1960–81.

The costs can be roughly calculated. £500 million in 1985–6. It has been worked out that **each job** created cost at least **£35,000**. The government has to spend more on welfare services in areas of high unemployment. The younger members of the community in Development Areas tend to **migrate** to find employment. Despite all the public money used, the **unemployment is**

still worse in the Assisted Areas and the gap with the prosperous areas is not closing—see Fig. 6.2.

The benefits have been in some new jobs and a slowing down of industrial decline in a more humane way perhaps. New **foreign** investment has been attracted by the incentives available, and Britain's place in the EEC. For instance, **Japanese investment** in Wales (seven factories providing 3000 jobs) has been used as a base for expansion into Europe. Exports from Japan directly would be subject to tariffs, but from within Britain, their cars and motorbikes are not taxed on entry.

The EEC has also helped in another way, through its Regional Development Fund. This gives **'disfavoured'** industrial and regional **grants** of up to 40 per cent of the capital cost of investment. For instance, it gave £600,000 towards £6 million Glendevon water treatment and dam project in Scotland.

Although the regional problem remains, without regional policy the situation might have been worse.

6.5 Summary

The location of industry refers to the location of factories and offices, although a large proportion of an industry is often concentrated in one geographical area. Factors influencing location such as power and labour supply have declined, whilst others such as market proximity and government aid have grown in importance making modern industry more footloose.

The regional problem consists of high unemployment, in some areas, congestion in others and inner-city decay. In practice the policy disagreements centre on the extent of government involvement rather than whether or not to intervene. Since 1979 government policy has been to reduce intervention.

Certain areas have been specially designated and firms locating in these areas are eligible for a whole range of incentives provided by the government. It is very difficult to judge the success of post-war regional policy, although all governments have pursued an active policy of some sort.

7 MARKETS

7.1 Introduction

'A market is **where goods and services are bought and sold**.' This need not be an actual place, although most markets can be located. For instance, the market for second-hand shares is the Stock Exchange in London. The main requirement for a market is that buyers and sellers can **communicate**—this may be done by telex, letter or word of mouth.

The term 'market' is used in many ways in Economics:

1 **Retail market.** People normally mean **stalls** from which goods are sold to the **final consumer**. Most towns have **traditional** market **days** in which itinerant traders sell their products.

2 **Wholesale markets.** In the chain of distribution (Unit 20) manufacturers sell to retailers through wholesalers. Their function is to **buy** the manufactured goods and raw materials and **distribute** them to shopkeepers. Most wholesale markets are in regional centres such as Sheffield, Birmingham, Manchester or in the national centre at London, e.g. Covent Garden (fruit and vegetables).

3 **Product markets.** In Economics, a market refers to the trade in a particular product when it is **made**.

4 **Factor markets.** The **factors of production** (land, labour, capital, enterprise) are sold to buyers who wish to make goods and provide services. Their demand is said to be **derived** from the demand for the final product, e.g. oil companies seek more divers if demand for oil increases.

5 **Geographical markets.** This refers to the **size** of the market in terms of potential customers. For instance, the market for 'self-pick' strawberries is limited by the distance people are prepared to travel and the price difference between self-picking and buying from a shop. As the sale of many raw materials, e.g. silver and primary products such as cocoa, is world-wide, these would be classified as international. In between local and international markets, there will be regional and national markets.

6 **Commodity markets.** The trade in basic raw materials and foods is centred in London, e.g. cotton, tea exchanges. The goods can be bought immediately at the prevailing price (spot) determined by demand and supply or at a future date at an agreed price. The latter system was developed to protect traders from price changes over time.

7 **Free market or market economy.** In Unit 2, the market or capitalistic economy was outlined. In it there was resource allocation and price determination as a result of **competition** between buyers and sellers. In contrast, in a collectivist economy there is usually a small range of goods, and prices are fixed by the state. Between these two extremes, most economies operate as mixed economies. In practice, the conditions under which trading takes place vary enormously. The main market structures are Perfect Competition, Monopoly and Imperfect Competition.

7.2 Perfect competition

This structure describes an **imaginary** situation in which no one buyer and no one seller can determine the market price and each has perfect knowledge of market conditions. It is characterized by:

1 **A large number of sellers.** Each seller provides just a small share of the total and this makes him unable to influence market price.

2 **Perfect information.** Each buyer has complete knowledge of the market. Such information means that no seller can raise his price as he will lose all his customers, assuming that they are rational.

3 **Freedom of entry into the market.** If firms in a market are making large

profits (abnormal), more entrepreneurs will be attracted into the industry. It is assumed in perfect competition that entry is easy and that there are no restrictions on entry (Unit 7.3).

4 **Homogeneous products.** All goods are identical and cannot be distinguished

5 **Many buyers.** Each consumer buys only a small proportion of the total goods available and thus cannot influence market price by their own actions.
apart. Any differences between products would make competition less than perfect.

6 **No government interference.**

7 **Perfect mobility** of goods/factors throughout the market. This assumes no transport and no training costs.

These assumptions were made when demand and supply were discussed in Unit 4.

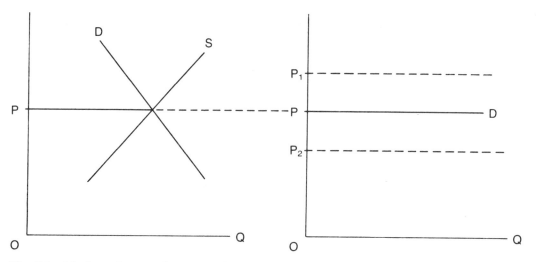

Fig. 7.1 Market price—perfect competition

Fig. 7.2 Individual firm's demand and supply in perfect competition

The demand and supply diagram in Fig. 7.1 shows market demand intersecting with market supply at **market** price P. Although the market demand curve is downward sloping left to right, the **individual** firm faces a **perfectly elastic** Demand curve as illustrated in Fig. 7.2. This is because each firm has to accept the market price and sell just at that price. If a firm tries to sell at P_1, it will price itself out of the market. It will get **no sales** as people will buy cheaper substitutes which they know about.

Conversely, if a firm tries to sell at P_2 it will **not make normal profit** because its supply is inelastic in the short run. The only effect of this price cutting will be to reduce total revenue.

In perfect competition, **market price = average revenue**—this is because all units of production are sold at the same price. For the same reason **average revenue = marginal revenue**.

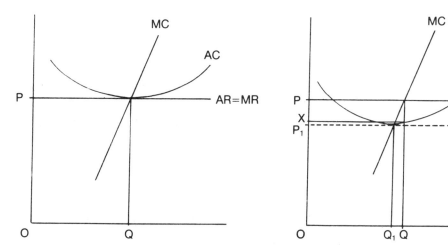

Fig. 7.3 Firm's output in perfect competition

Fig. 7.4 Effect of new firms entering perfect competition

When costs and revenue are combined, in Fig. 7.3, it can be seen that for **marginal cost** to equal marginal revenue (profit maximization, see Unit 5.5), **average revenue** must also **equal average cost**. Thus, in perfect competition, the firm produces output where AC = MC = AR = MR. It sells OQ at OP and makes normal profit. This position produces **normal profit** because normal profit is included within average cost (see Unit 5.5).

The firm's production in perfect competition will be at the **optimum** (lowest AC)—i.e. greatest efficiency.

For a short period of time, **abnormal profit** might be earned in perfect competition as in Fig. 7.4 at price P (orange shaded area PX abnormal profit on each of OQ sales). However, **new firms would enter the industry** because there are no entry barriers. This would lower prices probably until P_1 occurred and just normal profit was made (Q_1 output).

Perfect competition in the market economy

The general advantages and disadvantages of capitalism apply to perfect competition. In addition, there are some **specific advantages** to perfect competition.

1 **No excessive profits** are made because higher prices lead to no sales. In the long run there are new entrants and normal profits obtained (see Fig. 7.4).

2 **Production is at lowest average cost** in the long run. This produces efficiency. Inefficient firms cannot sell at the market price and so will be forced out of the industry.

Specific disadvantages to perfect competition

1 **Small-scale** production means less scope for economies of scale, thus higher costs than in other market structures perhaps.

2 As all **products are the same**, there is no incentive for research and development in a market and less consumer choice.

7.3 Monopoly

A monopoly occurs when the **supply of a product is controlled by one firm**. It is very rare in practice. In a **pure** monopoly, the one firm has no competitors and the good has no close substitutes. The government has a wider definition of monopoly in Britain. Its definition is 'where **a quarter of an industry** is controlled by one firm'. This means that the market structures of oligopoly and duopoly come within the supervision of monopoly.

A duopoly is two firms controlling an industry.

An oligopoly is a few large firms controlling an industry.

Causes of monopoly   'LAST'

1 **Legal protection.** Some monopolies are granted by law. Investors get patents (e.g. cats' eyes) which allow only them to make something. On a larger scale, NCB has the sole right to extract coal in UK, although it does allow others to mine under licence from it. Furthermore, it cannot stop people collecting coal washed up on the beach.

2 **Avoid wastage of resources.** Some industries are considered to be unsuitable for competition, e.g. gas, electricity. Competition would lead to duplication of resources (see Unit 3.2).

3 **Supply restrictions.** Geological and geographical features may mean that some minerals, e.g. gold, diamonds, are only found in a few parts of the world leading to natural monopolies. Within an area, a local monopoly, e.g. village shop, may develop where transport costs limit the size of the market.

4 **Takeovers.** One firm may emerge victorious from a competitive situation through technical efficiency and superior marketing strategy, e.g. London Brick Co. However, the Stock Exchange panel may examine proposed takeovers.

Forms of monopoly

Nationalized industries (see Unit 3.2). These are legal monopolies created by the **state**. Although having a monopoly in their own industry, e.g. provision of gas for heating, they may be competing with one another in a wider market, e.g. domestic heating. They are usually allowed because they operate in the **public interest** and profits in theory are returned to the people through lower taxes.

Cartels. **A group of firms** agree and arrange to **act together** in a market. They either restrict supply or fix prices.

> 1 In **theory**, the cartel sets up a **selling syndicate** (group) which sells on behalf of the members. The best example of this is the Milk Marketing Board which acts for farmers in UK.
>
> 2 In **practice**, the term 'cartel' covers **loose price fixing agreements and market shareouts**.

In 1986 ICI, Shell and thirteen other European petrochemical companies were fined a total of £35 million by the European Commission for running a price-fixing cartel. Between 1977 and 1983 they fixed the price of polypropylene, keeping it 15–40 per cent above the 'real' market level, mainly because the industry was making big losses.

Trade Associations. Firms in industry form an association to **look after their interests**. They may agree to **share out the market** among themselves, either by product or geographical area. Alternatively, they might decide a **common price**, thereby avoiding the cost of unnecessary advertising and subsidizing unprofitable parts of the market. Both would lead to greater profits. Such restrictive practices are now scrutinized by government (see Unit 7.4).

Characteristics

As the **monopolist's output = industry's output**, he faces a downward sloping demand curve. He is not tied to accepting the market price like a firm in Perfect Competition. He has a choice:

> 1 He can **fix price** and **make supply elastic** at that price and let quantity demanded determine the quantity sold.
>
> 2 He can **fix quantity sold**, thereby **making supply inelastic** and let quantity demanded determine the price.

The monopolist can only sell more by reducing price, because demand slopes downwards. This means that MR does not equal AR. MR is less than AR as illustrated in Fig. 7.7, because in order to sell more the price needs reducing.

However, monopolist still produces where MC = MR, so in Fig. 7.7 he supplies OQ at market price P (we are assuming S inelastic). The average cost of producing OQ is OC (where AC crosses S line). PC is **abnormal profit**, on each unit sold. A situation like this can persist in the long run because new firms cannot enter the industry.

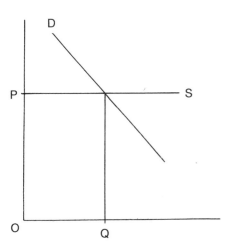

Fig. 7.5 Monopolist—fixing prices

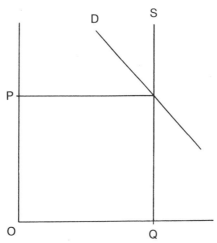

Fig. 7.6 Monopolist—fixing quantity

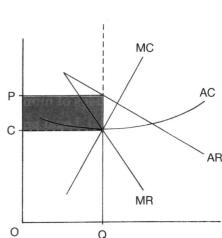

Fig. 7.7 Monopolist—output

Specific advantages 'WERE'

> 1 **Wasteful** competition is reduced.
> 2 **Economies** of scale enables production at lower average cost than several small competing firms.
> 3 **Research** and development can be undertaken as there is a secure market.
> 4 **Excess** capacity is avoided.

Disadvantages

> 1 High prices may be maintained to keep abnormal profits in the long run.

2 Lack of competition may lead to lower-quality goods.

3 Optimum production not obtained (not best use of resources) because production not at lowest average cost, unlike Perfect Competition.

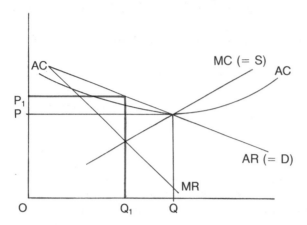

Fig. 7.8   Monopoly and perfect competition—efficiency

In Perfect Competition the market price would be where MC(S)=AR(D), where MC=MR too, i.e. in Fig. 7.8 price P, quantity Q.

However, in monopoly as MR is lower than AR, the market price is different P_1 Q_1. Thus production at Q_1 is **not at the optimum**, i.e. most efficient, lowest cost output. Thus best use of the resources is not obtained. A monopolist will produce there, as it is **maximum profit** which motivates him. However, this diagram assumes that the average costs of a monopolist are similar to those of a firm in perfect competition. This may not be the case as a monopolist can benefit from economies of scale and thereby lower costs.

7.4 Government and monopoly

Government control may be:

Direct

1 Breaking up a monopoly, by making it illegal, e.g. USA policy of trust busting.
2 **Nationalization,** e.g. electricity.
3 **Supervision** of activities of public corporations which are regularly accountable to a Minister and Parliament.

Indirect

4 **Establishing independent bodies** such as Monopolies Commission to **investigate/report on** monopolies and restrictive practices. Restrictive trade practices are agreements between firms which limit competition in price, range of goods or services available within an industry. This approach recognizes that some monopolies may be beneficial or only harmful in part.
5 Setting up a **court** to judge monopoly activities. If these activities are deemed to be against the public interest then they can be dealt with.

Summary of major legislation

Fair Trading Act 1973. This Act set up the Office of Fair Trading headed by the Director General. It protects consumers against **harmful** trading practices, monopolies and mergers. The 1948 Monopolies Commission was renamed the **Monopolies and Mergers Commission** in 1965.

Restrictive Trade Practices Act 1976. The Act consolidated earlier legislation. It covers the regulation of **restrictive agreements** relating to **goods** and **services** and enables judicial investigation by a Restrictive Practices Court, set up in 1956.

Resale Prices Act 1976. This brought together earlier legislation. It prohibits **collective** and **individual** resale price maintenance for goods (i.e. manufacturer telling shops what price to sell goods for, or else they would not supply them).

Competition Act 1980. It supersedes Price Commission (set up in 1977 with power to freeze prices while investigating price rises) and established a new 'competition reference' procedure. The Director General (OFT) investigates any **anti-competitive** activity. This is anything likely to restrict, distort or prevent competition. The Director General publishes a report and then either, (a) negotiates a **voluntary** undertaking with the firm to drop the practice within **two months,** or (b) refers it to **Monopolies and Mergers Commission** within a **six month** deadline. If the MMC decides that the activity is 'against the public interest', then the **Department of Trade can prohibit it.** In addition, the Department of Trade can refer nationalized industries and other bodies to the Monopolies Commission for examination of their **efficiency, costs and service.** He can ask the Director General (OFT) to investigate cases of 'major public concern'.

In 1983, the Department of Trade bargained with the Stock Exchange over its restrictive practices. It agreed not to investigate if the Stock Exchange dropped its minimum commissions and brought outsiders on to the Stock Exchange Council (see Unit 11.4).

The work of the Monopolies and Mergers Commission

This commission can investigate where one firm controls at least a quarter of the market (originally this 'rule' was one third) and mergers involving assets exceeding £15 million (originally £5 million). It can also look into mergers where the new organization will control at least a quarter of market. It **can prohibit** acquisitions and regulate prices.

Aims

1 It seeks to promote competition, in particular it stresses **consumer sovereignty, efficiency** and **reward to enterprise.**
2 It opposes most **entry barriers,** vertical integration and aggressive competition.
3 It acts as a deterrent against misuse of **monopoly power.** However, it does recognize the benefits of **economies of scale.** It also supports **abnormal profits** as a reward for research, development and the risk of investment.

Powers

1 It can impose sanctions, e.g. Hoffman Le Roche ordered to repay £3 million to NHS; Unilever and Proctor and Gamble were told to reduce prices by 40 per cent in 1975.
2 It can prevent mergers, e.g. Imperial Tobacco (who make Golden Wonder) and Smiths Crisps.

Work of Restrictive Practices Court

It enforces the 1976 Act. This act requires the registration of all agreements under which **two or more** persons support restrictions relating to the **price of goods, the conditions, quantities, processes or areas and persons supplied**.

It operates on the principle of **guilty till proven innocent.** It assumes all restrictive practices are against the public interest unless satisfying one of the **eight gateways.** These gateways or exceptions include:

1 Avoiding local unemployment.
2 Promoting exports.
3 Satisfying public interest.

Any restrictive practice not registered is illegal.

Achievements

1 Less than 1 per cent of all registered agreements have been found to be illegal— nearly all of the guilty ones were for price fixing.
2 Cartels have been swept away, e.g. ready-mixed concrete.

but

1 Price wars often follow the courts' decisions. These may benefit the consumer in the short term. However, in the long run, if the winner dominates the industry, then the consumer may suffer.
2 Recommended prices have been developed and many unofficial, informal arrangements still operate.

7.5 Imperfect competition

Sometimes called Monopolistic Competition this lies between the extremes of pure monopoly and perfect competition. There are **several market structures** collectively known as Imperfect Competition (or Monopolistic Competition), they are:

Monopolistic	**many firms**	⎞	**but** market limitations and
	very competitive	⎟	information restrictions
Oligopoly	a few firms	⎟	tendency to collusion and
Duopoly	two firms	⎠	monopoly behaviour

Examples: Monopolistic   furniture making   largest five firms = 25 per cent of market

            Oligopoly   canned beer   largest five firms = 80 per cent of market

            Duopoly   household detergents   largest two firms = 90 per cent of market

The percentage of the market supplied by five largest firms is usually called the concentration ratio. It has increased for nearly every industry in Britain in the last 25 years.

Monopolistic competition. The market is characterized by:

1 Price cutting, e.g. ZX81 computers—£100 → £69 → £49 → £39—inside two years, in response to competition from Spectrum, Tandy, Dragon, Vic 20, Electron, Oric.

2 Non-price competition, e.g. free offers, holidays, etc.

3 Packaging and advertising—these are often 20 per cent of total costs.

4 Consumer services often provided, e.g. 'interest-free credit'. The idea of such behaviour is to create brand loyalty which makes Demand curve more inelastic.

Oligopoly and duopoly. The temptation and the ability to co-operate have produced **less aggressive marketing**. For instance, one firm might take the lead on raising prices which others follow, e.g. petrol prices.

The behaviour of firms in these markets has occasionally been seen by the Monopolies Commission to be **'not in the public interest'**. This has been because of higher profits, inefficiency and prevention of new entrants.

7.6 Summary

A market is where goods and services are bought and sold. Perfect competition is based on certain assumptions and describes an imaginary situation where no one buyer or seller dominates the market. The advantages of perfect competition are those of capitalism in general with the addition of optimum production and no excessive profit. However, there is little scope for scale economies and less consumer choice.

A monopoly occurs where the supply of a product is controlled by one firm. In practice the legal definition specifies an individual firm controlling more than 25 per cent of its market. Monopolies can develop in several ways and result in advantages to the consumer. However, there are the disadvantages of high profits, high prices and less than optimum output.

Governments attempt to control monopolies and protect consumers through the Restrictive Practices Court, OFT and the Monopolies and Mergers Commission. In general monopolies and restrictive practices are assumed to be against the public interest unless it can be proved otherwise. Between the extremes of monopoly and perfect competition are several more Common Market structures including monopolistic competition and oligopoly.

8 MONEY

8.1 Introduction

Today, money can be obtained legally by:

1 Working for it, e.g. a week's wages.
2 Gaining an income for letting someone use your assets, e.g. rent for a flat.
3 Being paid by the state, e.g. Supplementary Benefit.
4 Receiving a gift, e.g. £5 for birthday.
5 Borrowing, e.g. a bank loan.

The last is repayable with interest, but 1–4 usually involve no further expense. These four sources of income enable a person to buy goods and services (consumption) and save money (savings).

8.2 Definition

'Money is anything that is **acceptable** to its users in an economic system.'

As most economic systems operate through trade, because people are not self-sufficient, the money has to facilitate the exchange of goods/services. These goods and services need to be valued and money is the measure which does that. Any profits made might wish to be saved for future use, thus money needs to keep its value.

It is often said that **'money is what money does'**. This means that anything can be used as money as long as it performs certain key functions.

8.3 Functions

There are four main functions of money. They can be remembered by the word **'SUMS'**.

Store of value. When people receive money the amount not spent is saved. People expect their savings to maintain their value for when they wish to spend them. Thus money should be capable of holding its value through time, so that the buying of goods in the future by savers does not put them at a disadvantage.

In the past, people hoarded gold because it kept its value. Clearly if inflation is rapid, the value of savings falls and money does not function efficiently as a store of value. This occurred in Britain in 1978 when the annual rate of inflation exceeded 25 per cent. Thus within one year the real value of £100 of savings was reduced by 25 per cent.

Unit of account. This is sometimes referred to as a **'measure of value'**. It means that all goods and services are valued in common units (e.g. £ and pence) which people accept and understand. This enables the easy comparison of products, e.g. £10 skirt = 20 × 50p blocks of chocolate. It also avoids the disadvantages of barter (see Unit 8.5).

Medium of exchange. This function means that the money is acceptable to the seller when the buyer pays for the good bought. Thus money enables exchange/trade to take place and barter is no longer needed (see Unit 8.5).

In a modern society a worker is paid wages in money (rather than goods) and this enables him to spend when and where he wants. Furthermore, the benefits of specialization can occur because surpluses can be sold.

Standard for deferred payments. Deferred means 'postponed'. Money allows for goods to be obtained one day and paid for on another day, or over a period of time, in an acceptable way. Thus it enables credit to be given to buyers and reassures sellers that they will receive the expected amount, valued in money, later. Credit thereby encourages trade. Thus, a car bought on hire purchase will involve the buyer in monthly repayments of money to the garage owner/HP company.

In the past when goods were paid for 'in kind'—by performing a service or receiving food/lodging—the payment was open to dispute, e.g. an itinerant gardener weeds a lord's lawn in return for his food/lodging for a week: How much food is he entitled to? What nature should his lodgings take?

8.4 Qualities

In order to perform the above functions, anything used as money needs to possess certain desirable properties. These characteristics can be remembered by the phrase '**ADDS UP**'.

Acceptability. This key quality means that people are prepared to accept something as money. Thus the Yap Islanders in the South Seas used to make payments in giant stone cartwheels which were kept under water. They facilitated the Store of Value function better than the other functions!

Durability. Money needs to be long-lasting, particularly in order to remain as a store of value and standard for deferred payment. Thus perishables are no good as money. It is probably because of this that people keep new crisp notes and spend old tatty ones.

Divisibility. The money used has to be capable of being divided into units, so that small amounts can be paid exactly. Thus, we have £1 which divides into 50p, 20p, 10p, 5p, 2p and 1p pieces. The development of cheques is making this quality less important, but it will remain whilst 40 per cent of the adult population do not have bank current accounts.

Stability. The maintenance of value over time is important for money to keep its store of value function, so that trust is maintained. If a currency loses its stable value then the economic system goes haywire. For instance, the hyperinflation of Germany in the 1920s led to wages being paid twice per day and money being quickly spent because its value was rapidly declining. Value is maintained if money is **relatively scarce**, e.g. sand or leaves would not be chosen.

Uniformity. If money is of variable quality then people may be wary of certain types of money. For instance in 1983, people were reluctant to hold £1 coins and preferred £1 notes. In the past coins with more precious metal in them were retained and others spent. Thus, today, all 10p pieces are indentical in shape, size, weight and content and this facilitates all functions of money except the Store of Value idea. Uniformity aids easy recognition of money.

Portability. Money needs to be easily carried around so that it can be exchanged for goods/services as required. In the past when workers were paid in tokens, which could only be redeemed at factory shops, they had no freedom of choice and were easily exploited. This was known as the truck system. Today cheques give a consumer flexibility and increased choice, because they are easy to transport and generally acceptable.

8.5 Historical development

Barter

Primitive communities in the past managed without money. Tribes produced just enough for themselves. Skills and abilities were pooled and production was amicably shared out. Some tribes in the Amazon jungle still operate in this way today.

However, as simple economic systems advanced through specialization and the division of labour (see Unit 5.2) groups and individuals often produced a surplus. This surplus was traded for the surpluses of other groups. Initially the trading was by barter—the **swapping of goods** or direct exchange. One tribe might have a surplus of apples which it could exchange for another tribes' surplus cow. There were three main problems with barter, which can be remembered by the word '**RID**'. You could say that barter was got **rid** of—because of its deficiencies!

Rate of exchange. Primitive traders had to agree how many apples were worth one cow. This involved haggling and dispute over the value of the swapped goods. It made trade difficult. Today, sellers fix prices and the consumer either accepts that price or does not buy—usually it is 'take it or leave it' which makes trade much easier and less time-consuming.

Indivisibility of goods. Some goods, such as apples, were capable of division into small quantities whereas others, such as cows, were only useful as a whole unit. As a cow could not be divided without losing its value, the person swapping it could not make an exchange if the other person offered only a small quantity of his surplus, such as a few apples. Thus, there was no flexibility in the bargaining when large indivisible goods were involved.

Double coincidence of wants. If the trader with apples wanted a cow then there was a possibility of exchange. However, finding someone who wanted what you had, and who was prepared to offer in exchange what you wanted, was not easy. Thus, one person's wants had to equal another person's needs, and vice versa, at the same time. This made obtaining the right combination of goods and services very difficult and time-consuming.

Early forms of money

Goods (or *commodities*). As the scale of trade developed, an easier method of exchange was needed within communities, goods with some intrinsic value to the people were used. Such goods were usually chosen because of their acceptability and stability of value. However, some goods, such as salt, cattle and tobacco, suffered from the disadvantage of variable quality and perishability.

The early American settlers in Virginia used tobacco as money for 200 years up to the mid-19th century. However, as the bales were cumbersome and people paid in the worst quality tobacco, public warehouses were provided to weigh, grade and certificate set quantities.

If trade in the communities using such goods was limited, the function of this money was as a Store of Value. However, if it was perishable then its primary function would be as a medium of exchange.

Rare objects. Some systems developed rare objects as money. Cowrie shells and dogs' teeth, which were easily divisible into convenient units, were graded into proper monetary systems. Although useful as a means of exchange this form of money lacked homogeneity and was susceptible to sharp fluctuations in value, as the market could be disturbed by new finds. For instance, in the Admiralty Islands, dogs' teeth were rare until Western traders flooded the market with some imported from China, and created inflation!

Precious metals. These came into use because their properties overcame the weaknesses associated with earlier forms of money. As gold and silver were attractive in appearance, fairly rare and non-deteriorating, they were readily acceptable. In addition, being portable and divisible into different standard sizes and weights, they facilitated exchange and acted as a clear unit of account. The general shortage of such metals meant that their value was maintained over time, enabling them to perform as a Store of Value also. A further advantage of gold was that it was acceptable in most countries and this encouraged international trade.

Paper money

The popularity of gold gradually reduced its usefulness as money. Its supply did not expand quickly enough to meet its demand. Furthermore, because gold was precious it was liable to theft. Thus people holding gold often left it for safe keeping with **goldsmiths**. They received a receipt for the gold deposit, which they took back in order to collect the gold when it was needed. The use of these goldsmith's receipts developed into bank notes. Thus the goldsmiths were, (a) creating money by giving credit, (b) earning profits by charging interest, and (c) taking risks by judging the credit worthiness of borrowers.

These functions are similar to those of modern **banks**. During the Industrial Revolution many goldsmiths were tempted into overlending, because of the profitability. They lent more money than their gold holdings and could not redeem receipts. This caused financial crises. Thus **the 1844 Bank Charter Act** gave the Bank of England the sole right of note-issue. Joint-stock banks, the successors of the goldsmiths, could not issue new notes. This Act also introduced the **Fiduciary Issue** which enabled the Bank of England (only) to issue bank notes without full gold backing. This issue has rapidly increased from the initial £14 million with inflation to £10,000 billion. It is not possible nowadays to go to a bank and ask for the gold equivalent (about 1/300 oz) of £1 note.

Cheques

In the early days of banks, some traders requested their 'bank' to pay a named sum to a particular person on a certain day. This was convenient, safe and saved the trader time. Such written instructions were the forerunner of today's cheque (see Fig. 8.1).

In 1882 the Bill of Exchange Act defined a cheque as a bill of exchange drawn on a banker payable on demand. The main advantages of cheques as money are:

1 Convenience—easy portability, divisible.
2 Time saving—avoids frequent withdrawals from bank.
3 Generally acceptable, if accompanied with a cheque guarantee card, although not legal tender.

Fig. 8.1 A typical cheque

Legal tender. This is money that a creditor has to accept in settlement of a debt. For instance, £s are legal up to any amount, but 10p coins can only be used up to £5 limit (i.e. 50 × 10p coins).

Cheque guarantee card. A small plastic card issued by a bank to those with cheque books (Fig. 8.2). These cards, which make cheques acceptable to most retailers, were introduced in 1966. The initial limit on the amount guaranteed by the Bank was £30. The current limit of £50 has been in force since 1977. The banks do not wish to raise the limit because most customers (not just an élite as originally) have these cards and fraud is costly to them.

Fig. 8.2   A typical cheque guarantee card

Fig. 8.3   A typical credit card

Coins. These are still an important form of money—for students and those purchasing goods under £5. They are produced by the Royal Mint. They are 'token money', as the face value of the coin (e.g. 20p) is worth more than the intrinsic value (value of metal in it, i.e. 2p). With inflation, there has been an increased demand for higher denomination coins and notes. In 1983 the £1 coin was introduced. This has now replaced the £1 note.

Credit cards

The development of credit has enabled people to 'buy' goods without using money. Informal credit ('on tick', 'on the slate') at the local shop still operates, but credit cards are now widespread. These enable the user to buy goods from a shop, if it participates in a credit card scheme, and instruct the shop to obtain a sum of money from the buyer's account. The transaction is completed by the buyer giving his credit card number and signing a standard slip of paper for the shopkeeper. The credit card company guarantees the money to the shopkeeper and in return takes a small percentage of the amount spent. Credit is the main form of money used to buy consumer durables.

Three types of credit card can be classified.

1 **Bank customers.** The banks have led the way by issuing Barclaycard (now VISA) and Access to their favoured customers. These two plastic cards account for 90 per cent of credit business. The main advantages and disadvantages to the **Customer** are:

Advantages	*Disadvantages*
(a) Wide range of outlets	(a) Established good credit record needed
(b) Buy now, pay later	(b) Interest charged, if repayment not made within the specified time (usually 3 weeks)
(c) Easier and safe shopping	(c) Minimum age 18 usually
	(d) High interest rates

2 **Businessmen.** Less common and more exclusive are credit cards for businessmen, e.g. American Express, Diners Club. Generally, these give more days interest-free credit and a lower rate of interest **but** their use is more restrictive and they apply more to services than to goods.

3 **Retailers' customers.** Most department stores and some other retailers issue their own cards which are often called 'credit cards', although some are more accurately classified as 'budget accounts' because they require regular repayment and are limited to one store or group of stores. The rate of interest charged varies enormously, whilst bank credit cards' interest rates fall within a fairly narrow competitive range. A typical credit card is shown in Fig. 8.3.

A major drawback from the point of view of credit-card companies is the increasing amount of fraud. In 1984, Access, Barclaycard, American Express and Diners Club lost £15 million through fraud. It is reckoned that on average a credit card is stolen every five minutes in Britain today.

8.6 Measurement of money

The total volume of money in the economy is important. Clearly, if the quantity of money in the system increases, and production is constant, this will cause inflation and the value of money will fall. However, **'what is money?'** is the subject of some dispute and there are several official definitions. The different measures are distinguished by their **'liquidity'**, i.e. how quickly they can be used to buy goods/services. Figure 8.4 illustrates the differences.

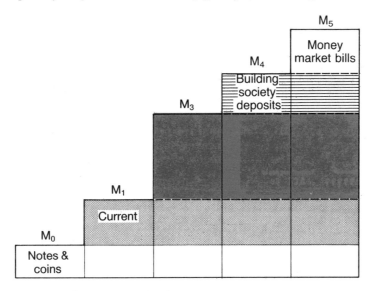

Fig. 8.4 Components of main money measures

The most liquid, M0, is termed 'narrow' money whilst the least liquid measure M5 is called a broad monetary measure.

M1 = notes and coins and private sector sight (current account) deposits. This narrow money stock has components which function both as a store of value and a medium of exchange.
M3 = cash and current account holdings and deposit account balances, in the private sector. M3 = 10 per cent cash, 30 per cent current account and 60 per cent deposit account and is a broader definition of the quantity of money in the system. As the distinction between current accounts and deposit accounts becomes less clear, the usefulness of M1 is diminishing.
M4 = M3 plus building society deposits.
M5 = M4 plus money market lending e.g. certificates of deposit.

M1 is the most liquid but smallest volume measure, whereas M5 is the least liquid but largest size. Many people treat **building society deposits** as 'money', mainly because they are a store of value. For instance, usually £250 can be withdrawn in cash without notice being given. However, **credit cards**, which are a means of exchange but not a store of value, are not included in any of the definitions.

In operating economic policies, the government often utilizes a **monetary target**. M3 has often been chosen and governments have tried to influence its growth. However, M3 has increased much faster than the other monetary aggregates. The growth has also been above the government's targets, e.g. in 1980–81 M3 increased by 18·3 per cent despite a 7–11 per cent planned target. It has been claimed that when a measure of money is officially adopted and control is attempted, the measure loses its meaning. This occurs because the banks often seek to maintain their profits, even if this means thwarting government credit restrictions.

In October 1983, the government discarded M3 as its main monetary target and replaced it with **M0**. This consists almost entirely of **notes and coins**. It has been chosen as it **should** indicate **changes in demand** in the economy. More cash in circulation (M0 increase) means more demand for goods and services, and the increased possibility of inflation.

However, the increased use and acceptance of plastic credit cards rather than cash may make M0 a less effective measure of demand. In 1986, it was discarded as too unreliable a target. The government now says it will take an overall view of all of the available money measures.

8.7 Summary

Money is anything that is acceptable to its users in an economic system. Anything may be used as money as long as it performs the four basic functions of money. In order to perform these functions certain characteristics are desirable.

Primitive economies managed without money but as they developed this barter system became inefficient and was eventually replaced by precious metals and paper money.

Money exists in several forms, such as coins, notes, cheques and credit cards. There are several measures of money, both broad and narrow. Recently M3 and M0 have served as official monetary targets but they have proved unreliable.

9 INFLATION

9.1 Recent history

Since 1970, inflation has become a major economic problem in Britain and most other developed countries (see Fig. 9.1). The annual rate of price increase started rising above the acceptable 1960s average of 4 per cent and reached a peak of 24.2 per cent in 1975. Thus, the main priority of the Conservative government elected in 1979, and re-elected in 1983 and 1987, was to reduce inflation.

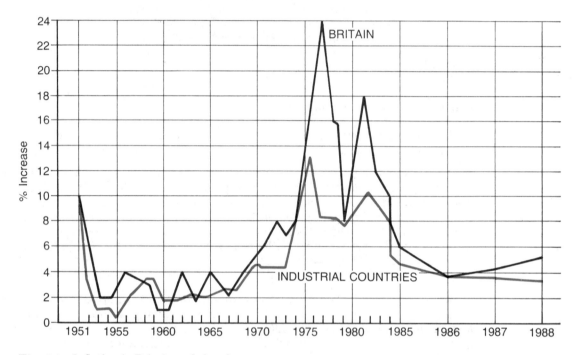

Fig. 9.1 Inflation in Britain and elsewhere

9.2 Definition

'A persistent general increase in prices'

The result of this tendency for prices to rise is that the value of money falls. The rising prices of goods and services mean that the **cost of living** has increased. If people's incomes do not improve, then they become worse off. When this happens we say that **real income has fallen**, as the same income purchases less. Thus, an increase in the cost of living will lead to a **fall in the standard of living**, if other things remain unchanged.

9.3 Types

Many different types of inflation have been described. However, the most common today and therefore the most important are listed below.

Creeping. A 'low' inflation rate which lasts for many years. This occurred in **Britain** and other industrialized countries in the 1960s and 1970s, with each trough being higher than the previous ones as shown in Fig. 9.1. The figure given for the annual percentage increase in this type of inflation has been revised upward over the years. 'Low' is now considered to be less than 10 per cent, whereas in the 1960s text books described it as 2–3 per cent!

Strato. A **'high'** but fluctuating inflation rate. It is a characteristic of **developing** economies, with rates of over 100 per cent common in bad years. South American countries are particularly prone to this type of inflation, partly because of their authoritarian government policies.

Hyper. **Short-lived** and unusually **high** rates of inflation, i.e. 1000 per cent per annum; e.g.

Israel 1986. Such astronomical rates are often caused by gross economic mismanagement and/or political crises. These may occur anywhere, but the best example was **Weimar Germany in 1923** when prices rose daily and people lost faith in the currency. The history books quote the famous example of a person putting down a basket of money and having the basket stolen and the money left! In times of hyperinflation, barter returns, as money ceases to function as a means of exchange and store of value.

9.4 Measurement

Inflation cannot be measured exactly, as its impact varies between people, places and times. For **example**:

1 Different people buy **different goods**—if the price of cheese doubles and price of jam remains unchanged, then people eating cheese sandwiches are affected more by inflation than people eating jam sandwiches.
2 The price of goods in **big towns** may be lower than in remote village areas, thus people living in towns suffer less from inflation and a higher cost of living.
3 In the **summer** months the price of fresh fruit and vegetables is much lower than in the winter and thus inflation in food is relatively slower.

The official figures can only be **estimates** because of such variations as these. They are **averages** which are calculated **monthly** and aggregated for yearly figures. There are several indices with the main one being the **Retail Price Index** (RPI). An index number provides a statistical method of measuring the average percentage change in the price of a set of **related goods and services** over a period of time. This is usually calculated from a **base year** of 100 (Jan 1987). The RPI was 111.0 on January 17, 1989.

Usefulness of RPI

1 **Information** is needed for government policy-making—the monthly movement of RPI can indicate the performance of a government's policies and enable more accurate forecasts of future trends. The Treasury estimates of inflation are 3 per cent out on average!
2 **General indication of the cost of living** is given by the RPI. This is often used by trade unions as a guide when making wage claims. It is also useful to businessmen when they are assessing future economic prospects.
3 **Certain government benefits** are determined by the RPI. Pension increases are now index linked by law and so RPI provides a standard measure.

Characteristics of RPI   'WEBB'

Weights are allocated to goods and services according to the proportion of family income spent upon them. In Fig. 9.2, the weight for food has declined since 1966, whilst one new general category, meals out, has been introduced. The weights are adjusted each January and changes reflect modifications to the spending pattern of the average family.

	1966	*1974*	*1979*	*1985*
Food	298	232	214	190
Alcoholic drink	67	82	82	75
Tobacco	77	46	40	37
Housing	113	108	124	153
Fuel and light	64	53	59	65
Durables	57	70	69	65
Clothing and footwear	91	89	84	75
Transport	116	149	151	156
Miscellaneous goods	61	71	74	77
Services	56	52	62	62
Meals out	0	48	41	45
	1000	1000	1000	1000

Fig. 9.2   Retail Price Index weights

Exclusions are made for pensioners and household heads earning at least twice the national average. This is done to maintain the 'average' approach to expenditure. Similarly, certain payments which are variable or non-measurable services (e.g. insurance premiums) are excluded.

Basket of goods is chosen. In 1914, when the price index began, it measured the changing price of necessities. Since 1945 it has been extended to include the bulk of consumer spending.

A **representative** sample of goods is obtained from the Family Expenditure Survey and data are collected for them. **Consistency** is maintained by reviewing the same quality of good each time; each month 200 people collect information on over 500 goods, covering each of the 11 categories in the index, using 270 middle-income families every fortnight.

Base year is selected. January 1987 was a new base year, as was January 1974. Typical years are chosen so that inflation is not measured from an unreliable base. For instance, 1973 would have been a poor year for revision of RPI because of the dramatic quadrupling of oil prices which was occurring at the time.

9.5 Method of calculation

The calculation of RPI can be explained simply by assuming that the index covers a **basket** of just three items—chips, coke and cigarettes. Each is weighted according to its relative importance in the family budget.

Item	Price	Weight	P. × Wt.
Chips	100	50	5000
Coke	100	10	1000
Cigarettes	100	40	4000
		100	10,000

Base year

$$\frac{10,000}{100} = 100$$

Fig. 9.3   RPI example—base year

If 50 per cent of the budget is spent on chips, 10 per cent on coke and 40 per cent on cigarettes, then the weights are as in the base year table (Fig. 9.3). Each item's initial price is represented by 100 in the price column of the index.

Item	Price	Weight	P. × Wt.
Chips	120	50	6000
Coke	140	10	1400
Cigarettes	110	40	4400
		100	11,800

Next year

$$\frac{11,800}{100} = 118$$

Fig. 9.4   RPI example—next year

In Fig. 9.4, the prices of chips have increased by 20 per cent, coke by 40 per cent and cigarettes by 10 per cent. The index number, which is an average, shows an increase of 18 per cent.

Item	Price	Weight	P. × Wt.
Chips	120	40	4800
Coke	154	10	1540
Cigarettes	132	50	6600
		100	12,940

Following year

$$\frac{12,940}{100} = 129.4$$

Fig. 9.5   RPI example—following year

Figure 9.5 shows the following year in which both spending patterns and prices have changed. People have spent less on chips (weight falls to 40) and 10 per cent more on cigarettes (weight rises to 50). The price of chips remained unchanged (120) whereas the price of coke rose by 10 per cent (140 + 14 (10 per cent of 140)). The government increased VAT on cigarettes causing a 28 per cent price rise and raising its index price to 132 (110 + 22). Overall, although the price index rose to 129.4, prices increased less quickly compared to the previous year (9.7 per cent, i.e. 11.4/118 as opposed to 18 per cent, i.e. 18/100).

Problems of measurement   'CRABS'

Changes in the nature of the goods and services used in the index may occur, although the weights and price remain the same. For instance, a $\frac{1}{4}$ lb bar of chocolate may contain less cocoa and more water, and so perhaps it becomes of lower quality. Thus comparisons become more difficult and less clear cut over time, as products change.

Range of households included in the survey will influence the weights. As patterns of expenditure depend on income, then different income groups have different baskets. For instance, if food prices rise rapidly, then pensioners, who spend a higher proportion of their income on food than average, will suffer more than the RPI indicates. Thus changes in RPI do not affect all groups equally.

Averages are used. In practice few people fall into this category and thus RPI is too simple and too general.

Base year soon gets out of date and unrealistic. For instance, the new base year of 1974 was 100 in the index, yet by April 1986, the index read 380.

Spending patterns change rapidly and so the weights and items need frequent revision. Factors such as:

1 Changes in taste, e.g. less spending on haircuts by men.
2 New products, e.g. video boom in 1980s.
3 Increased income—less spending on necessities, more spending on luxury services, e.g. meals out.

9.6 Effects of inflation

The impact of inflation is illustrated in Fig. 9.6.

Item	1976	1986	Percentage increase
Denim jeans	£9.70	£19.40	100
Colour TV	£274.00	£350.00	28
20 cigarettes	£0.46	£1.38	200
RPI	156	379.5	143
Average male weekly earnings	£65	£170	162

Fig. 9.6 Inflation—selected examples

The mnemonic **'BIRDS'** can be used to remember the effects of inflation.

Business confidence

Fluctuating rates of inflation make it difficult for entrepreneurs to **predict** the economic future and accurately calculate the returns on their investment in new plant and machinery. They may fear government action which may depress demand and thereby reduce likely sales. Less investment usually means more unemployment. A high rate of inflation requires them to seek higher profits or else they will lose in real terms. If high profits do not seem likely then businessmen may cease production and put money into less risky ventures, such as gilts.

International competitiveness

If the prices of exports are rising faster than competitors' goods, then a nation's trade will probably suffer unless the goods are inelastic in demand. Britain's world market share in manufactured goods has slumped, partly for this reason.

Alternatively, imports may be relatively cheaper than home-produced goods, e.g. consumer durables in a modern kitchen. By 1986, 99 per cent of dishwashers, 75 per cent of fridge freezers and 70 per cent of clocks were imported. The overall impact is:

1 Less trade for British firms and so less production and likely unemployment.
2 The balance of trade (on just goods) is in deficit.

Redistribution of income

Those people on **fixed** incomes or incomes not keeping pace with inflation (e.g. unemployed) will become relatively worse off as their purchasing power falls. Increases in food prices and rent tend to hit poorer families most, because they spend a higher proportion of their income on such necessities. Thus income in **real terms** is redistributed from poor to rich.

Some groups, often those in strong and successful trade unions, gain real wage increases whilst others such as teachers and bus drivers, which are weak and poorly mobilized, lose out.

Deflation

Inflation is frequently followed by economic depression when a government takes measures to curb rising prices. However, the deflation does not feature falling prices but **lower output** and **fewer jobs**. Prices are 'sticky' downwards, in that the main costs of production, particularly wages, are difficult to reduce, as people have come to expect rising wages and rising prices.

Savings

With inflation, the value of savings falls. This is compensated for by the interest given by financial institutions. However, if the rate of inflation is higher than the rate of interest received, savers are losing in **real terms**.

Conversely, borrowers paying a rate of interest below the level of inflation will gain, as the money which they repay is worth less than the amount borrowed. In these conditions, increases in demand for credit could lead to excess demand in the economy and further fuel inflation. Thus, generally, inflation discourages saving and encourages borrowing.

9.7 Causes of inflation

Although British inflation has moved up and down with the other industrialized countries, it has tended to be 50 per cent higher on average (see Fig. 9.1). The two main causes of inflation are known as 'demand pull' and 'cost push'.

Demand pull

Generally, this is caused by excess purchasing power—too much money chasing too few goods. Thus increases in demand **pull up** prices, as supply is fairly constant.

Supply may be unable to expand, to meet the increased demand, because of lack of capacity—insufficient space, inadequate machinery, shortage of trained labour. Generally, in the economy, a low level of unemployment indicates supply as being near its maximum.

Increases in demand may be created by the following.

Increases in the supply of money. Monetarist economists believe that increases in money supply lead to price increases after 18 months. The money available can expand through:

1 The commercial banks issuing **more credit** to consumers and businessmen and thereby raising aggregate demand in the economy as a whole, e.g. 1972–73 relaxation of credit control by government.
2 The government running (or increasing) a **budget deficit** where spending exceeds income and money is pumped into the economy. If the deficit is covered by borrowing from abroad, then it is likely to be more inflationary. When the government borrows from domestic sources it may reduce the banks' capacity to create credit and so money supply may remain largely unchanged.

A balance of payments surplus. A current account surplus can lead to increased spending power in the domestic economy. Britain has rarely suffered from this, but West German inflation 1980–82 was accentuated by its export earnings.

Tax reductions. These occur through:

1 Lower basic rates of income tax.
2 Increased personal allowances.
3 Reduced national insurance contributions.

They all reduce the government's tax revenue and increase individual spending power.

Demand pull inflation serves to increase demand for particular goods. For instance, tax rebates often stimulate the purchase of consumer durables. The demand for dishwashers shifts to the right in Fig. 9.7 and price rises to P_1.

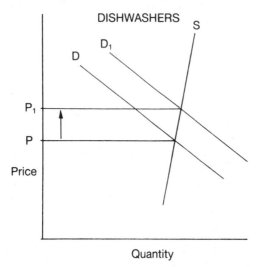

Fig. 9.7 The effect of demand pull inflation on a good

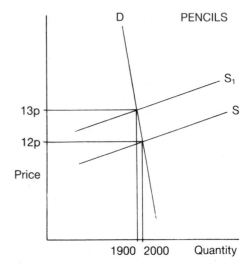

Fig. 9.8 The effect of cost push inflation on a good

Cost push

An increase in costs, not matched by similar higher production, which results in price rises is known as 'cost push inflation'. As producers set their prices in markets, they may decide to maintain profits and so **pass on** rising costs by raising their prices.

For example, a pencil sells for 12p, which is made up of 3p manufacturer's profit, 5p cost of production, 3p cost of distribution, 1p VAT. If production costs rise by 20 per cent (an extra 1p) then in order to **maintain** his 3p **profit**, the manufacturer needs to sell the pencil for 13p. However, this price rise will usually lead to a fall in quantity demanded, as in Fig. 9.8. Thus:

1 Manufacturer's **total profit has fallen** from 6000p (2000 × 3p) to 5700p (1900 × 3p).
2 Manufacturer's **profit percentage mark-up** has fallen from 33 per cent (3p/9p, i.e. profit/costs) to 30 per cent (3p/10p).

The factors which produce increased costs are as follows:

Imported raw materials. These may arise because of world **shortages**, particularly in the case of primary products like cocoa and sugar where the weather may devastate supply. Furthermore, the depreciation of the exchange rate (falling pound) serves to make imports more expensive and this may raise the cost of imports. Britain's **open** economy, which imports 30 per cent of GDP, and dependence on international trade, make her particularly vulnerable to this type of inflation. For instance, the quadrupling of **oil prices** in 1973 sent large shockwaves throughout the Western world, forcing up prices because of industry's reliance on oil for power.

Domestic costs. The main factor here is **wages**. Their impact varies between industries. In labour intensive services, e.g. Post Office, as wages account for 70 per cent of total cost, wage increases will probably be passed on in higher prices. Conversely, in **capital intensive** industries, such as petrochemicals, wage costs may be less than 10 per cent and less important than interest rate and fuel price changes. In these industries, high wage increases could be fairly easily absorbed. It is often argued that the increased power and greater militancy of **trade unions** in the 1970s forced employers to concede unrealistically high wage demands. These wage rises were then passed on in the form of higher prices because of the **monopolistic power** of the producers in many markets.

Poor productivity. If wage increases are matched by productivity improvements, the cost per unit of output does not necessarily rise. However, output per man has risen only slowly in the UK compared with the other major industrialized countries. This reflects low levels of investment, badly directed investment, a lack of modernization, old fashioned working practices and lack of labour mobility.

Profiteering. Some Marxists argue that businessmen who exploit labour anyway, raise their profits (which are a cost of production and thus added into the selling price) and cause inflation. In theory, this assumes that the demand for products is relatively **inelastic**, otherwise consumers would buy substitutes. In practice there is little evidence for this view as the 'real profits' of British industry fell during the 1960s and 1970s.

A combination of demand pull and cost push

As many factors in Economics are **interdependent**, the two main causes are likely to be intertwined and interacting. For example, increased raw-material prices may cause the price of consumer goods to rise. This cost push may provoke wage increases (further cost push) to maintain living standards or increased borrowing (demand pull) by businessmen to finance production.

Alternatively, making credit available to businessmen by an expansionary monetary policy (demand pull) may enable them to give in more easily to large wage demands (cost push). In particular, when there is a boom, firms may accept rapidly rising costs in order to supply the market profitably. Thus workers threatening strike action in pursuit of a wage claim, may obtain high wage rises because the extra cost to the manufacturer of the claim is less than the extra profit obtained by selling the product in an expanding market (opportunity cost!).

9.8 Control and policies

In modern economic society, inflation is **influenced** rather than controlled. It is certainly not within the government's capacity to cure it.

Restraints on government

Success for the government in the area of inflation control may have detrimental **side effects**, because economic policies do not operate in isolation, e.g. lowering inflation may increase unemployment which may have social and political consequences. Furthermore, the **time**

period involved is significant. There may be short-term hardships for society to bear in return for the long-term benefits.

Essentially the government needs to take a view on the cause of inflation, and choose suitable measures for that type. However, in practice, there is **not one cause** and as such the two broad theories may be intermingled.

Policies. Thus the possible policies proposed need to be qualified:

Reducing demand

Limit increases in the supply of money by:

1 **Curbing the banks'** ability to create credit—this can be done by a tight monetary policy (calling in special deposits, sales of gilts). However, the banks may thwart such policy as providing credit is profitable to them. If the credit limitation is successful, through high interest rates, this may lead to less consumer expenditure, lower production and more bankruptcies, which in turn increase unemployment.

2 **Reducing the budget deficit** or generating a budget surplus—a contraction in government spending will lead to less money in the economy via lower consumption and investment. But the policy means fewer public services thereby reducing the general standard of living, as well as probably redundancies in the public sector.

Obtaining a Balance of Payments balance or deficit. Extra imports and government expenditure abroad take money out of the domestic economy and thus reduce the inflationary pressure. However, this may bring about a Balance of Payments crisis. A falling pound makes imports more expensive and may encourage cost push inflation.

Increased taxation. Higher tax rates and lower allowances will increase government revenue and take more funds out of the economy, thus reducing **consumption** potential. Similarly, higher national insurance contributions raise revenue and cut spending. However, these measures may have **disincentive** effects on production and through lower consumption they serve to increase unemployment. As real incomes are cut, it may also lead to higher wage claims.

Limiting costs

Cost of imports reduced by appreciating pound. High interest rates relative to other countries may be used for this purpose. This is only indirectly under the influence of the Bank of England, although sensible and acceptable government policies can create confidence in the currency. In addition, the development of import substitutes and the discovery of raw materials (e.g. North Sea oil) can operate to minimize imported inflation.

Production costs could be subsidized to minimize their impact. The British Steel industry has complained that its international rivals are subsidized, thereby putting it at a competitive disadvantage. Certainly industrial electricity prices are subsidized in Germany.

Wage costs could be lowered/wage increases slowed down. The usual ways proposed for doing this are:

1 **Incomes policy.** The statutory control of incomes has been used in Britain in 1967, 1972 and 1975. It usually lays down an upper limit to wage settlements and thereby inhibits trade union bargaining.

2 **Reduction of trade union power.** The ability of many trade unionists to obtain wage increases above the level of inflation increased considerably in the 1970s. The increased use of the strike weapon and the development of the closed shop, combined with the unwillingness of successive governments to let unemployment increase, strengthened trade union bargaining power. The Conservative government of 1979 decided by legislation on picketing and strike ballots to curb this power. In addition, their deflationary policies led to moderation of wage claims as workers began to fear unemployment and accept low wage offers.

Raising productivity. Costs can be reduced if production is maintained with a smaller workforce or greater production is obtained with the same workers. Clearly, technological investment and production incentives can generate improvements. There was a spurt in British productivity in 1981–82 as labour was shed faster than output fell. British Steel, for instance, in certain plants, raised productivity by over 40 per cent in one year.

9.9 Summary

Inflation is defined as a persistent general increase in prices and has been a major problem in Britain since 1970. Three types may be distinguished: creeping, strato and hyper inflation. Although it cannot be measured exactly, the most useful estimate of inflation is the Retail

Price Index. It requires a base year, weights, a basket of goods and average households, although it may become distorted over time.

Inflation may have far-reaching consequences on business confidence, international competitiveness and income distribution. Although in practice the causes of inflation are likely to be intertwined, economists have identified two main causes, namely demand pull and cost push. In modern economies inflation can merely be influenced rather than controlled and it must be recalled that anti-inflation policies may have adverse side effects elsewhere in the economy.

10 BANKING

10.1 Introduction

Until 1979 there was no law to prevent any institution calling itself a 'bank', if it **accepted deposits and lent money**. The 1979 **Banking Act** classified all banking institutions into either:

1 **'Recognized banks'** such as Midland, Lloyds. This group contains three categories of bank—British, overseas and consortium (a bank set up by several other banks and including at least one overseas member).
2 **'Licensed deposit takers'** such as the 'Baptist Union Corporation' which can no longer use the word 'bank' in its name.

10.2 Types of bank

Commercial banks

These are the main clearing banks which have High Street premises. They all take deposits from the general public and because of this direct relationship, they are sometimes called **'retail'** banks. They are **public limited companies** (see Unit 3.3) which aim to make a profit, e.g. Midland averages £400 million per annum. The main commercial banks in Britain, which were initially called joint-stock banks, are Barclays, Lloyds, Midland, National Westminster, Coutts and Williams & Glyn's.

Merchant banks

These are banking brokers who bring together lenders and borrowers of large sums of money, e.g. firms. They operate in a **high risk** area and handle very large sums of money daily through their **international** transactions. They advise companies on money management, arrange short-term finance and accept/negotiate bills of exchange. They are thus **wholesalers** of money. Many of the merchant banks are **privately owned**, e.g. Rothschilds, and trade on their reputation and family name. Others are subsidiaries of the Commercial banks, e.g. Samuel Montagu (Midland). Seventeen merchant banks are known as **Accepting Houses** because they guarantee commercial bills for companies.

Savings banks

These banks are defined by their main function—savings. However, organizations like Trustee Savings Bank are **diversifying** into lending, etc.

National Girobank

The government created this bank in 1968. It is based on the network of **Post Offices** around the country. It operates like the other Commercial banks and is increasingly **competing** with them in services provided.

Discount Houses

Although these bodies do not have 'bank' in their title, they operate like banks. They borrow from the Commercial banks with very **short-term loans** (often overnight) and **lend for up to three months** (by buying Treasury Bills). They make a profit on the difference in interest rates paid and charged. Their skill lies in anticipating market trends. There are just ten discount houses left in Britain. No such institution exists in other countries. They survive because they are **specialist** and **convenient**. In addition, they protect the **Commercial banks** from the effects of sudden interest-rate changes.

10.3 Commercial banks

Functions—these can be remembered by **'CAST'**, if you are angling for the answer!

Customer services

The banks provide numerous services which are given detailed coverage in most commerce books. They are listed below together with the customers for whom they were designed.

Type of customer	Specific services
Most current-account holders	standing order, direct debit, bank giro credit, cheque guarantee cards, cash dispensers
Reputable current-account holders	credit cards
Anyone	budget accounts, savings accounts, deposit accounts
Any account holder	advice on insurance, investment, legal matters, references
Owner occupiers	mortgages
Travellers	foreign exchange, travellers cheques
Businessmen	night safe, bills of exchange, certificates of deposit, small firm advisory service, references, tax and legal advice.

11 million people have current accounts and deposit accounts
16 million people have just current accounts
3 million people have just deposit accounts
25 million have building society accounts

Advancing money

Banks lend to personal customers and businesses through loans and overdrafts usually for short and medium periods of time.

Loans. A formal means of borrowing usually over a **set period** of time at **fixed rate** of interest with **regular** (monthly) payments. The customer completes an **application form** for the Bank Manager. He needs to state the reason for wanting the loan, the amount and the time involved. He will have to give personal particulars of income, previous credit record, other existing credit commitments and character references. Banks look for customers to 'share the risk' by providing a proportion of funds from their savings, e.g. 25 per cent on a motor bike. If it is a large loan, the bank may seek **collateral** (a valuable asset to be left in bank's possession which can be sold to repay the loan if the borrower defaults on payment). Usually the customer has a separate loan account which he repays and his current account is credited with the total amount lent.

Overdrafts. Informal borrowing, usually for a very **short period** of time, mainly used by traders. The bank agrees to let the trader spend more from his current account than he has in it. Thus his account is said to be overdrawn, i.e. **'in the red'**. For instance, businesses often have to pay for goods before they are sold, and so need temporary finance to tide them over. An approved overdraft arrangement is a very **flexible** form of borrowing and firms may have overdrafts for years. **Interest** is charged on a **daily** basis on the actual amount overdrawn. Overdrafts are usually cheaper than loans for borrowing, but the rate of interest charged varies with the risk involved, e.g. new customers will pay more than established, reputable customers.

Credit cards

Safeguarding money

Originally goldsmiths (see Unit 8.5) performed this function. Today, money is held in either a **deposit** account or a **current** account. The main differences between these accounts are summarized below.

Characteristic	Current account	Deposit account
General function	transactions	savings
Frequency of use	regular	occasional
Services	cheque book monthly statements standing orders direct debits credit cards	statements twice a year
Withdrawals	no notice needed	7 days' notice for large sums
Gain/loss	charges quarterly	interest received twice per year
Minimum age	16	—
Average balance	£400	£800

Currently, the big banks do not charge current-account users unless they go overdrawn. Then, most services are charged for, with cheques being 30p each. In contrast, **interest is paid on some special current accounts**, e.g. where a minimum balance of £1000 is maintained and each withdrawal exceeds £250.

Transferring money

The banks move **cash** between branches to meet needs. For instance, a branch near to a market may well be a net receiver of cash when takings are paid in, whilst a branch on a housing estate may face more withdrawals than deposits. Thus, within a bank, cash needs to be transferred to where it is required.

In operating the clearing system, the banks transfer money, but in the form of cheques. Cheques today are written on printed forms issued by the banks. Clearing occurs in three ways.

Within a branch. A writes a cheque to B. Both have accounts at same branch. On the day when B pays the cheque into the branch, B's account is credited and A's account is debited.

Within a bank. A has an account at Hay Street branch and gives a cheque to C, who has an account at Sea Street branch of the same bank. C pays the cheque into his branch and his account is credited. The cheque is sent with other cheques drawn on different branches to the bank's **Head Office**. There, the cheques are sorted into the branches of origin and returned to them. Thus, **two days later**, A's branch will receive his cheque from Head Office and then debit his account.

Between different banks. A banks with Midland and pays a cheque to D whose account is at a Lloyds branch. This is illustrated in Fig. 10.1. The process usually takes **3 to 4 working days**.

The transfer between accounts is more complicated when two different banks are involved. At daily clearing, each bank totals up its accounts with every other bank. For instance, if the Midland has cheques worth £50 million drawn on Lloyds and Lloyds has cheques worth £40 million drawn on the Midland; then Lloyds owe Midland £10 million. However, they do not pay each other directly. Each has an account at the Bank of England and so £10 million is deducted from Lloyds account and £10 million is added to the Midland balance at the Bank of England.

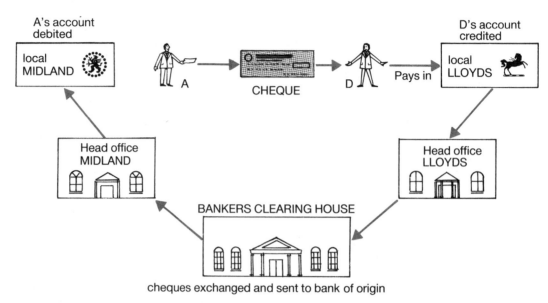

Fig. 10.1   Cheque clearing between banks

10.4 Balance sheet

Liabilities and assets

Liabilities are what banks **owe**. Thus, all **deposits** at bank are liabilities because the bank has to provide money when customers wish to withdraw either in cash or by cheque.

Assets are the ways in which the bank has used the deposits. Some deposits are **retained in cash**, but most have been **lent to individuals, companies and the government**. In deciding how much to keep in cash and how much to lend, the banks are guided by the principles of liquidity and profitability.

Liabilities		*Assets*	
Deposit accounts	62	Cash in tills	0.5
Current accounts	38	Balance at Bank of England	2
		Money at call	3
		Treasury and other bills	2
		Market loans	25
		Special deposits	0
		Investments	6
		Advances	61.5
	100		100

Fig. 10.2   Bank balance sheet £ %s January 1986

1 Cash in tills—notes/coins needed for everyday transactions.
2 Balance at Bank of England—each bank has a deposit at the Bank of England which enables clearing debts to be settled (see Unit 10.3).
3 Money at call—overnight lending to Discount Houses which can be quickly recalled at short notice.
4 Treasury bills—91-day loans to the government.
5 Special Deposits—the Bank of England, at the government's instigation, often requires banks to leave a fixed percentage of funds with them. It is not classed as a liquid asset and cannot be used.

6 Investments—longer-term lending, e.g. government stocks in £100 blocks for up to 25 years called 'gilts' (see Unit 11).

7 Advances—loans and overdrafts (see Unit 10.3).

Increasingly more foreign currencies are held and loans made.

Cash Ratio. The percentage of assets needed to be kept in cash and balances to meet immediate customer requirements.

Liquid assets. Those redeemable within one year.

Reserve assets. Between 1971 and 1981 the banks were supposed to maintain a reserve-assets ratio. This was $12\frac{1}{2}$ per cent of eligible liabilities (i.e. most deposits) and consisted of the most-liquid assets, except cash.

Illiquid assets. Those assets which cannot be quickly turned into cash because of longer-term lending or 'frozen' (i.e. special deposits) at Bank of England.

Profitability and liquidity

Liquid assets can be most easily transformed into **cash**. Thus money in the till is the most liquid asset. Alternatively, a loan which will be redeemed in five years' time is very illiquid.

Profitable assets are those which earn the banks most **interest**. Thus, loans are very profitable and money kept on the premises gains no return at all. Therefore, the **most-liquid** assets are the **least profitable**. The most profitable are the least liquid. The banks have to strike a balance between these two requirements on their balance sheet. Their customers desire ready cash (i.e. liquidity) yet their shareholders seek high dividends (from profitability). The banks may increase liquidity of investments by spreading their maturity dates out, i.e. a 20-year loan matures 1986, a 15-year loan matures 1987 and so on.

Interest and profits

As most banks are **public limited companies** they aim to make a profit for their shareholders. One way of doing this is through charging interest on **loans and overdrafts**.

The banks have a **base rate** to which they link the interest paid on deposits (e.g. base rate below 3 per cent) and the amount charged to borrowers (e.g. base rate above 2 per cent at least). The rates charged/given **vary** with the period of time involved and the status of the customer. Thus, if base rate is 9 per cent, then the interest paid may be 6 per cent and the interest charged at least 11 per cent, depending on the credit-worthiness of the customer. This gives at least a 5 per cent (11−6) **profit margin**. In addition, as a lot of money on deposit at the bank is in (non-interest bearing) current accounts, the profit margin may be a lot higher (i.e. 11−0 = 11 per cent).

Generally, when interest rates are high, the banks make larger profits because this margin on current account becomes higher. For this reason, in 1981, the Chancellor of the Exchequer imposed a 'windfall' profits tax on the major banks for just one year. In that year, the interest rates had been 17 per cent. It did also help him to raise finance for the government (see Units 15 and 19).

10.5 Credit creation

Theory. In order to explain simply how banks create credit, several **assumptions** have to be made: just one bank and a 10 per cent cash ratio. This means that any money lent will be spent and returned to the one bank. The bank needs to keep 10 per cent of its assets in cash. For example, a person deposits £1000 in cash. Another customer seeks a £9000 loan.

The bank, knowing that only 10 per cent of its assets need to be in cash (£1000) to meet regular withdrawals, can raise their assets to £10,000 by granting a loan of £9000. In Fig. 10.3 Stage b, the bank's liabilities are £1000 in deposit account and £9000 in current account. Thus there has been an expansion in bank deposits (deposit + current account) which is a **multiple of liquid reserves** (i.e. cash ratio) held by the bank. The multiple is nine times (9000 to 1000). This can be shown in diagrammatic form (Fig. 10.4).

Liabilities	Assets
Stage (a) £1000 (deposit)	£1000 (cash)
Stage (b) £1000 (deposit) £9000 (current)	£1000 (cash) £9000 (loan)

Fig. 10.3 Simple credit creation

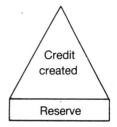 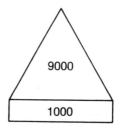

Fig. 10.4 Credit pyramid with 10 per cent cash ratio

Practice. There are many banks who differ in their ability to attract customers. The daily differences in settling the balances when cheques are cleared are fairly small and so their liquidity cash positions do not fluctuate much. There is a much looser link between liquid assets and liabilities created. Furthermore, there are other financial institutions, such as building societies, competing for deposits.

Limitations on credit creation

1 Demand for cash by customers fluctuates.
2 Government policy (see Unit 10.8).
3 Money is moved around by institutional investors (see Unit 11.2) to gain the benefit of a higher rate of interest when rates change. They move their funds in and out of the various savings institutions. For instance, if bank deposit interest rates fall and building society interest payments remain unchanged then funds may move into building societies.

10.6 Money market

The money market refers to the institutions which deal in **lending money** for **short periods** of time, up to **three months**. The lending is through Bills of Exchange for companies and Treasury bills for the government.

Bills of Exchange and Commercial Bills

On these, a trader promises to pay a sum of money (in return for goods received) on a certain date to a seller. The seller can sell the bill for cash to someone who will 'discount' it. **Discounting** means that a bank buys a bill (say £950) for less than its face value (e.g. £1000) knowing that it will receive the face value at a later date from the buyer who has promised to pay. Thus, the purchaser of the goods gets the goods immediately and 'accepts' them. Accepting means that the buyer gets his bank (for a small fee) to promise to pay the bill on his behalf when it matures (is due for payment). The seller of the goods gets paid immediately. The bank pays him, less their discount. This bank knows that the buyer's bank will pay them on the set (maturity) date, because the bill has been accepted. So each bank earns commission for what is effectively lending.

Treasury bills

These are short-term loans to the government. In return for a sum of money now (say £4800) the government promises to pay the lender £5000 in 91 days. Thus, the government gets **91 days credit at a cost**. The buyers of these bills are Discount Houses and Merchant Banks (see Unit 10.2). They make a profit (pay £4800, receive £5000) which is calculated as a **rate of interest**. The rate of discount is the rate of interest. In this example, 200/4800 for 3 months (roughly 4 per cent), approximately 16 per cent per annum.

Each Friday the Discount Houses **tender** (offer) to buy Treasury bills. If the tender price is low, then the rate of interest paid by government is high and Discount Houses make bigger profits.

10.7 Bank of England

It is the **central bank** and exercises general control over the banking system. It was founded in 1694 as a private institution, but it has always been subject to government influence. In **1946** it was formally **nationalized**. It has two main departments: the **issue** department which deals with note issue and the **banking** department which deals with the banking sector. There are a small number of private individual accounts there, too.

Functions 'BINGOES'

Banker's bank. All banks and other financial institutions (Discount Houses, Merchant Banks) keep **deposits** at the Bank of England. They are used in **clearing** to make payments between each other (see Unit 10.3). They are also used for making payments to the government. These balances form part of a bank's liquid assets and can be used to influence their lending policies (see 10.8).

Issue of notes. The Bank Charter Act, 1844 paved the way for the Bank of England to have the **sole right** of note issue in England and Wales. The Bank of England prints and releases notes and coin from the Issue Department to the Clearing Banks as necessary. There are **seasonal fluctuations**, e.g. Christmas, summer holidays.

Government accounts. The Bank of England acts as Banker to the government in the same way as the Commercial Banks service customers. It holds the government's balances. In so doing, it **(a)** pays out for government **expenditure** and receives in **taxation, (b)** manages the **National Debt** (see Unit 15) by issuing government stocks, paying interest and redeeming securities as they mature. As part of this function, Treasury bills are issued to raise short-term finance for expenditure because tax income is irregular. It mainly comes in towards the end of the financial year.

Operating Monetary Policy. The Bank of England assists the government in trying to control the economy. The Bank of England can influence **lending** and **interest rates**. Generally, in times of inflation, it tries to force up rates and discourage spending. The weapons for achieving these policies are outlined in Unit 10.8.

External functions. The Exchange Equalization account is operated by the Bank of England. This account contains Britain's gold and foreign currency reserves. It also services IMF loans.

Supervising the monetary system. The Bank of England aims to maintain a **stable and public confidence** in its efficiency. Thus in 1975, when several 'fringe banks' looked like collapsing, it organized a 'lifeboat' scheme to save them. The main clearing banks and the Bank of England lent funds to the secondary banks in trouble. This action showed the Bank of England as a **'lender of last resort'**. It also plays this part in its dealings with Discount Houses on a more frequent basis. Discount Houses may have to quickly repay the Commercial Banks and so need to borrow to do so (because they 'borrow short and lend long'). If no other source is available the Bank of England will step in and lend the money, but at a penal (higher than market) rate of interest.

10.8 Monetary control

Much of the discussion around monetary policy relates to two basic economic problems: **inflation** and **unemployment** (see Units 9 and 16). It has been argued that by reducing the supply of money (credit included) in the economy, inflation could be reduced. Alternatively, by raising the supply of money, unemployment could be lowered (through more spending).

The government can affect the **quantity** of money in the economy and the **cost** of borrowing money (i.e. rate of interest). In trying to change the quantity of money, the government will try to control the creation of credit. It will seek to increase credit to expand money supply and thus stimulate spending in order to lower unemployment. With the same aim the government might seek to **lower interest rates**, thus making borrowing easier.

GOVERNMENT INFLUENCES

The monetary weapons available and the techniques used have varied greatly since 1951. The mnemonic **'OARS'** is appropriate because they have given the government little power in steering the banks in the troubled waters of the economy!

Open market operations

The Bank of England buys and sells Treasury bills and other government securities in the money market. If the government wishes to **stimulate spending** it will get the **Bank of England to buy stocks**. The following process takes place.

1 Sellers of stock receive cheques from the Bank of England.
2 Thus banks' balances at the Bank of England increase (as their customers, the sellers, have gained income).
3 This gives each bank more liquid assets which enables the banks to expand credit (i.e. lend to borrowers who will spend the money). Thus the credit pyramid would have a wider base and larger top (see Fig. 10.5).

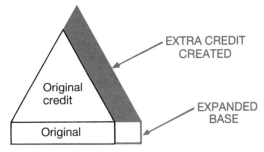

Fig. 10.5 Cost pyramid expanded with government buying of stock

In curtailing spending, the reverse process may be less effective. Would-be borrowers who cannot obtain credit from banks may go elsewhere. These other **financial institutions**, such as HP Finance Companies, are **not under the direct control of the government**. Thus they could expand lending when the government wanted it limiting.

Assets ratio

Post-war   8 per cent cash ratio
1951–71   28 per cent liquid assets ratio
1971–81 $12\frac{1}{2}$ per cent reserve assets ratio
1981   **monetary base** or modified cash ratio.

In theory, if the reserve assets of the credit pyramid is altered, the shape and size of the pyramid is altered. Thus in Fig. 10.6, less credit is created (7000) than in Fig. 10.4.

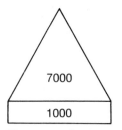

Fig. 10.6 Credit pyramid with $12\frac{1}{2}$ per cent reserve assets ratio

In practice, governments have not regularly changed the assets ratio as a monetary weapon. On average in 1971–81 the commercial banks kept $13\frac{1}{2}$ per cent of the assets in the necessary reserve form and this prevented small changes by the government being effective. These percentages were used to make open market operations effective, but they did not work in 1971–81 because banks kept at least 13 per cent as reserve assets. Thus, usually open-market and interest rates changed at the same time. The Bank of England bought stocks and interest rates fell, leading to more credit creation. The failure in practice of the assets ratio, open-market operations and interest-rate changes led the Conservative government to try a new system—the monetary base. For the first time the **'monetary sector'**, not just the banks, were included. The banks have to keep $\frac{1}{2}$ **per cent of their eligible liabilities** in a non-interest bearing account at the Bank of England. This is in addition to their normal liquid assets.

It is not yet clear how this system will operate because the government keeps intervening, despite their belief in competition and government withdrawal from the market.

Rates of interest

Postwar to 1971   bank rate
1971–81   minimum lending rate.

BR and MLR were the rate at which the Bank of England would lend to Discount Houses, as a lender of last resort. It was fixed weekly at $\frac{1}{2}$ per cent above the Treasury bill rate, thereby following interest rates in the market. However, on occasions the government did depart from this practice.

Importantly, **other interest rates** (such as bank base rate) were fixed from bank rate/minimum lending rate. Thus, if government increased MLR, then other interest rates in the economy rose, e.g. loans. This discouraged borrowing and reduced the money supply.

In August 1981, MLR was suspended, as the government did not want to 'lead' the market. However, in practice it still interferes.

Special deposits

These were introduced in 1960 to restrict bank lending. Each bank had to keep a **specified percentage of deposits at the Bank of England** in return for which it received interest. However, the special deposits did not count as liquid assets. So a call for special deposits meant cash was given up and so loans had to be recalled in order to keep the required assets ratio. The banks got round this though by keeping more than 28 per cent in liquid assets. Conversely, if the Bank of England wishes to encourage lending, it releases some of these captive deposits, thereby increasing the banks' liquid assets. This allows the banks to create more credit. **Special deposits have not been used since 1980.**

There are two other less important weapons of monetary control:

Funding

This describes government action of selling more long-dated stock and fewer (short) Treasury bills. This leads to banks holding a small percentage of liquid assets and thus having less potential to create credit.

Directives

The Bank of England may **advise** banks about specific things. For instance, they might ask banks to lend less to the personal customer and more to businessmen and exporters. Usually, the Bank of England's advice is accepted by the commercial banks and so an order (directive) is not needed. In practice, these weapons have been largely ineffective. Hence the introduction of the **monetary base**. However, it is too soon to say how effective this change has been.

10.9 Summary

There are several types of bank, ranging from licensed deposit takers through to merchant and commercial banks. The latter safeguard, lend and transfer money, and in the process provide specific customer services. They accumulate assets and liabilities and the banks' balance sheets reflect their desire to maintain profitability and liquidity.

The banks possess a tremendous ability to create credit and thus all governments pursue a monetary control policy. The Bank of England operates this policy using open-market operations and interest-rate changes mainly. Also, the Bank of England holds the government's accounts, issues notes, keeps our gold and foreign currency reserves and generally supervises the banking system.

11 SAVINGS AND INVESTMENT

11.1 Introduction

In Unit 10 we examined the Money Market where short-term loans are obtained. In this unit we turn to the **Capital Market**. This is the market for **large long-term** borrowers, particularly the government, local authorities and large companies. The funds for lending often come from the savings which the institutions below attract from many small savers.

Investment has two meanings.

1 Buying capital goods, e.g. machinery to make consumer goods.
2 Buying 'claims for money', e.g. putting money in a bank, buying shares in PLC, making deposits in a building society. These may be 'investments' in the sense that they may give extra income, but they are normally called savings.

In economics, **investment is capital formation**.

11.2 Borrowers

COMPANIES—MAINLY PLC

They take loans from savers occasionally but rely heavily on bank borrowing and undistributed profit (see Fig. 5.9). If a particularly large capital project needs financing a PLC may make a new issue of shares, e.g. Saatchi and Saatchi raised £26 million in 1982.

New companies seeking to become PLC (with shares quoted on the Stock Exchange) mainly make **new issues** of shares. They get the services of an experienced merchant bank (see Unit 10.2) to advise them on timing and method of issue. In doing so, it acts as an Issuing House. There are five methods of issuing shares available. They can be remembered by **'POP IT'**.

Prospectus. This gives detailed information about the nature of the business, its financial position and an application form for the shares at a given price. If the view of the investing public is favourable then the shares will be sold. This is more commonly known as a public issue.

Offer for sale. This is similar to a Prospectus, except that it is all done by the Issuing House who promise to take up any shares not sold.

Placing. All the shares are taken up by a few large investors, which is arranged by a merchant bank.

Issue to existing shareholders. This is known as a **'Rights issue'**. It enables existing shareholders to buy new shares in proportion to their holdings of old shares, e.g. 5 old shares = 1 new share plus 20p.

Tender. This is similar to issue by prospectus except that offers are invited above a minimum price. When all the bids have been received the shares are issued at the highest price which enables all of the shares to be taken up.

THE GOVERNMENT

As well as issuing Treasury bills in the Money Market (see Unit 10.6), the government's broker sells **gilt-edged securities**, e.g. 1993 Treasury Loan $13\frac{3}{4}$ per cent Stocks. This means that a loan to the Treasury paying $13\frac{3}{4}$ per cent interest each year will be repaid in 1993. These can be either **fixed or variable yield**. Occasionally, variable-yield stocks may be 'indexed' to the rate of inflation. The bonds are sold in **£100 units** by the government in two different ways.

Tap. Stocks are offered for sale at **specified price** and yield (interest). If they are not all bought, then the government sells them off gradually, as they are demanded. Thus, eventually the government gets the **price** it wants.

Tender. Government decides to sell a **particular quantity** of bonds on a certain day and invites offers. It then sells the bonds to the **highest bidders**. The government gets the quantity sold that it wants.

The amount borrowed by the government to finance public expenditure (see Unit 15) adds to the National Debt.

LOCAL AUTHORITIES

In order to finance expensive capital projects, many councils issue bonds. They tend to offer attractive rates of interest. They borrow over short-medium term in the £1000 to £10,000 range, usually from private individuals and institutional investors (below). In 1983 the total local authority debt from borrowing was £43 billion.

11.3 Savings institutions

Most of these institutions are large suppliers of funds to the capital market. They buy Government Stock and subscribe to new issues. In general, they seek, like banks, to earn more from **lending** than they pay out to savers.

The first four institutions listed below are private sector profit seekers, the fifth is private sector non-profit making (trustee status) and the sixth is public sector non-profit making. The banks were dealt with in Unit 10.2.

Insurance companies

They collect 'sums of money called premiums from people who take out insurance policies'. This money is invested in a portfolio (range) of paper assets, each earning **interest**. Insurance companies make their profit from wise investment rather than from underwriting risks (where the claims paid usually exceed the premiums income). The **Prudential** is one of the biggest investors in the stock market.

Investment trusts

These PLC **buy shares** in other businesses. They manage these investments by switching between profit uses. In effect, they are expert speculators in finance. Their funds come from people buying their shares as new issues, usually plus £1000. The Scottish Provident offer six investment funds and a mixed fund.

Unit trusts

These trusts attract **small savers** who buy units of a stated value in a trust, often by answering a **newspaper advertisement**. The trusts specialize in certain sectors of the stock market and spread their investments for safety. They are fairly flexible and allow units to be redeemed for cash easily, e.g. Kleinwort Benson.

Pension funds

Most workers contribute to private pension schemes, which top up the state pension. The funds are managed by boards of trustees who invest in a wide range of assets, from Government Stock to oil paintings. The aim is to obtain as big a return on the savings as possible. The National Union of Miners (NUM) pension fund holds £1.5 billion assets.

Building societies

They are **mutual institutions** owned by their members (depositors and borrowers), each of whom has one vote at the AGM. They are not intended to be profit makers because of their **Friendly Society** status, although they do make 'surpluses'.

The Chief Registrar of Friendly Societies checks building societies by vetting their **annual accounts** and regulating their activities. For instance, in 1984 the New Cross Building Society's business was transferred to a larger building society. Members' deposits and loans were fully guaranteed to maintain general confidence in building societies.

Since 1970 they have rapidly expanded and now hold £70 billion of personal savings, with half of all adults holding a building-society account. They offer **savings accounts** to lenders.

Since 1975 the building societies have offered high-paying instant-access accounts and attracted large investors. However, by offering instant liquidity they may become vulnerable when sums of money are shifted. At present building societies are supposed to keep a $2\frac{1}{2}$ **per cent reserve ratio**.

Home loans are given to borrowers. Of building society assets, 78 per cent are in **mortgages**, which are usually 20-year plus loans. The funds are provided by the deposits of the savers. The **rates of interest** offered vary over time and between different types of saving accounts. For instance, regular savers obtain higher returns. In addition, in Britain saving with building societies is encouraged by the government as the interest received is tax paid by the society.

	Assets (£ billion)	Shareholders (million)	Borrowers (million)	Number of branches
1983	14.1	6.5	1.1	577
1986	24.3	10.7	1.4	725

Fig. 11.1 Halifax Building Society growth, 1983–6

Between 1980 and 1983 the main clearing banks began to compete with building societies in providing mortgages. The building societies retaliated by increasing their **financial services**, e.g. Leicester began cheque clearing and issuing credit cards, as well as withdrawals/deposits through the Post Office. Future developments are uncertain. Figure 11.1 shows the growth of the largest building society.

Government savings schemes

Trustee Savings Banks are government supervised and non-profit-making. They are no longer simply savings institutions as they provide current accounts and participate in the Clearing House. They are designed for private individuals, charities and trade union funds rather than companies.

Savings Certificates of various types are issued by the government usually to raise finance for itself. They vary in rates of interest, terms and redemption dates.

National Savings Banks are government operated. They accept deposits in ordinary and investment accounts, which they invest in Government Stock.

11.4 Stock Exchange

People

The main Stock Exchange is in London but there are also regional exchanges. They are controlled by their members who elect a **council of 47 members**. This council tries to ensure that the 4000 members stick to the rules; it fixes entry fees, it vets new members, it approves new issues and investigates suspected malpractices.

All members have to pay 1000 guineas nomination, 1000 guineas in entry fee and 215 guineas yearly subscriptions. Since October 1986, there has been no distinction between stockbrokers and jobbers. They are both now termed **market makers** and deal directly with the general public. Most firms are **partnerships** and have **unlimited liability**. They follow a client's instructions and charge a **commission** for their service in buying/selling shares from jobbers. They give advice to their customers, based on their knowledge and experience of the stock market. There are about a hundred stockbroking firms now, compared with 300, 20 years ago. The brokers Cazenove act for Midland Bank. In performing the jobbing function, they hold shares in the same way as **wholesalers** store goods. They buy/sell in order to make a profit. Generally, they try to sell at prices higher than they buy in order to make this profit. Dealers tend to **specialize** in a narrow range of markets. Their work involves more risk than stockbroking as they may be left with shares that they cannot sell except at a loss.

Stocks and Shares
Ordinary Shares
Preference Shares } (see Unit 3.8)
Gilt-edged Stock

These shareholders receive **dividends**, usually calculated as a percentage of the nominal price of the share (i.e. original issue price), e.g. £10 Share, 60p dividend = 6 per cent. However, the share may have been £15 on the stock market so in fact it yields less than 6 per cent, i.e. = 60p/£15 = 4 per cent. Its **yield** = dividend/market prices.

Procedure

When shares/stocks are bought or sold, certain steps are involved in the transaction. You wish to buy **1000 ordinary shares** in Rentokil, and so contact a dealer. This may be done through your bank manager. He will contact dealers in the chemicals market. He will ask several dealers to **quote their prices** for 'Rentokil ordinary'. For instance, 107–112, $108\frac{1}{2}$–$112\frac{1}{2}$, 109–114 may be given. You want the **lowest selling price** quoted. In this case, 112 would be chosen ($112\frac{1}{2}$, 114 more expensive). The transaction is called the **'bargain'**. This agreement is binding, in accordance with the Stock Exchange motto **'My word is my bond'**; 20,000 bargains are made per day, averaging £50,000 each.

	750 × £1 shares				
	1983			1986	
Expenses	%	cost		%	cost
Broker's commission	3.0	22.50		1.65	12.37
Stamp duty	2.0	15.00		0.5	3.75
Contract stamp		60			10
VAT (on commission)		3.37			1.86
		£41.47			£18.08

Fig. 11.2   Cost of share buying in 1983 and 1986

The dealer informs you (the client) of the purchase and you have to pay at the end of the **account**, a two-week period into which the financial year is divided. The dealer will give you a **contract note** which lists the price paid, commission and date for payment. The cost of buying shares has fallen through lower stamp duty and more competition between dealers.

Prices

The stock market is usually claimed to be a **perfectly competitive** market because there are many buyers and sellers with excellent knowledge and rapid reactions to price changes. Check Unit 7.2 for the features of Perfect Competition.

Share prices are published daily. They reflect changes in demand and supply. For instance, jobbers will **'mark down'** prices of shares for which they have a plentiful supply. However, the prices in practice are caused by many wider, often non-economic, considerations:

Company prospects. They may be enhanced by:

1 Likely takeover by bigger company.
2 Beneficial government policies, e.g. increased spending by Department of Transport will probably help Wimpey Shares.
3 Optimistic statement by company chairman.
4 Political stability, e.g. the ending of a war or political crisis in a part of the world where a company's trade has been disrupted.

Company performances. Reduced profits, or lower profits than expected, together with low dividends are likely to cause a fall in demand for the share and thus a share-price drop.

General economic trends. Optimism about economy and government policies may stimulate confidence in share buying. Thus most shares may increase in value.

Political factors. Wars, crises and elections tend to depress prices generally because of the uncertainty created.

These factors may shift the demand for a share, as in Fig. 11.3.

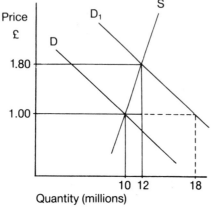

Fig. 11.3   Application of demand theory to share price changes

In this diagram, supply (S) is relatively inelastic. This means that some but not a lot of extra shares will be put on the market if the price rises. Many potential sellers may not know of the price increase and some jobbers holding shares may wish to keep their shares (perhaps expecting further price rises).

Demand is drawn as relatively elastic. The reason being that a small change in price may make a share much less attractive, as speculators work on tight profit margins and knowledge is nearly perfect. The shift to D1 is caused by anything improving company prospects/performance. At £1 per share the demand increases from 10 million to 18 million. However, only another 2 million are made available for sale and so the quantity supplied expands to 12 million. The excess demand cannot be satisfied and so the market price is bid up to £1.80, at which point demand = supply.

Speculators

Many stock exchange investors want a **regular income** through dividends. Others, though, seek a quick profit by anticipating changes in share prices. They want **capital gains**, from selling at a higher price than buying the shares.

1 **Bulls,** people who **buy** expecting **prices to rise** before they have to pay for them.
2 **Bears,** speculators who **sell** expecting **prices to fall**, usually within one period of account. This is so that they can buy back the same shares but at a lower price.
3 **Stags,** investors who **buy** new issues anticipating a price rise in oversubscribed shares, e.g. in 1982 Amersham was sold off by the government; 250,000 people applied for shares and 65,000 were successful. Once issued, the market price shot up and most of the 65,000 sold off their shares at a big profit. In November 1983 there were just 7717 shareholders, with the bulk of the shares in the hands of the big pension and insurance funds.

Functions 'MINGS'

Market for second-hand securities. The Stock Exchange brings together buyers and sellers. It enables sellers to obtain **liquidity** and buyers to get paper assets.

Indicator of business prospects. It is said that the Stock Exchange acts as a barometer of business confidence. This can be seen to some extent in the changes of the **Financial Times** (FT) **Index**. This measures **changes in share price** of the top 30 shares, such as Allied Brewery, BP, etc. There is also an All Share Index which is based on 750 share prices. This is calculated slightly differently but it moves in same direction as FT Index.

It is the **relative change** in the index, not its absolute level, which is **important**. For instance, an index number of 300 could mean different things. If it had reached 300 from 200 in a month then it would indicate **business confidence** growing. However, if it had fallen to 300 from 400 it would show pessimistic prospects in the market. Thus changes in FT Index indicate the health of the economy, to some extent.

The movement of share prices in a **specific sector**, say chemicals, may show depression or expansion in that part of the economy. In indicating expanding areas, it points to areas where funds might be channelled.

New issues are supervised. New public companies need Stock Exchange approval for their accounts, prospectus, etc. The fact that new issues can be **resold** on the Stock Exchange makes individuals and institutions more willing to take up new issues. They have a seal of approval and the chance to regain liquidity by selling the shares.

Government funds are obtained on the stock market. The government sells bonds/stocks to acquire finance for its spending on defence, education, etc. The sales of **gilt-edged** securities account for **80 per cent** of the turnover by value on the Stock Exchange.

Savings can be 'invested' on the Stock Exchange. Individual savings eventually find their way on to the stock market. It gives pension funds and insurance companies another profitable source for their funds in which they are protected (to some extent) by the supervision of the Stock Exchange Council.

Criticisms of the Stock Exchange

Short-term profit is more important to speculators than productive investment. Many 'investors' are interested in **capital gains** rather than dividends from profits. Thus shares may be bought for reasons which do not help the economy. For instance, companies have been taken over so that the **assets could be sold off** ('stripped'). This meant that production ceased and unemployment resulted. Similarly, investment funds may be channelled into empty property, as happened in 1973 when bank lending expanded.

The supervision of companies is weak. Shady activities such as false accounting, non-submission of accounts and **insider trading** occur and sometimes go unpunished. The **voluntary code** of the Stock Exchange is ignored by some company directors who trade in their company's shares, using their privileged knowledge to maximize capital gains and minimize capital losses. The Stock Exchange Council does not include outsiders and is a very weak policeman. In contrast, America's Securities and Exchange Commission can issue injunctions and take cash from companies if they misbehave.

It is an inaccurate barometer. The FT Index was increased to record levels in 1986. However, Britain with 3 million unemployed, falling manufacturing production and worsening trade was in a **depression**!

The average person in the street cannot participate. He cannot hope to have sufficient 'spare funds' to run the risk of share ownership. However, privatization has increased the number of individual shareholders to over 5 million.

It is a gambling club. The Stock Exchange was described by Tony Benn as a 'capitalist casino', where rich people bet on share-price movements.

11.5 Personal savings

People save for different reasons and in different places. However, they are all **giving up immediate use** of their money, and thus consumer satisfaction, in order **to obtain** a **future benefit**.

The government encourages personal savings for three main reasons:

1 It provides funds for **investment**.
2 It saves the government from having to provide some support for families when they fall on hard times. For instance, some state benefits, e.g. home help, are not subsidized if a person has savings of more than £1200. Thus, indirectly, personal savings **reduce government spending** a little.
3 It is thought to encourage the right **attitude to thrift** and self-discipline. Planned, regular saving means going without current consumption; it teaches people certain values such as self-sacrifice. This may indirectly limit pressure on the government if it does not fulfil its economic promises.

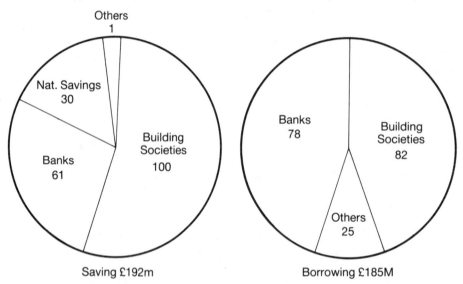

Fig. 11.4   Personal savings and borrowing 1985

GENERAL FACTORS INFLUENCING HOW YOU SAVE — 'MURT'

Money. How much you have, e.g. very small savers cannot use the Stock Market as £100 minimum is usually needed, in practice.

Use. What you want it for. Savings can be used to obtain a regular income, through interest and dividends obtained, or a lump sum at the end of a period of time. This sum may be quickly obtained through share speculation or eventually paid when a set period loan is agreed.

Risk. How willing you are to take a risk. Some savings institutions, e.g. banks, are much safer than others.

Tax. How much you pay. If the income from savings is taxed then its net value is reduced, e.g. bank deposits. However, saving in some institutions, e.g. building societies, is tax paid.

SPECIFIC FACTORS INFLUENCING SAVING — 'STILE'

Safety. Most savings institutions are directly or indirectly government backed and thus reliable.

Tax liability. The tax position varies between institutions and individuals. e.g. National Savings Certificates are tax-free.

Institution	Type of account	Interest (net %)	Percentage gross for basic rate taxpayer	Tax
Building Society	Ordinary share	6.0	8.57	Paid
	Instant access	7.5–8.5	11.0–12.14	Paid
	High interest term	9.0	12.8	Paid
Clearing Banks	Deposit	5.25	7.39	Paid
Local Authorities	1 year	7.75	10.5	Paid
	10 years	6.9	9.87	Paid
Trustee Savings	Deposit	5.0	7.04	Paid
National Savings	Ordinary up to £500	3.0	3.0	First £70 free
	Ordinary + £500	6.0	6.0	First £70 free
	Investment	8.05	11.5	To pay
	Income bonds	8.4	12.0	To pay

Fig. 11.5 Savings accounts (April 1986)

Interest. The rate of interest earned varies between savings institutions as illustrated in Fig. 11.5.

Liquidity. The speed with which savings can be turned into cash may be significant. For instance, the withdrawal of £500 from a bank account is much easier than redeeming a local-authority loan which may be committed for two years.

Easiness. The convenience of paying in and taking out money is important. The Post Office which administers National Savings has the advantage over banks and building societies in having more branches. The building societies have a slight advantage over the banks through Saturday opening and longer hours.

Places to save in short term

These give **immediate liquidity without penalty**:

1 **Commercial banks**   All safe.
2 **National savings**   All convenient.
3 **Building societies**   Building societies give best net interest.

Places to save in medium term

These give **maximum benefit** over a period of **up to seven years**:

1 **Government Savings Certificates/Bonds**
2 **Local Authority Loans**
3 **Save As You Earn**
4 **Building Societies Term Shares**

All safe and all convenient to buy.
Liquidity varies as in 2 and 4 you cannot withdraw but in 1 and 3 you can, with loss of interest/bonuses.
Interest varies but 3 pays best interest in times of high inflation.

Places to save in long term

These give **maximum benefit** over a period of **over seven years**.

1 **Unit trusts.** They are fairly safe as authorized by the Department of Trade and supervised, but the return cannot be predicted and there is the possibility of loss if units are sold at wrong time. It is a risky 'investment' as the units are linked to share prices. The earnings are taxable.
2 **Life assurance.** Very safe and convenient. However, liquidity is gained at a high cost. Endowment policies guarantee a sum of money which is not liable to tax.
3 **Government Stocks.** Safe, convenient and unexciting. Regular interest and a guaranteed capital gain on redemption.
4 **Gold coins.** Very risky as there are rapid fluctuations in the price of gold to which their value is linked. Cannot predict.

Other means of saving

Property, particularly **housing**. Very lucrative as:

1 Tax relief on monthly mortgage interest payments up to £30,000 per annum.
2 Asset increases in value (antiques, paintings and wine are saved for the same reason).

3 No capital gains tax on sale.

4 Mortgage repayments fall in real terms with inflation.

Premium Bonds. £5–£10,000 very safe but no interest, although a gambler's chance of a big prize.

Commodities such as cocoa, silver, potatoes can be bought and sold often without putting up the full amount (10 per cent of purchase price needed). Very risky and very specialized.

11.6 Summary

The Capital Market centred on the London Stock Exchange is the market for large long-term loans. The major borrowers are companies, the government and local authorities. The major suppliers of funds to the capital market are institutions. The insurance companies and pension funds invest the monies they collect from insurance premiums and pension contributions. Investment trusts and Unit trusts invest private money in a range of shares. Building societies specialize in providing advances for home loans. Government saving schemes raise finance for the government. The Capital Market operates primarily through the Stock Exchange. This is a market for second-hand securities which brings together buyers and sellers. Prices are basically determined by demand and supply and the FT Index of prices is said to be an indicator of business prosperity and confidence. Critics claim that the Stock Exchange encourages speculation, that it is inefficient and exclusive.

Personal savings can be put into a variety of schemes, the choice of which is primarily influenced by the interest earned, liquidity and ease of access.

12 POPULATION

12.1 British population growth

Population provides **labour** in a country and it is a source of **demand** for the goods and services which labour produces. Thus changes in the size and composition of the population have important economic effects on production and consumption. These changes need to be handled carefully so that a nation continues to make the best use of its **resources**.

In all types of economy, awareness of population change is important because it affects demand and supply. For instance, an increase in population requires more educational facilities, and so resources will need to be allocated into school building. In the long run, this increase brings about an expansion of the workforce which will need to be employed. Similarly a change in the structure of the population, with total population remaining constant, will influence demand and supply patterns. For example, more old people and fewer young ones (an ageing population) necessitates more retirement homes and fewer nurseries. Again, resources need to be reallocated from one sector to another. Such changes require **planning** to get the most efficient use of resources. Planning depends on accurate information. Hence every ten years, the government conducts a **census** (since 1801).

1981 CENSUS

Completion of the census form is compulsory and refusal can be subject to a £50 fine. After the 1971 census, 324 people were convicted and fined. The 1981 census cost £40 million and was briefer than 1971 version. There were 21 questions requiring box-ticking, such as:

Accommodation—do you live—

- ☐ in a caravan
- ☐ in any other mobile or temporary structure
- ☐ in a flat/maisonette
- ☐ in a permanent building with entrance from outside the building

This question was followed with enquiries about the number of rooms, tenure, amenities and vehicles.

Population information on date of birth, sex, address, was sought, together with the person's whereabouts on 5/6 April, their job, employment status, journey to work and qualifications. From census data, and that collected regularly on births and deaths, population trends can be projected and plans undertaken.

Usage of census

1 Housing—calculation of present and future needs from size and age of families.

2 Social capital—government grants to local authorities and NHS provision depend on number and needs of people in different areas.

3 Transfer incomes—government future spending on pensions and other allowances can be worked out from the information on families, marital status, etc.

4 Planning—the census will show changes in the workforce and the information can be used to plan offices, shops, public transport and leisure services.

BRIEF HISTORY OF UK POPULATION GROWTH

Year	Population (m)	Birth rate	Death rate
1066	1 (estimate)	—	—
1701	6 (estimate)	—	—
1801	12	37	27
1851	22	35	23
1901	38	25	15
1951	50	16	13
1988	56	13.5	11.2
2001	58 (projection)	—	—

Fig. 12.1 UK population growth

The history of Britain's population can be divided into three periods.

Pre-1801 very slow growth. There were **very high birth rates** and **very high death rates**, thus cancelling each other out. Life expectancy was low. The 18th-century increase resulted from **better food, clothing and living standards** caused by the agrarian and industrial revolutions.

19th Century—fast growth. The high birth rate remained constant but the **death rates fell** markedly. This produced a natural rate of increase, such that the population tripled in 100 years. The main factors causing the fall in death rate were **better sanitation**, prompted by government regulations, improvements in **medical knowledge** and techniques and greater awareness of public and private **hygiene**.

20th Century—rapidly declining rate of growth. The general trend has been a declining birth rate, with occasional sharp increases. For instance, the 1901 birth rate of 25 per 1000 had declined to 13.5 in 1988, but there have been occasional peaks, e.g. 21 in 1947 and 20 in 1964.

This **declining birth rate** has been caused by:

1 New and cheaper methods of **birth control** have been developed. In addition, birth control is now more socially acceptable and popular. Also, people are better informed.

2 Children have become more of an **economic liability** than an asset. The ending of child labour, compulsory education and the raising of the school-leaving age have all made large families more expensive to maintain.

3 The desire for **higher living standards** has made many couples defer child bearing until they have major material possessions, e.g. cars, videos, foreign holidays, etc. Providing for children means less for such luxuries and so the birth rate has fallen.

4 The **emancipation of women**, particularly since the 1960s, has meant fewer women in the home and more at work. The traditional woman's role as a mother now faces competition from career aspirations. This makes women less likely to want children. Furthermore, the extra income from female employment enables a higher standard of living for a couple, which they may be reluctant to give up in order to have children.

The **death rate** has fallen a little in the 20th century. It has been **fairly stable** for the last 30 years although the causes of death have changed. Heart attacks, cancer and suicide which are associated with modern living styles, have replaced the old killers such as perinatal and infant mortality, tuberculosis and pneumonia.

12.2 Size

Factors affecting population size:

Birth rate (fertility rate)

Ratio of total live births to the total population, usually expressed in 'births per 1000 of total population' per annum. The birth rate is influenced by the following.

1 Number of women of child-bearing age (16–45) in the population.
2 Number of children born per woman.

These two influences are determined by other factors, remembered by **'MALE'**.

Marrying age. If people marry later in life then there are likely to be fewer children reared. Thus a lower average age of marriage will raise the birth rate, other things being equal.

Attitudes to marriage and family size. The declining importance of religion and the increased emancipation of women have made marriage and large families less popular. For instance, in some Roman Catholic countries, such as the Irish Republic, where the contraceptive pill is banned, the birth rate is much higher than Britain. The desire for a better standard of living has meant an average of fewer children per family. Such factors affect the willingness of women of child-bearing age to have children.

Law. A minimum age of 16 for marrying means that most children are born to women of between 18 and 30 who are married. The social custom of children being born to married women means that changes in the age of marriage could influence the birth rate. Similarly, the accessibility of abortion and birth control, both of which the government may manipulate, can influence the number of live births. In China, because of the massive population, the government tries to restrict families to not more than one child.

Education. If people are better informed about the costs and duties of parenthood, it is likely that the birth rate will fall. Sex education in schools has indirectly contributed to the falling birth rate in the 1970s and early 1980s.

Death rate (mortality rate)

Ratio of total deaths to total population, usually expressed in 'deaths per 1000 of total population per annum'. The death rate is influenced by the following.

Health standards. If many basic services, such as refuse collection, water purification and efficient sewage disposal are provided, then death from infectious disease can be reduced. Such improvements in the late 19th century accounted for the dramatic drop in the death rate. They came about as the government took a more active role in society's welfare and enforced minimum standards by law.

Medical advances. New discoveries, drugs and inventions have enabled increases in life expectancy. The development of anaesthetics, antiseptics and radium in the 19th century and penicillin and sulphonamides in the 20th century, significantly reduced the death rate. The average life expectancy is now 74.

Food, clothing and housing. With the improvements in nutrition and self-care, the general standard of living of the population has improved. This is shown in the earlier maturity of children and the higher average height of the population. Thus the natural death rate in Britain is low and a further substantial decline is unlikely.

Migration

The difference between the number of people leaving a country (emigration) and the number entering (immigration). If immigration exceeds emigration, then a nation's population increases.

This factor has been of little importance in Britain. Between 1871 and 1931 (and since 1961) Britain was a **net emigrator**. However, the 1931 to 1961 period saw an inflow of immigrants, mainly composed of European refugees and new Commonwealth citizens. These immigrants came to Britain for various motives: escape from religious and political persecution, e.g. Jews from Germany, Asians from Uganda; to take advantage of economic opportunities, e.g. Pakistanis, West Indians; the attraction of a higher standard of living, e.g. Indians, Cypriots.

The net outflow since 1961 has been termed a **'brain drain'**, because the better educated and more skilled left. Their reasons were similar to those of the immigrants except that the persecution was claimed to be high rates of income tax which stifled business initiative and penalized people on high salaries. The lowering of income tax, particularly on higher incomes, by the Conservative government since 1979 has not produced any noticeable return of exiles: in fact the 1979 to 1982 outward migration accelerated!

Changes in the size of the population

Birth rate > death rate = **natural increase** in population
Death rate + net emigration > birth rate = **decrease** in population

Optimum size

In theory, there is an ideal population size for each country. This is the level of population at which **income per head is maximized**. This would mean that best use was being made of a nation's **resources**. The optimum size is not fixed but varies with a nation's resources.

If a country's population exceeds the optimum it is said to be **overpopulated**, e.g. Bangladesh, Mexico. Thus, those nations do not allow immigration and encourage lower birth rates. In contrast, Australia and Canada are underpopulated and they actively seek immigrants so that currently untapped resources, particularly land, can be utilized and output per head can be raised.

It is impossible to estimate the optimum-sized population for a country, because population size varies quickly. It takes time to collect information, and technology improves, making larger populations more sustainable. The optimum size is not just related to space. It needs to be considered in the light of **productive resources** and potential.

In 1798, **Malthus** predicted that the expansion of food supply would be inadequate to meet the growth of population and that **wage rates would fall**, because the supply of land was fixed (and MRP would fall—see Unit 13). But he assumed no technological progress, thus making his gloomy predictions inapplicable to the modern industrialized world. However, they have some relevance to the developing nations, who cannot control the population explosion.

12.3 Structure

AGE DISTRIBUTION

In looking at age distribution, it is useful to classify the population into three groups:

1. Those up to **school leaving age**; currently sixteen. They need health, welfare and education services but they do not produce anything. However, their upbringing can be viewed as an investment—a future producer, for society.
2. Those of **working age**; 16 to 65 men, 16 to 60 women. About one-fifth of this group between 16 and 22 are in full-time education and supported by the state. Furthermore, there are many housewives and unemployed people who do not add to the national income. The latter receive benefits. Thus about 45 per cent of the population are producers who pay taxes which can be put towards state services.
3. Those **above retirement age**; men +65, women +60. Although some pensioners stay in part-time/full-time employment, the bulk of this category need health and welfare facilities. They do not produce much of national income.

The percentage of population in each category is determined by, **(a)** changes in birth and death rates, and **(b)** changes in migration. For instance, the fall in death rate has meant a big growth in the retirement-age category; from 7 per cent in 1901 to 18 per cent in 1986.

Dependency ratio

Ratio of working population to the non-working (dependent) population. At present at least 40 per cent of the population (22 + 18) are dependent on the other 60 per cent (working population), to produce the goods and services needed to sustain them.

Working population

All those inhabitants at work or available for work. Its size will be determined by:

1 Total population size.
2 Ages of school leaving and retirement.
3 Percentage of non-workers within the working-age group.
4 Those at work beyond retirement age.
5 Age distribution of population.
6 Sex composition of population.
7 The number of married women in work.

An ageing population

Britain's population is ageing, and the average age is rising. The numbers leaving the workforce and retiring exceed those entering the workforce. This trend has been quickened by the schemes for early retirement and the expansion of further education.

The **economic effects** of the ageing population are as follows.

Changing spending patterns. As a population ages, the demand moves from goods associated with the young such as toys, towards products for the old, such as thermal underwear. Faced with a declining birth rate in the 1970s, Mothercare reacted by expanding their 'baby' range to cover children's clothes up to age ten. Conversely, Barratt Homes responded to the increasing number of elderly widows and widowers by developing single accommodation, e.g. the 'Mayfair' one-bedroomed house. State spending shifts from·child care and education towards home helps and old folks homes. Thus, some teacher-training colleges in the UK were closed between 1978 and 1982 because of the declining birth rate.

Increased dependence on working population. As there are more consumers and fewer workers, **taxes** may need to be increased to pay for the necessary services. This could act as a disincentive to production and **slow down** (or halt) **economic growth**. Thus the extra cost of pensions or education falls on a relatively small group who are working and earning, which it could be argued is **unfair**.

Less labour mobility. Younger people tend to be more energetic and enterprising. Thus an ageing workforce will tend to be less mobile between jobs and areas. Many workers made redundant from declining industries such as shipbuilding and steel are unlikely to be employed again, particularly those over age 45.

Less adaptive workforce. As older people are ingrained in their habits and trades, they are unlikely to seek or get retraining. Thus the nation's productive resources of labour are diminished.

These effects can be overcome if **productivity** and **technology** increase as they enable greater output per head of population. This can bring about a general increase in national income and raised living standards for all of the population.

SEX DISTRIBUTION

The sex distribution in the UK is of less economic significance than the age distribution, as long as male/female proportions are fairly similar. More males are born, but more women survive, particularly beyond age 45. This is explained by three factors.

1 **Work.** The physical exertion and mental pressure of work affects men more than women, as more men go out to work and they retire later. Thus more men die at, and from, work.
2 **Emigration.** More men leave Britain than women.
3 **Wars.** The majority of women in the population now has been caused by male deaths 1914–18, 1939–45. This factor is becoming less important and the age (50) at which women outnumber men is getting higher.

In 1986, the number of females (28.7 million) exceeded the number of males (27.3 million), although by 2001 it is predicted that the gap will be slightly narrower.

GEOGRAPHICAL DISTRIBUTION

The average density of 230 people per sq km in Britain is similar to West Germany and India. It is one of the denser parts of the world.

The history of Britain shows that before the **Industrial Revolution**, the population was located mainly in **rural** areas. The concentrations were on good **farming land** in the south-east beneath an imaginary line from the Wash to the Severn. The population moved into the northern parts of Britain rapidly during the Industrial Revolution, with the development of coal, steel, cotton and shipbuilding. In addition, Scottish and Irish immigrants also went there. This movement **northward** coincided with **urbanization**. Thus by 1901, three-quarters of the population lived in towns.

With the decline of these traditional industries, the population distribution again changed,

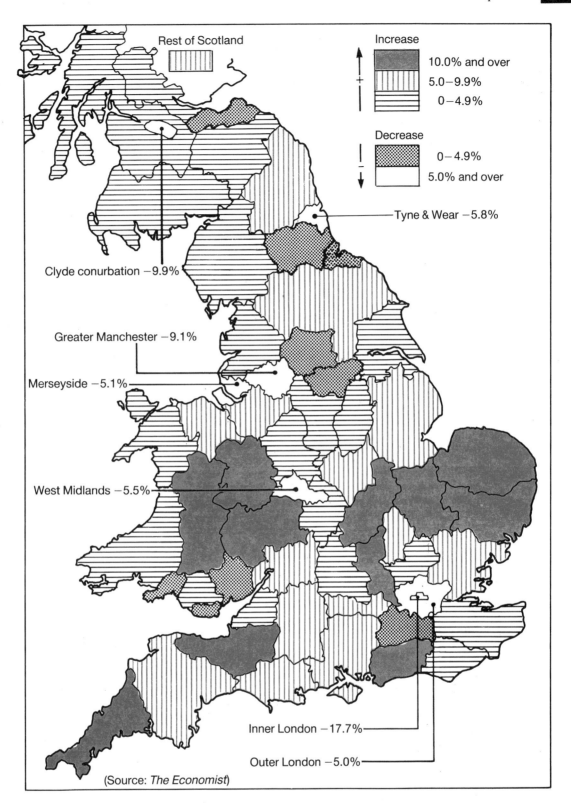

Fig. 12.2 Geographical mobility 1971–81

but it remained urban. Thus, between the wars and after 1945, the new **light engineering industries** of the **Midlands and South** attracted labour away from the industrial North.

The heavy concentration of people in urban areas continued until the mid-1960s, with 50 per cent of the population living in towns of over 50,000 inhabitants. However, the 1981 Census (and Fig. 12.2) show that the **big city areas lost population** to the more rural areas. For instance, Inner London's population fell by 17 per cent, Birmingham's by 8 per cent and Manchester's by 17 per cent. Places where population increased included new towns, such as Milton Keynes, and remote areas such as the Shetlands. **Overall from 1961 to 1981**, the population has increased in England, Wales and Northern Ireland and declined in Scotland. The main **regions of increase** have been West Midlands, East Anglia, Outer London, the South-East and the South-West. The areas from which people have migrated were North, North-West, Merseyside and Greater London.

OCCUPATIONAL DISTRIBUTION

The job distribution of the workforce depends on a country's stage of **development**. Underdeveloped countries typically have 80 per cent of their workforce employed in the agricultural sector, whilst developed nations have less than 10 per cent in this area.

Before the Industrial Revolution, Britain's workforce was largely agrarian. The development of industry necessitated **mobility** into engineering, mining trades, etc. In the 20th century as these occupations have declined, so workers have moved into assembly work and the service sector. Increasing prosperity creates more jobs in the tertiary sector of the economy and fewer in the primary sector (see Unit 5.2 and Fig. 5.1).

Sector	Millions employed		Percentage change
	1950	*1986*	
Agriculture, forestry, fishing	0.8	0.35	−56
Mining, quarrying	0.9	0.25	−72
Chemicals	0.5	0.34	−32
Food, drink, tobacco	0.8	0.60	−25
Construction	1.4	0.93	−33
Distributive	**2.1**	**3.35**	**+59**
Total employed	21.1	20.8	−1.4

Fig. 12.3   Selected occupational changes 1950–86

Figure 12.3 shows the faster decline of employment in the **primary** sector (agriculture, fishing, forestry, mining, quarrying) than in the selected secondary industries (e.g. chemicals, construction). The decline of employment varies between types of secondary industry, with some, such as electrical goods, doing better than other older ones like textiles. The growth in the distribution trades shows expansion of the **tertiary** sector. The public sector is an increasingly large employer in society, because of these trends and the expansion of the welfare state. An ageing population necessitates more state provision of benefits and services and thus employment in the tertiary sector will continue to increase in Britain.

Since 1980, more workers in Britain are **female, part-time and self-employed**.

12.4 Mobility of labour

Mobility is the **movement between jobs**. In an efficient economy it is easily achieved. In **Perfect Competition** (see Unit 7) it is assumed that labour is perfectly mobile, i.e. an unemployed miner can become a brain surgeon if a vacancy arises. This is clearly unrealistic. However, labour needs to be as mobile as possible, so that **fullest use** is made of it, like any other resource.

Types of mobility

The changing pattern of demand creates growing and declining firms and industries. Thus mobility may be

1 **Occupational**—different **job** but same area, same organization.
2 **Geographical**—different **area** but same job, same organization.
3 **Industrial**—different **organization** but same job, same area.

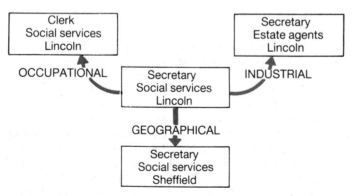

Fig. 12.4   Types of labour mobility

OCCUPATIONAL MOBILITY

Obstacles 'CARPET'

1. **Cost.** The cost of retraining may be a deterrent, so too might be relatively low wages when first starting a new job.
2. **Ability.** Many white collar workers 'dream' of being professional sportsmen **but** they do not have the basic skills.
3. **Retraining.** If this is lengthy and involves periods of time away from home, it may deter people from changing jobs.
4. **Personal reasons.** Personal preference for a particular job and dislike of the alternatives available may discourage movement. A highly specialist worker, such as a glass blower, may be proud of his skill and unable and unwilling to find other employment because of his narrow specialization.
5. **Employment prospects.** After age 45, many workers are on the 'scrap heap' because employers will not employ them. They are poor prospects for an employer as they only have a short working life (and probably out-dated skills).
6. **Trade Union resistance.** Trade unions are reluctant to admit retrained workers to certain jobs which involved lengthy apprenticeships. Furthermore, they may have a closed shop agreement whereby union membership is a prerequisite for employment. Similarly, professional bodies, e.g. solicitors, require certain qualifications before admission.

The obstacles of training, money and trade union resistance can be partly overcome by **government policies**. It has set up skill centres for retraining and paid wages well above the unemployment benefit rates. Since 1980, legislation has been passed to curb the closed shop and weaken trade union resistance. However, the overall effect of these policies has been **minimal**.

GEOGRAPHICAL MOBILITY

Obstacles 'FIBPEA'

1. **Family.** Moving areas poses family problems—changing children's schools, leaving aged relatives, missing close friends. Such factors may deter a worker from moving to another area.
2. **Ignorance.** Information of opportunities may not be available to a prospective migrant.
3. **Benefits.** For lower-paid workers with large families there is little incentive to move to a job because the state benefits may be nearly as much as his wage. Furthermore, redundancy pay may cushion the blow of unemployment, particularly in the short run.
4. **Prejudice.** Some people dislike certain parts of the country because of its image, e.g. 'dirty' North, 'snobby' South. Similarly, London is disliked because of the 'speed' of life and South Yorkshire because of the 'strange' accents!
5. **Expense.** It may be costly to move, particularly if the worker is buying/selling his own house. The cost of housing varies widely around Britain. Thus a worker moving from Humberside to the south might pay £20,000 more for a similar four-bedroomed detached house.
6. **Availability of accommodation.** Workers living in rented property may find it difficult to obtain council housing in the areas where the jobs are located, particularly if there are long waiting lists.

The obstacle of ignorance can be overcome by the better and wider publication of information through **job centres**. However, more people obtain jobs through agencies, such as Alfred Marks Bureau, than through job centres. Expenses may be partly met by **employers**, often government subsidized, but they present a big problem. Recent government policy to **reduce benefits in real terms** means that the differential between work and unemployment is slightly widening, and this might induce more mobility. The regional policies used to encourage geographical mobility are outlined in Unit 6.4. Their lack of success seems to be admitted by the emphasis placed on **increasing capital mobility**.

INDUSTRIAL MOBILITY

This is the easiest type of movement for a worker as it often involves no change of homes and no occupational adjustments. Movement from the public sector into the private sector may involve a change of attitude towards more **profits awareness** though.

An **expanding economy** facilitates industrial mobility. Since 1978, British unemployment has been rising, leaving no scope for industrial mobility (see Unit 16). The available vacancies have been mainly for skilled tradesmen and thus required mainly occupational (and some geographical) mobility. Sometimes, all three kinds of mobility needed to be combined in a single move.

12.5 World population

The total world population (1983) was 4.5 billion and growing. However, the rate of growth varies . In the **industrialized** nations, the natural rate of increase is **less than 1 per cent** per year. Britain's population of 56 million is almost stationary. In the **developing nations**, the rate of growth of population is $2\frac{1}{2}$ per cent per year.

In the developing world, the birth rate is 40 compared to a death rate of 10, whereas in the industrialized nations the respective rates are 17 and 10. Such differences are often explained by economic and social factors, such as income distribution and religion.

Within the developing nations, the **middle-income nations** (£200 to £500 per head per annum) which are better off have experienced falling birth and death rates. However, the death rate is falling faster so population is bulging, similar to 19th-century Britain. The high rate of population growth per head tends to lower income per head which creates a **poverty trap**. It has been calculated that 50 per cent of population in developing countries live in absolute poverty, i.e. they cannot afford the bare necessities of life.

The other consequence of fast population growth is the **lack of world resources** to feed and employ the population. In the last 25 years, supply has kept pace with food demand. However, the expanding areas of food production are not the regions of growing populations, i.e. North Africa needs food whilst Latin America has a surplus. Many developing nations have failed to raise their **productivity** and cannot sell enough to pay for food imports. They need **aid**. However, in 1983 the amount of aid sent by the industrialized nations (except the centrally planned!) to the others fell.

The world population problem has two aspects.

1 The **immediate** problem—to feed the starving, e.g. Ethiopia, Sudan. This is largely a problem of distribution as there is probably enough food in the world to feed everyone.

2 The **longer-term** problem—to slow the rate of population growth. This involves lowering the birth rate and increasing the productive capacity (and thus the standard of living) of the less-developed countries (LDC). A transfer of resources from the rich countries to the LDCs through aid and trade could facilitate this.

12.6 Summary

Information about the size, composition and distribution of the population is essential for economists and government because the population is a major source of demand for goods and services and is the recipient and user of a wide range of transfer incomes, government services and public goods. The size of the population is determined by changes in the birth rate, death rate and levels of migration. The structure of the population is affected by changes in age, sex, geographical and occupational distribution of the population. The Mobility of Labour refers to the ease with which labour moves between jobs geographically, occupationally or industrially. It is argued that any obstacle to mobility reduces a country's ability to respond to changing economic circumstances. The rate of growth of the world population varies significantly between the advanced industrialized nations and the developing nations.

13 TRADE UNIONS

13.1 Introduction

Wages and salaries

Wages are the payments made by an employer to the factor, labour, for its use. Wages are the **price of labour**. It is a general term which covers many different types of payment.

Usually 'wages' refers to payments made on an **hourly/weekly** basis which **vary** according to the work done. Extra work (overtime) is usually rewarded at a higher rate, because the worker sacrifices some leisure time in order to work, e.g. 'Time and a half' may be given (£3 per hour rather than £2 per hour) to a shop assistant for working on her day off. In the past, wages were paid to **manual** workers in **cash**.

Salaries, on the other hand, are usually paid **monthly** with the **same amount** being given each month. Any overtime performed was often considered to be 'part of the job' because salaries were paid to white collar **(clerical)** workers. In the past they were paid by cheque, unlike wage earners. However, increasing numbers of workers are being paid monthly and by credit transfer. So this difference between wages and salaries does not apply. To a firm salaries are a fixed cost whereas wages are a variable cost.

Earnings

The term **'earnings'** means the amount received from employment. This may be composed of a basic wage and certain bonuses. These extra payments may be for overtime, shift-working, etc. The **basic wage rate** is usually nationally negotiated and less than total earnings. The total amount earned during a period of time is known as the **Gross wage**. However, this is not the sum of money received by the worker. From gross wage, there are several **deductions** which are compulsory—national insurance, income tax and pension. The amount which is received after these, and any other deductions, such as savings and trade union subscriptions which are voluntary, is known as the **Net wage**. These are illustrated in Fig. 13.1.

Monthly pay		£900.00 ← Gross wage
Deductions		
National Insurance	81.00	
Income Tax	154.00	Compulsory deductions
Superannuation	55.00	
	290.00	
Trade union subscription	4.00	← Voluntary deduction
Total deductions	294.00	
Net pay	£606.00	Net wage

Fig. 13.1 Wages and deductions

13.2 Methods of payment

Time rate

Sometimes called 'Day' rate, this is the most common method of payment, e.g. most salaries and some wages. Workers are paid on the basis of **how many hours** (or weeks, months) they work, e.g. 40 hours at £2.50 per hour = £100 per week gross. The amount paid per hour may depend on the person's age, experience and responsibilities (see Unit 13.5). Any overtime is usually paid at a higher rate.

Time rate is paid where output is not easy to measure, e.g. teaching, and where the payment for speed may lead to lower standards, e.g. doctor. It usually enables quality output to be produced by the worker. However, it suffers from **three disadvantages**.

1 It is not easy to distinguish (and thus reward) **efficient** and inefficient workers.

2 It gives no **incentive** to work hard and encourages skivers.

3 **Supervision** of workforce is needed and this adds cost to the employer.

Piece rate

Workers are paid for **how much they produce**. Their output is counted or measured for the jobs or processes which they perform, e.g. an assembly line operative gets £4.20 per dashboard fitted to a motor car. He fits 50 in one week and so receives £210. Often a bonus may be given.

Piecework overcomes the three disadvantages of time rate and often enables a full use of capital but it too has disadvantages.

1 **Shoddy** workmanship may result from the accent on speed.
2 More needs to be spent on **inspection**, e.g. quality controllers.
3 **Strain** on workers of working at speed; also **boredom**.
4 **Wages vary** with jobs performed and this creates uncertainty for the workers.
5 **Disputes** may arise over the rate for the job and this may cause an industrial-relations conflict.

Fees

Professional groups, such as solicitors, charge fees for specific work done over a period of time, e.g. conveyancing a house.

Commission

Employees are paid a certain percentage of the value of their output. This is most commonly found amongst sales personnel who have a low basic wage, as an incentive to sell more. Insurance brokers receive, from the insurance company, a percentage of the premium paid on policies which they have arranged for the company.

Profit sharing

Some firms give their employees a share of the firm's profits. They may be in the form of free (or cheap) shares or an annual bonus. The idea is to strengthen the loyalty of the workers to the company, increase their efficiency and reduce potential industrial relations conflict.

13.3 Demand for labour

All workers incur an Opportunity Cost, i.e. what they could be doing if they were not at work. In order to compensate them for this sacrifice they receive wages. As with any other commodity in theory, the price of labour (wages) is determined by the interaction of Supply and Demand for Labour. The demand for labour is mainly influenced by the following.

The productivity of labour

No employer wants to purchase labour merely to have a factory full of workers. Labour will be demanded only if it can increase the firm's profits by increasing production.

Number of workers	Total output	Marginal physical product
0	0	—
1	10	10
2	22	12
3	32	10
4	40	8
5	45	5
6	46	1
7	45	−1

Fig. 13.2   Diminishing marginal productivity

Marginal Physical Productivity of labour is defined as the 'addition to total output resulting from the employment of one extra unit of labour'.

A farmer employs successive workers to harvest his crops. Figure 13.2 shows the effect on total output of increasing the level of employment. As employment rises so too does total output. Initially the farmer will benefit from increased specialization and more extensive use of fixed capital, e.g. combine harvesters. However, as further workers are employed each one adds less and less to total output until the seventh worker actually reduces total output. This may be because the employees now find themselves getting in each other's way.

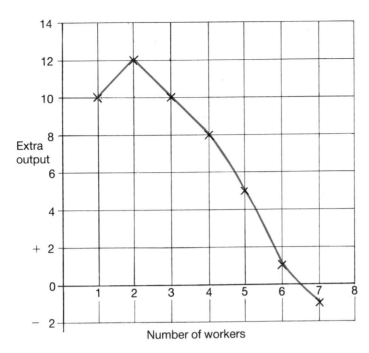

Fig. 13.3 Diminishing marginal productivity

The Law of Diminishing Marginal Productivity. This principle is clearly illustrated in Figs. 13.2 and 13.3. As successive units of a variable factor production (labour) are added to fixed factors, marginal productivity will start to decline and may eventually become negative, in the short run.

This principle plays an important part in determining the demand for labour. For example, in times of slavery employers will increase the labour force as long as there is some addition to total output, no matter how small—i.e. as long as MPP > 0. This situation is not necessarily unrealistic for in many Third World countries agricultural employment could be significantly reduced with no loss in output, i.e. MPP = 0.

However, in most situations labour is scarce and thus commands a price. A rational profit-maximizing employer will continue to employ additional workers as long as what they add to **Total Revenue** exceeds that which they add to **Total Cost**. However, in practice not all employers are rational and/or profit-maximizers.

The demand for the final product (which the labour helps to produce)

It is clear that there cannot be any sense in employing labour, no matter how productive, if the extra output (MPP) cannot be sold. Thus we can see that the Demand for Labour ultimately depends upon the Demand for the Final Product hence the Demand for Labour is a **Derived Demand**. For instance, between 1950 and 1986 the demand for steel fell from 18 million to 13 million tonnes per annum. In the same period the workforce was reduced from 300,000 to 55,000.

In Fig. 13.2 we will assume that a bushel of wheat can be sold for £10 and that wages for farmworkers are £75 per week.

The fourth worker adds £80 (8 units × £10, i.e. MPP × Price) to **Total Revenue**. Thus it is profitable to employ this worker because the addition to total **revenue** (£80) is greater than the extra **cost** of employing him (£75 wages). However, the fifth worker only adds £50 (MPP × Price) to Total Revenue whilst adding £75 to the wages bill, thus it is not profitable to employ him/her.

Marginal Revenue Product is defined as the addition to Total Revenue resulting from the employment of one extra unit of labour.

The MRP is calculated by MPP × Price. In the example above the MRP of the fourth worker is £80. From Fig. 13.2 we can see that the MRP of the seventh worker is £ − 10.

Thus we can see that MRP tells us whether or not it is profitable to employ successive workers. Therefore, we may regard the MRP as the Demand for Labour.

The MRP varies with market conditions. So far we have assumed that a firm's output can always be sold at a fixed price, i.e. the firm is in a perfectly competitive market (Unit 7).

However, in most markets demand theory suggests that in order to increase sales price must be reduced. In our example, for the farmer to sell the output of the last, or marginal, worker, the price of **all** the bushels must be reduced. In that case MRP will be equal to MPP × MR (rather than price). Thus MRP will decline steeply as both the extra output (MPP) and price obtained for it (MR) are falling.

The **demand for labour shifts** when

1 There is a change in demand for the final product, e.g. a fall in demand for ships leads to fewer shipbuilding workers, similar to MRP$_2$ in Fig. 13.4.

2 Labour becomes more productive, i.e. MPP rises. This will have the effect of increasing the demand for labour assuming other things remain unchanged. MRP$_3$ in Fig. 13.4 illustrates this.

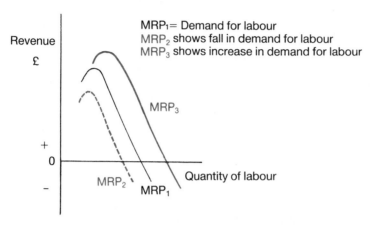

Fig. 13.4 Changes in marginal revenue productivity (MRP)

The shape of MRP curve

This is determined by the following.

The ease of substitution of factors of production. If capital can be substituted for labour then, in the long run, demand for labour will fall. For example, robots in the car industry take the jobs of people and thus MRP curve shifts to the left (Fig. 13.4 MRP$_2$).

Elasticity of Demand for the Final Product. This affects the shape of the Demand curve for labour (MRP). The more elastic is the demand for the final product, the **more elastic** will be the demand for labour. The elastic demand for toys, for example, or ice cream, has meant that the demand for workers in such industries fluctuates greatly unless other products are made to level out the demand for labour.

If there is an increase in demand for the final product there will be a similar shift in the demand curve for labour. A reduction in demand for the product will produce the opposite effect. This factor goes a long way towards explaining the considerable increases in unemployment in such declining industries as coal and shipbuilding.

13.4 Supply of labour

Labour is not a homogeneous factor, indeed it is characterized by **diversity**, e.g. a roadsweeper and a brain surgeon are both 'labour' to the economist although they clearly need different skills. As the wages of a particular occupation rise then more people will be willing to work in that industry. Thus the supply curve of labour **slopes upwards** from left to right as in Fig. 13.5.

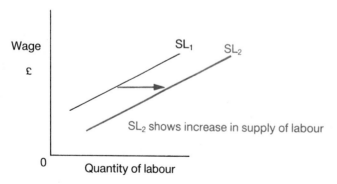

Fig. 13.5 Increase in supply of labour

General factors affecting the total supply of labour in the economy

Total population. This generally determines the potential labour force for an economy. An expanding population, sooner or later, creates an increase in the number of workers available for employment. The factors determining population growth are explained in Unit 12.

Labour law. School leaving age and retirement age will determine the actual number available for employment. The trends are towards a higher school leaving age and a lower retirement age. This makes more non-workers dependent on the workers in the society.

Immigration law. An increase in the number of immigrants raises the potential labour supply—see Unit 12.

Specific factors affecting supply of labour to a particular occupation 'PICTSE'

Pay. The wage rate offered will influence the quantity of labour supplied, e.g. low pay puts people off whereas high pay encourages. Thus many wish to be business executives but few want to be doormen.

Income in kind. Many jobs have perks and fringe benefits which are an indirect form of payment. For instance, the use of company cars, expense accounts, luncheon vouchers and cheap mortgages all save the employee from expenditure which others might have to undertake. In certain jobs the income such as tips and travelling expenses may be cash but does not form part of the gross wage which is taxed. Generally substantial perks are linked with high salaries rather than being compensation for low ones.

Conditions of employment. This may include dangerous, dirty and unpleasant work surroundings, or the need to work long and/or anti-social hours. Thus a night shift worker will be paid more than a day shift colleague in the same factory doing the same job to compensate him/her for incurring a greater opportunity cost in leisure terms.

Type of employment. Certain jobs are said to be more attractive than others offering similar remuneration because of the nature of the job. They may give 'job satisfaction'.

Society feels that teachers get privileged hours of work, nurses are virtuous and lawyers gain social standing. Conversely, other jobs such as dustmen, social workers and lorry drivers are of low status. If the attitudes in society and the tastes of workers change positively towards certain jobs then the supply curve will shift to the right, with more labour available at existing wage levels. Figure 13.5 shows movement from SL_1 to SL_2.

Security. Employment legislation has made most jobs more secure than in the past. For instance, 'on the spot' dismissal rarely occurs because warnings and notice need to be given to employees.

However, some specialized labour still faces a short or uncertain working life. For instance, actors, footballers, models, pop stars, etc., **can** earn very high incomes. However, part of this is compensation for the fact that they may only have a short working life, e.g. 3 to 4 years, or long periods of unemployment, e.g. an actor or actress may earn £200 to £300 for one or two lines and one day's work and then be unemployed for the next four months.

Entry requirements. The supply of labour is **limited** for many jobs by factors such as:

1 **Minimum qualifications** and training, e.g. degree to become a school teacher. Unskilled work is likely to be characterized by an elastic supply curve. SL_1 in Fig. 13.6. Road-sweeping requires no special skill. Thus only a small rise in wages would be needed to encourage a relatively large number of workers to become road sweepers. Alternatively a brain surgeon requires years of training and few people have the dedication and ability to make the grade. In this case even a large rise in salaries will be unlikely to raise the supply of brain surgeons more than a little. Thus the supply curve is relatively inelastic, i.e. SL_2 in Fig. 13.6.

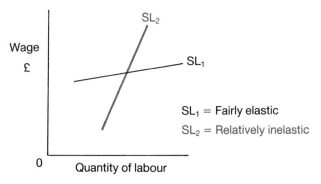

Fig. 13.6 Elasticity of supply of labour

2 **Trade union membership.** In some jobs you cannot be employed unless you have a 'union card', or agree to join a trade union. Such closed shops, e.g. journalism, enable the existing labour to restrict supply and strengthen trade union bargaining position.

Wage determination

In theory wages are determined by the interaction of supply and demand for labour as in Fig. 13.7. Wages can **increase** from either: **(a)** an increase in demand, or **(b)** a fall in supply. Alternatively in theory wages can fall through either: **(a)** a fall in demand, or **(b)** an increase in supply.

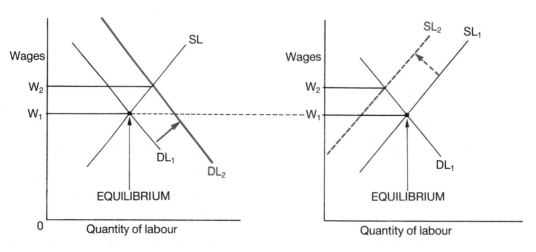

Firm A – Increase in demand for labour   Firm B – Fall in supply of labour

Fig. 13.7   Wage changes caused by shifts in demand and supply

The factors causing these demand and supply changes are termed **'compensatory wage differentials'**. Higher wage rates offered to attract labour (expand supply) eliminate shortages, e.g. if North Sea divers were not paid more than swimming pool attendants, there would be a serious shortage of people willing to work on North Sea rigs.

In practice wages have not fallen (in money terms) because of institutional factors, principally trade unions. They create **non-compensatory differentials** by interfering in the free workings of demand and supply. Similarly, minimum wage laws artificially raise wage levels. Three million lower-paid workers are in industries governed by 13 **wage councils** which set minimum rates of pay. However, some employers ignore the councils and government inspectors who check on pay regulations.

13.5 Wage differentials

Most of the reasons why some jobs are paid more than others can be explained using Supply and Demand factors. For example, the differentials between manual and non-manual largely reflect the relative education/training intensities of the two groups. Labour is not homogeneous.

The differentials between the wage rates paid to different people doing different jobs may arise **between** the following.

1 **Industries. Capital intensive** industries such as oil tend to pay higher wages to manual workers than labour intensive ones, because wages are a very small percentage of total cost. Similarly the workers in **growth** industries find it easier to get wage increases than those in declining industries, e.g. platers in shipbuilding fell from fourth to sixteenth in manual workers' pay league, between 1976 and 1984. **Public sector** manual workers are better paid than their private sector equivalents. Such differences between similar jobs which are created by employers are termed **relativities**.

2 **Job requirements.** Occupations requiring qualifications, training, skill, responsibility and risk are paid more than jobs which do not need these qualities. For instance, gross earnings for coalface workers in 1982 were £165.30 per week compared with £137.30 for chemical workers.

3 **Individual characteristics.** Where several people do exactly the same job, their gross pay may vary because of their age or experience. For instance, a new 17-year-old shop assistant will probably earn less than an experienced 40-year-old.

4 **Trade union power.** Strong and effective trade unions like NUM may be able to maintain, and even extend, their differentials compared with weaker groups such as toolmakers. Between 1976 and 1981 the pay differential between these two widened from £13 to £38.

Wage levels and wage costs

Employers are interested in reducing wage costs per unit of output rather than lowering wage levels as such. Thus if productivity were to rise by 20 per cent and wages by 10 per cent wage costs per unit would have fallen (by 10 per cent).

Britain's major European competitors, despite wage levels some 50 per cent greater than those in the UK, enjoy lower wage costs per unit of production. They have a high wage, high output, low-cost economy which provides growth and rising living standards, whereas a low wage, low output, high-cost economy offers merely stagnation and falling living standards.

13.6 Trade unions (aims, functions, types)

They are organizations of **employees** to represent their interests. One employee alone has no power but employees acting collectively are able to negotiate with employers on a more equal basis. They are formed, financed and run by the members. The average weekly subscription is 50p (1983).

At the end of 1982 there were an estimated **11.3 million** trade union **members** in the UK. This represented 40 per cent of the working people and 52 per cent of the employed labour force. The **number** of trade unions in Britain has fallen from 630 in 1965 to 350 in 1986. There are still 69 unions with less than 100 members, e.g. Pattern Weavers Society with just 70 members. The biggest unions are identified in Fig. 13.8. Each, apart from NALGO, has lost members since 1979 with the increase in unemployment being the main cause.

Trade union	Membership (thousands)	
	1979	*1986*
TGWU (Transport)	2070	1491
AEUW (Engineers)	1200	1001
GMBWU (Municipal workers)	965	847
NALGO (Local government)	729	766
NUPE (Public employees)	712	673
USDAW (Shop workers)	462	390
ASTMS (Managerial staff)	471	385

Fig. 13.8 Membership of largest trade unions

AIMS

Trade unions are concerned specifically with improving their members' **terms and conditions of work** and generally with improving the quality of life of working people. They also have wider **political** and economical **objectives**, such as seeking a redistribution of income and wealth and increased state planning in economic affairs. The main trade unions, apart from the NUT, are allied to the **Labour Party** and their members make a contribution to the Labour Party. This **political levy** is paid by more than 70 per cent of trade unionists. Some trade unions, such as NUM and TGWU, sponsor Labour Party MPs also, whilst the trade unions as a whole have a 40 per cent share in choosing the Labour Party Leader.

FUNCTIONS 'NIPS'

Negotiation. Trade unions bargain on behalf of their members and others (non-union members, ex-members and unemployed members) for improvements in **pay and conditions**. Empirical evidence suggests that hourly pay in an industry where the workforce is completely covered by a collective agreement is between 8 per cent and 20 per cent higher than the average wage in a non-unionized industry. If a trade union is able to **restrict labour supply** successfully it can force up wages (see Fig. 13.6). The extent of their success largely depends upon an inelastic demand for the final product. For instance, the NUM benefits from the inelastic demand for coal, particularly from power stations.

Shorter hours, longer holidays, cleaner working conditions, redundancy pay and job security are all features of trade union negotiations. They are part of their general responsibility to improve **job satisfaction** and the physical environment of the workplace.

Information. The trade unions provide important information and advice for management, the government and the nation. Their members' views on new developments within a firm influence management decisions. Similarly, they are closely involved with government economic planning through the National Economic Development Council (NEDC). They also attempt to educate the general public to the wisdom of their policies of full employment, state planning, increased pensions, wealth redistribution and free collective bargaining.

Persuasion. The unions are heavily into **Politics**. In the past they have persuaded their members to accept wage restraint during periods of voluntary incomes policy. This has involved close liaison with the government. Furthermore, because of union links with the Labour Party, they seek to convert people to their political views (outlined above), particularly at election time. The 1983 election, in which only 40 per cent of trade unionists voted Labour, indicates their diminishing success in this area.

Support. The early trade unions operated as **friendly societies**, providing benefits such as sickness and unemployment payments. However, since the Welfare State has taken over such provision, their social function of protecting workers from hardship has become less important. Nevertheless, many unions still have their own insurance schemes, pensions funds and retirement homes.

TYPES

Craft unions. The **earliest** trade unions, which grew up in the 19th century, were of this type. They contained **skilled** tradesmen who had usually served an **apprenticeship** and tried to maintain certain working **standards**. Initially they were some of the few workers who could afford to pay subscriptions.

They have **declined** in importance, because of their limited size and entry requirements. The **Electricians** (EEPTU) with 380,000 members is the largest craft union. As its members are spread across many industries it is not very powerful.

The craft unions are very conscious of their skills and qualifications. Thus they seek to maintain their **differentials** over unskilled and semi-skilled workers. Furthermore, they are often involved in **demarcation disputes**, as they try to maintain their sole right to perform certain jobs, which other less-skilled workers seek to do. With technological change, such 'who does what' conflicts have become more common in British industry.

Industrial. Most **types** of labour in one industry belong to **one union**, e.g. NUM contains both labourers at the coalface and skilled workmen. In the USA most unions are industrial. It enables **easier** and **tougher** negotiation, because there is only one spokesman for the workers and industrial action (e.g. strikes) can be more effective, assuming the union is united. However, the extent of an industry is sometimes difficult to define (e.g. engineering) and sometimes **conflicts** within a large union may occur because of the differing interests of various types of worker, e.g. guards versus ticket collectors in NUR.

General. In the late 19th century these unions developed to cater for **semi-** and **unskilled** labour, whom the craft unions would not admit, e.g. dockers. Traditional crafts declined with industrialization and mechanization and so general unions were formed to represent workers of **varying interests and skills**. TGWU, formed in 1918, is the largest union in Britain but it is difficult to control and often has **internal conflicts** between its members, e.g. seamen and dockers over cargo handling.

White collar. These unions are the most **recent** and fastest **growing**. They contain **non-manual workers**, e.g. NUT. They are dubbed 'white collar' because their members typically wear white shirts, rather than overalls, and work in offices rather than factories. Their expansion has been prompted by **envy** at the wage increase successes of manual trade unions and the **decline** in pro-management attitude. The increased number of jobs in the tertiary sector (see Unit 5.2) and the employment of workers with union traditions in these jobs has given impetus to unionization. Thus, white-collar unions account for 40 per cent of all trade unionists, with ASTMS among the largest unions. These unions have become increasingly **militant**, e.g. teachers' strike 1985–6.

Unions can also be classified into **open** (e.g. TGWU) and **closed** (e.g. Equity). Open unions do not seek to restrict membership entry to any particular occupation whereas closed unions do.

13.7 Trade unions (organization and methods)

ORGANIZATION

The following outline is a typical pattern, as union structures vary widely.

Each union member belongs to a **local branch**. These are based on large **factories** or several smaller firms in a geographical area. The members elect the local officials and discuss wages, membership and issues at their meetings. However, only 7 per cent of members actually attend branch meetings. In multi-employer branches average attendance is only 4 per cent.

The local branch send representatives to higher organizations, to sit on **district, regional or area committees**. These committees control the running of the branches in their area and occasionally negotiate local agreements with firms. The larger unions have **full-time paid officers**, such as district organizers, who deal with immediate problems and negotiate settlements.

The branches also elect delegates to represent them at the annual conference. The **conference** decides union policy. It also elects the **National Executive** which dominates union affairs throughout the year. For instance, it negotiates national minimum wages with

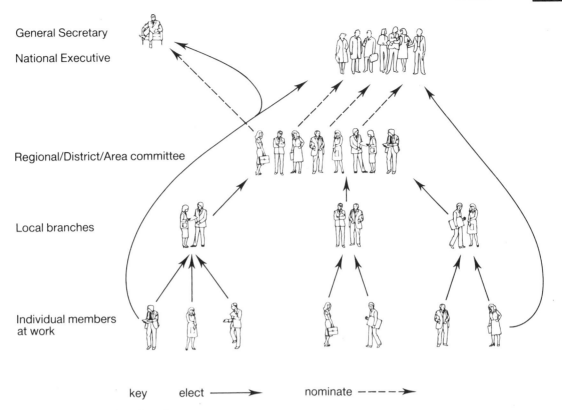

General Secretary

National Executive

Regional/District/Area committee

Local branches

Individual members at work

key   elect ⟶   nominate ----➤

Fig. 13.9 Typical trade union structure

the employer's federation. Usually, it alone has the authority to call the union out on strike. The **General Secretary** often acts as leader of the National Executive. He is elected by a ballot of members and is responsible for the daily affairs of the union.

Shop stewards

They are **elected** (in practice half are elected unopposed) by the men with whom they work on the 'shop' floor (on average 40 people). Shop stewards speak and **negotiate** on behalf of the men. It is their responsibility to bring worker **grievances** to the notice of management. They often operate separately from the official union structure. The main duties of shop stewards are distributing union information and recruiting new members. They used to collect subscriptions but now employers collect from over three-quarters of workers and charge the union up to 5 per cent of the amount for the service.

In large factories, the shop stewards may be given an **office**, a telephone and time off work to carry out their duties. They usually form themselves into a **shop stewards committee**, composed of shop stewards from the different unions operating in the factory. The elected leader of this committee is known as the **Convenor**. He acts as the spokesman for the workers in discussions with management.

The **influence of shop stewards has increased** because:

(a) More **wage** agreements are now made at **plant** and **company level** rather than industry-wide. This involves the shop stewards as negotiators more than full-time trade union officials.

(b) Management recognize and accept shop stewards much more than in the past, because 95 per cent of their work is useful and non-controversial. For instance, in some large firms, a shop steward may have secretarial help provided by the employer.

(c) Full-time shop stewards **outnumber union officials**. There were 3700 full-time and over 300,000 part-time shop stewards in 1983.

METHODS

Bargaining

Trade union activity centres around bargaining with employers, to improve the wages and conditions of the employees. Negotiations take place at national and local levels. The procedure undertaken is usually a union claim followed by a lower management offer leading to negotiation. Occasionally industrial action is taken and only rarely is the Advisory, Conciliation and Arbitration Service (ACAS) involved (see later).

    1 **National negotiations** involve groups of **unions** in an industry and the corresponding **employer's federation**. They often have voluntary agreed procedures for solving disputes. They discuss and decide **wage rates**, overtime rates, the length of the working week, training initiatives and so on. These then

apply throughout the **whole industry**. In some industries, minimum wage rates are determined by wages councils, e.g. catering, where the unions are weak.

2 **Local negotiations** are less formal and are carried out by **shop stewards** and individual employers. These negotiations may be in addition to the national agreements made, or instead of them. If they are in addition, the shop stewards may succeed in getting wage rates above the nationally agreed rate. Usually the local workplace agreements cover factors such as bonus payments, closed shop, working conditions, manning of machinery and holiday periods.

'**Free collective bargaining**' is a slogan which trade unionists use. They want the right to **negotiate without the interference of the government** and without the legal penalties being placed on them for industrial action. Thus the trade union movement is opposed to statutory incomes policy and most employment legislation which attempts to control them.

ACAS occasionally intervenes in industrial disputes. It was set up in 1975 to provide advice and solve complicated issues, through conducting its own enquiries and recommending a course of action. It does a lot of successful, unpublicized negotiating in which it brings disagreeing unions and management into acceptable solutions (conciliation). Also sometimes it decides the outcome of a conflict by arbitration.

Industrial action 'WOBS'

The most common types are:

1 **Working to rule.** The workers stick to the official rules and procedures which in theory determine working practices and safety. Normally these complicated rules may be bypassed or ignored by both employees and employers in the interests of speed and efficiency. The tactic of working to rule is often used by the railway unions in their disputes with BR Board, because it cripples the service by the delays caused.

2 **Overtime ban.** In jobs where regular overtime is worked by many employees who are low paid, a ban on overtime working may lower production and prove effective, e.g. bus drivers.

3 **Blacking.** Trade unions occasionally refuse to handle (or 'black') certain goods. This is often either for political reasons, e.g. dislike of a foreign government so its products are not handled, or to show sympathy towards another trade union, e.g. steel workers may refuse to handle coal when NUM are on strike.

4 **Strikes.** The refusal to work may be '**official**' or '**unofficial**'. Official strikes are backed by the union whereas unofficial ones are not. Official strikes tend to last longer and occur in larger organizations than **unofficial strikes**, which are usually **small-scale, brief, unpredictable** and confined to **one factory**.

Strikes have been termed 'the English disease' which is unfair as our strike record is 'fair to middling' among the major industrialized nations. The working days lost per employee 1968–77 in Britain was 0.45 compared with 0.02 in West Germany and 1.45 in Italy. However, this figure of about half a day lost per employee is much worse than for the period 1961–9. In contrast we lose 13 days per employee in absence through sickness. Strikes are not more frequent now and do not involve more employees **but** they tend to last longer.

LIKELIHOOD OF STRIKES

1 Major industries are **coal, cars** and **docks**. They account for 40 per cent of days lost but only 6 per cent of all employees work in them.

2 Small firms are less likely to have strikes than large firms.

3 More strikes occur in **manual** industries and few where there is abundant female labour. White-collar workers are more likely to ban overtime and work to rule.

4 Main cause is **pay**—60 per cent; 16 per cent demarcation; 16 per cent redundancies.

EFFECTS OF STRIKES

On the firm involved

1 Loss of production thus average costs raised.

2 Loss of revenue thus extra cost of borrowing.

3 Potential loss of market to rivals, particularly foreign.

4 Diminished reputation with customers.

5 Worse industrial relations in future.

6 Extra security/warehousing needed, raising costs, again!

On employees (strikers)

1 Loss of earnings, **but** (a) strike pay, depending on union funds (e.g. TGWU = £9 a week), (b) Social Security, depending on family size (e.g. married man with two children will receive £28 a week from the state, who 'deems' that he will receive £16 a week strike pay also (whether he receives it or not!)—this 'deeming rule' is a bone of contention with trade unionists—and (c) tax rebates.
2 Part-time jobs and moonlighting may be undertaken.
3 Loss of 'working habit' if unemployed for a significant period of time. In the long run, this means lower productivity when the striker returns to work.

On other firms

A strike in one firm may well affect others, in the same or associated industries. The car industry, because it is an assembly industry, can influence production and employment through the engineering industry, e.g. BL strikes lead to lay-offs in the components industry because half of the parts for BL cars come from outside. There are over 7000 suppliers including: Dunlop, wheels and tyres; BSC, sheet steel; Lucas, battery; Triplex, windscreen; Ferodo, brake linings; GKN, drive shafts.

Since 1982 legislation, a trade union involved in a dispute can lawfully call on its members to:

1 **Picket peacefully** at their own place of work.
2 Take **industrial action** only over disputes **'wholly** or **mainly'** about wages and conditions.
3 Take industrial action only at **other firms** if they are direct customers or suppliers of the firm involved in the dispute.

13.8 Government and industrial relations

The government may be **directly involved** in negotiations and disputes:

1 Where it is the **employer**, e.g. civil servants, 1981 strike.
2 Where it **provides funds** for the employer, e.g. nationalized industries depend on government for finance. So the government may exert pressure on employers to hold wage costs down, e.g. 1980 steel strike.
3 Where it intervenes as a **last resort**, e.g. Prime Minister invites the two conflicting groups to Downing Street for beer and sandwiches and tries to persuade them to compromise 'in the national interest'. If this fails, the government may 'strike-break' by sending troops in, e.g. Glasgow dustmen in 1980.

The government may be **indirectly involved** in industrial relations. Many of its fiscal and monetary **policies** influence employment in some way. More blatantly the government may affect the framework of industrial relations by its **legislation**. This has been increasingly the case since 1970.

BRIEF HISTORY OF GOVERNMENT—TRADE UNION RELATIONSHIPS

1945–69 consultation and agreement between trade unions and successive Labour and Conservative governments.

1969–74 confrontation. Labour (unsuccessfully in 1969) and Conservatives 1971, attempted to use the law to reform trade unions. The 1971 Industrial Relations Act created a Court which could try trade unionists but the employers were reluctant to use it. The Conservative government conflicts with the miners over incomes policy 1972 and 1974 intensified matters and partly contributed to the government's loss of office in 1974.

1974–8 co-operation. The elected Labour government made a 'social contract' with the trade union movement. In return for wage restraint and incomes policy co-operation, the Labour government repealed the 1971 Act, introduced 1975 Employment Protection Act and implemented several social reforms.

1975 Employment Protection Act. This set up **ACAS** to provide industrial relations advice, conduct enquiries and decide union recognition claims. It made trade union **recognition** by employers easier to obtain and demanded greater disclosure of information by employers. It gave employees better **terms of employment** such as longer notice of dismissal and greater consultation over redundancy and unfair dismissal.

1978–86 great hostility. In 1978 the trade union movement refused to co-operate with Labour government pay policy and called several damaging strikes which became known as the 'Winter of discontent'. In 1979 the Conservatives were elected to power with a mandate to curb trade union power. They pledged to introduce legislation, which the trade unions refused to discuss.

1980 EMPLOYMENT ACT

1 Limited picketing to the place of work. Thus **secondary picketing** by workers other than those involved in the dispute became illegal.

2 Provided state money for **secret ballots** by trade unions over industrial action (i.e. strikes).

3 Enabled the Secretary of State to publish **codes of practice**, particularly on the closed shop and picketing.

1982 EMPLOYMENT ACT

1 Limited **pickets to six** at each entrance to a place of work.

2 Allowed the introduction of **closed shop** (all workers having to belong to a trade union) if **80 per cent** of the workers are in favour. It provided also for regular reviews of closed shop by secret ballot.

3 Made **trade unions liable for damages** if they undertook action to enforce a closed shop.

4 Gave an **individual** the **right** to seek damages if dismissed for refusal to join a closed shop on grounds of conscience or personal conviction.

1984 TRADE UNION ACT

This law makes trade unions hold a **ballot** of members every 10 years to see if they are in favour of the **political levy** to the Labour Party. They also become liable for **damages** if they go on strike without first holding a **national ballot**.

It is clear that the **attitude** of the government to the trade unions depends upon which **political party** is the government. Generally, the **Labour** Party is **pro-trade union** for several reasons. There is a long history of mutual help between the Labour movement and trade unions. The Labour Party is financed (90 per cent) by trade unionists' subscriptions and its leaders are chosen through a system (electoral college) which gives the trade unions a 40 per cent say. Above all, they share similar political views of more state planning, less uneven wealth distribution and high suspicion of capitalism.

The **Conservative** Party is more **anti-trade union**. It dislikes its monopoly power in bargaining and its ability to disrupt the economy. In addition, the Conservatives support freedom of the individual which is diminished through the closed shop and threatened by mass picketing. However, the Conservatives are unlikely to outlaw the **closed shop** because some managements prefer it as it gives greater order to bargaining. Closed shops cover over 5 million workers and occur principally in the public sector, e.g. gas, electricity, water.

13.9 TUC and CBI

The Trades Union Congress (TUC) and the Confederation of British Industry (CBI) speak on behalf of the employees and employers respectively. They are often consulted by the government on economic matters.

TUC

It is a permanent organization set up in 1868 and now based at Congress House in London, consisting of trade unions representing over **10 million** trade unionists. There were 102 trade unions **affiliated** to TUC in 1983 and this included the major unions.

The trade unions send delegates to attend the **Annual Congress**. At this conference they formulate **policy** on a wide range of issues such as the economy, social policy, education, health and international affairs. The delegates also **elect** the **General Council**, which runs the TUC between conferences. Since 1983, this body has contained **52** members elected in 3 sections—large unions (at least 100,000 workers with each of 16 largest unions getting between 1 and 5 members according to its size), small unions (11 members in total from 81 unions) and 6 women members (elected by the whole congress). The voting is by **'block' voting**, which means that all a union's votes are given to the candidate/issue which the trade union delegation supports. For instance, a delegation may split 13 to 12 in favour of 'X' and against 'Y', but all its 25,000 votes go to 'X' (rather than 13,000 to 'X', 12,000 to 'Y').

The TUC may **participate** in economic decision-making. This is particularly likely if the Labour Party is in power. It will make proposals to any government and **prepare policies/ recommendations** on all legislation that may affect its members. In addition, the TUC is represented on many important bodies, such as National Economic Development Council, and in Parliament through its sponsored MPs and peers. Its spokesman is usually its **General Secretary** who represents the General Council.

The General Council also adjudicates between unions. In 1983 it threatened the print union SOGAT '82 with **suspension** unless it handed back 800 recently recruited Fleet Street workers to the electricians union. It rarely has to expel a member union. However, it often investigates and reprimands, but it cannot control its member unions. For instance, if a trade union refuses to negotiate, when the TUC advises, there is **nothing** the TUC can do, except continue to talk and persuade. In 1986 the TUC threatened to expel the EETPU.

CBI

This body represents **employers** and was created in 1965 from three smaller organizations. The firms belonging to the CBI contain about half of Britain's workers. It includes large and small firms and this occasionally creates disunity.

It has a less obvious political role than the TUC. Before **1974** it was hardly **consulted** at all by the government. However, in 1975 it bargained with the Labour government over its Employment Protection Act and gained concessions on Corporation Tax and planning agreements. It tends to take a less partisan stance than the TUC. For instance, between 1980 and 1981 it was very **critical** of the Conservatives' economic policy because of its effect on company profits and interest rates.

13.10 Summary

The demand for labour is a derived demand, based on the value of its MRP and the demand for the final product. The supply of labour is determined by the size of the population and the laws of a country, together with a range of specific factors which reflect the fact that labour is not homogeneous. These include the type and conditions of employment, employment legislation and entry requirements. Theoretically wages are determined by market forces and most differentials can be explained by demand and supply factors.

Trade unions exist to advance the interests of their members. They can be divided into craft, industrial, general and white collar. Elected shop stewards represent employees in the workplace. Most unions have a district, regional and national organization. National and local bargaining is the main feature of union activity. Industrial action may be taken to bring pressure to bear on employers. The number of strikes has fallen in recent years, although they tend to last longer and are most common in large manual industries.

Since 1970 governments have increasingly turned to legislation to control industrial relations.

The TUC and CBI speak on behalf of employees and employers respectively and are often consulted by government on economic matters.

14 NATIONAL INCOME AND STANDARD OF LIVING

14.1 The circular flow of income

In all economies using money, there are flows of income between people. These people can be represented as groups in a **simple model** (Fig. 14.1). In this model, **producers** pay an income to workers (who become consumers) for their production. The workers as **consumers** spend their income (expenditure) on goods which the producers sell. This simple model assumes:

1 No trade with the outside world.
2 No saving, as all income is spent.
3 All the output is sold.

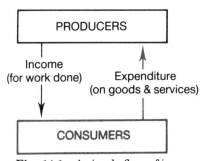

Fig. 14.1 A simple flow of income

The amount of economic activity in a community can be measured by examining the flows of income, expenditure and output in an economy. **In theory national income = national expenditure = national output** because each is measuring the same thing but in different ways. For instance, if an economy produces one bag of logs and one loaf of bread then:

1 National income = **money paid to the factors** that made the logs and bread.
2 National expenditure = **money spent** on logs and bread.
3 National output = **money value** of logs and bread **produced**.
4 The flow of income is said to be **'circular'** because, (a) the starting point is impossible to find in the model, and (b) one person's expenditure becomes another person's income.

A more complicated circular flow model is illustrated in Fig. 14.2. This model distinguishes different types of spending and introduces the following concepts.

1 **Investment.** Money spent on capital formation. The main capital items are provided by **producers** and they include factories, offices and shops. The **government** invests in **social capital** such as schools and hospitals, whilst **household** consumers buy houses and other capital assets.
2 **Consumption.** Money spent on goods and services by consumers and by national and local government. In the national income accounts these two groups are treated separately.
3 **Leakages.** The **spending** which is **not returned directly** to the **producers**. Represented by the solid arrows in Fig. 14.2, showing taxes, savings and spending on imported goods and services.
4 **Injections.** Spending by other than producers and consumers. Thus **government expenditure** on investment, consumption and transfer payments and the income from **exports**, add to the circular flow and raise national income. The injections are represented by broken arrows in Fig. 14.2.
5 **Overseas sector.** Payments made to overseas producers and the income received from overseas consumers both affect the flow of income. If export earnings exceed import spending then there is a net inflow of income—an injection into the circular flow.

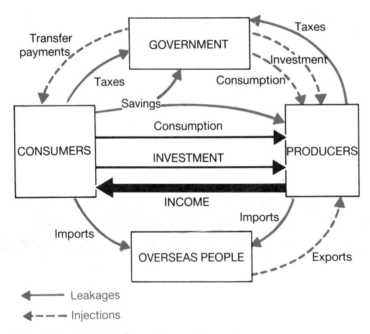

Fig. 14.2   Detailed flow of income

14.2 Measurement of national income

The national income of a country is the **total value** of the **goods** and **services** produced by a country's **resources** over a given period of time, normally **one year**.

National income is precisely measured by the government in three ways.

EXPENDITURE METHOD

This calculation adds together the **spending on consumption and investment** by consumers and the government. It adds on foreign spending on our exports and deducts our spending on imports. This adjustment gives the net **inflow or outflow of income from British trade**. Stocks of unsold goods and partially completed products need to be included because they show expenditure undertaken too.

There are two calculation **problems** which need consideration.

1 **Transfer payments.** These are payments such as **pensions** made by the government to people when production has not been given in return. They provide incomes for people who can thus undertake spending. However, as they are a transfer from taxpayer to government to beneficiary, they have to be **deleted** from government spending.

2 **Market prices.** The data on spending is collected from the prices paid by consumers. However, market prices are distorted by taxes, such as **VAT**, and subsidies. Thus from gross domestic spending **taxes** need to be **deducted** (as they artificially raise the value of the goods bought) and subsidies added. This then gives the value of production at factor cost.

The expenditure method is useful for detecting changing trends in consumption and investment. It may also show the effects of government policies such as tax raising and reduced public expenditure.

INCOME METHOD

This method adds up to the income received by the **owners of resources**. The share of income from employment is usually about 70 per cent of the total, and includes wages and salaries. Rent includes income from leased property and other assets. The surpluses of the nationalized industries and other government agencies are kept distinct from those of companies in the private sector.

The imputed consumption of non-trading capital is a small adjustment made for the free use of assets by people for themselves. However, if they let others use them they might charge and thereby earn an income, e.g. garaging a company car on your own premises. The three main problems with the income method are as follows.

1 **Stock appreciation** is an important **adjustment**. With inflation the stocks of goods may increase in value, without anyone touching them, e.g. Dunlop increases its tyre prices, thus making unsold tyres more valuable than previously. Thus stock appreciation is deducted from the income because it boosts company profits artificially.

2 **Residual error.** The main source of information for the income method is the Inland Revenue. However, they only know about what people declare as their income. It has been calculated that £15 billion per annum is earned in the **'black economy'** (see Unit 2.1). Thus, in order for gross domestic product at factor cost to be **equal** by all methods, a balancing figure called residual error is included in the table.

3 **Transfer payments.** They are left out of the calculations (as explained in the Expenditure Method).

OUTPUT METHOD

This method shows the contribution to Gross Domestic Product of the **different sectors of the economy**, as the values added by each industry are summed. The value-added output is the output of an industry minus the value of its inputs. Thus comparison with earlier years will reveal the expanding and declining sectors. As shown in Unit 5.2 and Fig. 5.2 manufacturing industry in Britain has declined and the service industries have expanded. There are four main **problems** with this method.

1 **Double counting.** We take the **value added** by each firm/industry in the calculations rather than the output of each. If we do not, double counting will occur. For instance, if a loaf of sliced bread retails for 40p that is the value of its production to national income; but if we add manufacturers sale price (say 30p) and retailers (say 40p) we get 70p. The value-added system of calculation thus gives 30p by manufacturer and 10p by retailer (40p sale price −30p purchase price = 10p value added) making a total of 40p. This avoids counting output more than once.

2 **Residual error.** As explained in income method.

3 **Adjustment for financial services.** It is impossible to allocate the amount of certain financial services (e.g. accountant's fees) at each stage of output in the production process. Thus, this adjustment is made when the total output value of the financial services sector is ascertained.

4 **Valuation of public services.** As many services, such as defence and education, are provided free for the nation it is very difficult to assess accurately the value added and the benefit gained, so they are valued at their cost of production.

INCOME, OUTPUT AND EXPENDITURE

The three methods operate differently up to the calculation of **gross domestic product at factor cost**. This shows the total value of goods and services produced **within Britain**. However, beyond that point the calculations are the same, as shown in Fig. 14.3.

Expenditure method	(billions)		Income method
Consumer expenditure	193.6	180.4	Income from employment
Government consumption	69.6	24.9	Income from self-employment
Gross domestic fixed capital formation	55.2	48.3	Gross company profits
Decrease in stocks	−0.5	8.5	Gross public corporation surplus
Total Domestic Expenditure	317.9		⎧ Rent and
Exports	92.4	19.7	⎨ Imputed consumption of
Imports	92.3		⎩ non-trading capital
Gross Domestic Product at market prices	318.0	−2.6	Residual error
Taxes	44.3	−5.5	Stock appreciation
Gross Domestic Product at Factor Cost	273.7		
Net property income from abroad	+6.9		
Gross National Product	280.6		
Less capital consumption	−38.3		
National Income	242.3		

Fig. 14.3 National income calculation by expenditure and income methods 1984

Gross National Product

This gives the total value produced by all **British-owned resources**, both at home and abroad. Thus to GDP at factor cost, we need to **add net property income from abroad**. This total is composed of income earned abroad by British residents less corresponding payments out to foreigners. It is always a positive figure for Britain.

National income

During the year in the course of production, the nation's **capital assets** will be used, thereby wearing them down and lowering their value, e.g. machines depreciate in value with use. The usage of these assets is known as **capital consumption** and it needs deducting from GNP to give national income.

The gross capital formation in Fig. 14.3 represents total investment and thus includes capital consumption, which is the amount of capital undertaken to maintain our existing capital stock. Thus the difference between gross capital formation (£42.2 billion) and capital consumption (£33 billion) is the net (new) investment during the year.

14.3 The use of national income calculations

The final figure for National Income is really only an **estimate**. Much of the calculating is based on approximations and samples, whilst some activities are under-recorded.

Furthermore, it does not allow for inflation. An increase in national income may occur through higher prices without an increase in production. National income may increase by 10 per cent but if prices rise by 10 per cent then the nation is no better off. Thus, a nation needs to increase its national income in **real terms**. Real national income is national income at constant prices.

Real disposable GDP per head rose by $2\frac{1}{2}$ per cent between 1972 and 1982. However, this average masks ups and downs, i.e. 5 per cent rise from 1978 to 1980 but 2 per cent fall from 1981 to 1982.

GOVERNMENT INFORMATION

The data collected can enable the government to judge the effectiveness of its previous policies, e.g. effect of tax changes on consumption. The trends can be used to identify new problems and plan new initiatives.

ASSESSING CHANGES IN STANDARD OF LIVING WITHIN BRITAIN

The standard of living is a relative concept. It shows whether people are **'better off'** when compared, either with other people, or with other periods of time. National income statistics are used as a basis for such comparisons. However, they are subject to many **qualifications**.

Limitations 'TRIP TIPS'

Tax. An increase in the **burden** of taxation and national insurance over time means that a higher national income per head is needed to maintain the same standard of living. For instance, increased income tax when national income is constant means lower disposable income. Conversely, lower taxes for everyone may make people better off without increases of income.

Regional differences. The cost of living may vary within a country. For instance, it is much more expensive to live in **London** than elsewhere in Britain particularly because of the cost of housing. Similarly, in 1988 average earnings in the South were £40 higher than in the North.

Inflation. As mentioned above, adjustment has to be made for **price changes**. For instance, between 1953 and 1988 the average weekly wage rose from £8 to £180 per week but a family car increased in price from £750 to £6000. Thus we compare using **index numbers**.

Population. An increase in total national income may be achieved because the population rises, through (say) immigration. Thus we need to look at **output per head** unless a false comparison is being made. As Britain's population has now stabilized, this point is becoming less important.

Technical changes. The invention of labour-saving devices, improved machinery and better entertainment facilities may enhance the living standards of producers and consumers by making their jobs easier. As we value the output rather than the method of its creation, technical changes may give people an easier, less stressful working life and more enjoyable leisure time. A reduction in the **working week** and an unchanged national income represent an improvement in the standard of living.

However, although mass production techniques may raise the quantity of goods available, the **quality** may fall, e.g. 'plastic' bread and weak beer!

Income distribution. An increase in national income per head does not mean all people are better off. A few may be considerably better off and most might be a little worse off. For example, government tax changes 1979–80, which reduced the high rates of tax on very high earners and increased expenditure (VAT) tax for all, widened the post-tax differentials in Britain.

Personal differences. People's needs are different. For instance, pensioners spend a much higher proportion of their income on food and housing compared with well-off households. Thus, the income levels needed to sustain a decent standard of living vary between groups in the community and they change over the years.

State services. If the government reduces the free or subsidized services which it provides to the community then the population will be worse off. Such services have been termed the **'social wage'**. They are paid for out of taxation and people receive them according to their needs, without apparently having to 'pay' for them. Thus, changes over the years in state spending and provision will affect living standards.

MAKING INTERNATIONAL COMPARISONS OF LIVING STANDARDS

It is useful to make comparisons with other countries because it shows a nation's **economic development**. International **league tables** are devised on the basis of national income per head. In 1986 Britain stood nineteenth with £6000 GNP per head. The table was headed by Kuwait (£13,800) with USA eighth (£8200) and USSR twenty-fourth (£3500).

There are many **problems** of such comparisons. They can be remembered by 'SPICE PAWS'.

Spending habits. These differ between nations because of their needs. For example, **cold climate** countries need to spend more on heating than warm nations and thus require a higher national income to maintain the same standard of living.

Prices. As rates of inflation differ between countries then adjustments should be made for relative prices. For instance, the **cost of living** in Britain is still less than in Western Europe and America so the national income differential becomes less in **real** terms.

Income distribution. The average figures calculated give no idea of the range and distribution of income. For instance, Kuwait has the highest **average** national income but 95 per cent of the population receive less than what would be considered as low wages in Britain. The wealth is concentrated in the hands of a few wealthy sheiks.

Composition of output. A modern society may use many resources for military purposes which contribute little to the immediate welfare of the people. It could be argued that by changing the pattern of output from **defence** to health and education, the standard of living could be improved without national income changing. Thus a pacifist nation probably can sustain a similar standard of living to a militarist one, but with a lower level of national income.

Exchange rates. National incomes are measured in domestic currencies and then **converted, usually into dollars**. However, because exchange rates are **volatile** and often subject to irrational forces (e.g. election jitters), the process of conversion and the timing of the conversion can significantly affect the result. For instance, if the dollar moves strongly against the pound but not against other currencies, then the national income of Britain, as measured in dollars, appears much worse in comparison.

Political factors. Some **intangible** and unmeasurable factors may be important in people's lives, e.g. **freedom of speech**, religion and association. In some nations no political opposition is allowed, and in others the rule of law is not maintained, thereby diminishing the life of the people, e.g. USSR, South Africa, The Lebanon, etc.

Accuracy. The data collected can vary in its quantity and quality. The integrity of the officials and the resources devoted to collection will determine the accuracy of the estimates. Some nations, e.g. China, are most reluctant to publish basic economic information. The figures published by others, e.g. USSR, may be doctored for political reasons.

Wealth. Although income mainly determines living standards, wealth accumulated in the past can be influential. A nation with a stock of roads, hospitals, schools **(social capital)** and houses, is much better off than a developing nation that needs to develop such assets. The developing nation has to forgo consumption (which effectively determines current living standards) in order to invest in capital.

The average net wealth (assets – debts) in Britain in 1985 was £35,000. Each household averaged £40,000 of assets, mainly in the form of financial assets, housing and consumer durables, compared with £5000 of liabilities. Wealth, as well as income, determines the ability to buy **consumer durables**. Britain is well endowed with telephones (527 per 1000 people in 1984), television sets (457 per 1000 people) and computers (most per head in the world).

Social indicators. The quality of life has become an important issue, bearing on the standard of living. Increases in **pollution**, violence, **crime**, heart disease and **pornography** are seen as diminishing the standard of living. Conversely, falls in infant mortality, shorter hospital waiting lists, less emission of lead and fewer patients per doctor all indirectly make us better off. The extent of these factors **varies widely** between nations, again complicating international comparisons. For instance, Japan's national income has exceeded Britain's but few would argue that its standard of living is better because of its pollution and low level of state provision of services.

CALCULATING ECONOMIC GROWTH

See Unit 14.4.

14.4 Economic growth

MEASUREMENT

Economic growth is the **percentage increase in total output of the economy at constant prices**. Such increases mean that real incomes have improved and so probably have living standards. Thus the raising of the standard of living is closely tied to economic growth.

However, the measurement of growth in percentage terms creates **complications**. Britain's average 2 per cent growth rate of the 1970s does not mean that we are worse off than Spain whose economy grew by 6 per cent. The GNP per head increase in Britain was £200 per year whilst Spain's was just £40. This was because Britain has a **larger base** (starting point) from which the percentage was calculated. Clearly, a nation with a strong, developed base has less chance of a high **percentage** improvement but more likelihood of a large **absolute** increase.

ARGUMENTS FOR 'PENS'

1 **Poverty.** Increases in national income can lead to reduction of poverty in society. There is less resistance to the sacrifice of higher taxes paid by high-wage earners which may be needed to relieve the poverty.
2 **Efficiency growth.** Encourages efficiency and best use of resources.
3 **National prestige.**
4 **Standard of living.** Growth is necessary to maintain/improve living standards.

ARGUMENTS AGAINST 'SWAP'

1 **Social costs**, such as congestion, noise, crime, pollution, and the loss of beautiful countryside, may increase in the pursuit of economic goals. These costs often have to be paid for by the state.
2 **Waste disposal**, particularly nuclear, becomes more difficult and **dangerous**.

3 **Attitudes** may become **carefree and complacent** and develop with growth because people have high standards and little incentive for improvement, e.g. **'throw away' lifestyle**; it is also claimed that much modern employment is depersonalized because of automation. These attitudes, and the increased freedom resulting from higher living standards, may cause more **selfishness** and less trust and co-operation in society.

4 **Private affluence** and **public squalor**. If the benefits of economic growth go to a small sector of society then these groups may become very wealthy. Alternatively, the rest of the community will be relatively badly off. The strength of this argument rests on the distribution of income and wealth in a nation and the attitude of the government.

MEANS OF GROWTH

Economies need to make use of **idle resources** in order to grow. Once these have been utilized, an economy can only grow through **increased productivity**, i.e. greater output per person. This can be achieved by the following.

1 **Increased quantity of investment.** It usually means diverting resources from consumption to investment. This may be difficult to manage because it means giving up increases in living standards at the present in order to gain greater increases in the future. It may be a problem of political will.

2 **Higher quality of investment.** More productive and effective capital construction aids growth. Britain's investment in the public sector, particularly in defence rather than communications (which benefit **all** firms in the country), has been criticized because the goods produced are not marketable.

3 **Technological progress.** Technology can be improved by research and development leading to more efficient machinery and new inventions, e.g. robots and computers. Each year General Motors in America spends more on research than the whole of India does! The main criticism of Britain in this sphere has been the failure to market inventions, although Sinclair's success with computer technology is a notable exception.

4 **Quality of labour.** A general improvement in health and better training and education both serve to make labour more productive.

5 **Quantity of labour.** The size of the working population ultimately limits growth. For this reason many under-populated countries (e.g. Australia) and rapidly expanding nations have encouraged immigration (Unit 12).

6 **Incentives.** Labour output per head can be raised by various inducements, e.g. bonuses, profit-sharing. These tend to be short-lived rather than fundamental changes in the economy.

BRITAIN'S GROWTH

Britain's relatively poor post-war growth performance has been analysed and several causes suggested.

1 **Frequent changes of government policy.** These have disrupted business planning and deterred investment.

2 **Lack of finance.** British banks have not ventured enough risk capital into British manufacturing. They have preferred to lend to property companies and speculators rather than more productive investors.

3 **Low productivity.** Caused by inadequate training, a lack of flexibility in working practices, trade union selfishness and a fragmented workforce all at **shop-floor** level. In addition, **middle management** is often underused and not sufficiently rewarded. At **senior management** level, the dominance of the class system, unwise investment and incompetence have been variously quoted as problems which create poor productivity.

4 **Late entry into EEC** meant that Britain did not get toeholds in the European market when its competitors did. It has been calculated that Britain's entry raised the rate of economic growth by 0.3 per cent per annum, via the stimulus to exports. Over the period 1972–8 North Sea oil contributed 0.5 per cent to GDP growth.

5 **Low level of investment.** The percentage of income which is invested in Britain is much lower than our industrial competitors. The high interest rates and the high exchange rate, particularly 1979–82, have hit recent investment, particularly in manufacturing. UK fixed investment is 15 per cent of GDP (1980–5 average) whereas in 1974 it was 20 per cent. The decline has occurred most in steel, chemicals and mechanical engineering. In 1980, 69 per cent of the investment was

done by the private sector and 31 per cent by the public sector (of which nationalized industries accounted for 17 per cent). UK investment has also been of poor quality, e.g. we get a lower return per pound invested than West Germany, our machines are more likely to break down and our workers are less-well trained.

However, the OECD estimated Britain's growth in 1986 at 2½ per cent, which was still sluggish compared with most of our industrial competitors. In 1987 and 1988 British economic growth increased to over 4.5 per cent in advance of our major rivals. Britain's change in real GNP seems to fluctuate less than most other nations, meaning that we **suffer less in slumps** but **gain less in booms**.

14.5 Distribution of wealth

A distinction must be made between income and wealth.

1 **Income** is a **flow** of money—usually received on a **regular** basis (Unit 13).

2 **Wealth** is a **stock** of assets—these are accumulated over a period of time, either from saving or inheritance. A person's wealth is measured at one point of time. It includes assets which have a **monetary value**.

The general distribution of wealth in Britain is rather more even than in countries such as France and the USA. This is because there are few excessively high top incomes. However, in Britain it is very difficult to 'break into' the top groups because of:

1 **The large council housing system.** In Britain land is the basis of the top people's wealth and 40 per cent of population do not live in their own property. The Conservative government, however, is encouraging people to buy their own council houses, often at much less than their market price.

2 **The progressive income tax system.** As incomes rise above the poverty line, the government takes an increasing proportion in taxation. This prevents the build-up of fortunes out of earned income and makes for relative income equality.

The percentage share of total personal wealth held by the most wealthy one per cent of the UK population declined from 61 per cent in 1923 to 23 per cent in 1980, but increased to 24 per cent by 1985.

Britain does not have a wealth tax, which is an **annual** tax on the value of personal wealth above a certain threshold level. France and Sweden have such taxes. However, Britain has a tax on **inheritance**. For instance, when a person dies and leaves more than £118,000 worth of assets, the government takes a percentage as a death duty. The scale is progressive as the amount left increases. However, the many exceptions allowed and the current law on trusts and covenants means that the tax take is low and its effectiveness in redistributing wealth is limited. Thus wealth in Britain is largely determined by inheritance as large stocks of assets are handed down through rich families.

POVERTY

The opposite of wealth is **poverty**. The definition of poverty is not clear-cut because the **poverty line** changes through the years with movements in earnings, prices and social behaviour. For instance, in 1955 a television set was considered to be a luxury, but in 1983 51 per cent of the population regarded it as a necessity!

Poverty is measured by using the **supplementary benefit level** which averages two-thirds of the national average wage. The benefits paid vary with **family circumstances** but are supposed to be sufficient to allow people to 'keep themselves reasonably fed, and well enough dressed to maintain their self-respect and to attend interviews for jobs with confidence'.

The line below which people are considered to be poor, is usually drawn at **120 per cent** of supplementary benefit level. Thus if a single parent with one child receives £50 per week then the amount needed for them to be out of poverty would be £60 (i.e. 120 per cent of £50).

The 1983 Market and Opinion Research International (MORI) Survey defined poverty in terms of the **necessities needed for a decent life**. The items which most people deemed to be essential were heating for living areas (3.23 million families without), indoor lavatory, damp-free home (4.3 million without), bath not shared with other families (1.1 million without), money for public transport, three meals a day for children (7.0 million without).

On this basis, the poor in Britain are concentrated within five vulnerable groups:

1 Single-parent families (900,000)
2 Unemployed (3 million)
3 Elderly
4 Disabled and sick
5 Low paid

4½ million elderly
3 million adults
2½ million children

14.6 Housing

Housing is a basic need which can be secured by either **renting** someone else's property (private landlord or local council) or **buying** your own property. Whether a house is rented or bought (using a mortgage), it results in expenditure for the occupant. Some of the costs are **fixed** each year e.g. council house rent, and rates on a owner-occupied house. Other costs are **variable** e.g. council house decoration, owner-occupied mortgage repayments.

A distinction can also be made between the **capital** expenditure on housing and **current** expenditure. Capital expenditure refers to the money outlayed on buying or creating the asset if it is brand new. Private houses appreciate in capital (resale) value over the years. Current expenditure is the spending undertaken on the upkeep and running of the property: this may mean regular repairs and renewals. In the case of council houses the council pays, but for private property the owners must foot the bill.

Buying	*v*	**Renting**
1 A capital asset which appreciates		1 Low cost accommodation
2 Tax relief on mortgage payments so you are subsidized		2 You do not pay directly for repairs
3 You make your own decisions over the property		3 Outgoings are fixed and do not fluctuate with the rate of interest
4 You can sell to raise capital if necessary		4 There is less worry as you are only the tenant and not the owner

14.7 Summary

The circular flow of income model shows the flows of money between different groups of people in the economy. The basic model is a closed system involving producers and consumers. A more complex model takes account of leakages and injections. National Income is the total value of goods and services produced by a country in one year. It can be measured by the Expenditure, Income or Output method. National Income calculations are used by governments and organizations to judge the effect of economic policies, to assess changes in living standards and to make international comparisons of living standards. The figures are also used to calculate economic growth, because the latter is seen as the way of increasing living standards and improving efficiency. Opponents of 'growth' stress the social and environmental costs involved.

Economic growth takes place through increased productivity. Britain's poor growth record since the war has been blamed on government policies as well as the practices of private firms and financial institutions. The government seeks to influence the levels of wealth and poverty through the taxation and transfer payment systems.

15 PUBLIC FINANCE

15.1 Public expenditure

This term refers mainly to **government spending**, which has become a much larger proportion of national income in recent years (see Fig. 15.1). Public finance refers to the revenue raised to pay for this expenditure. In 1969 central government revenue exceeded expenditure leaving a budget surplus. However, in every year since, expenditure has exceeded revenue, causing a **budget deficit**. In 1979 the Conservative government came to power committed to reducing the budget deficit and lowering the government spending as a percentage of GDP. By 1988 it had become successful. The term **fiscal policy** is used to describe deliberate changes in taxation and public expenditure.

		Central government		
Year	*Expenditure* *£ billion*	*as percentage of GDP*	*Income* *£ billion*	*as percentage of GDP*
1963–4	11	36	9	30
1973–4	32	43	26	36
1985–6	140	46	112	39
1987–8	158	39	161	40
1989–90 (est)	194	43	206	45

Fig. 15.1 Public expenditure, taxation and GDP percentages

	As percentage of total spending	
Category	*1972–73*	*1989–90*
Social security	20	30
Defence	12	12
Education, science, arts	13	12
Health and personal services	10	14
Industry and employment	8	4
Scotland	6	5
Housing	6	1
Transport	4	3
Agriculture, fishing, forestry	2	2
Other expenditure	19	17

Fig. 15.2 Public expenditure by category

Figure 15.2 shows the main areas of public spending. The major change which has occurred in the last decade is the large increase in the proportion of public money spent on **Social Security**. This has been a direct result of Britain's ageing population, which partly explains the increase in the health and personal services category. A significant fall is in the housing category and this reflects the stable population and the increase in owner-occupation. More money is spent on all of the categories now, than in 1972–3, reflecting **inflation**.

REASONS FOR PUBLIC EXPENDITURE   'PERM'

Public goods. They are defined as 'those goods/services which will not and cannot (in reality) be provided by the free market'. Examples are defence, law and order, roads and street lighting. The main reason why the free market does not provide these goods is that it is **impossible to exclude** nonpayers from benefiting from the provision of these goods and services. For instance, if you do not purchase an entrance ticket to the cinema then you are prevented from seeing the film being shown. However, if you refuse to purchase the services of the **armed forces** it would be impossible to defend your neighbour, who has paid, without defending you at the same time. For this reason, if public goods are provided at all it must be by the government through taxation.

In the 19th century most public expenditure was on public goods, particularly defence, but nowadays it is a small share of the total. However, since 1979 (and the Conservative government) defence spending has increased its share of the total which had fallen to 11 per cent (in 1978–9).

Economic efficiency. Governments often feel the need to intervene in the economy either to increase efficiency or to reduce the production of economic 'bads', e.g. pollution, whose costs are paid for by society, rather than privately by those responsible.

In order to raise efficiency, a **new motorway** might be constructed which will probably lower the transport costs for firms using it. Other similar policies such as regional grants and youth training schemes also have **social aims**, i.e. reducing unemployment. The extent of government intervention aimed at increasing economic efficiency depends on political values. A socialist (Labour) would argue that **nationalization** leads to a better use of resources. In contrast capitalists (Conservative) dispute this view and thus privatize parts of the public sector.

Relief of poverty. Income is provided for many **disadvantaged** groups in society, so that they are not dependent on charity, e.g. widows, pensioners, students, unemployed, etc. They receive **benefits** from the state. Supplementary benefit is designed to ensure a minimum standard of living for those who do not have full-time jobs. It covers pensioners, single parents working part-time and the disabled, as well as the unemployed.

Not all of the available benefits are taken up by those who are eligible for them. For instance, only 74 per cent of those who qualify for supplementary benefit actually claim it. Many benefits have a lower **take-up rate** than this, e.g. free school meals 15 per cent. These benefits are termed **'transfer incomes'** because public funds taken from taxpayers are given to the needy.

Merit goods. They are defined as 'those goods considered to be so important that they are provided by the state at **zero** (or subsidized) **price'**. The two most important examples in Britain are **education** and **national health**. These services are also provided by the free market (i.e. public schools such as Eton, and private nursing homes) but for the majority of the population they are too expensive. In contrast, the government may deter or prevent **demerit goods**, such as addictive drugs, which it considers to be harmful.

15.2 Taxation—aims and principles

AIMS OF TAXATION 'MARS'

Management of the economy. Taxation and public spending have been used to regulate the economy. In general a higher **budget deficit** seems to reflate the economy because more money enters the circular flow. This stimulates spending and increases the demand for workers, thereby probably **lowering unemployment**. However, some economists (notably the Monetarists) argue that such reflation leads to **inflation**, unless there are substantial increases in productivity. Thus, generally, lower taxation and more spending reflates, whilst higher taxation and less spending deflates.

Alteration of income distribution. Taxes can be used to redistribute income in society. The **Labour Party** as a government tends to seek a reduction in income inequality by **progressive** taxation (see Unit 15.3). Thus it is likely to raise income tax, particularly the rate on large incomes. In contrast, the **Conservatives** since 1979 have reduced the basic and top rates of income tax (from 83 per cent to 60 per cent) and nearly doubled VAT which is **regressive** (see Unit 15.3). This has effectively redistributed income to the higher earners. Such a policy is justified by their desire to increase incentives and encourage investment.

Raise revenue. The original aim of taxation was to gain income, usually for the state to fight wars. The contribution of the main taxes towards government revenue is illustrated in Fig. 15.3.

Tax	As percentage of total tax income	
	1972–3	*1989–90*
Income Tax	31.1	23.1
National Insurance	15.3	18.2
Rates	11.1	9.9
Petrol and diesel	7.1	5.1
Corporation Tax	6.7	10.3
Purchase Tax	6.5	—
Value Added Tax	—	14.9
Tobacco	5.4	3.2
Beer, wines, spirits	4.9	2.8
Vehicle licences	2.3	1.7
Death duties	2.2	0.5
Capital Gains Tax	1.3	0.6
Petroleum Revenue Tax	—	2.1
Other	6.1	7.6

Fig. 15.3 Income from different taxes

In the last decade several important changes have taken place. **VAT** has replaced Purchase Tax and become an important source of income. Also, **Petroleum Revenue Tax** has been introduced (1974) and, together with several other taxes on North Sea oil, it is likely to raise £9 million in a typical year. **National Insurance** (see Unit 15.4) has become more important, whilst the shares of **income tax** and **excise duties** on petrol and diesel, tobacco, and beer, wines and spirits have fallen.

Specific objectives. Governments sometimes use taxes to discourage certain harmful activities. For instance, in the 18th century **gin** was taxed to deter excessive drinking which had been increasing the death rate. This policy of **discouraging 'vices'** such as smoking and drinking persists today and the taxes on them raise over £6.0 billion. Of the price of a packet of cigarettes 70 per cent goes in tax, raising £1 billion a year.

Similarly, government spending can be used to encourage certain effects. From 1967 until 1975 a **regional employment premium** was paid to manufacturers in development areas (see Unit 6.3) for each employee. This **subsidy** encouraged employment in these depressed areas and was a disincentive to firms thinking of locating in other areas.

PRINCIPLES OF TAXATION

Adam Smith's four canons or principles of taxation are still relevant today.

Certainty. It is argued that the easier taxes are to understand the less will be the incentive to evade them. The many exemptions from Capital Transfer Tax (see Unit 15.4) have encouraged evasion, which is unfair to those who pay, and a loss of revenue for the government. Some people say Capital Transfer Tax is a 'voluntary tax'. If people know what is **expected** of them (i.e. when and how much they pay) then there is less aggravation, e.g. PAYE (see Unit 15.4).

Convenience. Governments should consider the **circumstances** of tax payers and levy taxes when it is more convenient. Thus income tax is deducted through PAYE weekly or monthly at source (i.e. when paid) rather than collected yearly. The latter arrangement would require great organization and disciplined saving by the taxpayer. The self-employed often find paying income tax six months after the 'year end' onerous, because a lump sum is required. Nowadays local rates can also be paid monthly because payment is easier that way, for both ratepayers and councils.

Economy. The receivers of tax want a system in which **collection is cheap**. If a tax costs a lot to gather then the yield from it is reduced. For instance, in 1982 it was calculated that the collection of dog licences had cost over four times the amount received.

Equality. This principle is difficult to interpret. Most people argue that taxes should be based on the **ability to pay**. Thus, people bear a fairly equal **burden** rather than all paying the same amount. Those on higher incomes pay more tax (and usually a higher proportion of their income) than those on low incomes. This progressive tax idea for income tax is also **practical**. Equal tax demands for all people would hurt the least well off who probably could not pay and incur high administration costs, e.g. taking non-payers to court.

15.3 Taxation—types

Taxes are classified in two ways.

    1 Who pays the tax—**Direct and Indirect**.
    2 The economic effects—**Progressive, Regressive, Proportional**.

DIRECT AND INDIRECT TAXATION

Direct taxes. The **burden** of paying the taxes falls **upon** the income of those from whom the tax is collected. For instance, **income tax** is paid by employees, corporation tax is charged on company profits, and rates are levied on property owners. Income tax and corporation tax are collected by the **Inland Revenue**.

Indirect taxes. The **burden** of taxation does **not** fall upon those from whom the tax is collected. **VAT** (see Unit 15.4) is an indirect tax, which is collected from manufacturers, wholesalers and retailers (see Unit 20) but as it is included in the final price it is the consumer who really pays when he buys the good/service. The **Customs and Excise Department** supervise taxes on expenditure.

PROGRESSIVE, REGRESSIVE AND PROPORTIONAL TAXATION

The **average rate of tax paid** varies between different income levels and different types of tax.

Progressive. The **proportion** of income taken in tax **rises as income increases**, above a certain minimum level. Income Tax in Britain is progressive because taxable income up to

£20,700 is taxed at 25p in the pound but taxable income above £20,701 is taxed at 40p. Thus, a single person with a gross income of £6785 has a taxable income of £4000 (6785−2785) which is taxed at 25p. His total tax bill is £1000 (£4000 × 25p) which is 14.8 per cent (1000 ÷ 6785 × 100).

In contrast, another single person with a gross income of £26,785 has a taxable income of £24,000 (26,785 − 2785). The first £20,700 is taxed at 25p and the other £3300 is taxed at 40p. This gives a total tax bill of £6495 (5175 + 1320) which is 24 per cent (6495 ÷ 26,785 × 100).

Allowances	1988–9
	£
Single and wife's earned income allowance	2785
Married allowance	4735
Additional personal and widow's bereavement allowance	1590
Single age allowance	3400
Married age allowance	5385
Age income limit	11,400

Income tax rates (%)	1988–9
	£
25	0–20,700
40	+ 20,701

Fig. 15.4 Income tax allowances

Regressive. The **proportion** of income taken in tax **falls as income increases** (i.e. the average rate of tax falls). **VAT** is regressive because it is charged at uniform rates (see Unit 15.4) irrespective of the purchaser's income.

For instance, if a relatively poor person with an income of £100 per week buys a bouquet of flowers for £11.50 (£10 + £1.50 VAT) then he pays 1.5 per cent (1.50/100) of his income in tax. A much richer person with an income of £500 per week buying a similarly priced bouquet of flowers pays 0.3 per cent (1.50/500) of his income in tax. Thus, the higher a person's income the smaller the percentage of it which will be paid in tax.

Proportional. The **same proportion** of income is taken in tax at all income levels. National Insurance payments by employers used to operate in this way between certain minimum and maximum limits. It was 9 per cent between £95 and £385 per week.

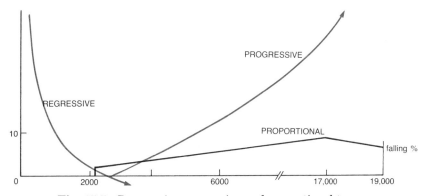

Fig. 15.5 Progressive, regressive and proportional taxes

15.4 Taxes on income, expenditure and capital

The main taxes levied in Britain can be classified into three categories.

TAXES ON INCOME

Income tax

Introduced 1799 for incomes over £60 per year, discontinued in 1815, and reintroduced in 1842 at 7d (2.9p) in the pound. It has since varied between 2d (0.8p) in 1875 and 10/- (50p) during the Second World War. Each taxpayer is given certain **tax-free allowances** depending upon their family circumstances (see Fig. 15.5). The difference between their gross income and tax-free allowances is their **taxable pay** – the first £20,700 being taxed at the basic rate of 25 per cent. After that the tax charged on extra income increases up to a 40 per cent maximum.

Advantages 'FAYRE'

1 **Fairness.** As it is levied according to the ability to pay, income tax is **equitable**. Thus very low earners pay no tax and very high earners pay much more than the basic rate.
2 **Automatic stabilizer.** As incomes rise generally, so does the total amount paid in income tax. The increased taxation acts as a withdrawal from the circular flow, slowing down the increase in consumption. Conversely, a fall in income during a depression will mean less tax for the government (and lower withdrawals). This **prevents rapid fluctuations** in the economy.
3 **Yield.** Income tax is a **large revenue** raiser, at least £30 billion annually.
4 **Redistribution of income.** As income tax is **progressive**, it takes more from the rich than from the poor. If some of the tax revenue is used to provide free benefits for the poor then income has been redistributed.
5 **Efficiency.** It is easy to operate through PAYE (Pay As You Earn) and **difficult to evade**. The cost of collection is **cheap**—1.7 per cent of the yield from PAYE but 6.0 per cent of the yield from self-employed and rent incomes.

Disadvantages 'DEALS'

1 **Disincentive effects.** It is often argued that high and progressive income-tax rates discourage extra work by employees and deter entrepreneurs. For these reasons, the 1979 Conservative government cut income tax at all levels. There is not much actual evidence that these changes have encouraged greater production and brought the return of famous 'tax exiles'. In general it is very difficult to measure people's responses to tax changes as they react differently in different situations at different times. For instance, someone using overtime earnings to pay for a future foreign holiday may work more as tax rates rise because he gains less from each hour of overtime worked. In contrast, somebody with nothing to save for may react to a tax increase by substituting leisure for work.
2 **Evasion** and **avoidance**. Tax evasion, which is not paying the tax required, is **illegal** and the Inland Revenue employs inspectors to catch offenders. However, tax avoidance is **legal** and involves the self-employed and companies employing accountants to reduce tax liability. It is claimed that high direct taxes channel effort into avoidance and evasion.
3 **Less savings.** The income tax system in Britain is said to encourage consumption rather than savings. In the long run, a low level of savings (17 per cent of GDP in Britain, compared with 31 per cent in Japan) reduces the flow of funds available for investment and thus limits the potential for economic growth (see Unit 14.4). In particular, the tax relief given to private pensions, house loans (mortgage relief costs £3 billion per year) and life assurance encourage specific savings but these do not go towards productive investment.

National Insurance

National insurance contributions are made by both employees and employers. People earning up to the lower limit of £43 per week pay nothing. Those above £43 pay 2 per cent on the first £43 and 9 per cent on the rest, up to an upper limit of £325. In practice, national insurance is a tax on earnings and a **tax on jobs**, because every time a firm takes on a full-time employee it has to pay the employee's contribution. It is unpopular with business. However, it is popular with the government as a **revenue raiser** because its contribution to total revenue has doubled in less than 20 years.

Corporation tax

This direct tax on **company profits** was introduced in 1965 to replace Profits Tax. The standard rate of **35 per cent** is charged on profits in excess of £750,000. Companies can claim tax relief for many business costs, e.g. interest paid on loans. Small companies are charged at a lower rate: 25 per cent on profits up to £150,000.

TAXES ON EXPENDITURE
Value-added tax

VAT is levied upon the **net** value added at each stage of production for certain goods and services. This is illustrated in Fig. 15.6. It was introduced in **1973** as a replacement for purchase tax and to bring the UK in line with the EEC prior to our entry. It is essentially a tax on **consumption**, e.g. in 1984 the Chancellor introduced VAT on hot takeaway meals such as fish and chips.

There are three levels of VAT. There is the **standard** rate which is 15 per cent on many goods and services, e.g. meals out. Some goods and services, e.g. food and power are **zero-rated**. This means that VAT is not payable at the retail stage and that any VAT paid at earlier stages of

Stage of production	Buying price	Value added £	15 per cent Tax £	Selling price
Primary producer	—	40	6	46
Manufacturer	46	40	6	92
Retailer	92	20	3	115

Fig. 15.6 VAT at different stages of production

production can be claimed back. Other goods and services, such as education and insurance, do not have VAT charged at the final stage, but VAT paid earlier cannot be reclaimed. This is the **exempt** category.

Advantages 'FACE'

1 **Flexible.** VAT can be easily and quickly changed, as happened in 1979.

2 **Automatic stabilizer.** As most **consumer durables**, particularly luxuries, are subject to standard rate VAT, increases in consumption expenditure bring about greater tax revenue. This prevents a too rapid surge into a boom (and vice versa during a slump).

3 **Cheap.** The administrative costs of VAT are low. In 1976 they were 2 per cent of the yield but now they are only **1.2 per cent of the yield** (mainly because VAT is now at a higher rate). The low collection costs are partly explained by the work done by the VAT payers (i.e. business) who virtually act as 'unpaid tax collectors'.

4 **Effort unaffected.** VAT is not usually 'seen' by the consumer because it is included in the purchase price. Increases in VAT by making goods more expensive may encourage **extra effort** so that the goods can be afforded.

Disadvantages 'DIRE'

1 **Disliked by business.** Firms bear the **cost** of record keeping and VAT calculation, because the law says they must. In addition VAT inspectors may check their accounts and search their premises. These aspects have made VAT unpopular with small businesses.

2 **Inflationary.** The existence of VAT and any increases, such as 1979, are inflationary because **prices rise** in order to maintain profit margins and pay the costs of record keeping. It is possible that trade unions may respond to such price increases by demanding higher wages to maintain living standards.

3 **Regressive.** Even though many basic necessities, e.g. food, are zero rated, VAT hits the lowest paid hardest (see Unit 15.3). Clearly poor people pay less VAT than rich people because they do not buy as many 'vatable' goods or they buy cheaper goods, but they still pay a higher proportion of their income in VAT. Thus VAT seems to be **inequitable**.

4 **Evasion.** The Black Economy (see Unit 2.1) has thrived since VAT was introduced. VAT payment is evaded by activities such as charging a lower price for **payment by cash** without a receipt (e.g. car mechanic servicing motor car) and the **bartering** of services by professional people (e.g. accountants and solicitors).

Protective (customs) and excise duties

These taxes are collected by the Customs and Excise department and levied **in addition** to VAT on several important goods, e.g. alcohol, tobacco. Before 1973 (EEC transitional entry) the **excise** duties were taxes placed on **domestic** goods and **customs** duties were taxes levied on **imported** goods. However, since we have 'harmonized' with the EEC the terminology has changed. All duties for **revenue purposes** are now termed **excise** which is payable on both **home produced and imported goods**.

Protective duties refer to customs duties on **non-EEC** goods (rather than just non-British as in the past) and are generally in line with the **Common External Tariff**. This change has arisen because there is a free market within the EEC and so Britain cannot levy customs duties on goods from (say) France. Britain imposes tariffs on cheap textiles from South Korea and Taiwan, as part of a Multi-Fibre agreement (since 1977).

TAXES ON CAPITAL

Inheritance tax. This replaced Capital Transfer Tax in 1986. It has been called a '**Gifts** tax' because it is payable on gifts made during a lifetime and on **transfers of personal wealth** at death. It is intended to reduce the inequality of wealth distribution by taxing its transfer. Gifts made within seven years of death are taxed (e.g. three to four years at 80 per cent whereas six to seven years at 20 per cent).

In 1988, the first £118,000 left was tax free, and after that 40 per cent of each pound was taxed. There are many **exemptions** for birthday and wedding gifts (£5000 tax free), business owners and donations to charity. These concessions have encouraged tax **avoidance**, particularly through trust funds, and given CTT the label of a 'voluntary tax'. It contributes a very **small**, declining amount of tax revenue and the collection cost is 3 per cent of the yield.

CTT is a tax on inheritance rather than wealth. Britain does not have a wealth tax, unlike France and Sweden where a tax is paid annually by those owning assets above a certain value.

Capital Gains Tax. This tax is charged on **profits** made when certain **paper assets**, such as stocks and shares, are sold. Profits of less than £5000 per annum are exempt whilst allowances are made for inflation. The revenue earned by the government from this tax is thus slight and **diminishing**.

OTHER TAXES

Rates. See Unit 19.5.

Petroleum Revenue Tax. Prior to 1975, production from the UK's offshore gas and oilfields was subject only to **Royalty** payments and Corporation Tax. Since then companies have paid PRT and Advanced PRT which together now take about 75 per cent of an oilfield's net revenue, after certain costs have been deducted. The **complicated system of allowances** permits oil companies to recover most of their capital expenditure within a few years of the oil first flowing. The main advantage of the tax is clearly its **yield**—£10 billion estimated for 1984–5. In contrast, it is argued that very high rates of tax may deter future investment. This income is very susceptible to falls in oil price, e.g. 1986.

15.5 Incidence of taxes

The incidence of a tax occurs in two ways. The **formal incidence** refers to the taxpayer who has to **pay the tax over** to the government. For instance, VAT is collected by the retailer and remitted to the government every three months. The **real incidence** refers to the person who has to **bear the burden** of the tax. For instance, whilst a retailer may collect and pay over VAT, he may be able to pass on the tax by raising the price of his goods and not losing any customers. Economists are concerned with this eventual real impact of certain taxation, particularly where it affects demand and supply.

Expenditure taxes, such as VAT, may **distort** the prices and quantity supplied of goods. Such taxes shift a producer's supply curve to the left as shown in Fig. 15.7. At each price the producer is now prepared to **supply less** because part of his sales income goes in tax. The supply schedule shows that at £2 price before tax was introduced 15 units were supplied, but since taxation of £1 per unit, only 10 are put on the market. The suppliers' total revenue before tax was £30 but now after tax it is only £10 (£20 total revenue less £10 tax). In order to achieve a net revenue of £30, the supplier needs to produce 15 at £3. In that way he pays £15 (15 × £1 tax) to the government and keeps £30 out of the £45 total revenue.

The original equilibrium price was £3 with 20 units supplied. The imposition of tax has caused a fall in the quantity demanded to 17 units and rise in price to £3.30. This result has been caused by the **shape of the demand** curve (i.e. its elasticity). The real impact of the tax is shown by the shaded areas in Fig. 15.7. The price rise to £3.30 shows that the consumer has to pay an extra 30p because of the tax. On each sale, the supplier has to pay £1 to the government and so really he bears 70p of the tax (£1 to pay but gets extra 30p from customer). It is mainly because the **demand curve** is so **elastic** that the bulk of the burden falls on the producer. In Fig. 15.8, the demand curve is **perfectly inelastic** (and the supply data is the same as in Fig. 15.7) and so the incidence of the tax falls completely on the **consumer**. In practice, taxes on expenditure should be placed on goods (such as tobacco, alcohol?) where demand is inelastic so that the revenue aimed for is obtained.

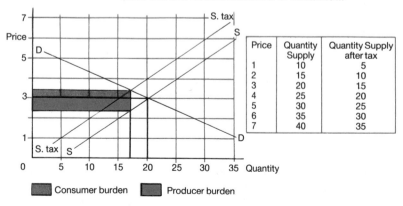

Price	Quantity Supply	Quantity Supply after tax
1	10	5
2	15	10
3	20	15
4	25	20
5	30	25
6	35	30
7	40	35

Fig. 15.7 Tax incidence and effect of a tax on supply

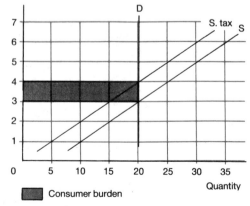

Fig. 15.8 Tax incidence and inelastic demand

15.6 The Budget and PSBR and government policy

THE BUDGET

Each year the Chancellor of the Exchequer, on behalf of the government, prepares a budget in which he outlines the **following year's** public expenditure and public revenue **plans**. Occasionally, there is a mini-budget mid-way through the financial year, in the autumn. There is now also an **Autumn Statement** outlining possible options for the following March budget and laying down economic policy objectives.

The budget has become an important economic weapon for the government in the pursuit of certain objectives (see Unit 19.1). In the past governments sought either to **balance** the budget, or create a **surplus** or produce a **deficit**. With a surplus budget, government income exceeds expenditure.

In simple theory, a **balanced budget** has no overall effect on the level of economic activity because the amount withdrawn through revenue is matched by the amount injected by expenditure. In the inter-war years a balanced budget was aimed for as a sign of **good housekeeping**. **Keynes** was one of the first to suggest deficit budgets—the idea being for the amount by which expenditure exceeded revenue—to stimulate demand. Thus, deficit budgets could be used to lower unemployment which had been caused by low demand. However, too large a deficit, by increasing spending possibly faster than output and possibly on imported goods, created two problems—**inflation** and **balance of payments deficits** respectively. Thus, in order to reduce these problems, **surplus budgets** were sought when expenditure was less than revenue and the level of demand fell. In the 1960s the alternation of these types of budgets was known as 'stop–go'. The government was trying to regulate the economy through **fiscal** (taxation–spending) policies. It was trying to manage the level of demand.

PUBLIC SECTOR BORROWING REQUIREMENT (PSBR)

PSBR is the **difference** between **the income and expenditure** of the **whole of the public sector** each year. This includes the activities of nationalized industries, public corporations, local authorities and central government departments. A **budget deficit/surplus** just refers to the **central government**.

The increase in public spending in the **1970s** has made PSBR inevitable every year until now. Thus the economic argument has shifted away from surplus/deficit towards **how large/ how small** a PSBR (fiscal stance). The main reasons for the **increasing size** of PSBR have been:

1 Effects of **inflation** on spending, particularly on necessary services.
2 **Political spending** commitments, e.g. Labour to social services, Conservatives to defence, and law and order.
3 **Unwillingness**, for political reasons, of successive governments to **raise taxation** in line with the increases in spending—increased rates of income tax before election time is political suicide!
4 **Ageing population.** This has raised the social security share of public expenditure significantly (see Fig. 15.2).
5 **Increased unemployment,** particularly since 1979. Each unemployed person costs the state approximately £7000 per year in lost tax revenue and paid benefits.
6 **Debt interest**—each PSBR raises the National Debt (see Unit 15.7) upon which interest needs to be paid. As debt interest is 11 per cent of total public sector expenditure it usually exceeds the PSBR on its own.

The PSBR is a **forecast** for the next financial year. The actual amount borrowed (out turn) is often several billions different from the planned total. Changes in the economy may distort the estimates. For instance, greater unemployment than forecast may increase government expenditure and lower government revenue, thus making PSBR larger.

The significance of PSBR

Year	PSBR– } PSDR+ }	Percentage of GDP	National Debt £ billions	Percentage of GDP
1972–3	−2.5	3.9	49.6	77.4
1976–7	−8.5	6.8	88.5	70.1
1978–9	−9.2	5.4	108.1	63.6
1980–1	−13.2	5.7	136.4	58.6
1984–5	−10.1	3.1	190.0	55.5
1989–90 (est)	+13.8	3.0	184.2	39.0

Fig. 15.9 PSBR and the National Debt

Figure 15.9 shows the 1980s tendency to PSBR, which was first reversed in 1988–9 when a PSDR was created. **Monetarist** economists argue that the rise of PSBR has caused inflation.

In order to finance the public spending, the government has needed to borrow money. In so doing it has increased the supply of money in the economy thus generating inflation (see Unit 9.7).

Another consequence has been **higher interest rates**. In order to borrow, the government needs to offer lucrative interest rates. It is argued by some that investment funds have been attracted by these rates on government stock (gilts, savings certificates, etc.) and diverted away from productive industrial lending. This view claims that private sector investment has been '**crowded out**' by the public sector.

The Conservative Party as government takes the view that a high and rising PSBR is a 'bad thing'. It argues that PSBR should fall as a proportion of GDP. On the other hand, the Labour Party is less concerned about the overall size of PSBR. It points out that Britain's PSBR is a very small percentage of GDP compared with most of our competitors and that it is falling in **real** terms (i.e. allowing for inflation). In addition, it disputes the inflation argument, giving the **demand for money** fed by profit-seeking banks and other credit providing institutions as alternative causes of the inflation. The Labour Party dismisses the crowding-out argument and cites the **conservatism of British management** and its unwillingness to invest, as explanations.

PUBLIC SECTOR DEBT REPAYMENT (PSDR)

In the financial year ending March 1988, public sector income exceeded public sector spending by £3 billion. This created a PSDR. In 1988–9 the PSDR exceeded forecasts and jumped to £13 billion. The main causes were:

1 Public assets sales, which count as negative spending. They increased to approx £5 billion annually in the late 1980s, as a result of the expanding privatization programme.

2 Housing budget capital receipts from local authorities, which lowered housing expenditure. They were about £2 billion in 1987–8 and 1988–9.

3 Increased VAT receipts. They resulted from a consumer credit boom, particularly in 1988–9, which unexpectedly raised the government's income.

A PSDR enables a government to repay part of the National Debt. In future years this means lower debt interest repayments, as the capital sum has been reduced, and thus slightly lower public spending.

15.7 National Debt

The National Debt is the **total** amount **owed** by the **central government** to people both in Britain and abroad. The debt has been accumulated over the years. Whenever there is a PSBR the debt increases. Each year, **interest** is paid to the lenders and, intermittently, **capital** is repaid. However, some debt is undated (e.g. $2\frac{1}{2}$ per cent Consols have no redemption date or value). Obviously as the debt increases in size so does the amount paid in interest. However, in **real terms**, the National Debt has become less significant.

Most of the debt is owed to **domestic residents** who hold Treasury bills, medium- and long-term Government Stock and various savings certificates. Less than 10 per cent is owed abroad fortunately, because interest and capital repayments are an outflow from the British economy and a drain on the Balance of Payments.

15.8 Summary

Public expenditure is undertaken by governments on behalf of the nation to provide goods and services which might otherwise not be provided by the free market or which might only be available in limited quantities and/or at high prices. Revenue to pay for government expenditure primarily comes from taxation. Taxes can be classified as direct or indirect and are levied on income, expenditure and capital. Adam Smith's canons of taxation can still be applied to today's taxes to assess their worth.

The annual Budget statement outlines the government's income and expenditure plans for the forthcoming year. The PSBR records the size of the public sector's overall surplus or deficit. A deficit had existed every year until the late 1980s when government policies were successful in creating a PSDR. The National Debt increases in the years in which there is a budget deficit. Most debt is held by UK residents.

16 UNEMPLOYMENT

16.1 Introduction

Unemployment has become a serious economic problem, particularly since 1976 when the percentage of the working population unemployed exceeded 5 per cent and the numbers went over 1 million. As well as labour, capital and land may be unemployed. The unemployment of any factor incurs an **opportunity cost** through the waste of a valuable resource.

The unemployment of the 1980s has been compared with the 1930s. However, although the total numbers involved are similar, there are several important **differences**.

1 The percentage unemployed in the 1930s was **higher**, because the working population was lower (fewer women workers in particular).

2 The unemployed in the 1930s was much more **regional**. For instance, current blackspots show 30 per cent unemployed in certain towns, e.g. Hartlepool, compared with 80 per cent, e.g. Jarrow in 1930s.

3 **Most occupational groups** were affected in the 1930s with skilled, unskilled and white-collar workers all suffering significantly. This happened because world trade declined in volume by a quarter and GDP fell by a sixth. However, in the 1980s the unemployment has been more concentrated in certain sectors (e.g. steel) and occupations (e.g. unskilled manual labour).

4 The effect in 1980s has been felt most amongst the **young**, and amongst **older men**.

16.2 Characteristics

PEOPLE

'YOU' and **'ME'** is an appropriate mnemonic, as it is important to know who the unemployed are. Five main groups can be identified.

Young people. A quarter of those aged 16–25 are unemployed. This has happened because firms are **unlikely to recruit** young workers during a recession because:

1 The **training** costs are high before the young workers become fully productive.

2 The **wage rates** are too high. Trade union power in the 1970s pushed up wages, making young labour less cheap and thus less profitable to employ.

In contrast, firms are **more likely** to make young workers **redundant** because:

1 Young workers are **less experienced**/less skilled.

2 The **'last in, first out'** principle is used by employers when shedding labour, as it rewards loyalty and seems fairer. Young workers are often 'last in'. Thus young workers have experienced several short-lasting jobs.

3 It is **cheaper** to lay off the young, as large redundancy payments do not have to be paid. Thus the middle-aged are kept on the payroll.

Figure 16.1 shows the unemployed in each age group (January 1989).

Age group (thousands)

	Under 25	25–39	40–59	Over 60	All
Males	388.6	521.1	519.1	42.1	1473.2
Females	207.2	197.6	194.0	0.8	601.1
	595.8	718.7	713.1	42.9	2074.3

Fig. 16.1 Unemployment by age group January 1989

Older men. There are also more older men, usually aged over 55, unemployed than on average. For instance, if cuts in a firm's labour force are necessary then the **declining productivity** of older workers makes them 'natural' targets. Those unemployed after age 50 are unlikely to want (or be considered for) **retraining** and many have taken early retirement anyway.

Unskilled workers. These workers have borne the brunt of the unemployment. However, as a percentage of total unemployed, the manual workers' share has fallen and that of craft workers has increased. Unskilled workers are most prone to be replaced by **new technology**. They are also most likely to be employed in (or made redundant from) **labour intensive** industries suffering structural decline. Their relatively **low productivity** makes them likely victims of a recession.

Married people with families. There is a direct link between family size and unemployment, if single people who have the highest rate of unemployment (mainly because of their youth) are discounted. Families with four or **more children** are four times **more likely** to have the **male parent unemployed** than families with one child or no children. There are several sociological explanations for this. However, the main economic reason is the '**unemployment trap**' created by low wages and social benefits. Some potential workers with large families are only slightly better off in work than unemployed. Thus, such workers have little financial incentive to find employment.

Ethnic minorities. There are proportionally more **non-whites unemployed** than whites in most age groups. For instance, a male West Indian school leaver with five GCSEs is twice as likely to be unemployed as a similar white classmate. Almost no whites with degrees are employed in manual work yet 20 per cent of ethnic minority degree holders work manually. Apart from being unfair, it is a serious waste and misuse of scarce resources.

DURATION

The length of time unemployed is very important. A short period unemployed is a **financial burden** to the state and a waste of resources. However, a longer period of unemployment incurs a bigger financial sacrifice, **social costs** and a **deterioration of an economic resource**. In 1955 the average spell of unemployment was just under one month, now it is nine months! The young are less likely to be unemployed for a very long period but those over 55 face longer periods of inactivity. Half of those aged over 60 have been on the unemployment register for over one year. In general, over one-third of total have been unemployed for over one year and 60 per cent for at least 26 weeks.

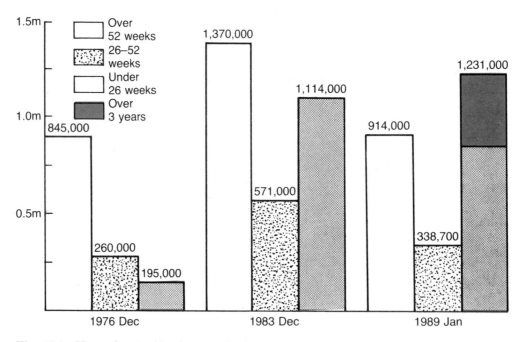

Fig. 16.2 Unemployment by duration (1976–1989)

REGIONS

The extent of unemployment varies between regions. Generally, the further you go from London and the South-East, the worse the problem has become. It is mainly associated with the decline of traditional industries, e.g. steel, shipbuilding (see Unit 6.3.). As a result of high unemployment, **assisted areas** have been created. It is interesting to note that **Scotland** made a small relative improvement in its position because of North Sea oil and its success in attracting high-technology electronics firms.

INDUSTRIES

The **manufacturing** sector of the economy has suffered much more unemployment than the service sector. For instance, employment in manufacturing in 1983 had fallen to three-quarters of the 1976 level. This shows the **de-industrialization** referred to in Unit 5. The **steel** industry suffered particularly badly losing three-quarters of its workforce between 1980 and 1983. Also between 1950 and 1981 employment fell by 50 per cent in shipbuilding, 61 per cent in agriculture, 61 per cent in mining and 64 per cent in textiles.

The **service sector** has maintained its employment levels. This partly explains why the South-East had the lowest rates of unemployment in the 1980s.

THE NEW EMPLOYED—PART-TIMERS

The labour market now has many more part-timers. There are 5 million people working less than 30 hours per week. Between 1951 and 1981 3.7 million more part-timers were employed but 2.3 million full-timers lost jobs. Of the extra part-timers 3 million were **women**, most being employed in the **service** sector.

Employers demand part-timers so that they can:

1 Make better **use** of their **labour**, e.g. maintain production over longer hours by retiming work schedules to avoid loss of output through things such as meal breaks.

2 Use **capital equipment** more fully, e.g. use machines more hours per day without paying overtime rates.

3 Provide a **better service**, e.g. retailers late-night opening.

If a full-time shop assistant is replaced by three part-timers, the firm can save eight hours/week. They can reduce wage costs, because part-timers are often paid less, kept on low grades and do not require National Insurance contributions. Also legislation relating to redundancy, unfair dismissal and maternity leave only applies to those employed for over 16 hours per week.

16.3 Costs

There are costs to the individual and society when unemployment occurs. These can be remembered by the highly appropriate (but contrived) mnemonic **'DESTITUTES'**.

DEterioration. Labour, like land, deteriorates if not used. An increasing sense of frustration, apathy and uselessness lead the long-term unemployed to 'a not caring less attitude'. They fail to organize themselves, miss appointments and shun work. This makes them 'unemployable'. Thus their previous experience and training is wasted.

STandard of living. When workers lose their jobs, their incomes fall and this lowers living standards. Some may receive redundancy pay which might cushion the fall but most of the unemployed have to **cut back their spending**—thus the demand for goods and services falls. A single person currently receives around £30 per week Supplementary Benefit which is one-sixth of the average industrial wage. The fall in spending may create further unemployment elsewhere in the economy.

Income Tax. As the number of unemployed people rises so the revenue received by the Inland Revenue falls (through less tax and more rebates). This may make the government's PSBR target (see Unit 15.6) unobtainable because their income falls; and when Supplementary Benefits are paid their spending increases.

Unemployment benefit. A whole range of **social benefits** become available to unemployed people, e.g. free school meals, welfare milk, rate and rent rebates. Their provision increases public expenditure. It is calculated that each unemployed person **costs** the state **£6500** per year through lost tax revenue and benefit payments. These are just the **direct** costs. There are also indirect economic costs, such as extra administration involved, and social costs.

Total Economic activity. A major **opportunity cost** of unemployment is the goods and services which could have been produced by the unemployed. Consequently, real GDP in UK actually declined in 1980–1. Thus economic growth is handicapped in both the long and short term by the unemployment of resources.

Social costs. There are many dimensions to the cost to society as a whole of unemployment. There is a link between rising unemployment and **crime**. The Handsworth riots of 1985 and other **violence** were not unrelated to unemployment. Similarly, increased divorce, **suicide**, heart attacks and stress-related diseases tend to rise with unemployment. For instance, the suicide rate among the male unemployed is twice that of employed men. Although individuals suffer, society bears much of the cost through health, police and law services, which are paid for with taxpayers' money.

16.4 Measurement

Since 1983, the unemployment figure has been based on those **claiming unemployment benefit**. It used to be calculated from those **registered** as unemployed. Furthermore, the figures given are **seasonally adjusted**. This allows for large increases in the summer, when students leave school, and enables an underlying trend to be identified.

Each month the government discloses the '**official** figures' relating to unemployment. Most economists accept that they are not the '**true** figures'.

The actual measurement is an **understatement**, because of:

1 **People not registered** but available for work. It is reckoned that nearly all men but only 67 per cent of women register for employment. For instance, many **women** do not qualify for unemployment benefit but would take a job if offered one—thus they are 'available, able and willing to work' (usual definition) but unable to find paid employment.

2 People seeking **part-time** employment.

3 **Men aged over 60**—from December 1982 they did not have to claim, thus 250,000 were removed from the figures. However, undoubtedly some are able-bodied and want work if it is available.

4 **Some employees** are kept in employment by their firms (even though not fully employed) to avoid, **(a)** redundancy payments, **(b)** loss of skilled men who may be needed when the economy recovers—if these men were lost then new workers would need recruitment and training—and **(c)** litigation from workers against unfair dismissal.

5 **Government job creation** and **training schemes**, e.g. Youth Opportunities Scheme (1978–82), Youth Training Scheme (1983 onwards)—see Unit 16.7.

Thus, some economists and critics of the government claim that the true total is about 5 million unemployed. However, others argue that this is an **over-estimate** because it does not allow for:

1 **People changing jobs**—each month slightly over 320,000 join the register and slightly less than 280,000 leave it.

2 Many of the unemployed are **incapable** of work—because of ill health, age, lack of skill.

3 Others are **unwilling to work** (about one-tenth of total)—they may be 'work-shy' or they may find Supplementary Benefit sufficient.

4 Some are in the **wrong place** but unwilling to move, e.g. a crofter in the Orkneys.

Between 1979 and 1982 the population of working age **rose by over half a million** whilst the number of employed and registered unemployed **fell** by over half a million. This indicates that over one million people have disappeared from the labour market. The categories of people so discouraged from employment seem to be women, ethnic groups and young people. Since 1986, however, the total unemployed has fallen dramatically. This resulted from the rapid economic growth in the British economy.

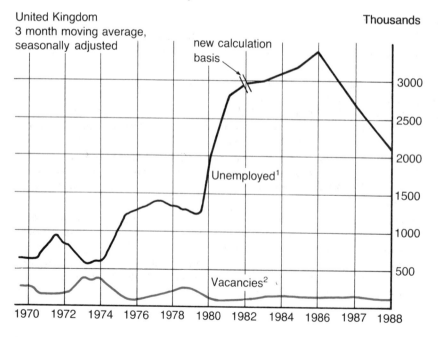

United Kingdom
3 month moving average,
seasonally adjusted

Thousands

new calculation basis

Unemployed[1]

Vacancies[2]

1970 1972 1974 1976 1978 1980 1982 1984 1986 1987 1988

[1] Excluding school leavers.
[2] Vacancies notified to unemployment offices.
(Source: *Employment Gazette*, Department of Employment)

Fig. 16.3 Unemployment and vacancies

VACANCIES

Undercounting also affects the statistics of vacancies. The Department of Employment estimates that it records about one-third of the job openings that actually exist. Thus, the vacancies figure in Fig. 16.3 should perhaps be over 400,000 in 1988. If there was **perfect mobility** of labour there would be no vacancies.

16.5 Types

The unemployment problem is, in reality, **several** different problems. A useful insight into these problems may be gained by classifying unemployment into several types.

STRUCTURAL

Long term changes in **demand** and/or **supply** cause this type. For instance, if a particular skill, e.g. roof thatching, or product, e.g. matches, suffers a drastic fall in demand then labour becomes unemployed. Competition from other countries, e.g. **cotton textiles** in Britain facing cheap Third World products, cars from Japan, may depress the British industry and lead to redundancies. Thus changes in the structure of economic activity, prompted by different consumption patterns, create unemployment. In other industries, demand has expanded but supply is fulfilled by **capital**, such as robots and greater mechanization and so labour is needed much less.

Some parts of the UK suffer greatly from this type of unemployment, e.g. North-East (coal, iron and steel, shipbuilding, in decline), West Yorkshire (textiles). As these industries are **localized** in certain areas, structural unemployment is linked with **regional** unemployment, which is essentially geographical.

Structural unemployment is always present in an economy. There appears to be more in British economy now than in the 1960s and early 1970s.

DEMAND DEFICIENCY

This modern term has largely superseded 'cyclical' and 'general' unemployment. It is suggested that total demand in the economy is insufficient to purchase all the goods and services which would be produced if there were full employment. It occurs when **total spending** in the economy **falls** and tends to affect most industries, occupations and regions. It is often associated with a decline in **world trade** and growth. With its open economy, Britain is particularly susceptible to this type. It partly explains the large increase in unemployment since 1979 in Britain. Government policies of controlling money supply and limiting public expenditure have contributed to the demand deficiency and could again be partly blamed for the rise in unemployment.

FRICTIONAL

This type is sometimes known as **'search'** unemployment. It refers to people **changing jobs** and the period of transition from one job to another. As it is temporary, there is little hardship. A lot of frictional unemployment indicates a healthy and dynamic economy. It shows **labour** being **mobile** and moving from declining to expanding sectors. Currently in Britain the low level of vacancies and the mismatch between job specifications and the unemployed's skills (or lack of them) suggest that there is little frictional unemployment.

NATURAL

Monetarist economists argue that there is a 'natural rate of unemployment' which is defined as 'that rate of unemployment at which **inflation is constant**'. This is a very controversial viewpoint which suggests that a government can only reduce unemployment below the natural rate for short periods and then at the cost of accelerating inflation. This view underlines Conservative government thinking on unemployment.

TECHNOLOGICAL

Improvements in science and technology have made it possible to replace workers with **machines** (labour with capital) in specific industries, e.g. robots building motor cars. The service sector is perhaps less susceptible to this type of unemployment, particularly where personal contact is important, e.g. estate agents, solicitors.

On available international comparisons, the UK appears relatively sluggish in its record of **investment** in new technology. This perhaps suggests that there is more of this type of unemployment still to come in the British economy. On the other hand, in the long run technology **creates more jobs** than it destroys, on American evidence. For instance, computers need hardware and software.

SEASONAL

Certain jobs are only available at certain times, e.g. Santa Claus at Christmas, strawberry pickers in July and August. This type of unemployment is of **little** economic importance. Many such jobs are taken on by part-timers or occupational pensioners; the holiday season is lengthening, e.g. Christmas pantomimes now run from up to four months in some places; and seasonal workers have diversified to other times of the year, e.g. ice-cream salesmen.

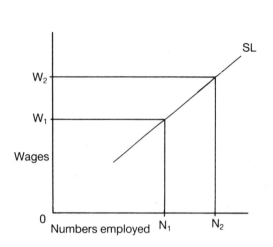

Fig. 16.4   Wage rates and the supply of labour

Fig. 16.5   Wages, trade unions and unemployment

VOLUNTARY

This is said to occur when people are unwilling to work to existing **wage rates**. In Fig. 16.4 if W_1 is the existing wage rate then N_1-N_2 people may be said to be voluntarily unemployed as they will only supply their labour at wage rate W_2. Some argue that a high level of **Supplementary Benefit** and other free services encourages voluntary unemployment.

In contrast, **involuntary** unemployment occurs when workers are willing to work at existing rates but cannot find employment. Figure 16.3 seems to indicate that the great majority of Britain's unemployment is involuntary, because there are so few vacancies.

16.6 Causes

Several causes of unemployment have been implied in the different types explained in Unit 16.5. However, five main underlying causes can be identified. They can be remembered by the word **'WILTS'**.

WAGE RISES

It can be argued that the quantity of labour demanded by firms falls as wage rates increase. (See Fig. 16.5.) Clearly, if trade unions can achieve **higher wages** then this may be at the expense of some unemployment. In Fig. 16.5 if trade unions restrict supply (SLT) then wages will rise and the quantity of labour demanded will fall to N_2. This creates unemployment (N_2-N_1). The present Conservative government claims that by demanding higher wages workers 'have priced themselves out of a job'.

However, it is clear that wage levels are a major determinant of the demand for labour. Labour is a **derived demand** based, particularly in the private sector, on the demand for the **final product**. If demand for the final product falls (i.e. structural changes, demand deficiency unemployment) then firms will seek less labour, irrespective of the wage rate. Furthermore, in capital-intensive industries, e.g. oil, labour is a small **proportion of total cost** and so high wage increases can be more easily absorbed.

A further argument against the view that excessive wage rises cause unemployment is that real wages in West Germany are about 50 per cent higher than in UK but unemployment is considerably lower.

INFLATION

Throughout the 1980s our rate of inflation was higher than that of our competitors. This made British **exports relatively** more expensive and **imports relatively** cheaper. Both of which would probably lead (assuming demand not inelastic) to a **fall** in the **market share** of British products and thus fewer jobs for British people. Higher rates of inflation in certain industries can cause structural decline, e.g. in textiles.

Furthermore in attempting to cure Britain's inflation problem, the government since 1979 has adopted policies which lead to greater unemployment. For instance, less grant given to local authorities has led to a fall in their manpower from nearly 3 million to $2\frac{1}{2}$ million.

LACK OF DEMAND/OUTPUT

If the growth of an economy slows down, then demand declines and workers are laid off. Unemployment follows changes in **economic activity** with a lag of 12–18 months. Thus GDP rose by $3\frac{1}{2}$ per cent per annum between 1966 and 1973 but then slowed down because of the oil crisis. This probably started the rise in unemployment in late 1974 and early 1975 (see Fig. 16.3).

Between 1974 and 1982 there was little world growth, made worse by the **1979 oil crisis**. This crisis could explain the take-off of unemployment in Britain in 1980 and its slowing down in early 1984, when the world economy recovered from depression.

This lack of demand in the world, and domestically, leads to redundancies. The redundant workers will **spend less** and thus the demand for other products falls, causing further job losses. Some economists (called Keynesians) maintain that it is the government's responsibility to increase spending (by fiscal and monetary policies) so that unemployment is soaked up. This lack of demand/output is probably the **main** cause of Britain's recent unemployment. An international trade war or policies of **protection** (see Unit 17) make matters worse.

TRADE UNIONS

The increased power of trade unions in the 1970s (Units 13.7, 13.8, 13.9) may have contributed to unemployment in two ways.

1 **Wage rises**, obtained by trade union militancy, may have fuelled inflation in some sectors.
2 By maintaining established **working practices**, rigid **demarcation** and **closed shops**, and by resisting certain new innovations (e.g. printworkers), trade unions have not helped manufacturers to raise their efficiency. This may have contributed to rising costs and prices, leading to lower sales and less employment.

SOCIAL SECURITY

Some economists believe that 'high' levels of unemployment and supplementary **benefits encourage unemployment**. If these benefits were lowered then unemployment would be reduced as workers would not refuse jobs where the wages made them only slightly better off. The present level of benefit seems to these economists to be an **incentive** to stay unemployed until a very lucrative job comes along, hopefully or indefinitely.

In 1982 the government took away earnings-related benefits and made unemployment benefits taxable in an effort to reduce the **real** value of benefits. However, there are still some people, often with large families and low incomes when in employment, who can get almost as much income from being unemployed. This **unemployment trap** affects about 5 per cent of the unemployed.

Married man with two children			
Income when unemployed		*Income in work*	
Supplementary benefit ⎫		Wage	100.00
Child benefit ⎬	67.85	Child benefit	14.00
Unemployment benefit ⎭		Rent rebate	7.32
		Rate rebate	2.41
Rent and rates (paid)	20.00	Tax	−9.73
		National insurance	−9.00
Net income	£87.85	Net income	£105.00

Fig. 16.6 Wages and social benefits (April 1986)

Figure 16.6 shows how a worker's income is replaced by various benefits and tax rebates if he becomes unemployed. In this particular example, his out-of-work income is 84 per cent of his in-work income. This is known as the **replacement rate**. The average rate is 66 per cent in the short run and 50 per cent in the long run. The benefit to the family of employment, in this case, is £17.15 per week (£105 minus £87.85). However, the costs of working such as travel, extra clothing, etc., make the net gain even less.

Professor Minford (Liverpool University) claims that such generous unemployment benefits set a floor for wages in the whole economy. Firms find it hard to recruit workers, wage rates do not fall and supply exceeds demand causing unemployment.

Other causes of the present high unemployment levels might be as follows.

1 The significant increase in the working population over the last few years.
2 The new technological revolution—combined with labour immobility and insufficient retraining facilities.
3 The tight monetary policy of the government.
4 The strong pound plus fierce competition from Japan, etc., having reduced exports and increased import penetration.
5 Certain industries having entered the recession heavily over-manned, therefore making a large labour shake-out inevitable.

16.7 Policies

There are no 'cures' for unemployment but some remedies may be less ineffective than others. The ideal solution is for the UK to make sure that it is producing the goods that people want much cheaper, better and faster than our rivals. The policies proposed depend upon the view taken of the **causes** of unemployment and the **types** that have resulted. The policies can be divided into two approaches: general remedies and specific measures.

GENERAL REMEDIES

Structural unemployment. In the **short run**, this can be minimized by increasing labour mobility, both occupationally and geographically, e.g. improved **training** facilities (see Unit 2).

Also in the short term the impact of decline can be lessened by government assistance—this may be by subsidy or overt **protection**, e.g. Multi-Fibre agreement since 1977 protecting British textiles from cheap imports.

The long-term remedy is a vigorous, expanding economy in which new industries develop. They replace the declining sectors. Thus Britain in the 1980s needs to develop **new technology** and **service** industries for the future.

Demand deficiency unemployment. The remedies here rather depend on the **cause** of the unemployment. Clearly if excessive wage increases are the problem then a reduction of **trade union** power may be one answer (see Unit 13.9). **Incomes policy** could be another (Unit 13.6). Both of these may involve deep government intervention through changes in the law.

If a lack of output is the cause then several approaches are possible—**increased government spending** through a larger PSBR (see Unit 15.6), expansion in **world trade** through international cooperation (Unit 17.6), **lower interest rates** (see Unit 9.8) and **increases in money supply** (see Unit 9.8) all help.

Frictional unemployment. This type is less serious than the previous two. However, **lower welfare benefits** and **more efficient** job centres could cut 'search' unemployment. A government survey in 1981 showed that four-fifths of the unemployed finding jobs did so **without** the help of job centres.

Natural unemployment. The answer here is simply reduce the level of **inflation** because it causes the unemployment (see Unit 9.8). The usual ways advocated by the monetarists are through restricting the growth of money supply and higher interest rates. They seek to lower 'inflationary **expectations**' (e.g. large annual pay rises) by their predictions and policies. This policy also involves the limitation of **trade unions**' power, because they make unrealistically high claims and in the 1970s they achieved substantial wage increases.

Technological unemployment. In some economies, technological advance has not created excess unemployment. Job preservation and opposition to innovation are short-term ways to stave off this problem **but** they damage the economy's productive capacity. Ideally, alternative employment needs to be available—this occurs if there is **retraining, mobile labour, government assistance** and **investment** (both public and private).

Seasonal unemployment. Very minor and largely acceptable.

Voluntary unemployment. This type of unemployment is publicized as consisting of 'work-shy' skivers living it up on social security! The reality was about 10 per cent of the 1978 total in a Job Centre survey. The proportion is probably much smaller now as unemployment has increased, the real value of **social benefits has fallen** and the replacement rate has fallen. Also, Health and Social Security unemployment review officers have proved very effective in finding **fraudulent claimants** and deterring doubtful claimants.

In the short term the measures above may have improved the incentive to work. However, they also harm those involuntarily unemployed. The advocates of tax and social security harmonization seek administrative changes so that benefits can be better directed to the needy without encouraging the fraudulent.

Again, in the long run, economic growth is the answer (see Unit 14.4).

Regional unemployment (see Unit 6.3).

A general solution for each type might be **work sharing**.

SPECIFIC MEASURES

The growth of unemployment is bad both economically and politically. Thus, successive governments have taken specific measures to **reduce the total** number unemployed. Critics call this 'massaging the figures' so that the problem does not seem as bad as it really is—see Unit 16.4.

These programmes began in 1976 and reached a peak of over 1 million in early 1981.

The **Youth Opportunities Programme** ended in 1982 and was superseded by the **Youth Training Scheme**. Both were aimed at finding 'employment' for school leavers. The YTS is now a two-year scheme.

Youth Training Scheme (YTS)

Advantages

1 Useful **training**, particularly in big organizations. In the YTS each trainee has a three-month off-the-job training spell in the year. However, much of the training has been criticized as 'traditional'.
2 It teaches the **'work habit'** and gives experience of working life and dignity to individuals.
3 It keeps 500,000 teenagers off the streets and **reduces the social costs** associated with juvenile delinquency.
4 Some of those trained find **employment**. The YOP Scheme claimed a 40 per cent success rate, and YTS 54 per cent.
5 Better-**quality** workforce is developed.

Criticisms

1 YTS trainees **replace adults**, raising unemployment in other age groups.
2 **Cheap labour.** The employer receives £1950 grant per person. He pays £1250 in wages (£25 per week), has administration costs of perhaps £150 and should use the remaining £550 for training.
3 **Public cost.** £1 billion per year.
4 **Artificial, not real jobs.** Few will get permanent employment and will become disillusioned. The YTS may postpone the problem.
5 **Lower wages** for young people because YTS is cheap employment. However, some might argue that this lowers costs and expectations and helps minimize inflation (thus being a benefit).

Government intervention

The government has intervened in the labour market in three ways.

1 Measures to increase **quantity of labour demanded**—the **Young Worker Scheme**. This scheme pays employers a grant of £15 per week if they employ young people aged 18–21, paying them less than £50 per week. However, these 'jobs' are not new—90 per cent would have existed anyway. In demand terms, they represent a movement along a demand for labour curve (W_2–W_1 in Fig. 16.5).
2 Measures to **reduce the supply of labour**, e.g. **early retirement** and work sharing. The **Job Release Scheme** pays males over 62 and females over 59 a tax-free allowance on early retirement provided they are replaced by someone currently registered as unemployed. From the point of view of national output and growth, reductions in supply (and compensating increases in leisure) are less desirable than increases in the demand for labour.
3 Measures to reduce the **registered unemployed**. YTS (see above). In 1988 the government merged several schemes in a new initiative called Employment Training, with guaranteed training for the unemployed for six months. Payment of Supplementary Benefit to people in further education on a **part**-time basis has encouraged more to stay on in education rather than enter the job market. The **Enterprise Allowance Scheme**—those unemployed between 18 and 65, who have £1000 to invest in their own business venture, receive £45 per week from the government for one year.

POSSIBLE SIDE EFFECTS

It is important for the government to identify the correct cause(s) of increased unemployment because if the wrong remedies are applied the problem may be **aggravated** rather than relieved. However, **economists disagree** over the relative importance of the different causes and types. For instance, the Conservative government (since 1979) has blamed world recession for the increase whereas the Labour opposition attributes at least half of the fault to the government's economic policies. These policies were designed to deal with a **different problem, inflation,** but in so doing they have made unemployment worse. This happened because demand was reduced, through restrictions on money supply and public spending, and this resulted in increased unemployment.

In contrast, it can be pointed out that a policy to directly lower unemployment through increased public expenditure may have undesirable side effects too. It could increase inflation and cause Balance of Payments difficulties by sucking in imports (rather than creating jobs in UK). Similarly, if increased wages have led to unemployment then higher public spending by increasing demand for labour will do nothing to slow down wage rises.

16.8 Summary

Unemployment in the UK has risen sharply over the last 12 years. There is significant regional variation with the highest figures in regions with traditional manufacturing industries. The increase is most marked amongst school leavers, older men, unskilled manual workers and ethnic minorities. The average duration of a period of unemployment has also increased. Private, economic and social costs of unemployment affect individuals and society.

Unemployment is measured by those who claim benefit, although this total is argued by some to underestimate, and by others to overestimate, the real total. It can be classified into seven types with five underlying causes. Policies adopted to deal with unemployment depend upon the government's view of its type and cause. There are two approaches: general remedies and specific measures. Policies to deal with unemployment can have undesirable side effects upon other indicators such as inflation or the balance of payments.

17 INTERNATIONAL TRADE

International trade is essentially an extension of **specialization** from **individual** and **regional** to an **international** level. Nations specialize in the production of goods and services and then exchange them for the output of other countries. A country's particular national interest is often best served through international co-operation but there may well be occasions when governments choose to intervene in the trading process in order to protect national interests— as they perceive them.

International trade differs from domestic trade in that **foreign currencies** are used. Thus a British importer of French wine will need to pay the French seller in francs. His bank will deal with the arrangements.

17.1 Advantages of international trade

The case for free international trade may be recalled by the mnemonic **'SMILE'**.

SPECIALIZATION

Since resources are unevenly distributed throughout the world it follows that different nations will have differing abilities to produce goods and services. In the same way that the **division of**

labour in domestic production has led to considerable increases in living standards, so too can specialization on an international scale.

In theory nations specialize in the production of goods for which they have a **natural advantage**. For instance, Canada uses its land and climate for wheat growing. Some countries acquire advantages. Britain's pop music industry is internationally respected and successful; thus it benefits our balance of payments (invisible account).

Assumptions. To demonstrate potential gains from trade we make some simplifying assumptions:

1 The world consists of two **countries** each producing two products. In Fig. 17.1 the countries and products illustrated are those referred to by David Ricardo, the 'father' of much of the economics of international trade.

2 Production takes place in **two** production units which are homogeneous (e.g. factories, farms, etc.).

3 All factors of production are **perfectly mobile**.

4 There are **no barriers** to trade, thus there is perfect competition.

5 Transport **costs** are **zero**.

	Annual output per production unit	
Country	*Wine (000 barrels)*	*Cloth (000 metres)*
England	5	10
Portugal	10	5
World output	15	15

Fig. 17.1 Output before specialization

Absolute advantage. In Fig. 17.1 it is immediately apparent that England is more efficient at producing cloth while Portugal is more efficient at producing wine. Figure 17.2 shows the result of each country specializing in producing only the product in which it has an **absolute advantage**. World output has increased by $33\frac{1}{3}$ per cent (15 to 20 = $\frac{1}{3}$).

	Annual output per production unit	
Country	*Wine (000 barrels)*	*Cloth (000 metres)*
England	0	20
Portugal	20	0
World output	20	20

Fig. 17.2 Output after specialization

Thus world output of both goods has been increased **without** using any more scarce resources. However, this benefit will not be realized unless international trade takes place, and goods are exchanged. Failure to trade will mean the only people to benefit will be, (a) alcoholic nudists in Portugal, because Portugal has more wine but no cloth, and (b) fashion-conscious teetotallers in England where cloth production has doubled but there is no longer any wine production!

	Annual output per production unit	
Country	*Wine (000 barrels)*	*Cloth (000 metres)*
England	7	13
Portugal	13	7
	20	20

Fig. 17.3 Output after specialization and exchange

Figure 17.3 shows that by exchanging 7000 metres of cloth for 7000 barrels of wine, both nations end up better off than in Fig. 17.1 (before specialization and trade). Thus, from specialization and trade, at this exchange rate, England has gained 2000 barrels of wine and 3000 metres of cloth.

Comparative advantage. It is somewhat unrealistic to expect the situation described above to occur very often in the real world. Far more likely is a situation in which one country is more efficient than its trading partner in producing a whole range of goods.

Country	Changes in output	
	Textiles (000 garments)	*Computers (000s)*
England	100 ($\frac{1}{20}$ C)	5 (20 T)
India	50 ($\frac{1}{25}$ C)	2 (25 T)

Fig. 17.4   Comparative advantage example (opportunity cost)

In Fig. 17.4 England is more efficient in the production of both textiles and computers than India. On the face of it there seems to be no basis for mutually beneficial trade. However, an examination of the **opportunity costs** of production proves otherwise.

The opportunity cost of producing 5 computers in England is the 100 garments which could have been produced instead. Thus the opportunity cost of 1 computer is 100/5 = 20 garments. Figure 17.4 shows all the opportunity costs.

It is clear that the opportunity cost of producing computers is the **reciprocal** (1/?) of the opportunity cost of producing textiles (i.e. $1/\frac{1}{20}$ = 20). This will always be true in a two-good model and is an important check on whether your own workings are correct.

From the example, we can see that the opportunity cost of producing computers is **lower** in England than in India, thus to the economist, England has a **comparative advantage** in production of computers. Put simply, England does not have to give up as much (only 20 textiles) to make computers as India does (25 textiles). Similarly India has a comparative advantage (lower opportunity cost) in the production of textiles. England may be said to have a **comparative disadvantage** (higher opportunity cost) in producing textiles (England gives up $\frac{1}{20}$ of computers whereas India only gives up $\frac{1}{25}$).

Economic theory predicts that international trade will be mutually beneficial if countries **specialize according to their comparative advantage(s)**.

This is a little harder to demonstrate than the gains from specialization according to absolute advantage. It will be necessary to assume there are a large number of 'units of production' in each country. Specialization thus involves England transferring production out of textiles into computers whilst in India the process is reversed. Suppose England switches three units of production from textiles into computers, whilst India transfers seven units from computers into textiles. Figure 17.5 shows the net results of such a change: 1000 more computers and 50,000 more textiles. Again through trade at a suitable exchange rate both nations can gain.

Country	Changes in output	
	Textiles (000 garments)	*Computers (000s)*
England	− 300	+ 15
India	+ 350	− 14
Net change	+ 50	+ 1

Fig. 17.5   Comparative advantage and specialization gains

It might be noted that in practice, specialization leads to the benefits of large-scale production (see Unit 5). Such **economies of scale** mean that when all of a nation's resources (Fig. 17.2) are concentrated on one product rather than half of them (as in Fig. 17.1) output is **more** than doubled. Thus in Fig. 17.2 world output of wine and cloth would exceed 20,000 giving each more benefit.

Conclusion. If countries specialize according to their comparative advantage then total production from a given set of resources will be increased. Furthermore, the greater the degree of specialization the greater the potential gains from trade. These potential gains explain why so many economists and politicians are supporters of free international trade and opponents of any attempts to restrict this trade.

MONOPOLIES

International trade enables foreign competitors to enter domestic markets which would otherwise be controlled by monopolists or oligopolists. All other things being equal (see Unit 17.5) this increase in **competition** will benefit the consumer through lower prices and improved efficiency (see Unit 7). For instance, British firms do not have to buy British steel and can import from elsewhere, notably West Germany.

INCREASED CHOICE

There is an obvious benefit from international trade in that a country may gain access to goods or services it cannot produce itself. However, a more significant aspect of increased choice lies in consumer demand for foreign alternatives to domestically produced goods. For example, even though the UK produces, and indeed exports, motor vehicles, British consumers obviously value being able to choose Japanese or European vehicles. However, the price of increased consumer choice may well be increased unemployment in domestic industries.

LINKS WITH OTHER COUNTRIES

To the extent that international trade increases both understanding and, more importantly, economic interdependence, trade may be said to be a force for international harmony. On the other hand it is, regrettably, true that conflicts of commercial and business interests have led to international crises, e.g. the European supplying of Soviet pipeline in 1982 angered the USA. Britain and France have clashed over milk, beef and apples in recent years.

ECONOMIES OF SCALE

The size of the market represents the most important restriction to the **division of labour**. By opening up new markets, international trade creates new opportunities to exploit economies of scale. Thus more trade between nations is beneficial to countries involved, although they do not always see the immediate gains. The scope for specialization and economies of scale may be limited by transport costs, national considerations and protectionist measures (Units 17.6 and 17.7).

17.2 Patterns of UK trade

COMMODITY STRUCTURE

Traditionally the UK has been thought to possess a **Comparative Advantage** in the production of manufactured goods and a **Comparative Disadvantage** in the production of food and raw materials. Economic theory would, therefore, predict that we would export manufactured goods and import food and raw materials (see Unit 17.1).

Exports—Description	1955	1975	1980	1985	1987
Engineering products	36.5	45.3	37.5	32.9	21.9
Machinery	21.1	30.4	25.3	22.0	8.2
Road motor vehicles	8.9	9.5	6.7	4.7	6.1
Other transport equipment	5.7	3.4	3.5	3.8	4.7
Scientific instruments	1.2	2.0	2.0	2.4	2.9
Semi-manufactures	29.7	24.0	22.7	25.8	19.2
Chemicals	7.8	10.9	11.2	11.6	13.2
Textiles	10.1	3.7	2.9	4.3	2.3
Metals	11.8	9.4	8.6	9.9	3.7
Other semi-manufactures and manufacture	12.6	12.6	13.4	9.3	35.3
Non-manufactures	21.2	18.1	26.4	32.0	23.6
Food, beverages, tobacco	6.5	7.3	6.9	6.6	6.9
Basic materials	5.6	2.7	3.1	2.6	2.5
Fuels	4.6	4.2	13.6	21.8	13.5
Other	4.5	3.9	2.8	1.0	0.7
Total	100.0	100.0	100.0	100.0	100.0

Imports—Description	1955	1975	1980	1985	1987
Food, beverages, tobacco	36.2	17.7	12.4	11.3	10.7
Fuel	10.4	17.7	13.8	13.0	6.5
Industrial materials and semi-manufactures	47.9	34.1	35.2	30.8	25.4
Finished manufactures	5.2	28.3	35.6	41.2	53.3
Unclassified	0.3	2.2	3.0	3.7	4.1
Total	100.0	100.0	100.0	100.0	100.0

Fig. 17.6 UK exports and imports by commodity 1955–87

In Fig. 17.6 we can see that the traditional picture of UK trade remains true as far as **exports** are concerned. There are two notable exceptions.

  1 The growth of **North Sea oil** into a major UK export.
  2 The decline of **textile** exports and **engineering products**.

In Fig. 17.6 we can also see in 1955 the notion of Britain as an **importer** of food, etc., and industrial materials was largely accurate. However, by 1980 the picture was very different.

Finished manufactured goods are now the most important single category of imports whilst finished and semi-finished manufactures now account for over 70 per cent of total imports. The food category has plummeted dramatically to 11 per cent.

Significance of changing trade patterns. It should be noted that given the **low income ineiasticity** of demand for **primary products** and fairly stable population, it is not surprising that the percentage of food imports has declined.

The increasing importance of **manufactured goods** may be seen as inevitable as world and UK incomes rise. Both France and West Germany are more dependent on imported manufactures than the UK. However, certain aspects of the UK's recent trading performance do give rise for concern. Britain is now a **net importer** of manufactured goods (imports exceed exports).

The last year in which there was a surplus on balance was 1982. Of all the individual industries listed, only metal goods seems to be going against the general pattern of increased imports.

It may be possible to explain this trend by suggesting that our **Comparative Advantage** now lies in **services and oil** rather than manufactures. However, it is clear that once the oil has run out the **import penetration** and consequent **de-industrialization** process (see Unit 5) will have so weakened our manufacturing sector that the UK will suffer serious balance-of-payments problems (see Unit 18).

AREA STRUCTURE OF TRADE

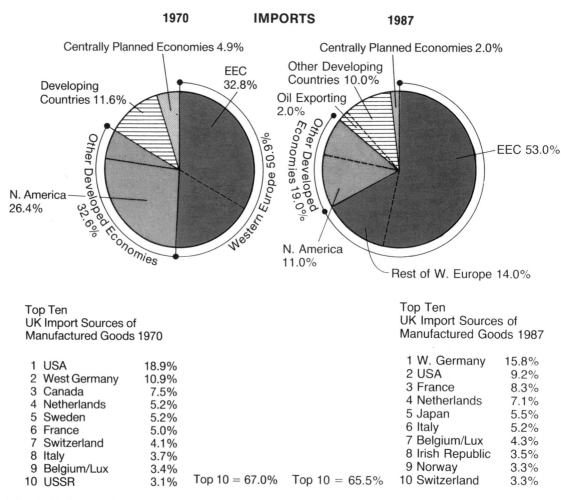

Fig. 17.7 UK Imports (manufactured goods) by area

Top Ten UK Import Sources of Manufactured Goods 1970			Top Ten UK Import Sources of Manufactured Goods 1987	
1 USA	18.9%		1 W. Germany	15.8%
2 West Germany	10.9%		2 USA	9.2%
3 Canada	7.5%		3 France	8.3%
4 Netherlands	5.2%		4 Netherlands	7.1%
5 Sweden	5.2%		5 Japan	5.5%
6 France	5.0%		6 Italy	5.2%
7 Switzerland	4.1%		7 Belgium/Lux	4.3%
8 Italy	3.7%		8 Irish Republic	3.5%
9 Belgium/Lux	3.4%		9 Norway	3.3%
10 USSR	3.1%	Top 10 = 67.0% Top 10 = 65.5%	10 Switzerland	3.3%

Imports

Britain's EEC partners have become far more important to the UK in terms of both imports and exports as can be seen from Figs. 17.7 and 17.8. Manufactured imports from the Common Market have risen much faster than UK sales to Europe since our entry in 1973. West Germany, France, Italy, Belgium and Luxemburg increased their percentage and moved up the top-ten table.

Perhaps the most significant change has been the rise of manufactured imports from Japan from nowhere to fifth. On overall trade a small UK–Japan trade surplus in 1970 was turned into a deficit in excess of £3 billion in 1988.

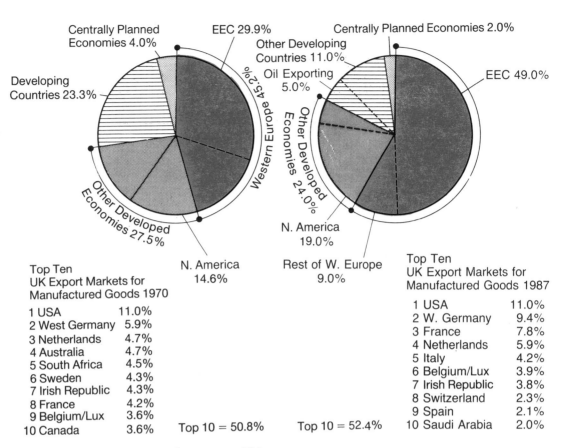

EXPORTS

1970   **1987**

Centrally Planned Economies 4.0%

EEC 29.9%

Centrally Planned Economies 2.0%

Other Developing Countries 11.0%

EEC 49.0%

Developing Countries 23.3%

Western Europe 45.2%

Oil Exporting 5.0%

Other Developed Economies 24.0%

Other Developed Economies 27.5%

N. America 14.6%

N. America 19.0%

Rest of W. Europe 9.0%

Top Ten
UK Export Markets for Manufactured Goods 1970

1	USA	11.0%
2	West Germany	5.9%
3	Netherlands	4.7%
4	Australia	4.7%
5	South Africa	4.5%
6	Sweden	4.3%
7	Irish Republic	4.3%
8	France	4.2%
9	Belgium/Lux	3.6%
10	Canada	3.6%

Top 10 = 50.8%

Top 10 = 52.4%

Top Ten
UK Export Markets for Manufactured Goods 1987

1	USA	11.0%
2	W. Germany	9.4%
3	France	7.8%
4	Netherlands	5.9%
5	Italy	4.2%
6	Belgium/Lux	3.9%
7	Irish Republic	3.8%
8	Switzerland	2.3%
9	Spain	2.1%
10	Saudi Arabia	2.0%

Fig. 17.8 UK Exports (manufactures goods) by area

Exports

Although the USA and West Germany remain our two largest single markets the shares of our EEC partners have risen to the detriment of the old Commonwealth. In 1987 Australia, Canada and South Africa had disappeared from the top ten. Sweden's decline as an export market also reflects Britain's entry into the EEC because Sweden remained outside in EFTA to which Britain used to belong.

It should be clear that, given the nature of **international specialization**, there is an obvious link between changing commodity structures and changing area structures.

17.3 The terms of trade

The terms of trade represents the purchasing power of a country's exports in terms of imports. It shows the **price** changes of **goods** in international trade rather than volume changes. It compares the average change in the price of exports with the average change in the price of imports. The calculation is through **index numbers**. The figure for the terms of trade is a percentage based on the movement of two index numbers (one for imports, one for exports).

Year	Terms of trade index
1972	121.2
1975	100.0
1977	100.1
1979	106.3
1980	100.0
1983	98.6
1985	99.2

Fig. 17.9 Terms of trade

The **Measurement** formula is

$$\frac{\text{index for export prices}}{\text{index for import prices}} \times 100.$$

Thus in 1972 the value of terms of trade was 121.2. The two indices are **weighted** averages (adjusted for the volume of trade in each product). The export weights reflect the importance of the different categories of goods which Britain exports. As with the retail price index (see Unit 9) a base year is chosen (in Fig. 17.9 it is 1975) and variations in the index show changes of price since that date. The two basic **causes of price increases** are:

1 **Production** costs rising. The seller in order to maintain his profits may have to raise his market price. In Britain's case higher domestic costs of production lead to more expensive exports.

2 **Exchange rate** rises—since fixed exchange rates were abandoned (see Unit 18.4), freely fluctuating rates have greatly affected prices in world trade. For instance, if the pound rises in value, then British exports go up in price, e.g. at £1 = $1.50, a £4000 British car sells in the USA for $6000; but if the exchange rate rises to £1 = $1.60 then a £4000 British car now sells at $6400—a price increase of $400. Changes in demand and supply patterns influence exchange rates. For instance, North Sea oil artificially raised the value of sterling, which in turn raised export prices and cheapened imports—this improved the terms of trade for Britain.

If the terms of trade index **is rising**, then it shows that export prices are increasing faster than import prices. For instance, between 1977 and 1979 the terms of trade increased from 100.1 to 106.3. The terms of trade are then said to be **favourable** to us. Each pound earned from a given quantity of exports can pay for a greater volume of imports. Conversely, a fall in the terms of trade between 1979 and 1982 means that more British goods will need to be exported to pay for a certain quantity of imports.

This supposedly favourable movement in the terms of trade indicates a **worsening** of Britain's **competitive position**, as it shows dearer exports and cheaper imports. Thus, where our exports compete with foreign goods in a third market then we will lose trade.

17.4 Government control

In view of the advantages of international trade it may seem surprising that governments seek to regulate international trade. Countries often place national interests before international interests and so protect their trade.

REASONS

The reasons for such intervention can be remembered by the mnemonic **'BRIDES'**.

Balance of payments. If a country is faced with a persistent balance of payments **deficit** (see Unit 18.3) it may attempt to reduce its import bill by imposing import controls (see Unit 17.6). The danger is that trading partners affected by the import controls may retaliate and thus British export demand will fall, making the protecting nation no better off.

Revenue raising. Just as domestically produced goods attract **indirect taxation** so too will imported goods such as wines, spirits and tobacco. Revenue raising is not a major objective of import controls. If it was then duties are likely to be levied on goods with an **inelastic demand**. The disadvantage of such tariffs is that domestic consumers pay higher prices and the cost of living is raised.

Infant industries. It is argued that new industries need protection. This argument is particularly applicable to Third World countries where newly formed manufacturing industries may not be able to grow fast enough to fully realize **economies of scale**. Also, they may face competition from the already industrialized nations. Import controls, therefore, allow the 'infant industries' a breathing space during which they can expand and exploit scale economies and thus compete on an equal basis. The main **problems** with this line of argument are:

1 Protection from competition may merely encourage inefficiency.

2 When does the infant come of **age**? It is hard to imagine domestic industry ever being totally willing to give up the benefits of protection.

For instance, Britain has protected its film industry from American competition since the 1930s, by restricting the percentage of American films which could be shown in British cinemas.

Dumping and unfair competition. Much of the protectionist argument centres on the claim that other countries indulge in 'unfair competition', particularly **dumping**. This tactic involves **selling exports** at **artificially low prices**. This may be done to benefit from economies of scale in production or to gain a toehold in the market, e.g. Japanese excavators sold for export at 45 per cent of the production cost.

Many protectionists would prefer free trade but are concerned by what they see as the unfair practices of some of our trading partners. Objectively it is very difficult to decide what constitutes 'fair trading' and what does not. In the 1984 lamb dispute with France, a central factor in the French farmers' case was that Britain, in subsidizing her farmers, was guilty of unfair competition. The Americans have said the same about British steel. One is tempted to conclude that 'fair trade', like beauty, 'is in the eye of the beholder'!

Employment. Since 1973, in Britain, a major argument for protection has been either to maintain home employment or to minimize the increase in unemployment. In demonstrating the advantages of international specialization (Fig. 17.2) we assumed both homogeneous units of production and perfect factor mobility. We thus envisaged that textile mills and textile workers would instantaneously become computer plants and operatives as the UK specialized according to its comparative advantage.

However, in the real world, such assumptions are unrealistic because of factor immobility. In the West Riding of Yorkshire, only a tiny fraction of workers made redundant by the decline of the textile industry have even the remotest chance of finding work in the new computer firms such as Systime. Thus the price paid for cheap foreign textiles has been **extensive localized unemployment**. In contrast to our hypothetical examples (Figs. 17.1–17.4) the gains from trade may well be outweighed by other **costs**, which may be indirect. Thus to limit the public cost of unemployment (and ease pressure on PSBR) and reduce social costs, protection may be encouraged.

The Multi-Fibre agreement limiting cheap textiles into Western Europe was adopted in 1975 to ease the unemployment problems threatening declining textile industries.

A number of politicians and economists, notably the New Cambridge group, have advocated **selective import controls** to maintain and increase employment levels. Protectionists further argue that if import controls successfully reduce unemployment then national income will increase, thus enabling Britain, as a nation, to afford to purchase **more imports**. Thus the effect of import controls may **not** be to reduce the volume of imports but to increase national income, in the **long run**.

Strategic reasons. In times of international conflict certain products may be considered 'essential', making home production desirable even when other countries are more efficient. Since the Second World War the UK has 'artificially' encouraged the development of home-produced foodstuffs by heavy subsidization of agriculture. Similarly for **security** reasons the export of high technology products to Comecon is restricted. Also the export of natural gas from Britain is prohibited. An obvious difficulty with this line of argument is that what is considered to be 'essential' may well be largely a matter of opinion.

POST-WAR TRENDS

1945–72 Trade became more free. The main reasons for this liberalization were:

1 Removal of quantitative restrictions.
2 Reduction of tariffs of manufactured goods through successive 'rounds' of cuts, e.g. 1973 Tokyo round.
3 Convertibility of currencies achieved in 1950s.
4 Rules, conventions and procedures established by international organizations such as GATT and IMF.
5 Enlargement of the EEC and agreement with other states bringing about more free trade in Europe.

Despite these changes, **agriculture** has remained **protected** and the trade in **services** is still not very liberated.

Since 1973 'New Protectionism'. Since the oil crisis and the decline in world growth (see Unit 14.4) newer, more **subtle**, restrictive devices have been introduced instead of tariffs and quotas. Trade is now **'managed'** by many governments in certain ways. For instance, selective temporary tariffs, voluntary export restraint agreements and export subsidies mean that half of world trade is not free, compared with 40 per cent in 1974.

17.5 Methods of protection

TYPES OF IMPORT CONTROL

One of the main forms of import control also serves as a mnemonic for the others **'QUOTAS'**.

QUOtas. There are restrictions on the amount of imports. They may refer to either the total quantity or total value of a commodity which may be imported during a given period of time. They may also refer to the quantity or value which may be imported from a particular country or group of countries.

GATT (see Unit 17.6) has tried to stop quotas. However, it has allowed **exceptions** for nations with balance of payments difficulties and industries suffering injury. It has also been undermined by the signing of **voluntary export restraint** agreements (VERA).

In recent years the Japanese car industry has voluntarily negotiated with Britain a limit of 12 per cent of all domestic UK car sales. Britain also limits T-shirts, radios, cutlery and watches from other less-developed nations.

Tariffs. These are taxes placed on imports. They may be **ad valorem** (i.e. a given percentage of import price) or **'specific'** (i.e. a set amount per unit such as per bottle of wine). Tariffs levied on goods with an **elastic** demand will be more effective in reducing the volume of imports, whilst those levied on goods with an **inelastic** demand will raise revenue rather than reduce imports.

Administration. A 'hidden' form of import control is the use of deliberately obstructive bureaucratic **procedures**. For years European exporters have complained about Japanese use of red tape (form filling) to slow imports into Japan. In 1983 France retaliated by insisting that all Japanese videos imported into France had to be processed through the customs office in Poitiers. This tiny office has a staff of only eight officials, thus the processing is a slow business!

This subtle form of protection has become more commonplace since 1973. Before 1979 Britain used exchange control to deter imports (Unit 18.3).

Specifications. The less visible the protection the less likely it is to invite retaliation. For this reason, recent years have also seen a proliferation of **technical and safety regulations** imposed by many countries. For example, Rowntree-Mackintosh are required to produce several different shades of Smarties in order to satisfy food-colour regulations in many countries. Similarly the American fuel emission regulations have acted as an indirect barrier to Rover and Jaguar exports. Italy will only allow garments to be imported through certain customs posts. In many cases, governments and other public bodies will purchase only from domestic producers.

DISADVANTAGES OF IMPORT CONTROLS—'WIRE'

Welfare loss. Unit 17.1 showed that unrestricted international trade leads to an increase in production and thus in total economic welfare. Thus the greater the barriers to trade the greater this loss of welfare.

However, individual nations are concerned with how the welfare gains are **distributed**. If a nation feels that it is not sharing in these gains but losing out then it may protect itself.

Inefficiency. Protection from international competition may encourage inefficiency in a number of ways. Within specific firms and industries it may prevent or delay the introduction of modern technology and encourage overmanning, etc. On a general economic level it may encourage an inefficient allocation of resources by delaying the movement of resources out of declining and into expanding industries.

REtaliation. The imposition of import controls may provoke trading partners to take similar action. For instance, British efforts to keep French UHT milk out were followed by French moves to stop British meat imports.

ENCOURAGING EXPORTS

Since 1973 exports from Britain have been artificially stimulated by:

1 **Subsidies.** Exporters can claim VAT refunds. This makes their goods artificially cheaper than otherwise and probably more competitive in world markets.

2 **Export credits.** British government bodies and banks give cheap loans to British exporters to tide them over, until the goods are paid for by the foreign buyers. Also, the Export Credits Guarantee Department gives cut-price insurance against nonpayment by foreigners. This enables exporters to be paid (by ECGD) even if the buyer defaults.

3 **General advice/information.** Official support is often given for export deals. This is done by Ministerial influence, British Embassy contacts and trade fairs.

17.6 International economic organizations

GATT

The General Agreement on Tariffs and Trade was founded by 23 nations in 1947. It is now composed of over 80 (noncommunist) countries and based in Geneva. It lays down rules for international trading. The broad **aims** are twofold.

1 **To reduce tariffs.** There have been a series of **'rounds'** in which tariffs were cut. By 1967 the average tax on manufactured goods had been reduced to 7 per cent. This was further lowered by the Tokyo round launched in 1973 and concluded in 1979.

2 **To eliminate quotas.** This was most successful up to 1973 but 'VERAs' (see Unit 17.5) have recently undermined this aim. GATT rules allow **exemptions** on a **temporary** basis if, (a) a nation has balance of payments difficulties, (b) home producers suffer injury.

The weaknesses of these allowed exceptions are that they are difficult to disprove and tend to become more than temporary, e.g. Multi-Fibre agreement since 1974!

The **importance** of GATT is **declining** for several reasons.

1 **Regional trade groupings** such as the EEC are growing. They have their own regulations which may contradict GATT, e.g. EEC has a common external tariff (see Unit 17.6). Fifty per cent of world trade takes place within Western Europe.
2 **Exemptions** to GATT are increasing. This undermines the principle of equal treatment which GATT has tried to develop. The 'New Protectionism' since 1973 has been counter to GATT's aims.
3 **Under-developed nations** are critical of GATT (see UNCTAD). In 1971 the Generalized System of Preference (GSP) was introduced to help poor nations. The rich countries gave tariff concessions to the less developed without expecting them to reciprocate (i.e. make tariff cuts in return). However, the benefits of this were lost with the 1973 oil crisis which made the under-developed world bigger debtors than before. They feel that GATT has not adequately catered for them. In particular, the new protective measures since 1973 during the world depression hit the poor nations more than the rich.
4 **Trade in services** has been largely ignored.
5 **Agricultural trade** is still restricted.

UNCTAD

In 1964, 77 poor nations set up a United Nations Conference on Trade and Development (UNCTAD). It holds conferences every **four years** to pressurize the developed countries to help the poor. UNCTAD wants:

1 Free **access** to world markets. GSP (above) went some small way towards improving their access. The Lomé conventions agreed with EEC in 1975 and 1979 gave 60 less-developed nations free access to EEC.
2 Commodity agreements to **stabilize prices** (mainly primary products). For instance, over 80 per cent of Zambia's export earnings are from copper. Thus if the price of copper falls dramatically, the economy of Zambia is badly affected.
3 One per cent of GNP of developed nations to be given in **aid**. They have achieved little success with this as Britain gave £176 million (0.53 per cent) in 1964 but £1400 million (0.34 per cent) in 1980.

TRADING BLOCS

There are two types of group (which GATT allows).

Free trade areas. There are **no internal restrictions** on trade **between** members. However, each member decides its **own external** policy in relation to trade with non-members. Examples are EFTA (European Free Trade Area) of which the UK is a former member and LAFTA (Latin American Free Trade Area).

Customs unions. A customs union is a **free trade area** where members agree to adopt a **Common External Tariff** to be levied on all imports from non-members. The European Economic Community is a customs union (see Unit 17.7).

SUPPLIERS' ORGANIZATIONS

Producers sometimes co-operate in a **cartel** to exploit a world market. The Organization of Petroleum Exporting Countries (OPEC) is a good example. In 1973 they forced a fourfold oil price increase, by making supply elastic at an agreed (high) price (P_1). Figure 17.10 shows the increase in total revenue (gained black area exceeds lost red area) which was achieved because D was very **inelastic**.

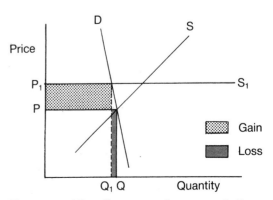

Fig. 17.10 The effect on total revenue of oil price changes

Since 1979 OPEC has **lost** its **power** because of:

1 **Disagreement** among the members. Unity is important. If price is agreed then one member selling cheaper creates competition, breaking the monopoly. Britain has done this with North Sea oil since 1981. Similarly, if supply levels are agreed and one member exceeds its 'quota' this makes supply more elastic and destroys the monopoly position again. Iran and Iraq have done this to gain extra revenue for war financing (against each other!).

2 The **fall in world demand** for oil. This demand is derived from the level of world production. If output does not continue growing substantially, then oil demand falls. This declining market means less for each oil-producing nation, unless it acts unilaterally to increase its market share. Such action breaks the unity of the cartel, and has weakened OPEC. In 1986 the oil price fell from $30 to $8 per barrel.

The world economy can be divided into four major trading groups:

1 **OECD** (Organization for Economic Co-operation and Development). Containing 24 leading industrial nations including Britain, they account for 62 per cent of world trade.

2 **OPEC.** Fifteen per cent of world trade.

3 **Developing nations.** Thirteen per cent of world trade.

4 **COMECON.** Communist economies which are centrally planned. This group includes Eastern Europe, Cuba and other communist states. They are responsible for 10 per cent of world trade.

17.7 The European Economic Community

In 1957 the **Treaty of Rome** created the EEC. It was composed of Belgium, France, West Germany, Holland, Italy, Luxemburg who had previously combined in the European Coal and Steel Community (ECSC) since 1951.

The UK joined the EEC on 1 January 1973 as did Eire and Denmark. The Labour government completed its renegotiation of British membership conditions in March 1975 and the issue was subsequently ratified by a referendum in July 1975. However, our participation remains a controversial issue and at the very least it remains a possibility that a future government may bring us out of the market. As well as the nine nations named above Greece (1981), Spain and Portugal (both 1986) are also members now.

MAIN FEATURES OF COMMON MARKET

Free trade within the market. There are no customs duties between members. However, there may be more subtle protective measures (see Unit 17.5). This market of just under 330 million people should enable large-scale investment and economies of scale resulting in lower prices for consumers.

Common External Tariff (CET). Most imports from outside the market face this tariff. The exceptions include 14,000 tons of New Zealand meat imported under licence into Britain, and agreements with associate members.

Common Agricultural Policy (CAP). This seeks to increase agricultural earnings and to eliminate fluctuations in prices and supplies. Farm products are guaranteed an **intervention price**. If the market price falls below this the Community guarantees to buy excess supplies at the intervention price. Imported foodstuffs are taxed so that they are above the intervention price.

CAP subsidizes farmers and by doing so it has created excess production, e.g. butter mountain, wine lake. CAP accounts for two-thirds of the EEC budget. Its effect on Britain has been:

1 To raise food prices (faster than otherwise but only slightly).

2 Many small efficient British farmers have become extremely well off. They have ploughed up hedgerows to get more land for agricultural production. Their output and incomes have increased.

3 The Budget expenditure on CAP means less for other EEC programmes from which Britain might benefit, e.g. regional and social funds.

4 Disproportionately large budget contributions, e.g. £1.5 billion in 1989–90 compared with much lower amounts pre-1987.

Generally, it would seem that there has been a redistribution of income from British taxpayers and consumers to the farming sector. However, consumers have probably benefited indirectly from the increase in economic growth (0.15 per cent a year) as a result of joining the EEC.

Free movement between nations, of capital and labour. For instance, entry visas and work permits are no longer required but passports remain. In 1979 Britain ended exchange control which has made capital movement much easier.

In 1992 a **Single European Market** is planned with the removal of all limits on free trade amongst members. The European Commission has devised 279 directives in order to reduce **financial** and **technical barriers** to trade. Furthermore, all European-made goods after 1992 should conform to common standards and regulations on health and safety. In some cases, British products will need to be modified to meet European-wide standards. For instance, the familiar three pin electrical plug could be replaced by the two pin European equivalent. It is hoped that national qualifications will be recognized in other countries and that this will encourage greater labour mobility. The development of the Channel Tunnel in 1993 should also hasten this process.

EEC FINANCE

The EEC is financed by 'its own resources', i.e. 90 per cent of all import duties and agricultural levies from non-EEC sources (the remaining 10 per cent covers administrative costs) are put into the EEC. It also receives a proportion of VAT receipts.

The UK contributes about 20 per cent of EEC revenue **but** our GNP is only 16 per cent of EEC total. Thus in recent years, British governments have attempted to negotiate temporary reductions in our contributions. For instance, in 1981 Britain received over £800 million refund. However, a permanent solution requires the reform of CAP.

BRITISH TRADE WITH EEC

The volume and value of UK exports to, and imports from, the EEC have increased since British entry. From 1973 to 1980 deficits were made on total EEC trade. In 1981 and 1982 surpluses were made but since then deficits have returned.

It is difficult to believe that the UK economy has benefited from EEC membership, because its performance has been so poor over the last decade. The evidence is, however, that the UK economy would have done and would do **even worse outside** than inside the EEC.

17.8 Summary

The economic case for free trade is based on the theory of comparative advantage. This brings lower costs, increased output and greater choice.

Over the last 30 years the UK has become a net importer of manufactured goods although manufactures still form the biggest single group of exports. The EEC is now our biggest market for exports and the biggest source of our imports. The terms of trade represent the purchasing power of a country's exports in terms of imports. The effect of changes in the terms of trade on the balance of payments depends on the elasticity of demand for imports and exports.

Governments seek to regulate trade for national reasons such as the protection of employment or to raise revenue. In the post-war period trade restrictions eased but the world recession since the early 1970s has led to more protectionism. Imports can be regulated by quota, tariff or an administrative/technical regulation.

GATT and UNCTAD were set up to promote freer and fairer trade. Other groups exist to exploit a world market, e.g. OPEC. The EEC was set up in 1957 and UK joined in 1973. The EEC is a customs union financed by import duties and member contributions.

18 BALANCE OF PAYMENTS

18.1 Balance-of-payments accounts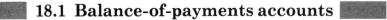

In the same way that companies calculate their profits and losses, so nations calculate their trading positions. However, for **nations** the calculations are larger and more complicated. For instance, imports into Britain need to be paid for in **foreign currencies** whose value now fluctuates daily. Thus, exchange rates have a big influence over the balance of payments.

The Balance of Payments is a national account, showing the **financial transactions** of **one nation** with the **rest of the world** over a **period of time**. Although monthly figures are calculated, quarterly and yearly totals are more useful indicators of trends, because the official figures (particularly invisibles) are often revised. This is caused by the use of estimates and the different dates for collecting information. The statistics are collected by the government. The format of the accounts has been changed over time, but the basic intention remains the same.

If total payments exceed total income, there is a net outflow of funds and vice versa. All nations seek a **net inflow**, but obviously they cannot all achieve it, because everybody's surplus is equivalent to someone else's deficit. Thus, 1973–7 surpluses in the oil-rich countries were matched by deficits in the industrialized world (except Japan and West Germany) and the developing world.

The Balance of Payments is divided into two sections:

1 Current Account.
2 UK External Assets and Liabilities.

The **current balance** should equal the **balance on transactions** in assets and liabilities, after the **balancing item** has been inserted.

1987

Current Account	£ billion	UK External Assets and Liabilities	£ billion
Visibles	−10.5	Transactions in assets	−76.2
Invisibles	+7.5	Transactions in liabilities	+73.9
		Net transactions	−2.3
		Balancing item	+5.3
Current balance	−3.0		+3.0

Fig. 18.1 Balance of Payments Accounts

CURRENT ACCOUNT

This part of the balance of payments is regarded as the most **important**, as it shows a nation's trading strength. If payments are greater than receipts, there is a **deficit** which is undesirable. This account is subdivided, as shown in Fig. 18.1 into:

1 **Visible** Trade—trade in **goods**.
2 **Invisible** Trade—trade in **services**.

Visible trade

The money earned from British **exports of goods** (e.g. tractor sold to Zambia) is **credited** (added) to this account, whilst payments for **imported goods** (e.g. Japanese car sold in Britain) are **debited**. The difference between the totals is known as the **balance of trade**.

In most years, Britain has suffered a visible trade deficit which reached a peak in 1988 of £20.5 billion.

This massive deficit has accrued since 1986 because of:

1 **Increased import penetration**. For instance, imports now account for one quarter of total UK demand in volume terms.

2 **The loss of market** share by British exporters. For example, the UK share of world trade in manufactures was 6.5 per cent in 1988, compared with 9 per cent in 1978.

3 **The decline in oil revenue.** Oil helped to produce a visible trade surplus in the early 1980s. However, with oil production in the North Sea past its peak and falling world oil prices, oil's net contribution to the Balance of Payments account in 1988 was only £2.5 billion.

4 **Deindustrialization of the UK economy.** The rundown of the British manufacturing base in the early 1980s has resulted in a massive import bill for manufacturers. The manufactures section on its own in 1988 equalled the current account deficit at £14.5 billion.

A sophisticated analysis of the accounts subdivides the visibles between manufactures, oil and others. As can be gathered from the above it is only the 'others' part that has a surplus.

Invisible trade

The income earned from the sale of British services abroad is known as an invisible export, e.g. an insurance premium paid by a Greek shipowner to a Lloyds broker. When British residents spend money on foreign services, e.g. a week's accommodation in Benidorm, they are creating invisible imports, because payment is going out of Britain. The main invisibles are as follows.

1 **Government expenditure** on embassies, contributions to EEC and other international bodies, military bases/forces abroad, and overseas aid. These all create a substantial **deficit**.
2 **Interest, profits and dividends.** These earnings from loans, companies and shares, respectively, earn substantial **surpluses** for the British economy (in 1985, £3 billion).
3 **Other financial services.** The earnings of solicitors, brokers, merchants and pension funds investments also contribute benefits to the invisible account.
4 **Transport.** Britain's former dominance as a passenger carrier by sea, particularly, and air has disappeared and payments are now roughly **equalled** with earnings in most years.
5 **Tourism.** This covers the expenditure of travellers abroad. From Britain's point of view, the debits and credits roughly **balance**.
6 **Private transfers.** Individuals transfer money to other countries. Most industrialized nations contain migrants who remit funds to relatives in their family of origin. Such monies are a small but slowly increasing deficit in the invisible account.

A large **invisible surplus** has always been a feature of the British current account in modern times (see Fig. 18.2). The figure is subject to **great fluctuation** and frequent revision. However, the general trend has been upward, with a peak reached in 1987 of £7.5 billion. The decline to £1.76 billion in 1982 reflected the low levels of world economic activity which created significantly fewer interest, profits and dividends earnings and the temporary increase in value of pound sterling. A decrease in pound's value is good for the invisibles, e.g. at £1 = $2.4, a $2400 insurance premium earns £1000, but if the pound depreciates to $2.0, the same $2400 is worth £1200 (£ × 2400/2.0). Thus, assuming the demand for British services is inelastic in America a **depreciating pound** raises extra income.

Britain's successful trade in services (invisible) has been explained by:

1 The expertise accumulated over the years.
2 London housing the world's largest insurance market and key markets in agricultural products and metals which often do not touch British soil.
3 The British reputation for probity (honesty) and variety.
4 Huge amounts of overseas assets held by UK firms and institutions.

This invisible trade success may be more limited in the future as there is likely to be extra competition particularly in banking and insurance.

Current Account balance

The balance of trade (visible) and net invisibles are added, as in Fig. 18.1, to give the current account balance. The net figure may be plus or minus. A **deficit** (−) on the current account is a warning that the **nation is spending more than it is earning**, in the short run, e.g. 1973, 1979. This usually leads to changes in government policy if the deficit is persistent. It is like a person living beyond their income – in the short run great but in the long term disastrous!

UK EXTERNAL ASSETS AND LIABILITIES

This section of the accounts records **capital** movements by governments, firms and individuals. Transactions in **assets** refers to purchases by British residents of various capital assets e.g. buildings, shares, and lending abroad by UK banks. They involve an **outflow** of resources, and thus are denoted in the accounts by a minus (−). This means that UK holding of foreign assets has increased e.g. in 1987 by £76.2 billion.

Transactions in **liabilities** shows the inward 'investment' by foreigners in similar things. It is represented by a plus (+) to indicate an **inflow** of resources.

Changes in the **official reserves** are also included in this section of the accounts. A minus (−) figure (as in 1987) shows that official reserves have been used to either **pay off** central bank **debts** or to **make loans**. If new net borrowing was undertaken by the central bank it would be represented in the liabilities section of the accounts.

Assets	£ billion	Liabilities	£ billion
Direct	−15 372	Direct	+5 954
Portfolio	+6 973	Portfolio	+10 094
Lending by UK⎫ Banks overseas⎭	−50 296	Borrowing by UK⎫ Banks overseas⎭	+52 806
Official reserves	−12 012		
Others	−5 479	Others	+5 015
	−76 186		+73 869

Net transactions = −2317

Fig. 18.2 UK external assets and liabilities

Investment

The two types of 'investment' identified in the account are **direct** and **portfolio**. Direct refers to the purchase of physical capital e.g. **factories**, whilst 'portfolio investment' is the acquisition of paper assets e.g. buying **shares** on a foreign stock market such as Wall Street. It is interesting to note that in the 1987 account more UK portfolio assets overseas were sold than bought and this produced a surplus (+).

In the 1980s the general trend has been for inward investment to outweigh outward investment. This has been caused by:

1 **British entry into the EEC** which has encouraged American and Japanese investment. Their firms could then sell in Europe without having to pay tariffs, which would be imposed if they had exported from home.

2 **North Sea oil.** By making the pound a strong, 'petrocurrency', this encouraged investors to regard investment in Britain as relatively safe, compared with industrialized nonoil producers, such as France.

3 **High interest rates** attract hot money, whilst generous regional aid induces real capital investment.

In the **short run**, net inward investment **benefits** the balance of payments accounts because official financing is not needed—reserves can be accumulated and borrowing repaid. However, in the long run, it may be detrimental. The profits, interest and dividends from the investment are remitted abroad and become invisible imports, thus weakening the current account.

Balancing item

This is an accounting device to cover errors and omissions. A balancing figure is **added to** or **subtracted from** the combined balances of the current and transactions accounts. The balance of payments accounts **always balance** because the current and transactions account totals should be equal. As the latter figure is more accurate than the **varied data** in the other two accounts, the balancing item is calculated from it and is used to make the two totals the same. It is a **net** figure. A positive balancing item usually shows unrecorded net exports.

18.2 Balance-of-payments problems

A country has a balance-of-payments problem when a section of its accounts are in regular deficit or surplus. Deficit problems are more serious than surplus ones, as surpluses usually result from successful international trading, whilst deficits indicate failure. Persistent imbalances indicate that the balance of payments is in **fundamental disequilibrium**. This usually requires the **government** to undertake rectifying policies.

The **seriousness** of a deficit depends upon its size and the section of the accounts in which it occurs. A **Balance-of-Trade** deficit has plagued Britain for decades but whilst **net invisibles** covered it, the problem was not too great. However, if the **Current Account** balance became negative, because net invisibles did not supersede the deficit trade in goods, then the alarm bells started ringing. This was because such a deficit, if large, showed trading weakness and tended to depress the exchange rate.

1970–1980. Up to 1980, **Britain** faced intermittent balance-of-payments crises, caused by current-account **deficits**. In 1967, sterling was **devalued** by 14.3 per cent and this contributed to a steady improvement in the current account. However, after 1971, because of the accelerating inflation and the expansion of credit in the economy, imports zoomed. In 1972, the government **floated** sterling in order to get a lower exchange rate (which would hopefully reduce imports by making them more expensive and encourage exports by making them relatively cheaper). This did not work for many reasons—1973 rising oil prices, faster growth from our competitors, lower inflation of our trading rivals. However, the world depression created by the **oil crisis 1973–4** dampened the demand for imports, as did reduced public expenditure (undertaken under IMF instructions), whilst a further sterling depreciation stimulated exports, resulting in a moderate surplus in 1978.

1980–1985. Britain gained a balance-of-payments **surplus** on current account. This was caused almost solely by North Sea oil. On-stream oil had reduced oil imports and increased oil exports. Although goods and services were imported for the oil exploration and construction work and invisible debits occurred through remitted foreign company profits, the overall impact was beneficial. In addition expenditure on imports was decreased because of the recession and this helped. The disadvantages associated with a surplus were as follows.

1 It **masked underlying weaknesses** in the economy. In Britain's case, the oil revenues may only be significant until 1990 and the non-oil visible trade is declining markedly (see Unit 18.1, page 139).

2 It led to an **unwanted rise in money supply**. This may have prevented internal monetary policy from working and stimulated inflation.

3 It was used to **finance current consumption** rather than future investment. The government used taxes from oil sales to increase existing living standards at the expense of investment in new industries and technology, e.g. 1983 British Rail electrification was put off because the government feared that it would raise public expenditure, but Social Security was paid to 3 million unemployed.

4 **Excessive inward investment** took up opportunities which domestic firms should have been developing; and led to a long-term drain on the invisibles through interest, profits and dividends sent abroad in the future.

5 It caused an **exchange-rate appreciation**, but this decreases the competitiveness of visible exports in world markets and increases the attraction of imports.

1986 onwards. Britain had a large and growing current account deficit as explained in 18.1.

However, governments find it much easier to live with surpluses than deficits. They give the appearance of successful economic policies, prestige and political strength. In 1986 oil prices tumbled dramatically from $30 per barrel to $10. This reduced government income and weakened Britain's Balance of Payments.

18.3 Balance-of-payments policies

Governments are expected to remedy persistent balance-of-payments **deficits**, particularly those on current account. The policies adopted depend on the causes. From British experience, the most **common causes** appear to be:

1 An overvalued exchange rate making our goods uncompetitive.

2 Domestic spending exceeding domestic output, leading to inflation, which made imports relatively cheap and exports relatively dear.

3 An excessive supply of money in the economy causing inflation.

4 Structural weaknesses in the economy.

POLICIES 'DEDECTS'

DEvaluation or depreciation

These mean a reduction in the foreign exchange value of a nation's currency. Thus, in 1949 the pound value was lowered from $4.03 to $2.80 when there was a system of **fixed exchange rates**—this was a **devaluation**.

However, since 1972 (see Unit 18.4) exchange rates have floated. If an exchange rate **floats** downwards, the fall in value is known as a **depreciation**, e.g. during winter 1983–4, £1 fell from $1.80 to $1.20.

The **role** of the **government** varies between devaluation and depreciation. In the case of devaluation, the government applied to the IMF (Unit 18.6) for permission to lower its fixed exchange rate as a **last resort**, after trying other policies to reduce the deficit. When exchange rates are floating, demand and supply factors cause the rate to fall. However, a government can affect them by its policies, thus having an **indirect influence**. For instance, a government may act to raise interest rates, which should attract demand for pound and thereby slow-down/stop a depreciating pound.

The effects of devaluation and depreciation are the same—**cheaper exports** and **dearer imports**. The following example illustrates how this results: at the exchange rate of £1 = $2, a British export priced at £5 sells for $10 in USA, and an American import costing $20 sells for £10 in Britain. If the exchange rate falls to £1 = $1, then the British export now sells for $5 (i.e. $5 cheaper) and the American import is priced at £20 in Britain (i.e. £10 dearer). Thus devaluation/depreciation restores competitiveness to a nation's goods. However, the Balance of Payments only benefits if proportionately more exports are sold and many fewer imports are bought. The likelihood of this occurring depends on the **elasticity of demand** of the goods being traded. Devaluation/depreciation is only effective if the demand for **exports** is relatively **elastic** and the demand for **imports** is relatively **elastic**. This is because in these cases, the total revenue from exports will increase and the total spending on imports will fall, giving a net gain. There is little evidence that the elasticity of demand for imports and exports are sufficiently elastic to have a big impact, in Britain's case.

The effectiveness of depreciation/devaluation is further **limited** by other factors.

1 The ability of domestic suppliers to meet the extra demand created by cheaper exports and home consumers switching away from imports to British goods. If home **supply** is **inelastic**, then the advantage of depreciation may be lost.

2 **Inflation.** If the costs of production in Britain are rising faster than elsewhere, the price advantage from devaluation may be lost.

3 Price is just one factor. The **conditions** of **demand** (Unit 4.2) might change, or be more important in some markets, e.g. in engineering the design, safety and efficiency of a product may be more important than its price.

4 Other nations may **retaliate** by lowering their exchange rates, thus nullifying the impact. In 1949 most countries did retaliate, but in 1967 only a few did.

DEflation

This is a general policy designed to reduce the **level of spending** in the economy. In doing so, it will curb the **demand for imports** in particular, as Britain tends to suck in imports during boom periods. It can be operated through fiscal and monetary policies. The government can cut its own **public spending, raise taxation** and increase National Insurance contributions so that less money is available for spending on imports. Alternatively, a monetary policy of **credit control** can be introduced to curb spending. It is further argued that the fall in purchasing power will affect domestic producers who may switch resources towards seeking export markets, thereby further benefiting the balance of payments. An additional effect of the government's deflationary policies 1979–82 was to **weaken trade-union bargaining power** by introducing the fear of unemployment. This may have produced lower wage increases and restrained costs.

Deflation has been tried many times in the British economy. It tends to be a short-term policy. As balance-of-payments crises have recurred, it would indicate that deflation is not a long-term solution, and not effective. The **costs** of deflation make it unpopular because spending cuts lead to **unemployment** and **falls in output**. In turn these changes make it self defeating because taxation revenue falls and public spending, through Supplementary and other benefits, increases, which is what the government did not want. Also, it clearly conflicts with policies designed to stimulate growth by depressing business optimism and lowering investment, both public and private.

Control of money supply

The monetarist economists believe that uncompetitiveness in international trade can result from domestic inflation caused by an excessive growth in the supply of money in the economy (see Unit 9.7). If Britain's inflation rate outstrips her trading rivals, then we suck in imports and lose export markets, thereby probably creating a deficit.

Thus, the supply of money could be controlled by **raising interest rates**, to deter borrowing, and **restricting credit**, using the usual monetary weapons (see Unit 10.8). Both policies would reduce spending on imports and strengthen employers' resistance to wage demands thereby lowering domestic costs of production and making British goods more competitive. In addition, higher interest rates attract **capital inflows** and temporarily strengthen the capital account. However, they may raise the exchange rate and make our goods less competitive too! This policy has similar consequences to deflation—namely lower output and increased unemployment.

Trade controls/incentives

This policy is less general and more **specific**. It involves direct measures aimed in certain areas.

Tariffs (see Unit 17). These can be used to raise the price of imports and, if demand is elastic, choke off the demand for imports. As a member of GATT, Britain can make little use of this option. However, in 1977, we imposed a duty on certain Japanese steels.

Quotas (see Unit 17). These can be introduced to limit the quantity of imports, thereby strengthening the balance of trade. The British Government has tried voluntary quota restraint with Japanese cars, with some success. However, GATT does allow the imposition of quotas on a temporary basis for a nation with balance-of-payments difficulties. Britain currently has restrictions on cheap clothing from South East Asia.

Exchange control. Capital account deficits created by **investment outflows** can be countered by exchange controls. In 1947, the government introduced controls over overseas transactions, restricting the amount of currency available for investment abroad. This meant that British citizens buying shares and British companies building factories overseas needed government permission to obtain the necessary foreign currency. In 1979, the government relaxed this policy and finally abandoned it so that British resources could be more freely invested overseas. On average £2 billion has flowed out each year since.

The Labour Party is pledged to re-establishing exchange controls. They also form part of the **alternative economic strategy** based on trade controls and expansionary public spending which has been proposed (by the 'new' Cambridge School of Economists) to generate domestic economic growth.

Administrative controls. There are many non-tariff barriers to trade which are not easily dealt with under GATT rules. Frequent changes in a country's **laws** and administrative **procedures** on **health standards, invoicing** procedures, **safety specifications** and product designs can be used by unscrupulous governments to keep out competitive imports. **France** and **Japan** are renowned for such tactics. Some people argue that Britain should adopt similar 'unfair' trading practices, in order to improve its visible trade.

Subsidies. Governments may subsidize exports to make them more competitive. This is not allowed by GATT rules, but the subsidies may be disguised as payments for services. Thus **West Germany** subsidizes its **steel** industry in particular and industry fuel bills in general. **British exports are exempted from VAT** which is a subsidy as it reduces the costs of production. Export credits (lending funds to buyers of British goods) are subsidized by most governments. In a normal year this subsidy costs British Government £500 million. Apart from direct help, the government, through the Department of Trade promotes **trade fairs,**

exhibitions and publicity to aid British exporters. There is a good case for raising this currently low-budget activity, so that more indirect financial and advisory help can be given.

Structural changes

Certain parts of the British economy are weak. It is argued that it is in these **sectors** where changes ought to be made. The declining manufacturing industries, such as textiles, shipbuilding, coal and steel, should not be supported with funds which could otherwise be spent on **investment in new industries**, e.g. information technology. The government could give a lead in this direction by its spending policies and attitude.

General **underlying problems** such as low investment, low productivity and high wage costs per unit could also be tackled. The 1979 Conservative government was elected to make radical changes in Britain's economy in order to overcome these problems. So far, it has used monetary policy and trade-union legal reforms to invigorate the **supply side** of the economy. Labour productivity has clearly improved but this has been more through unemployment and less from higher output. However, direct government action in several areas of the economy is unlikely because the Conservative Party believes in less, not more, government participation in economic decision-making.

18.4 Exchange rates

An **Exchange Rate** is 'the **external value** of a currency **expressed in another currency**' (or as a weighted average of the currencies of its **main** trading partners), e.g. £1 = $1.56 (or £1 = 86.2 trade weighted index).

In international trade, foreign currencies are needed for the payment of imports. Thus, the exchange of currencies is vital for **trade**. For instance, a British garage owner importing cars from Japan will require his bank to obtain yen and pay the seller with them; thus, the rate of exchange between the pound and the yen must be established. This rate may be determined by the conditions of demand and supply on a daily basis. This is known as a **freely fluctuating** or floating exchange rate.

Floating exchange rates

The **theory assumes** that a currency is demanded for just **trade** (rather than speculation), i.e. to purchase imports. Also that demand and supply elasticities are perfectly **elastic**.

In Fig. 18.3 the D and S curves for a currency show the amounts that traders wish to buy and sell at various prices (exchange rates). The **lower the exchange rate**, the **greater the demand** for pounds and the lower the supply of pounds. The demand for pounds is a **derived demand** reflecting the demand for British exports. Similarly, the supply of pounds is produced by the demand for British imports. Thus, if the exchange rate falls from 1.50 to 1.25, the supply of pounds will fall (Q_s) because imports become more expensive and so their quality demanded falls (fewer pounds supplied). Conversely, the quantity of pounds demanded will rise (Q_d) because exports become relatively cheaper.

A change in the conditions of demand, such as a new government or North Sea oil raising confidence in the nation's trading performance, will raise the exchange rate. In Fig. 18.3, the increase in demand to D_1 causes the exchange rate to rise to $1.75.

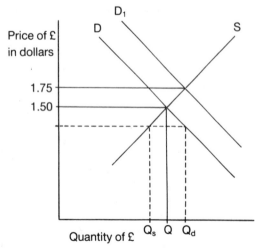

Fig. 18.3 Floating exchange rate changes

Advantages of floating rates

1 **Artificially high** exchange rates are not possible and the rate is subject to demand and supply. For instance, in 1978, Japan had a $17 billion current account

surplus similar to USA's deficit. In 1979, Japan had a current-account deficit because the yen appreciated against the dollar. This appreciation made Japanese exports more expensive and less competitive, leading to their contraction and the reduction of the surplus.

2 Market prices reflect changes in demand and supply and thus lead to **efficient use** of world **resources**.

3 The exchange rate ceases to be a policy objective. In order to maintain a favourable exchange rate, governments may adopt domestic policies such as deflation to prevent balance-of-payments deficits. Thus internal **fiscal** and **monetary policies** are **freed** from external trade limitations if rates float.

4 As any balance-of-payments deficit will be corrected by automatic exchange-rate adjustments, there is no need to tie up **resources** in **reserves**. Instead, they could be used internally for (say) investment.

Disadvantages

1 **Currency speculation.** This has two effects:

    (a) Hot money flows into a country forcing artificially high exchange for a short period. It then leaves for elsewhere causing violent fluctuations in the external value of the currency. This weakens the stability of the system.

    (b) Speculators may rush to sell a weak currency and force its price down, before buying back at a lower price and making a **capital gain**.

2 **Inflation has been encouraged** because floating rates transmit inflation and weaken the government's resolve to control domestic expenditure.

3 Increased business **uncertainty** reduces trade because traders cannot be sure of the exchange rate which they will receive when goods are sold, because the rates are ever changing.

Since the floating of the major currencies, 1972, these disadvantages have not been borne out. Traders can guard against the risk of exchange fluctuations to some extent by buying currency in the **forward market** at a certain rate. Similarly, governments can minimize these fluctuations by **intervention**. They use reserves to buy their currency in order to maintain and/or raise demand artificially, thus keeping the exchange rate up. If the currency is too strong, they sell it and buy foreign currencies, thereby replenishing reserves.

Consequences of floating

1 However, markets have tended to **'overcorrect'** exchange rates. In 1981, the pound appreciated from $1.80 to $2.45 in six months. This fast rise was bad for trade and investment.

2 Another criticism has been the emergence of **'dirty floating'**. This is where a government has an exchange-rate target, and intervenes in the foreign exchange market by buying or selling in order to maintain this target. This is considered 'dirty' if the desired exchange-rate target is artificially low, thereby giving its national goods a competitive advantage. An artificially low rate may thus stimulate employment. However, it will also raise import prices and worsen inflation. Thus, in dirty floating, the government makes a 'trade-off' between a rate of inflation and the number of people unemployed.

3 The effective exchange rate of the pound, measured by an index of currencies weighted to reflect British trade steadily fell down to 77.1 in 1988, as shown in Fig. 18.4 below.

Year	*Value*
1972	123.3
1975	100.0
1981	94.9
1984	82.0
1986	75.0
1988	77.1

Fig. 18.4 Effective exchange rate in the pound in selected years 1972–88

4 In March 1979, the **European Monetary System** (EMS) was created. Britain did not join. All the major European nations link their currencies to each other and to a central rate, expressed in terms of a European currency unit (ecu). The EMS operates like managed flexibility within certain bands.

18.5 International Monetary Fund

The IMF was created in **1944** at the Bretton Woods Conference, which met to establish a stable system of international exchange. The World Bank was also set up at the same time.

The IMF has **138** member countries. The centrally planned nations, such as the USSR, are not members. Each member pays subscriptions, called **quotas**, determined by the size of their economies. They pay three quarters in their **national currency** and one quarter in **reserves**, such as gold, dollars and SDRs (Special Drawing Rights—see below). It is run by a board of 21 executive directors. Six directors are appointed by the big economies, e.g. the USA, West Germany, and fifteen elected by the other members.

FUNCTIONS 'SAL'

Supervision and surveillance of exchange rates. Initially, the IMF supervised the fixed rates adopted and gave approval to devaluations. However, after the ending of managed flexibility in 1971, this role became less important. The IMF now **recommends** exchange rates for economies, when lending to countries with exchange-rate problems. It also recommends domestic economic policies to be adopted, usually lower public spending and domestic credit limitation. It usually objects to nations attempting to get an artificially low exchange rate in order to gain a competitive advantage at the expense of the rest of the world.

Advice. IMF **consults** and helps its members. It seeks stability in exchange rates. However, its **influence** over countries, such as Japan and West Germany, with persistent trade surpluses, is limited.

Lending. The IMF aimed to promote world trade by increasing international **liquidity**.

1 When nations went into **temporary** balance of payments **deficit** they could borrow from the IMF for short periods, during which they tried to rectify the problem. Each member could borrow so much **automatically** and obtain extra credit at the discretion of the Fund. The stand-by credit to Britain in 1976 was given subject to certain conditions. The money comes from the quotas which each country subscribes when it joins. The IMF has also created **special oil facilities** for borrowing by countries specifically hit by the oil price rises of 1973 and 1978.

2 The reserve role of the dollar has limited the growth of international liquidity and so the IMF has sought an alternative. It developed **Special Drawing Rights** (SDR), which is a kind of paper money. Its value is based on a basket of 16 major trading currencies and holders of SDRs receive interest. The IMFs supply of SDRs is 10 per cent of total world reserves (see Fig. 18.5). However, many countries lack **faith** in SDRs (and, as with all money, acceptability is important).

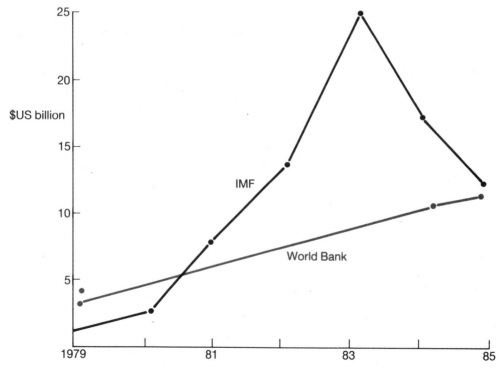

Fig. 18.5 IMF and World Bank lending

These functions are carried out in order to meet certain general objectives.

1 To promote international monetary co-operation.

2 To encourage/establish stability in exchange rates and balance of payments.

3 To seek full convertibility between currencies and an ending of exchange controls.

4 To lend its resources to maintain international trade/liquidity and so discourage trade restrictions as a means of resolving balance-of-payments crises.

THE WORLD BANK

The World Bank, or International Bank for Reconstruction and Development, was created in 1944 at Bretton Woods. Its main purpose is to provide aid to developing countries for capital projects, e.g. dams, airports etc. It is composed of most major nations, except the eleven centrally planned, and raises revenue from its members and by issuing bonds. In 1984-5 it spent £11.16 billion.

Figure 18.5 shows that as the IMF's lending has declined so the World Bank's has increased. The world's two largest debtor nations in 1986 were Brazil and Mexico who each owed over $100 billion. In each case at least one third of their export earnings went in debt interest payments.

18.6 Summary

The Balance-of-Payments account shows the UK financial transactions with the rest of the world. It is comprised of the Current Account, Capital Account and Official Financing. The UK always has a surplus on the invisible account whilst the visible account has moved between surplus and deficit over the years.

Throughout the 1970s the UK experienced regular crises on the balance of payments, but rising oil exports since 1980 have improved the current account balance. Remedies for balance-of-payments problems may focus on the value of the pound, the domestic economy, or trade restrictions.

The Exchange Rate can be fixed by the government or allowed to float and be determined by market forces. Most EEC members belong to the EMS which links their currencies together. The IMF, established in 1944, seeks to promote international monetary cooperation, whilst the World Bank provides aid to developing countries.

19 GOVERNMENT POLICY

19.1 Objectives

In a mixed economy such as Britain's, the government has a very important role to play. As explained earlier (see Unit 3.1) the two major parties disagree over the best **size of the public sector**. (Labour favours a larger public sector, Conservatives a smaller one.) The government's annual expenditure (1984-5 £128 billion) is at least 46 per cent of GDP and therefore very substantial and influential. Even the Conservative Party, which believes in less interference in the economy, realizes that the government has a major role to play. All political parties have a general desire to **raise the standard of living** of society. This could be done if certain **aims** are achieved.

1 A low level of unemployment.

2 A low inflation rate.

3 A surplus on the Balance of Payments.

4 An improvement in economic growth.

5 A realistically valued exchange rate.

Since 1945 successive British Governments have sought to achieve these rather **vague** aims. Prior to 1971 the fifth aim was unnecessary as we had a fixed exchange rate (see Unit 18.4).

These aims are extremely **difficult** to achieve individually, and almost impossible to attain simultaneously. Thus, a government usually lays down a **priority**, for example between 1967 and 1970 Labour's objective was to remove the balance-of-payments deficit; and between 1979 and 1983 Conservatives have aimed to reduce the inflation rate. In recent years, the priorities have **varied between political parties**. For instance in 1987 the Conservatives saw inflation as the main priority but Labour stressed the reduction of unemployment. Figure 19.1 gives a summary of the main party's election proposals for the economy. It shows Labour's specific commitment to a less unequal distribution of income and wealth. However, it is not included as a general aim, because the Conservatives do not agree with it.

CONSERVATIVES	Main priority remains to reduce inflation. Control of public spending, borrowing and money supply.
LABOUR	'Massive' rises in public spending. Annual national economic assessment agreed by TUC and government on how to distribute national income.
ALLIANCE	Increased government borrowing to reduce unemployment.

Fig. 19.1   1987 Election proposals for the economy

In practice each aim usually involves a **specific target**. For instance, in 1979 the Conservative government promised to 'reduce inflation to single figures', a lower rate than that which occurred in the previous five years. In order to achieve this it devised a medium-term financial **strategy** which incorporated several economic indicators, e.g. growth of money supply M3.

However, the targets may change. In 1977 the unemployment of 1 million people was thought to be a 'shameful failure'. If this target were achieved in 1990 it would be heralded as a 'fabulous triumph'. Thus, changing **economic circumstances** lead to revised targets. A total of 2 million unemployed in 1989 has made 1 million seem a desirable figure and unemployment at that level would now be seen as a 'success'.

19.2 Limitations

The effectiveness of a government's action is curtailed in many ways. These limits can be remembered by **'COPPIT'**.

CONFLICT BETWEEN AIMS

A policy which leads to the achievement of one aim may prevent the obtaining of another. For instance, a low level of unemployment could be achieved by massive public expenditure financed by borrowing and credit creation (fiscal and monetary policies). However, the rapid increase in the money supply would probably lead to higher inflation and so the inflation goal would not be obtained. There are potential conflicts between many of the objectives.

OPEN ECONOMY

As a nation dependent on trade and committed to more free trade, the British economy is **vulnerable** to world problems. For instance, a world economic recession will intensify British problems because the export markets will decline, thereby weakening the balance of payments and probably the exchange-rate value, as well as raising unemployment. The growth in unemployment in Britain between 1979 and 1983 was attributed to two factors—government policy and world depression. It could be argued that the openness may 'blow a government's policy off course' by introducing an unconsidered factor which distorts its calculations and policies, thus preventing the fulfilment of an economic aim.

It has also been argued that balance-of-payments problems, made worse by fair and free trading, have led to undesirable domestic policies, such as deflation, which have prevented the achievement of improved economic growth. Some have proposed a 'Siege Economy' in which Britain would withdraw from the EEC and erect trade barriers, behind which public spending would be increased substantially to generate economic growth. This forms part of the **alternative economic strategy** championed by some economists and left-wing Labour politicians. Furthermore, a high rate of economic growth may make wealth redistribution easier, but the balance of payments worse.

PREVIOUS POLICIES

A government often does not have much room for manoeuvre because of the policies which it has inherited and the substantial commitments that all governments have. In the short term, a government has to carry out the spending plans for the current financial year. After that it is less tied, although much **financial spending is long term** (e.g. motorway construction) and needs to be continued. Also, much of public spending is in the form of transfer payments (e.g. pensions) and these cannot be cut or stopped. For instance in 1983, the Conservative government slowed down the increase in spending on social-welfare programmes but only in the face of much opposition and criticism. Only about 20 per cent of public expenditure each year is subject to government discretion.

Even in the field of legislation, a new government is rather limited. Much legislation is introduced irrespective of which party is elected and the power of the **civil service** may minimize a government's impact. For instance the 1980 and 1982 Employment Acts were less radical than many Conservatives wanted and had promised. Similarly, between 1980 and 1984 several privatization proposals were scaled down.

INFORMATION

The government lacks perfect knowledge of the economy. It collects many **statistics**, related to its targets and general aims, but their accuracy leaves a lot to be desired. For instance, the **Balance of Payments figures**, which are published monthly are based on estimates, later often revised substantially. The export earnings from insurance premiums accrued at Lloyds are particularly difficult to calculate, as the accounting is done over a three-year period (to balance good and bad years). **Similarly**, the **'black economy'** indicates the problem with domestic statistics.

The information received is **out of date**, because of the time needed for collection. Things may change between the date of collection and the time when the figures are analysed. Governments therefore tend to base decisions on **trends** rather than figures in isolation.

Economic decisions also require information about the **future**. This type of information is very susceptible to error because it is based on **assumptions** and **predictions**. For instance there are various models of British economy and each will give different **forecasts** from the same input data.

Generally, there is plenty of reasonably accurate information available but government post-war policies indicate that either, (a) the inter-relationships between the figures are not very well understood, or (b) the wrong conclusions are drawn and thus the wrong policies are applied.

TIME

From the point when a policy decision is made, time elapses before the policy is implemented and carried out. During this period of time **circumstances** may have changed which may make the policy unnecessary. Some policies do not have immediate effect. For instance, changes in income tax usually take three months to implement and six months before they have any **impact**. So timing is clearly very important.

The 1979 Conservative government came to power aiming to bring about a 'fundamental change' in attitudes to work. They claimed that this would require two terms in office (i.e. up to ten years). This made their economic policy **long-term** and dependent on political factors such as winning another election inside five years—which they did in 1983. Thus, the Conservative government will have the time it needs. However, often this is not the case, for example in 1970, 1974 and 1979 when governments fell from power without lasting the full five years.

19.3 Methods

The government plays several roles in society. Each entails a type of action which can be influential. They can be remembered by the word **'LEST'**.

Legislation. The state passes laws which affect the economy, e.g. Equal Pay 1975 raised the costs of production because women had to be paid the same as men when doing comparable jobs. Most government policies have some legal aspect to them, including the need for Parliamentary approval.

Employment. The Government is a major employer—30 per cent of the labour force are employed in the public sector. It often sets an example to other employers in the economy for instance in incomes policy and wage restraint.

Spending. Public expenditure and government planning are vitally important in a mixed economy. Cuts in public expenditure in real terms affect the private sector and can be used to achieve certain economic objectives; for example to reduce consumption, to prevent tax increases, or to reduce the supply of money.

Trouble shooting. The state often acts as a mediator between groups in society. For instance, in industrial relations it provides services (such as ACAS) to resolve disputes between trade unions and employers. Since 1979 the Conservative government has been less interventionist.

TYPES OF POLICY

Fiscal. The use of public spending and taxation (see Unit 15). Very general policy.

Monetary. The use of interest rates and credit creation (see Unit 10.8). Very general policy.

Industrial. The use of specific policies affecting different aspects of British industry, for example:

> 1 **Manpower.** Trade union law (see Units 13.8 and 13.9), incomes policy (see Unit 13.6).
> 2 **Competition.** Monopolies legislation (see Unit 7.4), privatization (see Units 3.1, 3.2 and 2.4), small firms (see Unit 5.8).
> 3 **Regional policy.** See Units 6.3 and 6.4.

International. The use of specific policies affecting British trading relations with the rest of the world:

> 1 **Balance of Payments.** See Unit 18.3.
> 2 **Exchange rates.** See Unit 18.4.
> 3 **Trading.** See Units 17.4 and 17.5.
> 4 **Membership of international bodies** (e.g. IMF) and trading organizations e.g. EEC (see Unit 17.6).

Social. Many social policies have economic implications, and vice versa. For instance, the relief of poverty could be tackled by massive public spending and negative income tax. Each of these policies would have far-reaching effects on inflation and incentives.

The main social areas with economic links are:

> 1 **Housing.** Owner occupation is encouraged by the government through its provision of tax relief on mortgages. It gives incentives to home improvement through grants; and provides central government revenue to local authorities for the building and maintenance of council houses. In 1979 the Conservative government began the controversial policy of council house sales at reduced prices.
> 2 **Health.** The state provides the National Health Service, which consumes 10 per cent of public expenditure. The role of the NHS is influenced by population needs. Thus Britain's ageing population (see Unit 12.3) will require more health care and increased public expenditure in that field.
> 3 **Pensions.** As these are provided out of public funds, although based on workers' earnings-related contributions, their rising cost imposes an economic burden (as with health care).
> 4 **Poverty.** Many politicians and economists believe that poverty can only be alleviated by increasing the size of national output, so that all people can benefit from an improvement in living standards. The uneven distribution of income is seen by others as a problem which makes poverty relief difficult.

Overall, there is a general belief that certain social problems can be minimized by increased public spending. Such spending is easier to fund if **economic growth** is achieved (see Unit 14.4).

19.4 Problems and policies

In addressing an economic problem, it is unusual to find only one policy in use. More often than not **several policies** are involved, in achieving the objective, or **several** objectives. These policies may have **side-effects** which make other aims impossible to achieve.

The wisdom of using certain policies may be questioned. **Different schools of thought** may vary in their support and underlying variations may be political as well as economic. For instance, the Monetarist economists, who support Capitalism, believe that strict control over the money supply will lead to a reduction in the rate of inflation. They are prepared to accept cuts in services and greater unemployment in order to achieve their inflation goal. Conversely, Keynesian economists, who believe in greater state involvement in society, consider money-supply policies deflationary and misplaced, because they see an unemployment goal as more important.

| | **General policies** | | |
Aim	Fiscal	Monetary	Other
Bring down the level of unemployment	Increase public spending Lower taxes	Create more credit Lower interest rates	Investment grants Industrial training Tariff barriers
Lower rate of inflation	Higher taxes Less public spending	Reduce credit Lower interest rates	Incomes policy Lift trade controls Encourage competition
Balance of Payments improvement	Higher taxes Less public spending } deflation	Limit credit Raise interest rates	Tariff barriers Exchange control
Greater economic growth	Lower Income tax Inc. Govt. spending Reduce Corp. tax	Easy and cheap credit	Privatization Help small firms Encourage competition
Higher valued exchange rate	Cut public spending	Raise interest rates	

Fig. 19.2 Summary of economic aims and some possible policies

Figure 19.2 provides a simple summary of some policies which have been proposed to achieve certain aims. More detailed explanations appear in the relevant units. The trade is not all-embracing, and on careful study some policies may be seen as contradictory.

It is also possible to outline the effects of certain **specific policies**. In 1985 one (averaged) economic model predicted the effects outlined in Fig. 19.3. Although the actual calculated impact varies between different economic forecasters, they usually all identify the impact in the same direction. Thus most economic models show that lower interest rates reduce unemployment but by varying amounts.

	Unemployment	*Output* (%)	*Prices* (%)
Two-points cut in Interest rates	−10,000	+1	−1.6
Extra £2 billion government spending	−60,000	+0.3	+0.6
Income tax cuts of £2 billion	−51,000	+0.3	—

Fig. 19.3 Specific policy effects

19.5 Local government

There are several types of authority. There are **47 non-metropolitan counties** in England and Wales which are responsible for planning, transport, police, fire service, social services and education. These counties are divided into **districts** with responsibility for housing, local planning, environmental health and leisure services. There are **36 metropolitan districts** which are responsible for education, social services, housing, local planning, environmental health and leisure services. Since 1986 when the metropolitan counties were abolished, there are Boards appointed to run the other main services (such as planning, transport, fire and police) which are provided across the districts, e.g. South Yorkshire passenger transport executive.

Since 1986 London has had a system of its own composed of various agencies and boards which are responsible for transport, planning and housing, the Inner London Education Authority (ILEA) and 32 London Boroughs which provide all of the other local services, except the police.

The term 'Local Government' is used to cover all the elements of this diverse structure and all the different types of local authority. In total, local government accounts for 20 per cent of public expenditure and employs just over **2 million people**. Out of the total spending, roughly **80 per cent** is **current expenditure**, i.e. annual expenditure on consumption, such as teachers' salaries, dustmen's wages and maintenance of old folks' homes. The most expensive provisions are education and personal social services which account for two thirds of **current** spending. The other 20 per cent of the total, which is a declining proportion since recent central government policy changes, is **capital expenditure**. This is investment, mainly in housing (council houses) and social assets such as schools.

Each year, local authorities **budget** (plan) their spending in the light of what they need to provide in their area. They usually intend to spend more than the central government wishes them to spend. However, their **actual spending** in total is about 3 per cent less than they planned. Central government has become increasingly concerned over the growth of local government expenditure. The growth in real terms after allowing for inflation has been very slight (1 per cent per year on average).

LOCAL REVENUE

	1973–4	*1983–4*	*1987–8*
Rates	30	26	31
Government grants	49	53	46
Other income	21	21	23

Fig. 19.4   Local government sources of income

GOVERNMENT GRANTS

The Rate Support Grant given by the government is now the largest source of local authority finance. It was 61 per cent of the total spending from 1978 to 1979, but it has declined somewhat to 50 per cent (1986–7). The system of grant allocation has been reviewed and changed since 1981. As local authorities carry out many policies and laws on behalf of central government, central government makes a substantial contribution towards them and requires certain minimum standards and nationwide uniformity. In addition, the government may give financial assistance in emergencies, e.g. in cases of flood damage. Since 1981 it has also told local authorities what they should be providing and how much it should cost, based on a standard formula. This is known as **grant related expenditure**. Each authority now gets a **'block grant'** for this expenditure.

Before 1981 the Rate Support Grant was based on the past spending patterns of authorities. Each authority was paid a grant on the basis of their **needs** (the services they had provided) and their **resources** (income from rates). Under the new system, local authorities which overspend government targets will have their **grants cut**.

Central government can control local authority spending by:

1 Financing a smaller percentage of its local expenditure, i.e. **less block grant**.
2 Allowing less for inflation than necessary, i.e. setting a **cash limit** of 5 per cent when inflation is 8 per cent so that economies have to be made.
3 **Penalizing** them for over spending, e.g. in 1983–4, £292 million of Rate Support Grant was withheld from big overspending councils.
4 The government can also **change** the **formula** by which the grant is distributed to local authorities. For instance, the present subsidy to domestic ratepayers in Wales is greater than it is in England.
5 Rate-capping. Local authorities are prevented from raising their rates above a certain level, by the Government.

RATES

Rates are a local tax on property. All property in an area is given a **rateable value**. This is the estimated annual rent (less the cost of upkeep) that the property is worth in its present condition and location. It is assessed by the Inland Revenue department. An authority will know the total rateable value of its area, say £10 million. It estimates each year how much income it needs from rates, say £8 million. It can then fix the rate in the pound necessary to raise the required amount of revenue. This is called **the rate poundage** and in this example it is 80p in the pound. Thus a houseowner whose property has a rateable value of £300 pays £240 per year (300 × 80/100) in rates.

Rateable values are reviewed every five years, whilst the rates may be changed (and usually increase) annually. The rateable value of an individual property will increase when **improvements**, such as central heating, are made. Rates are charged at a higher rate on business premises but church and agricultural land is exempt. Commerce and industry contribute over 55 per cent of the rate income.

Advantages of rates

1 **Easy to collect.** A twice-yearly bill is sent and payment can be made in instalments (unlike VAT).
2 **Cheap to administer.** An annual calculation of rates per property (rather than monthly as with PAYE). Administration is $2\frac{1}{2}$ per cent cost of yield.

3 **Difficult to evade.** Ownership or use of a property is easy to establish and check upon.

4 **Large, reliable sources of income.** This is also fairly stable.

Disadvantages of rates

1 **Unfair.** Not related to income or spending and not everyone pays. Roughly one third of households are not ratepayers directly. Businesses pay whether they are profitable or loss-making.

2 **Regressive**. The system tends to hit the less well-off more than it does the better-off (e.g. a large house may mean a large family rather than a large income), although **rate rebate** schemes do operate.

3 **Penalizes improvements.** Improvements lead to higher rates being paid.

4 **Highest in poorer areas.** The inner city areas have few valuable properties and need to provide more services. So rate poundages are higher, often as high as £2.50 in the pound.

5 **Unequal.** The same type of property may incur vastly different rates in different areas, e.g. rates in Cardiff are nearly half as much as those in the West Midlands (for the same type of property) and less than half of those in London.

The Conservative government in 1984 introduced a system of 'rate-capping'. This was intended to limit rate increases by local authorities, thus reducing the local authority's ability to raise its revenue.

OTHER INCOME

Local government also obtains income from the amenities and services which it provides. It receives **rents** from council-house tenants, **fees** from leisure centres, and **payments** such as bus fares and from the use of other **facilities**. Many of these services are run at a loss and thus subsidized from the rates and from government grants.

LOANS

Capital expenditure is usually financed by borrowing. The money is raised publicly from the Public Works Loan Board and privately by the issue of bonds. Large capital projects such as housing estates usually require the central government's financial approval.

ALTERNATIVES TO RATES

A community charge (poll tax)—all adults on the electoral register will have to pay tax, which will be gradually phased in (during 1990s). This will produce more rate payers and so spread the rates burden more fairly perhaps. This system was introduced in Scotland for the financial year beginning April 1989.

Local sales tax. Unless the tax on sales was levied at a fairly high level it would not raise sufficient income to replace rates. It would not be very stable and would involve much administration. However, such taxes are used in the USA and they are generally fairer than rates.

Local income tax. This would only be a partial source of revenue, rather than a direct replacement for rates. It would seem to be fair and suitable, but subject to fluctuations, regional differences and central government interference.

Assigned revenues. In this system, all the revenue would be raised by central government and certain amounts would be given (assigned) to local authorities. It would seem to be fair, suitable and practical, but it would end local government independence. So for political reasons it is unlikely to be adopted.

Reformed rates. It is likely that rates will survive, but in a modified form. The valuation of property on a **capital**, rather than **rental** basis, could be introduced. Consideration of **multi-member** households paying higher rates than single occupants might be attempted; and the **rebate** scheme could be changed. A nationally set **business** rate could be introduced to ease the rate burden on business and make it similar all over.

19.6 Summary

All political parties agree on broad aims for the economy but different priorities exist between parties. When carrying out their policies governments are limited by a number of factors. Any government plays a number of roles in society and has a range of policies which they can implement to achieve their aims. A major problem is the side effects of a policy which can adversely affect other areas of government activity.

Local government is responsible for specific services which vary between the differing structures of local authorities throughout Britain. Their income comes principally from the Rate Support Grant, which is now the largest source of local government revenue, and local rates. Alternatives to the rating system are currently being considered.

20 CONSUMPTION AND DISTRIBUTION

20.1 Introduction

The aim of this unit is to cover several topics which are not 'mainstream' economics but which appear in some syllabuses, particularly of the 'Social Economics' type.

Topics such as retailing are among those which **overlap** Economics and Commerce. The treatment will be to identify the main aspects of a topic, apply economic concepts where appropriate and show the links with other units. If more detailed knowledge is required (e.g. Unit 20.4 Retailing) then a specialist **Commerce** book should be consulted.

The distribution of primary products **differs** from manufactured goods in two respects. First, many raw materials are extracted and grown in different parts of **the world** a long way from the manufacturers. For instance, tea grown in India is made into a saleable commodity in Europe. Therefore specialized **commodity markets** (see Unit 7.1) have been established so that firms can buy the materials months before they need them (to allow time for transport).

A second difference relates to **government interference**. For certain primary products in Britain, the government is involved in the distribution. This is very different from public corporations (see Unit 3.2) where the government is concerned with the manufacture **and** distribution. The government performs a wholesaling function though the **Milk Marketing Board**. The intention is to control the output and sale of this vital product, as well as to help the farming community. The government, through the board, **fixes prices**, grades and tests goods, packs and transports the milk and decides on the terms of sale. Thus, all farmers receive the same price for the same quality milk irrespective of transport costs (MMB collect the milk churns).

The MMB's factories store and use any surplus milk not sold retail. They advertise milk to encourage sales, e.g. 'Drinka Pinta Milka Day' and 'Milk's Gotta Lotta Bottle'. They also conduct research into cattle breeding and milk production, so that better-quality milk can be produced.

20.2 Distribution

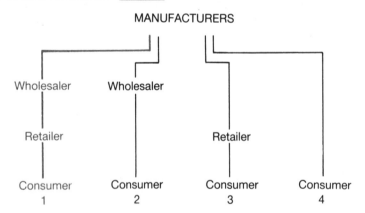

MANUFACTURERS

Wholesaler   Wholesaler

Retailer   Retailer

Consumer   Consumer   Consumer   Consumer
1   2   3   4

Fig. 20.1 Different patterns of distribution

The main effect of division of labour is that the goods produced by specialist workers need to be transferred to consumers. There are several **different routes** which goods can take. These are illustrated in Fig. 20.1 with the red route being the **traditional pattern**. In this pattern (1) the manufacturer sells in large quantities to wholesalers who redistribute them in smaller quantities to a larger number of retailers. The retailers then sell in ones and twos to the consumer. Most **fruit** and **vegetables** are distributed in this manner.

In distribution pattern (2) the **retailer** is omitted. His functions are undertaken by the wholesaler. Increasingly, **consumer durables**, e.g. furniture, dresses, etc., can be bought in this way, usually through the medium of a newspaper/magazine advertisement. Many wholesalers around big cities sell directly from their warehouse premises. The reasons for this development are:

1 Lower overheads—expensive High Street sites not needed.
2 Lower prices—the retailer's profit margin disappears, so cutting out a profit mark-up, often as high as 50 per cent of cost price. Lower prices attract customers.

3 Reduced transport costs. However, this saving may be balanced by the extra expense on advertising.

The **wholesaler** is omitted in the third pattern (3), in Fig. 20.1. His function is usually performed by the retailer who has large premises, particularly for storage. Supermarkets, e.g. Tesco, and discount stores, e.g. Trident, which utilize the **advantages** of **large-scale production**, buy in bulk direct from the manufacturers and usually sell in single units to the consumer, e.g. bread and electrical goods respectively. Some manufacturers prefer to sell directly to a retailer so that their product can be pushed, more than a wholesaler would. Other manufacturers have established their own retail outlets.

In pattern (4) both the **wholesaler** and **retailer** are **eliminated**. The manufacturer will carry out the functions of both, except in the case of mail order, where the agent acts like a retailer, by collecting money and organizing the distribution of information and goods. Avon cosmetics are sold in this way. Again the manufacturer has control over sales promotion and can benefit from **economies of scale** (see Unit 5.6).

Each of the functions in the process of distribution needs to be rewarded. It receives **profit** for adding value and providing products in the form at the time required. The profit gained is usually termed the **profit margin**, or **mark-up**. Figure 20.2 shows the different stages in the distribution process and hypothetical profit margins at each stage.

	Activity	Cost (p)	Profit Per unit (p)	Profit Mark up (%)
Manufacturer	Creates good	40	—	—
	Sells to wholesaler	50	10	$\frac{10}{40} = 25$
Wholesaler	Performs functions	60	—	—
	Sells to retailer	80	20	$\frac{20}{60} = 33.3$
Retailer	Performs functions	85	—	—
	Sells to consumer	102	17	$\frac{17}{85} = 20$

Fig. 20.2 Different stages in distribution process

20.3 Wholesaling

The wholesaler provides many functions. Some mainly benefit the manufacturer whilst others help the retailer.

SERVICES PROVIDED FOR MANUFACTURER 'CARS'

Convenience. It saves him **time/money** by buying in bulk—if there were no wholesalers then each manufacturer would have to deal with each retailer. This would mean more orders, invoices, statements and representatives. The wholesaler also saves manufacturers the trouble and expense of more staff, packing costs and so on, e.g. 1 manufacturer to 400 retailers = 400 orders. **But** 1 manufacturer to 10 wholesalers (to 40 retailers each) = 10 orders.

Advertising. The wholesaler markets the manufacturer's goods and advertises them, usually informally. Also he gives feedback to the manufacturer on sales of his goods and he pushes new products.

Risk bearing. The wholesaler provides a ready market for the manufacturer's output. He bears the manufacturer's risk of not being able to sell his goods and gives him prompt payment (which enables the manufacturer to finance the next batch of goods).

Storage. Wholesalers provide **warehousing facilities**. Manufacturers need to sell goods quickly. The wholesaler enables them to do this because he buys their output in bulk and stores it until required by the retailer.

SERVICES PROVIDED FOR RETAILER

Warehousing. Without wholesalers, retailers would have to buy in much larger quantities, and store them on their own premises. The wholesaler is a reservoir, or source of supply, for retailers. He has a wide selection of goods from many different manufacturers and saves the retailer's time and effort of having to visit and receive many manufacturers.

Breaking bulk. Wholesalers break large quantities down into smaller quantities which are more manageable. Some packaging is often undertaken, e.g. potatoes. In addition, the grading of goods is occasionally done.

Price stability. The wholesaler buys stock and releases it gradually over the year. This may eliminate wide price fluctuations. If no one held stocks and all flooded on to the market at once, there would be falling prices, e.g. excess supply (see Unit 4.3). Later, there would be a shortage and prices would sharply rise.

Credit. Few retailers pay cash immediately. Most pay monthly or on a sale or return basis. Thus the wholesaler takes the risk that the retailer may default and gives him short-term credit.

Delivery. If wholesalers deliver goods they save the retailer the expense of having under-utilized lorries.

Information. Wholesalers tell retailers about new products/bargains.

TYPES OF WHOLESALER

Wholesalers can be classified according to either, (a) the range of goods which they handle (1) and (2), or (b), their trading practices (3) and (4). There are:

1 **General wholesalers.** They serve a local or regional market, normally stocking a very wide range of goods. They have much capital tied up in stock and operate on a fairly large scale.

2 **Specialist wholesalers.** They concentrate on a much narrower range of goods, usually a particular trade. For instance, a builder's merchant who supplies local builders and hardware shops.

3 **Conventional wholesalers.** Traditional wholesalers deliver goods to retailers who pay for them on a monthly credit basis.

4 **Cash and Carry wholesalers.** In the early 1960s some wholesalers began to offer lower prices to retailers if they paid cash and collect their goods. This saved the wholesaler the costs of delivery, salesmen, bad-debt provision and credit control. It enabled the retailer to collect goods when necessary and pay lower prices (although he had to bear the delivery costs, he lost free credit and he needed to plan ahead). Many small-scale independent retailers utilized 'cash and carry' because they can better compete with supermarkets. The catering trade is particularly well suited to this type of operation.

20.4 Retailing

As the retailer is the last link in the normal chain of distribution, he provides essential functions for the manufacturers/wholesalers on the one hand and for consumers on the other.

SERVICES FOR MANUFACTURERS/WHOLESALERS

1 **Breaking bulk.** Wholesalers deal in large quantities which they sell to retailers. The retailers break this bulk and usually sell the products in single units.

2 **Quality control.** In handling the goods, retailers, particularly of electrical goods, check that they are 'fit' for selling. Usually unworkable equipment and damaged goods are withdrawn or sold off cheaply. Such action may preserve a manufacturer's reputation for quality.

3 **Information.** Retailers, through their comments and orders, feed back to the wholesalers how goods are selling. This may determine future production and planning.

4 **Selling goods** in the quantity, at the place and at the time required.

SERVICES FOR CONSUMERS

1 **Variety of goods.** Retailers usually sell several brands of each good. By doing this, they give consumers a choice.

2 **Local supplies.** Retailers are usually located near their customers (except hypermarkets). They provide easy access for customers. Without retailers, consumers would waste time and money travelling to wholesalers' and manufacturers' premises.

3 **Credit.** Most retailers give credit to encourage sales. For small amounts it may be an arrangement to pay the local shopkeeper at the end of the week. On large items such as a motor car, it will be a formal contract. However, supermarkets operate on a 'cash and carry' basis.

4 **Delivery.** Very large organizations, such as department stores who can afford the overheads of a transport fleet, deliver large items such as furniture etc., to their customers. At the other end of the scale, local corner shops may deliver goods for certain (usually aged) familiar customers, as part of their service. However, with the development of transport, particularly the family car, fewer retailers provide a delivery service nowadays.

5 **Advice.** Most retailers help customers by giving them the benefit of their detailed knowledge and experience of products, e.g. DIY shop giving advice over types of paint.

6 **After Sales Service.** Retailers often deal with complaints on behalf of the wholesalers/manufacturers. By law they must replace or repair faulty goods or give refunds. In performing these functions they clearly help the consumer, too.

---

1 Department stores, e.g. House of Fraser
2 Specialist multiples, e.g. BHS, Halfords
3 Mail order, e.g. Littlewoods
4 Discount stores, e.g. Comet
5 Independents, e.g. Roberts Stores, North Thoresby
6 Voluntary groups, e.g. Spar
7 Variety chain, e.g. Woolworths
8 Co-op retailer, e.g. local Co-op
9 Supermarket, e.g. Tesco
10 Superstore, e.g. Asda
11 Hypermarket, e.g. Carrefour

Fig. 20.3 Types of retailer

TRENDS IN RETAILING

Large-scale outlets. Many retailers are getting larger, in size and turnover, to benefit from **economies of scale**. For instance, supermarkets (over 2000 sq ft) have been superseded by **superstores** (over 25,000 sq ft) who can make even better use of specialist staff and gain big discounts from suppliers (because of the volume they buy and sell). As yet, hypermarkets (over 50,000 sq ft) have not been developed as extensively in Britain as in Europe. The consequences of such changes in the size of retailers have been fewer independent retailers and fewer small shops (see Fig. 20.3). Chains, such as Tesco, have closed their smaller stores e.g. 1975–85 Tesco closed over 400 out of 800 branches. Most chains now sell more and better-quality 'own label' goods than previously. They buy these from major producers. Retailers' powers have thus grown at the expense of the manufacturers.

Consumers have benefited through lower prices and easier shopping, i.e. all at one go, called **'one-stop shopping'**. Large, edge-of-town developments can give rise to 'local monopolies'.

Competition has intensified. There are plenty of retailers competing in the main markets. Some features of **Perfect Competition** (see Unit 7.2), such as many sellers and identical products, are relevant to the type of market structure in retailing. No one firm dominates food retailing, with Sainsbury's at 13 per cent having the largest market share.

In other respects such as **branding** and **advertising** (see Unit 20.5), retailing shows characteristics of **Imperfect Competition** (see Unit 7.5).

Most products are now better marketed because of the competition and also because of the development of **self-service**. When consumers are choosing their own goods, without the advice of an assistant in many cases, attractive packaging can be crucial. Many families buy prepacked **convenience food**, such as frozen peas, meat, chips etc., because husband and wife may be both at work and the meals need quick preparation. Thus the growth of private transport, labour-saving devices, refrigerators and working women have revolutionized retailing.

In order to increase sales and make a better return on assets, many retailers have moved out of their traditional markets. For instance, **multiples**, such as Marks & Spencer, have moved **upmarket** and begun competing with department stores in luxury goods. In contrast, many **department stores** which previously catered mainly for middle- and upper-class customers, are moving **down market**. They are selling less-expensive products and trying to appeal to better off working-class consumers. The gradual breakdown of social class in Britain and the general improvements in living standards have made such a policy necessary and possible.

Department stores such as Debenhams and House of Fraser have attempted to make better use of their **floor space**. As shoppers are less willing to be lured into lifts, many upper floors are being converted into offices (to earn rent). In addition, space has been let to specialist sellers such as booksellers, opticians, tailors and (even) the Electricity Board. In 1982 these concession holders accounted for over 20 per cent of the sales in Debenham's 70 stores.

Diversification. In making better use of their resources large retailers have tended to diversify into different product areas. Many **specialist** chain stores have become **variety chain stores**. For instance, W. H. Smith started as booksellers but in recent years they have moved into electrical games, computers and records. In 1982–3 a quarter of W. H. Smith's profits came from wholesaling and this side of their business was expanding much faster than the retailing side.

Food retailers, such as Asda, have diversified. As the income elasticity of demand for food is low/inelastic, then in order to increase turnover Asda needs to shift into other income-elastic markets such as consumer durables, wine, etc.

These trends have led to the **demise of the small shop**. Some such shopkeepers have responded by joining voluntary groups/chains such as Spar. This has enabled them to benefit from bulk buying and advertising, but in doing so they forfeit independence.

20.5 Advertising

Advertising makes distribution easier, because it informs consumers about the products and services. In 1986 £3200 million worth of advertising was undertaken (see Fig. 20.4). Over 90 per cent of the advertising expenditure is through newspapers and television. The buying and selling of advertising space in these media is very **competitive**. To be successful, advertising needs to be at the **right time**, in the **right place** and at the **right price**.

Media	Percentage of total 1962		Percentage of total 1986	
Newspapers				
National	22 ⎫		16.5 ⎫	
Regional	24 ⎬	70	21.5 ⎬	61.3
Periodicals	24 ⎭		23.3 ⎭	
Television		24		32.7
Posters and transport		4		3.8
Radio		0		1.8
Cinema		2		0.4
		100%		100%

Fig. 20.4   Advertising media (1962 and 1986)

AIMS OF ADVERTISING

Higher sales. As higher sales usually mean greater profits then most businesses seek this. As sales rise, overheads become lower per unit of output and **average cost falls**. For instance, if fixed costs are £20,000 and variable costs £5 per unit sold, sales of 4000 units cost £10 each

$$£20,000 + £5 \times 4000 = \frac{£40,000}{4000}$$

However, if sales increase to 6000 units, the cost of each item falls to £8.33

$$£20,000 + £6 \times 5000 = \frac{£50,000}{6000}.$$

If advertising is successful it reduces average cost of production.

Increased company turnover can also be obtained through promoting **new products** and generating a popular **company image**. An increasing amount of advertising is company-wide rather than just concentrated on one product. Most advertising is **persuasive**. It aims to persuade people to buy one good or service rather than another. Firms **compete** for a share of a market for their particular **brand**.

Some advertising to increase sales is undertaken on behalf of the **whole industry**. This is known as **generic** or **collective** advertising. In these advertisements the general product, such as milk, is advertised, rather than a particular dairy, e.g. Express, Co-op, Clover.

Information. Most advertisements provide some information, even if it is only a brand name. However, some advertisements are intended to inform rather than persuade. For instance, **government departments** issue advertising on health, road safety and crime prevention with the general aim of advising people. In 1988 the government spent over £70 million; and the nationalized industries, often in competition with one another (e.g. gas versus electric), spent a similar amount.

Other mainly **informative** advertising can be found in technical and trade journals. There are over 1000 directories, in addition to the Yellow Pages, which accept business advertisements. Informative advertising usually states the **facts**, e.g. date/time/place of an event rather than making claims for goods or services.

COST OF ADVERTISING

The rates charged for advertising depend on the medium used. Television is more expensive than newspapers because it tends to attract a larger audience and has more visual impact.

The rates charged for TV adverts vary with the TV station (13 different ones), the time of day, the likely viewers and the length of the advertisement. A 30-second advert on Anglia TV may cost around £1000 whereas a similar advert on Thames TV during a James Bond film will cost about £30,000. Occasionally, companies make special deals with the television network. For instance, the Shadows Silver Album advert only cost £60 for one minute. This was because ITV was given 30 per cent of the record sales.

Similarly, there are several factors which determine **newspaper** rates—the size of the advertisement, the position in the publication, the day of the week and if it is coloured. For instance, a one-page spread in a local newspaper may cost about £1000 whereas a colour page in the *Sunday Times* magazine costs about £14,000.

Public companies in Britain spend millions of pounds annually on advertising. **Proctor & Gamble** who make cleaning materials such as Bold, Ariel and Fairy Liquid spend about **£50 million per year** on advertising. This works out at roughly 20 per cent of the cost of the product. They are clearly trying to promote brand loyalty and gain an increase in demand. Thus they are trying to make the demand curves for their products more **inelastic**.

ADVANTAGES OF ADVERTISING 'SPECKS'

1 **The Standard of living** is increased because advertising introduces new products to consumers.
2 **Prices** are kept **lower.** The competition of advertising forces firms to make prices lower than they would otherwise be.
3 **Employment** is created. The advertising industry provides jobs for many people.
4 **Costs** are lowered because advertising enables larger-scale production (see Aims).
5 **Knowledge** of goods/services is increased by the existence of advertising. It may give people a better choice of goods.
6 **Subsidized** newspapers, television and periodicals result, because advertising revenue keeps their prices down. For instance, 50 per cent of the *Radio Times'* revenue is from adverts. The *Woman's Own* magazine takes £15 million in advertising revenue annually. **Free** newspapers now exist because they are financed by the advertisers.

DISADVANTAGES OF ADVERTISING 'CREW'

1 **Creation** of unnecessary **needs** can be done by persuasive advertising, e.g. people lived healthily without double glazing before its introduction. Improvements in the standard of living mean that more 'luxuries' can be advertised and sold as 'necessities'.
2 **Raised prices** may be the result of advertising. The extra costs caused by advertising may not be covered by the increased sales.
3 **Exploitation** may occur. Certain products may be advertised in such a way as to suggest to people that if they do not buy the product then they are not treating their family properly. Similarly the advertising in a glamorous way of potentially harmful practices such as drinking and smoking may be encouraging reckless attitudes and behaviour.
4 **Wasteful use of resources** may take place. If a firm/firms in a stable industry advertise just to maintain their market shares (e.g. bread) then they are perhaps not making the best use of their resources. In the long run sales are not likely to rise and they might do better by using the money elsewhere, in research, or by lowering prices. For instance, in 1981 the Army spent £$3\frac{1}{2}$ million on recruiting soldiers, using the slogan 'Join the Professionals NOW!'

ADVERTISING AGENCIES

Most individuals organize their own advertising without specialized help. Most large firms who want a **national campaign** lack the necessary skills that are needed to devise, make and place advertisements. So they consult advertising agents such as Saatchi and Saatchi, who are perhaps the best-known name. One of the biggest and widest ranging agents is McCann-Erickson, whose accounts cover beer (Carling Black Label), groceries (Tetley, Shredded Wheat), clothing (Levi jeans), milk (Milk Marketing Board) and cigarettes (Rothmans).
The **functions** of advertising agents are to:

1 Find out about the product and its market.
2 Plan the campaign.
3 Produce the advertisements.
4 Place the advertisements in the media.
5 Advise the producer about the image and brand perceptions of the good/service.

ADVERTISING STANDARDS AUTHORITY

This body was created in **1962** to oversee the advertising industry. It is composed of people from within advertising and outsiders. Its job is to protect the consumer from misleading and harmful advertising. In order to do this, it devised a **code of practice**, telling advertisers how to operate. These rules have often been revised. For instance, beer advertisements should no longer glamorize the habit of buying large rounds in a pub or suggest that a drinking man is more attractive to women! Anyone shown drinking must appear to be over 21.

The ASA investigates **complaints** against adverts which people find misleading. In addition, ASA publishes helpful leaflets for the producers of goods, so that they do not infringe the code of advertising practice. The ASA also advertises itself through its 'legal, decent, honest, truthful' adverts.

20.6 Marketing

Advertising and selling in large organizations is handled by a marketing department. They seek to co-ordinate work in several departments so that the good or service has public appeal. Their work covers four areas.

Market research. Firms need detailed information about their product and its rivals in the market. Thus, they collect such information through questionnaires, reports on the use of sample products, experiments in small areas with new goods and tests in shops. The information accumulated is used to plan the following activities.

Branding. A 'brand' is the **maker's** name for their product, e.g. **Heinz** beans, **Crosse & Blackwell** beans, **H.P.** beans. Often manufacturers in their advertising emphasize the brand name rather than a specific product because they make many different products, e.g. Heinz soup, Heinz tomato ketchup, etc. They are encouraging the shopper to select goods by **brand name** rather than by the quality of the product. They seek **consumer loyalty**. This differentiation between products shows imperfect competition (Unit 7) and attempts to make demand for the manufacturers' products more inelastic. 'Branding' tends to cause intense competition generated through advertising.

Occasionally, branding is done by **retailers**, e.g. Marks & Spencer sell their **'own-label'** food products. They do not produce the goods but they place large orders with manufacturers on condition that they are labelled with their name. By omitting the wholesaler and getting bulk discount they are able to sell at **below market prices** and increase turnover. The manufacturer also benefits as he has an assured order.

Packaging. The way in which goods are presented to the consumer has become increasingly important and costly. The advent of **self-service** requiring customers to select their products stimulated manufacturers into attractive and eye-catching packaging, in order to raise sales. Thus packaged food, such as fish fingers, cornflakes etc., is often sold because of the way it is made to **appeal** rather than on the nutritional value of the contents. With certain products, such as perfume, the packaging costs may be half of the total cost. However, generally the extra cost of packaging is less than the cost of selling (employee's wages, etc.) so the consumer does not suffer because of it.

Sales promotion—the branded, packaged product needs to be convincingly, and persuasively promoted. Most manufacturers allocate a **'budget'** (proportion of the firm's yearly expenditure) for such publicity. The marketing department has to decide how to spend the money which it is allowed. The normal regular means of sales promotion for many consumer goods is by using a **salesman** to tour existing and potential buyers (usually retailers/wholesalers). He may provide information, display material and give free samples which can be used to attract the consumer. In return, he will receive firsthand information on best-selling lines and stocks and he can feed this back to the manufacturer. Thus, he is a vital link in the chain of distribution.

20.7 Consumer protection

The expansion in the **role** of the **government** in a mixed economy has meant that today consumers are much better protected than in the 19th century. **Unscrupulous traders** are now less likely to 'get away with' cheating their customers. Many laws have been introduced to protect consumers from practices such as:

1 Incorrect weights and quantities being sold.
2 Failure to replace faulty products.
3 High fixed prices exploiting weak consumers.
4 Misleading claims about goods.
5 Dangerous substances contained in products.

With the growth of interdependence in society, in place of self-sufficiency, people became more dependent on others and the need for government supervision of trading relationships emerged.

CONSUMER LEGISLATION—A BRIEF SUMMARY

Sale of Goods Act 1893 (updated 1979)

Under this act:

1 Goods must be of **merchantable** quality, i.e. fit for normal use.
2 Goods must be **as described**, whether this is written or verbal.
3 Goods must suit the **purpose** for which they were sold.

In the event of these conditions not being fulfilled then the consumer has three rights—the 3 'R's—**refund, replacement** or **repair**. However, this Act does not totally apply to private sales (as in classified adverts) or to the sale of second-hand goods (although they should be in a 'reasonable' condition for the price charged).

Food and Drugs Act 1955

1 It is illegal for sellers to offer for sale food which is **unfit** for human consumption.
2 The premises must also be **hygienic**, e.g. no smoking when food is handled.
3 Products must be **correctly labelled**, with the contents correctly described.

The local **public health** department enforce this act.

Weights and Measures Act 1963

1 It is illegal for goods to be less than the **weight stated** on the package or materials.
2 Certain common foods, such as tea and butter, may only be packed in **standard sizes/weights.**
3 Weighing machinery should be working accurately—this is checked by **Trading Standards Officers**.

Trade Descriptions Act 1968

1 It is a criminal offence for a trader to describe goods or services **falsely**, either in words or pictures.
2 It limits the ability of traders to offer **spurious 'bargains'**, price reductions, and claims, e.g. watches that let in water cannot be sold as 'waterproof'.

The Trading Standards Officers also enforce this Act.

Unsolicited Goods and Services Act 1971

It is illegal for traders to **demand payment** for goods supplied which have not been ordered. The householder has the right to keep the goods if they are not collected within **six months**. If the householder **writes** to the sender asking for the goods to be collected, he/she can keep them, if they are not collected in **one month**.

Consumer Credit Act 1974

This Act refers to goods bought on credit and costing less than **£5000**. It gives the consumer four basic rights—remembered by **'WRIT'**.

1 **Withdrawal.** If a buyer goes to business premises and signs a credit agreement then he/she is totally bound by the contract made. However, goods bought **at home** are subject to a **5-day 'cooling-off'** period during which the buyer can change his/her mind. This was introduced to stop unscrupulous door-to-door salesmen.
2 **Retain possession.** Once **one third** of the price has been paid by the buyer on credit, the **seller** cannot repossess the goods without going to **court**. The court may allow the seller to retake the goods or it may allow the buyer to repay on slightly different credit terms.
3 **Information.** The customer should receive **written details** of cash price, HP price, goods description, frequency/amount/number of repayments and their rights and duties under the Act. In addition, a buyer on credit has the right to see a copy of any file which a **credit reference agency** has about him/her for 25p fee.
4 **Termination.** The borrower can end the agreement once he has paid **half** of the repayments **but** the lender gets the goods back. The hirer may have to pay for any damage done to the goods. In some agreements, the lender has the right to terminate the loan by giving at least seven-days notice.

Credit Trading Act 1976

This Act enhanced the rights of buyers in three more ways:

1 All businesses lending money or giving credit had to be licensed. Licences are issued (and refused) by the Office of Fair Trading (see below).
2 Buyers can **repay** the loan at any time and get a **rebate**.
3 Lenders must show on the agreement the true cost of the credit, namely the **Annual Percentage Rate** (APR) of the total charge for credit. 'Total Charge' means interest **and** any administrative charges. For instance, £100 borrowed for one year at 10 per cent interest (flat rate) has an APR of 22.2 per cent. This arises because the APR is based on the average amount owed rather than the total amount owed. The amount owed decreases each month and this makes the actual interest rate higher.

ORGANIZATIONS HELPING THE CONSUMER

Function	Type of body		
	Government	*The industry*	*Voluntary*
General supervision	OFT	Trade Associations	—
Proper manufacture and performance of goods	BSI DC		Consumers Association
Selling/services and complaints	Trading standards CAB	Trade Associations Consultative Councils	Consumers Association

Fig. 20.5 Consumer protection organizations

Office of Fair Trading. Created in 1974, this is a **central government** body which looks generally at trading practices. It can get the law changed to meet new problems which arise, e.g. Credit Trading Act 1976. Its main activities are to **'WIPE'** out unfair trading by:

1 **Warning**/prosecuting traders who persistently commit offences.
2 **Issuing**/withholding licences to credit traders.
3 **Publishing** useful information advising people of their rights and where they might get help.
4 **Encouraging** trade organizations to set up **codes of practice**.

Trading Standards/Consumer Protection Departments. Local **councils** set up such departments to investigate consumer complaints about goods/trading practices in their area. The local **Environmental Health Department** performs a similar function related to dirty premises where food/drink are prepared.

British Standards Institute. This body lays down desirable standards of manufacture and performance for a large range of goods. Approved products are awarded the **kitemark** and a safety mark where applicable.

Design Council. British goods, which are well designed, of high quality, are very safe and most efficient, qualify for the Design Centre label.

Both the Design Centre and the BSI are partly backed by government funds. Both aim to protect the consumer by ensuring high standards in the **manufacturing** of goods.

Citizens Advice Bureaux. There are over 700 CAB in Britain, which offer **free** and **confidential advice** to the public. They are partly funded by the government. They deal with family, legal and private matters as well as trading problems.

Trade Associations. Most trades and professions have such organizations, e.g. Association of British Travel Agents, British Insurance Association. Their members usually abide by **voluntary codes of practice** in their dealings with consumers. These codes outline the **correct complaints procedure** and how firms should deal with customers generally. The firms in the industry pay for the trade association to function, which may mean investigation of complaints, **arbitration** between buyer and seller and (possibly) **compensation** payments.

Consumers Association. This is a **private** organization set up in **1963** to protect and inform the public about goods and services. In return for an annual fee, members receive *Which?* magazine. This explains the good and bad points of products, carries out its own tests, and recommends 'best buys'. Such reports are respected by manufacturers/retailers and have thus been influential.

Consultative Councils. The government has insisted that each **nationalized industry** should set up a consumer council to keep a check on its operations. The councils receive **complaints** and offer advice, but are generally accepted as not being very effective watchdogs, e.g. Post Office Users National Council.

20.8 Credit

When people buy goods and services they can **pay** either immediately in **cash** or by **credit**. In the latter case, payment may be delayed for days (e.g. with a cheque until it is cleared—see Unit 10.3), for weeks (e.g. with a cheque card—see Unit 8.5) or for months/years (with a loan—see Unit 10.3 for bank loans).

Retailers in buying goods from manufacturers often receive **trade credit**. The goods are paid for within a month of obtaining them. A retailer paying sooner may receive a discount for prompt payment.

Consumers have many possible **ways** of obtaining credit. They vary with the individual's needs, circumstances and credit-worthiness. They are briefly explained below (more detail will be found in most Commerce textbooks).

MEANS OF CREDIT

Cheques. They give credit until the cheque is cleared, usually three days at the most **but** they are interest free! (See Unit 10.3.)

Credit cards. They provide short-term credit but may be expensive with high rates of interest, e.g. 24–30 per cent APR, and a temptation to overspend (Unit 8.5).

Retail budget accounts. Large shops may operate their own credit system, requiring regular fixed repayments but giving high spending limits.

Monthly accounts. Traders often allow acceptable and trusted customers to have goods/services which they can settle for at the end of each month, e.g. garage petrol.

Trading checks and vouchers. Companies such as Provident have agents who allow people tokens which can be used in certain shops. The consumer pays for the token with interest over time. This system is usually very expensive to the borrower, with interest rates of 60–80 per cent APR, although he/she may be allowed a limit up to twenty times the regular sum agreed.

Bank loans/overdrafts. Interest low, and fairly long repayment period, but not available to nearly half the population, without bank accounts (see Unit 10.3).

Personal loans. These may be given by money lenders, pawnbrokers and finance companies. In each case the interest charged is **high**.

Mail-order catalogue. A popular way of shopping with repayment allowed between 20 and 40 weeks. There is no credit charge but the same goods could be cheaper in the shops and choice is limited.

Insurance policy loan. Insurance Companies are prepared to give loans of up to 90 per cent of the current 'cash-in' value of certain policies. Repayment is made when the policy matures and interest is charged on the loan.

Mortgages. Very long-term credit for buying property, but a bargain (see Unit 11.3) because the asset bought with the mortgage appreciates.

Second mortgages. These are offered by some finance companies. They are long-term credit but are very risky as the lender has the right to repossess the borrower's home if repayments are not made. Such lenders are not as sympathetic about personal problems as building societies and banks.

TYPES OF CREDIT

Hire purchase agreements. The shop/dealer may put up the money for the goods or an agreement may be arranged with a finance company. Normally a **deposit** is paid and instalments of equal amounts are paid monthly over a period of time. However, the buyer is only the **hirer** until **all** the repayments have been made. The buyer has the advantage of immediate use of the good, and prompt after-sales service, but he may pay fairly high interest charges.

Credit sales agreements (sometimes called **Extended**). When the goods are purchased the **buyer immediately** becomes the **owner**. The advantages/disadvantages of credit sale are similar to hire purchase **but** the repayment period is usually shorter and ownership may be an important factor to the buyer.

Advantages of buying on credit

1 Immediate use of goods, rather than waiting and paying cash.
2 Repayment can be spread out over a longer period of time.
3 More expensive goods can be afforded, because often only a deposit (or small regular repayment) is needed. This improves the standard of living.

Disadvantages of buying on credit

1 Interest to be paid, at varying rates. Consumers lack perfect knowledge of all available credit.

2 Temptation to overspending.

3 Commitment to regular repayments may be a problem if income falls (e.g. unemployment).

Advantages of selling on credit

1 More sales than otherwise. People who could not afford the full price may be able to buy on credit. Increased turnover may lead to economies of scale in manufacturing.

2 Customers find credit to be habit-forming and often continue to shop at the credit-givers shop even when the original purchase has been paid off. Thus it may produce consumer loyalty.

Disadvantages of selling on credit

1 More administrative cost for the retailer—records, reminders and debt collection.

2 Capital tied up in debts which can be expensive.

3 No market for returned cheap, second-hand goods.

20.9 Summary

This distribution of goods usually involves a wholesaler and retailer each of which provide specific services. Over the last 25 years there have been marked changes in the retailing business mostly associated with the benefits of large-scale operations.

Advertising is a key part of distribution. It is a highly organized business which makes extensive use of the media. Advertising agencies are used increasingly by large firms. The industry has its own watchdog, the Advertising Standards Authority.

Government legislation, private and professional organizations, seek to protect the interests of the consumer. Trade and consumer credit are important for both retailers and consumers.

21 TYPES OF EXAMINATION QUESTION

Objective questions

The main feature of such questions is that there is only **one** correct **answer**. Thus, they do not require personal judgement by the examiner. If there is room for disagreement over the answer then the question is not objective. Generally, most objective questions are brief and specific. As a result often only **one mark** is given to each.

Objective questions are of two main types:

SHORT ANSWER

A **word, phrase** or **sentence** is needed to answer the question. For example:

1 Name one source of local authority finance—rates.

2 What do the letters ACAS stand for?—Advisory, Conciliation and Arbitration Service.

3 What is a Demarcation Dispute?—a disagreement between two trade unions over which type of worker should perform a certain job.

Questions 1 and 2 test the recall of factual knowledge. Question 3 assesses the ability to explain an idea (i.e. demarcation) which is probably more difficult.

Sometimes a **calculation** is required. For instance, from a list of taxes and the amount collected for each, a candidate might be asked to calculate 'How much direct taxation is collected?' Such questions require the application of understanding to a simple problem. There is just one correct answer.

MULTIPLE CHOICE

In GCSE Economics, the main types of multiple choice question used are: **(a)** simple completion, **(b)** multiple completion, and **(c)** matched response.

Simple completion. The most common objective test item asks for the candidate to select **one** from several possible responses in order to correctly finish a statement. For example:

The most liquid of a commercial bank's assets is/are:
(a) advances to customers *(b)* commercial bills *(c)* Government bonds *(d)* money at call

The correct answer is *(d)*.

Multiple completion. Candidates select **one** or **more** statements which may 'correctly' answer a question. They then select a code letter for the 'correct' pattern of responses from a table of directions as illustrated below:

Directions Summarized				
A	B	C	D	E
1 only correct	1 and 2 only correct	3 and 4 only correct	2, 3 and 4 correct	1, 2, 3, 4 correct

For example:

Which of the following is/are most likely to cause cost push inflation?

> **1** An increase in supplementary benefit payments **2** An increase in VAT
> **3** A rise in wage rates **4** A rise in raw material prices

As 1 is inappropriate and 2, 3, 4 may cause cost push inflation then D is the answer.

Matched responses. This type of question requires a candidate to match the correct answer from a list against a question. Often, as below, a list of words is given and a candidate chooses the correct definition from another list. Some Boards require that the number of words given should exceed the number of definitions.

Match the following explanations about industrial location to the correct description below: Bulk increasing, enterprise zones, industrial inertia, bulk decreasing, intermediate areas.

A An industry which tends to locate near its raw materials _____
B The original reasons which established the industry in a place having disappeared _____
C An industry locating near its market _____
D Certain areas such as inner city areas chosen by the government for aid _____
E Areas that do not qualify for the full range of government assistance _____

As Multiple Choice questions give candidates a chance of guessing the correct alternative they have been criticized. However, it is argued that their use enables a wider coverage of the syllabus in an examination, particularly when a wide choice is allowed in essay sections.

In a five-option, multiple-choice question, a candidate with no idea has a 20 per cent chance of guessing correctly (i.e. 1 in 5 chance). A candidate's chances can be improved if he can discount one or more of the alternatives as definitely wrong. Thus, if a candidate can definitely eliminate two options as wrong, he can improve his chances to 33 per cent by guessing (i.e. he guesses between 1 in 3, with two options definitely wrong). The best chance is 50 per cent (i.e. 1 in 2) with three alternatives being excluded from the guess. Some examination boards have banned true/false questions because there is a 50 per cent chance of success.

In the multiple-completion type question, the elimination of 'wrong' alternatives is more crucial. For instance in the second example, the knowledge that 1 is not appropriate immediately eliminates answers A, B and E leaving a choice between C and D. Notice that if the candidate 'knows' that 2 applies he can select answer D, even though he may not 'know' that 3 and 4 statements answer the question. Thus, this type of question may reward intelligent deduction as well as understanding of Economics.

Data response

According to National Criteria 'all candidates are expected to be able to handle data relating to various aspects of economic life, including the use of statistical methods, the preparation and interpretation of tables, graphs and diagrams'.

The extracts of data, upon which questions are based, can be either narrative, statistical or diagrammatic.

Some teachers transform newspaper cuttings into exercises as practice for such extract questions. This is done also to make candidates more aware of up-to-date changes and new developments in economics.

My general **advice** to candidates would be

1 Read a quality newspaper and examine the illustrations, tables and articles on the financial pages.
2 Watch TV programmes related to the subject as they will familiarize you with the jargon and issues.
3 Carefully read the extract and try to relate it to the topic (topics) notes which you studied at school. Recall of your notes might give you some clues for answering the parts indirectly based on the extract.

NARRATIVE

This type of extract tests the economic literacy of the candidate. It is used as a peg upon which several questions are hung. The example below seeks certain knowledge, understanding and judgement about the Stock Exchange.

Spurs share issue. There was a big rush to buy shares in Tottenham Hotspur FC. The club issues 3.8 million new shares of £1 each. Sheppard and Chase, the club's stockbrokers, reported that the issue was $4\frac{1}{2}$ times over-subscribed. They now have the problem of allocating the 3.8 million shares amongst 12,859 people and institutions who applied to buy shares in the football club. It seems likely that all those who applied will receive the minimum subscription of 100 shares and that above this everyone will receive 15 per cent of the shares they applied for.

Experts think that the large number of applicants was not just made up of Spurs supporters, but that 'stags' who speculate in the new issue market were well represented among the applicants. The 'stags' will probably make a 'killing' because stockbrokers expect the £1 shares to kick-off at £1.20 each when dealing starts on the Stock Exchange next Thursday.

1 What type of business can sell shares through the Stock Exchange? (1)
2 How much money will the club raise through making the share issue? (1)
3 Suggest two reasons why Tottenham Hotspur might be making the share issue. (2)
4 What evidence is there to show that the club could have sold more shares? (2)
5 Name two 'institutions' which buy shares through the Stock Exchange and explain where they obtain their funds from. (4)
6 (a) What are 'stags'? (1)
  (b) Why might they be expected to make a 'killing' on Spurs shares in the following week? (3)
7 On what grounds do people often criticize the Stock Exchange? (6)

This type of question usually has an incline of difficulty. Marks are often given in brackets after each subsection of a question. The opening questions are relatively easy for single marks and the last question demands more thought and organization which is rewarded with more marks. However, a well-prepared student who has thoroughly revised has no need to fear such questions.

The marks given in parentheses after a subsection of the question provide useful advice to a candidate. For instance, the 6 marks for part 7 means give either 6 arguments briefly or 3 arguments (× 2 marks each) more thoroughly. The latter being most likely in this case.

STATISTICAL

Figures can be presented in various ways, i.e. pie charts, histograms, tables, lists, etc. They are given as data which needs interpreting. The interpretation is usually done in a structured way through several questions.

Useful tips when faced with statistical data are as follows.

1 Look at the **title** and **date** of the data. These often provide useful clues for discussion-type questions. For instance, a set of statistics showing the average total unadjusted unemployment 1980–4 (in thousands)

1980	1981	1982	1983	1984
1664	2520.3	2916.9	3104.7	3159.8

is rather limited in the time covered and perspective. It gives no detail regarding duration of unemployment, age structure, sex structure and total population size. Also the word 'unadjusted' in the title is significant, as it indicates that seasonal fluctuations have not been allowed for.
2 The **source** of the data may also be useful, particularly if a question requires

judgement. The recognition of a biased source, e.g. newspaper, pressure group, government statement may well be rewarded.

3 Examine the **trends** in the figures. If you are asked to comment on the data then consider, **(a)** the highest and lowest figures, **(b)** the first and the last piece of information, **(c)** changes in the data—if smooth or uneven, and **(d)** averages and departures from the average.

4 Consider the **absolute** and **relative** changes which have occurred. You must know the difference between absolute and relative change. For instance, the data showing Retail Prices (percentage increase on previous year)

1980	1981	1982	1983	1984
18.0	11.9	8.6	4.6	5.0

shows that the greatest fall in inflation in absolute figures was 1980–1 (6.1, i.e. 18.0–11.9) but relatively speaking inflation fell by the largest percentage in 1982–3 (46.5 per cent, i.e. $4.0 \div 8.6 \times 100$)

5 Notice the **unit of measurement**. Data can be in normal numbers or in index numbers. Thus in answering a question seeking the average increase in unemployment 1981–2 (from the data in **(1)** above), the correct answer is 396,000 (not 396.6) because the data was presented in thousands (see title).

6 When making **calculations**, show your working out, as credit may be given when there is a mathematical error if the correct principle is applied. This may happen with calculations of elasticity.

There is also **specific advice** about the method of approach which can be given with certain types of data.

Table of figures

1 Look **along rows** and **down columns**.
2 Look for **similar changes** among different variables.
3 Look at **first and last data** to discern the overall trend.

For instance, the data showing Asda's performance 1979–83

	1979	1980	1981	1982	1983
Sales £ billion	0.79	0.99	1.19	1.31	1.52
Pretax profit £ million	41.00	49.90	51.40	60.80	77.40
Margins (%)	5.18	5.00	4.32	4.65	5.09

shows that sales and profits have increased in a similar way but there is no clear relationship between (profit) margins and sales. However, it might be discerned that reductions in (profit) margins slow down profit increases (1979–81) and higher (profit) margins raise profits more quickly (1981–83).

Histograms (and pie charts)

1 Compare different blocks (or shares) for largest and smallest.
2 Check if they are divided up by percentages or absolute amounts.

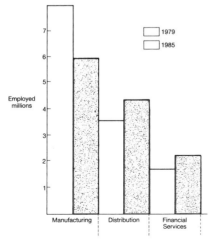

This data shows that manufacturing employment decreased by 2 million between 1979 and 1985 but the number of employees in distribution and financial services increased.

DIAGRAMMATIC

Diagrams are a distinctive feature of economics. Occasionally they are used in examination questions, as below:

The diagram indicates the original demand and supply curves (D and S) for a particular Commodity X, which is complementary to another Commodity Y.

1 What is a complementary good? Give two examples of pairs of complementary goods.   (4)

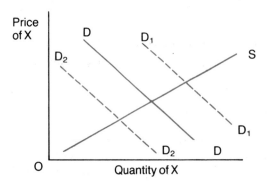

2 Assume there is an increase in the supply of good Y, other things being equal. Starting from the original demand and supply curves for Commodity X, which curve best illustrates the new situation? Explain your answer.   (6)

Part 1 of this question can be answered without the diagram. Part 2 gives a choice between D_1 (correct) and D_2. It requires understanding of the relationship between complementary goods, knowledge of certain economic assumptions, and application of a concept.

Some economic questions seek the construction of demand and supply diagrams from given data. For example:

The information below refers to the demand and supply schedules for potatoes:

Price (P)	Amount demanded (m tons/week)	Amount supplied (m tons/week)
15	30	62
14	35	60
13	41	57
12	45	53
11	49	49
10	53	45
9	57	41

1 On the graph paper provided, draw the demand and supply curves for potatoes.   (4)
2 What would be the equilibrium price?   (1)
3 What would be the effect of the government fixing a price of 10p per lb?   (2)
4 Assuming demand remains unchanged, what effects will a 2p per lb tax on supply have?   (3)

In this question part 1 requires accurate drawing and labelling of the demand and supply curves. They could be used to confirm the equilibrium price of 11p (part 2). On the diagram, the fixed price could be shown. This would make part 3 easier to visualize and describe. Similarly, the fall in supply caused by the tax could be illustrated on the diagram. It would show the increase in price and fall in quantity demanded vividly (part 4).

Generally, when displaying information, a diagram (or histogram or pie chart) should have a title and clearly labelled axes and curves (and blocks or shares). In addition, a diagram should be drawn neatly and plotted accurately, as should blocks and shares in histograms and pie charts. Different colours could be used for effect, if time permits.

ESSAYS

These are still popular and a widely used method of assessment in economics. The analysis of syllabuses and examinations shows that for GCSE over 40 per cent of the final marks are gained on essay questions. This is less than in the past. Also, increasingly the essays are subdivided and structured, so that the 'art' of essay-writing is now less important. However, the subdividing of questions has tended to increase the reliability of the marking, which is to the student's benefit.

The main tips which I would give you are:

1 **Only answer questions on topics which you have revised.** If you do not do much revision your choice, and therefore your chances, will be limited.

2 **Briefly plan your answer.** For instance, if a question seeks the advantages and disadvantages of large-scale production, and why small firms manage to survive, jot down the relevant mnemonics—**'MATEFIT'**, **'LICE'**, **'SWIRL'** and **'FIT'**.

3 **Include relevant points and facts.** It is no good writing down information which you have learned if it does not answer the question. I know that it is galling to spend time revising and not be able to use the knowledge to impress the examiner. However, you just have to accept that this happens. For example, in the question above, it is no good writing about the limitations on small-firm expansion because it is not needed. Examiners are looking for relevant information. They also seek some **balance**. If a question specifies advantages and disadvantages, then each should be treated fairly equally. Thus, by over-concentration on one part of a question, to the detriment of the rest, you will be limiting the number of marks which you will receive.

4 **Include examples and diagrams.** These should be used to illustrate and enhance your answer. Diagrams are particularly necessary in answering questions on Demand/Supply and markets. They should be clearly labelled along the axes and accurately drawn. Examiners are usually impressed by relevant and up-to-date examples. They should be learned beforehand. There are many given in this book.

5 **Do not use headings and noteform.** You should not use headings for sections, but you should write in continuous prose. You should not use numbers to distinguish points as it is bad style and looks like a remembered list. Furthermore, try not to use 'Firstly...' 'Secondly...' 'Thirdly...'. Instead, it is better to begin each paragraph differently such as—'Firstly...'; 'A second point...'; 'Another advantage...'; 'Finally...'.

6 **Do not write long sentences.** This is a very common fault with many students. In long sentences, separate points get amalgamated and credit is lost. Short sentences make the points better.

Questions

UNIT 1

The following article was published recently in a local newspaper. Study the article and answer the questions which follow.

The Future of the Health Service

In a debate at Gateley Town Hall last night, many people complained about the state of the National Health Service. Long waiting lists to see specialists and for operations were mentioned. The closure of hospital wards was criticized. 'More money must be spent on the health service if it is to operate efficiently' said Mr John Davies, himself a former nurse, who had left the profession because of low wages. Mrs Joan Pelling, a member of the government, insisted that more money than ever before was being spent on health. 'Of course we could spend more' she said, 'but where would the money come from? Do you want higher taxes? Or should we take the money from other social services, and leave them short? Let us seek improvements to the health service by improving efficiency'.

(a) Give *four* reasons why Mr Davies might believe that more money should be spent on the National Health Service. (4)

(b) The ideas of scarcity, choice and opportunity cost are central to the problem of allocating resources. Explain how these ideas are relevant to the provision of health services. (9)

(c) The article mentions long waiting lists for operations. It is often possible to reduce waiting time by paying for private operations.

Do you think health care is better provided privately or by the government through a National Health system? Give reasons for your answer. (10)

NEA Economics, Summer 1988

UNIT 2

Mr Gorbachov is said to have adopted a more liberal policy in the USSR. It is reported however that so far none of his proposals have changed things for the average person. Basic food and clothes are in short supply, exhausting hours are wasted each week in queues and the weekly wage is very low.

(a) The USSR is often referred to as a command economy. What does this mean? (4)

(b) What disadvantages are there to the consumer from living in a command economy? (5)

(c) How does a market economy differ from a command economy? (6)

(d) What disadvantages are there to the consumer from living in a market economy? (5)

MEG Economics, Summer 1988

UNIT 3

Levels of public ownership

Legend:
- ● More than 75 per cent
- ◕ 75 per cent
- ◐ 50 per cent
- ◔ 25 per cent
- ○ Less than 25 per cent

Country	Posts	Telecoms	Electricity	Gas	Oil Production	Coal	Railways	Airlines	Motor industry	Steel	Shipbuilding	Country
Austria	●	●	●	●	●	●	●	●	●	●	NA	Austria
France	●	●	●	●	NA	●	●	◕	◐	◕	○	France
W. Germany	●	●	◕	◐	◔	◐	●	●	◔	○	◔	W. Germany
Netherlands	●	●	◕	◕	NA	NA	●	◕	◐	◔	○	Netherlands
Italy	●	●	◕	●	NA	NA	●	●	◔	◕	◕	Italy
Japan	●	◐	○	○	NA	○	◕	◔	○	○	○	Japan
Spain	●	◐	○	◕	NA	◐	●	●	○	◐	◕	Spain
Sweden	●	●	◐	●	NA	NA	●	◐	○	◕	◕	Sweden
UK	●	○	●	○	○	●	●	◕	◐	◕	●	UK
US	●	○	◔	○	○	○	◔	○	○	○	○	US

Source: *AMEX Bank Review*

From *The Financial Times*, 1986

Study the information given above and answer the following questions.

(a) Explain the term 'public ownership'. (2)

(b) (i) In which country is the level of public ownership lowest?
(ii) How are resources likely to be allocated in this country? (2)

(c) (i) What percentage of the motor industry in the UK is under public ownership?
(ii) How is the rest of the industry owned? (2)

(d) Give *two* reasons why some industries are under public ownership in almost all countries. (2)

(e) Give *four* possible economic reasons for the changes in the level of public ownership in the UK during the 1980s. (6)

NISEC Economics, Summer 1988

UNIT 4

In a local market the demand for ready picked strawberries on one day was as follows.

Price (pence)	Quantity demanded (punnets)
35	800
40	700
45	600
50	500
55	400
60	300

(a) (i) On the diagram below, draw and label the demand curve for strawberries on that day.
(2)

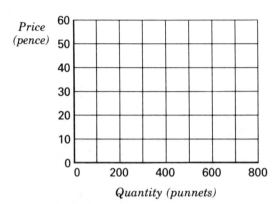

(ii) The supply of strawberries on that day was fixed at 500 punnets. What, in theory, was the equilibrium market price? (1)

(iii) In theory, what effects would a fall in supply to 400 punnets per day have on the local market? (4)

(iv) What factors might affect the supply of strawberries onto the local market? (4)

(b) On 20th July a farm in the area had the following strawberry sales:

Self picked: 600 punnets at 30 pence per punnet
Ready picked: 50 punnets at 60 pence per punnet

(i) Calculate the farm's total revenue on 20th July. Show your working. (2)

(ii) Suggest *two* reasons why more self picked strawberries than ready picked were bought. (2)

(c) Strawberries are sold at the Wimbledon tennis tournament in late June for £2.00 per punnet. Self picked strawberries can be bought in late July for 30 pence per punnet. What economic reasons do you think explain these price differences? (6)

NEA Economics, Summer 1988

UNIT 5

Refer to the graph opposite, then answer the following questions.

(a) (i) What is the total cost of production at an output level of 20,000? (1)

(ii) Calculate the average cost per computer at the same level of output. (1)

(b) (i) What are total variable costs at an output level of 65,000? (1)

(ii) Give *two* examples of variable costs which any firm making home computers would have to meet. (2)

(c) (i) Explain the term 'profit'. (1)

(ii) What profit does the firm make at an output level of 50,000? (1)

(d) Explain why total fixed costs are shown as a horizontal line on the graph. (2)

(e) (i) What is meant by 'economies of scale'? (2)

(ii) How might a firm such as Quasar Systems achieve economies of scale? (3)

(f) Discuss the likely future effects of a £2 million investment in automated machinery by Quasar Systems upon:

(i) its costs of production; (3)

(ii) its employees. (3)

SEB Economics, Summer 1988

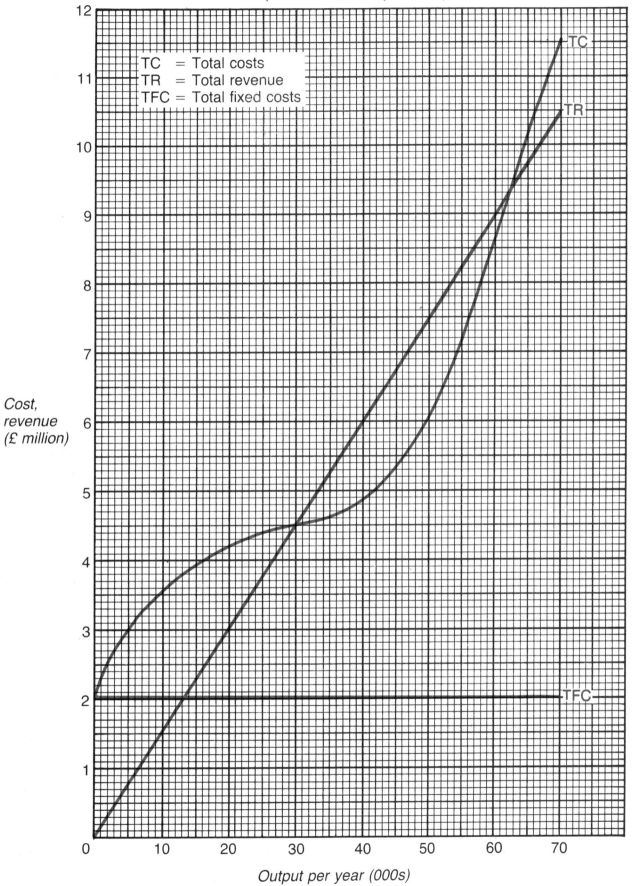

Costs of production and revenue from sales of home
computers manufactured by Quasar Systems

TC = Total costs
TR = Total revenue
TFC = Total fixed costs

Cost, revenue (£ million)

Output per year (000s)

UNIT 6

Study the map and information below and answer the questions which follow.

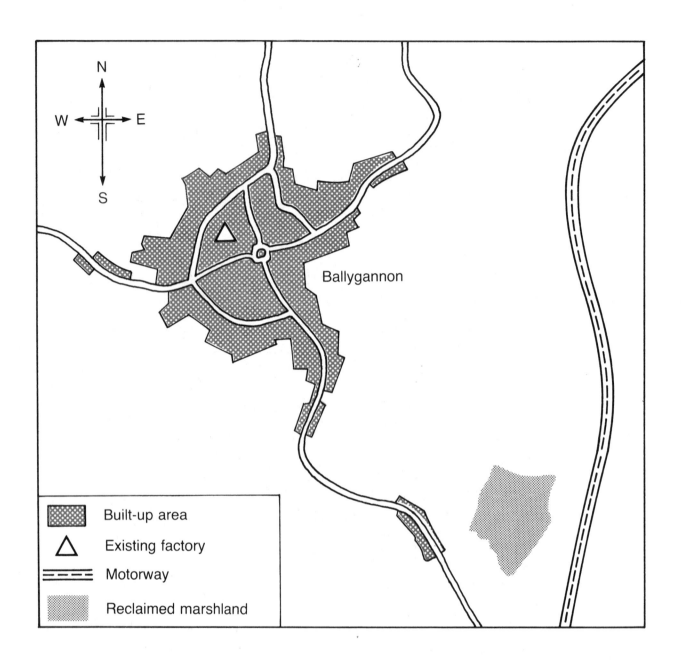

Ballygannon is a town of 150,000 with a flourishing central business centre. To the south-east of the town, about 20 miles away, is an area of relatively cheap reclaimed marshland. A sausage making factory using locally produced and imported meat has been operating near the town centre of Ballygannon for about a hundred years. The factory sells a quality product to an increasingly expanding market in this part of Northern Ireland. To profit from the increasing demand it needs to double its present weekly output of 45,000 kilos of sausages.

(a) Give *two* possible problems which the firm could be faced with in increasing the size of its existing factory.   (2)

(b) Give *two* benefits the firm might gain if they concentrated all the production at a new location in the south-east.   (4)

(c) Suggest *three* reasons why the firm might find the proposed new factory site unsuitable.   (3)

(d) Give *two* reasons why workers are sometimes unwilling to move with their firm to a new location.   (2)

NISEC Economics, Summer 1988

UNIT 7

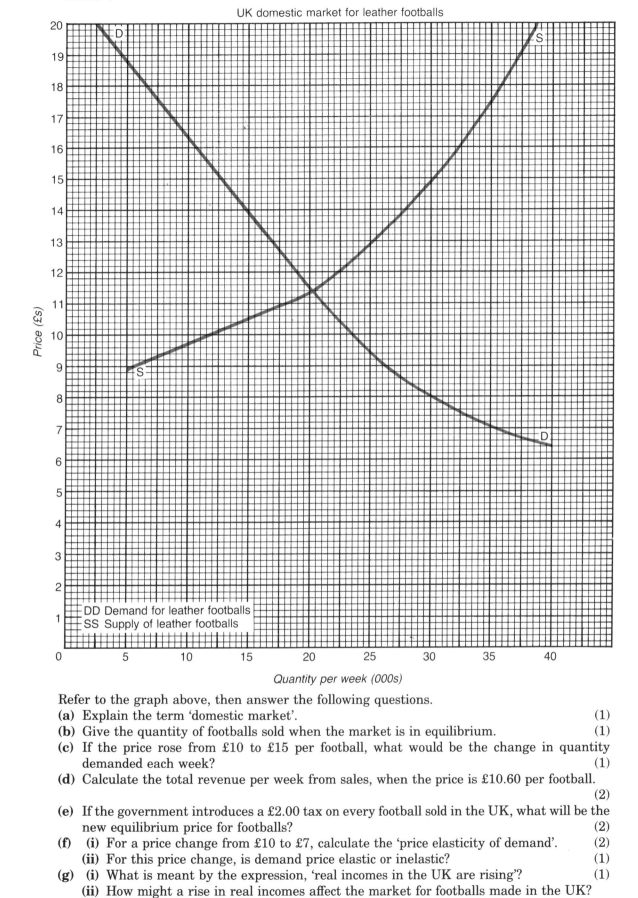

UK domestic market for leather footballs

Price (£s) — vertical axis

Quantity per week (000s) — horizontal axis

DD Demand for leather footballs
SS Supply of leather footballs

Refer to the graph above, then answer the following questions.
(a) Explain the term 'domestic market'. (1)
(b) Give the quantity of footballs sold when the market is in equilibrium. (1)
(c) If the price rose from £10 to £15 per football, what would be the change in quantity demanded each week? (1)
(d) Calculate the total revenue per week from sales, when the price is £10.60 per football. (2)
(e) If the government introduces a £2.00 tax on every football sold in the UK, what will be the new equilibrium price for footballs? (2)
(f) **(i)** For a price change from £10 to £7, calculate the 'price elasticity of demand'. (2)
    (ii) For this price change, is demand price elastic or inelastic? (1)
(g) **(i)** What is meant by the expression, 'real incomes in the UK are rising'? (1)
    (ii) How might a rise in real incomes affect the market for footballs made in the UK? (3)
(h) What are the likely economic effects on the UK football manufacturing industry of:
    (i) a merger of important firms making footballs in the UK; (3)
    (ii) an increase in the number of working days lost through strikes in this industry? (3)

SEB Economics, Summer 1988

UNIT 8

In the following statements, five methods of payments are mentioned.

    A Most supermarkets will not accept payment by credit card but will accept cheques.

    B Many high street stores will accept credit cards but some only accept their own store's charge card.

    C Many telephone boxes only accept phonecards and not cash.

(a) Only cash would normally be included in the money supply. Explain why each of the other methods of payment would not be regarded as money. (4)

(b) Explain the reasons behind *two* of the above statements: A, B and C. (8)

(c) **(i)** Why is cash becoming a less important part of the money supply today? (4)

     (ii) Explain *two* economic effects of the rise in the use of credit. (4)

SEG Economics, Summer 1988

UNIT 9

The diagrams below show the proportion of income spent on various items used in the government's Index of Retail Prices for the UK.

    The General Index (diagram A) sets out to measure changes in the prices of the goods and services we buy, using a 'basket' of the items, such as clothing, which are bought by an average income family. The government also measures changes in the cost of living for various groups such as pensioners, as shown in diagram B.

    The numbers on the diagrams represent the 'weights' given to each item.

Retail Price Index (excluding housing)

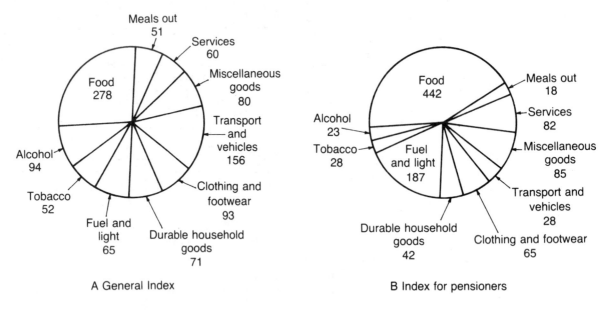

A General Index   B Index for pensioners

(a) What is meant by 'the cost of living'? (3)

(b) Name the *two* items which account for the highest proportion of expenditure by:

    (i) people in general; (2)

    (ii) pensioners. (2)

(c) **(i)** Give *one* reason why the proportion spent on services is higher for pensioners than for the community as a whole. (2)

    (ii) Give *one* reason to explain the difference in the proportion spent on transport and vehicles between pensioners and people in general. (2)

(d) Describe *one* of the difficulties in constructing a representative price index for all consumers. (3)

(e) For what purpose might the government use the Retail Price Index for pensioners? (3)

LEAG Economics, Summer 1988

UNIT 10

Consider the following information about accounts with banks and building societies in October 1986.

	Interest rate (%)	Days notice for withdrawal	Minimum amount (£)
Banks			
Current account	0	0	0
Deposit account	5.0	7	1
High interest cheque account	7.0	0	2500
Building Societies			
Share account	5.5	0	1
Instant access	7.5	0	500
90 day	8.5	90	500

(a)   **(i)** Which account offers the greatest return on savings?   (1)

     (ii) Which account requires most notice before savings are withdrawn?   (1)

     (iii) Which account requires the largest minimum amount to be deposited when the account is opened?   (3)

(b) Why do banks and building societies pay interest to savers?   (2)

(c) Why do the rates of interest differ between the various accounts?   (3)

(d) Both banks and building societies accept deposits and make loans. Explain *two* ways, other than interest rates, in which banks and building societies compete with each other.   (4)

(e) Is competition between banks and building societies good for:

     (i) ordinary households;   (3)

     (ii) the economy as a whole?   (3)

     Explain your answers.

NEA Economics, Summer 1988

UNIT 11

(a) From the advertisements for jobs shown give *one* example of each job which is paid by the
 hour, by the week, and annually. (3)
(b) Explain which of the jobs shown would have the greatest appeal to:
 (i) a young single person; (3)
 (ii) a person with three children and a mortgage. (3)
(c) (i) Give *two* examples of non-monetary (fringe) benefits from the advertisements. (2)
 (ii) Why do firms offer non-monetary benefits? (3)
(d) Many people use part of their income for savings. Why do people save rather than spend?
 (6)

                   MEG Economics, Summer 1988

UNIT 12

Study the population pyramids given below which show the age structure of the population of
two countries, A and B, in 1981, and then answer the questions that follow.

Age structure of population, 1981

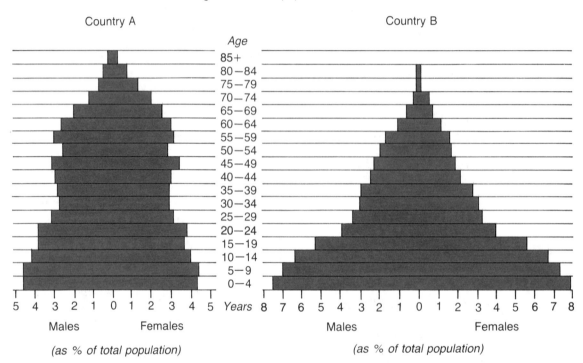

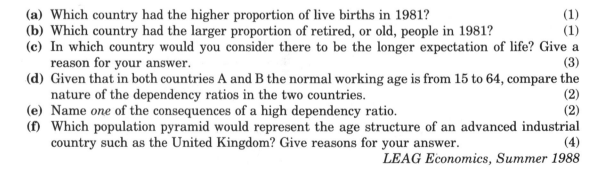

(a) Which country had the higher proportion of live births in 1981? (1)
(b) Which country had the larger proportion of retired, or old, people in 1981? (1)
(c) In which country would you consider there to be the longer expectation of life? Give a
 reason for your answer. (3)
(d) Given that in both countries A and B the normal working age is from 15 to 64, compare the
 nature of the dependency ratios in the two countries. (2)
(e) Name *one* of the consequences of a high dependency ratio. (2)
(f) Which population pyramid would represent the age structure of an advanced industrial
 country such as the United Kingdom? Give reasons for your answer. (4)

                   LEAG Economics, Summer 1988

UNIT 13

Below is a table which sets out unemployment and trade union membership between 1980 and 1985.

	Unemployment (million)	*Trade union membership (million)*
1980	1.6	12.9
1981	2.4	12.1
1982	2.8	11.6
1983	3.0	11.3
1984	3.0	11.1
1985	3.2	10.7

Source: *Annual Abstract of Statistics*

(a) **(i)** Explain the link between trade union membership and unemployment. (2)

(ii) Give *one* other reason for falling trade union membership. (2)

(b) If you were a trade union official, explain how you might respond to decisions by your firm to introduce:

(i) new labour-saving machinery; (4)

(ii) more flexible working practices such as those operating in Japanese owned companies. (4)

Give reasons for your response in each case.

(c) Explain the arguments for and against a young worker joining a trade union. (8)

SEG Economics, Summer 1988

UNIT 14

In 1980 the United Kingdom's national income was about £200 000m. By 1985 it was about £300 000m.

(a) **(i)** Do these figures mean that everybody in the United Kingdom was better off in 1985 than they were in 1980? (1)

(ii) Explain the reasons for your answer to part **(a) (i)**. (3)

(b) If a country's production of goods and services increases from one year to another, economic growth is achieved. What are the advantages of economic growth? (8)

(c) The smoke from coal-fired power stations causes air pollution in the form of acid rain.

(i) What costs are created by air pollution and who bears these costs? (4)

(ii) What can governments do to reduce the amount of air pollution? (4)

SEG Economics, Summer 1988

UNIT 15

(a) What is meant by 'the Budget'? (3)

(b) Describe *three* main items of central government expenditure. (6)

(c) For what economic reasons may the central government wish to change the rates of:

(i) income tax; (3)

(ii) indirect taxation? (3)

(d) What is a 'deficit budget', and why do governments sometimes plan for such deficits? (5)

SEB Economics, Summer 1988

UNIT 16

The diagram below shows unemployment rates in the 11 regions of the United Kingdom, and in the United Kingdom as a whole, over the years 1982 to 1987.

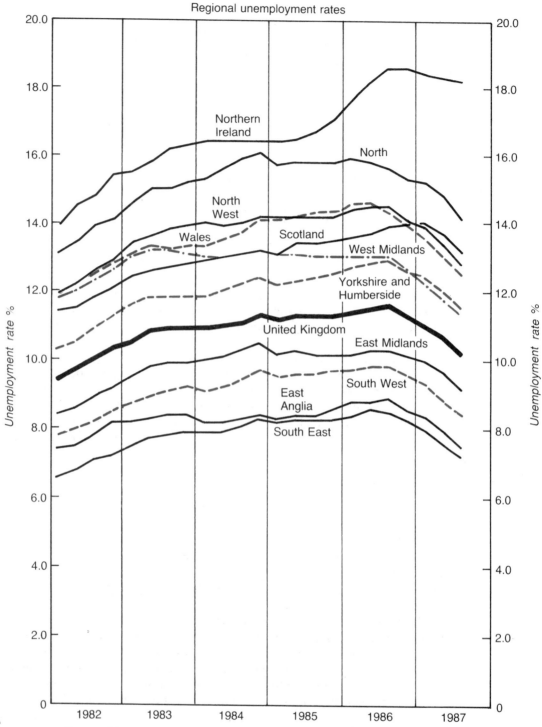

Regional unemployment rates

Source: *Economic Trends No. 410*, Central Statistical Office, December 1987

(a) From the data above:
  (i)   which region had the highest percentage rate of unemployment in 1985? (1)
  (ii) which region had the lowest percentage rate of unemployment in 1985? (1)
  (iii) what was the percentage rate of unemployment in the United Kingdom as a whole at the end of 1986? Give your answer to the nearest whole number. (1)
(b) Use the data shown in the diagram above to compare unemployment in different regions between 1982 and 1987. (6)
(c) Why do some regions have higher rates of unemployment than others? (8)
(d) What policies do you think the government should follow to reduce the differences in regional unemployment rates? Explain your answer. (8)

NEA Economics, Summer 1988

UNIT 17

Study the cartoon and photograph below.

(a) Name *two* of the advantages of international trade illustrated below. (2)

(b) Explain why the purchase of Japanese radios and hi-fi equipment in Britain may cause redundancies here. (4)

(c) Describe *two* methods by which a government can make it more difficult for foreign firms to sell their goods in this country. (4)

(d) Explain how, if labour can switch easily from one type of job or industry to another, trade with other countries can help to create jobs in Britain. (6)

LEAG Economics, Summer 1988

Source: *Illustrated Economics*, P. Donaldson, BBC, 1975

Source: *The Independent*, 24 December 1986

UNIT 18

Read the passage below and then answer the questions which follow.

Interest rates explained

Many people ask why the mortgage rate has to change and why interest rates go up, with rather more ups than downs in recent years.

'Interest' is the price of money borrowed and money must be considered a commodity like anything else. When it is in demand or in short supply, the price goes up. And vice versa.

So what affects supply and demand and why should the ordinary British householder have to suffer? Well, these days money itself is far more international and influenced by what's happening in the world. For example:

1 Excess rainfall in Florida ruins the orange crop.
2 Growers descend on their banks for loans to sustain them until next season.
3 Demand forces up Florida interest rates to borrowers. Interest rates to investors follow suit.
4 Across the USA, interest rates rise to prevent funds being moved to Florida banks.
5 Investors, seeing higher interest rates available in the USA, start moving their short term investment funds from London to New York.
6 The value of sterling falls on the foreign exchange markets.
7 The Bank of England steps in to increase basic interest rates, to stop the movement of funds away from sterling.
8 British investors prepare to move savings from places like building societies to other financial institutions offering higher rates.
9 To retain these investors' funds, building societies have to increase the interest rates they pay.
10 To retain the societies safety 'margin', your mortgage rate has to go up.

Source: *Walton and Weybridge Informer*, 19 February 1987

(a) What is a mortgage? (2)
(b) Illustrate on a diagram, labelling one axis *interest rates* and the other *quantity demanded and supplied*, how interest rates would change due to 'excess rainfall in Florida'. (4)
(c) Explain why investors would 'move' some of their money to New York. (3)
(d) Explain exactly why the value of sterling falls on the foreign exchange market. (4)
(e) How would the Bank of England's action stop the fall in the value of sterling? (3)

LEAG Economics, Summer 1988

UNIT 19

Much local government revenue is raised from the rates. There are proposals for rates to be replaced by a community charge or poll tax. This is where each person over 18 will have to pay a fixed amount (say £200) in tax to the local authority each year.

(a) (i) Which groups of people pay rates? (2)
    (ii) How is the amount each rate payer pays calculated? (2)
(b) Explain fully the disadvantages of the rating system. (8)
(c) How would a change from rates to a community tax or poll tax affect:
    (i) working parents, with three grown-up children earning wages, living in the same house; (4)
    (ii) people on high incomes? (4)

SEG Economics, Summer 1988

UNIT 20

The fastest selling item in any supermarket in the UK is said to be Whiskas cat food. Thousands of pounds are spent each year on advertising this product.

**Whiskas supermeat.
In tests, 8 out of 10 owners
who expressed a preference
said their cats preferred it.**

(a) What effect does advertising Whiskas pet food have on:
   (i) the magazine publisher?   (3)
   (ii) the makers of a rival cat food?   (3)
   (iii) the management of a supermarket?   (3)
(b) The above advertisement appeared in a national magazine. State *two* other methods of advertising a product like Whiskas.   (2)
(c) Where does the money come from to pay for these advertisements?   (3)
(d) (i) How does a buyer, for example of cat food, benefit from advertising?   (3)
   (ii) How does a seller, for example of cat food, benefit from advertising?   (3)

MEG Economics, Summer 1988

▆▆▆ Answers ▆▆▆

There now follow suggested answers to the GCSE questions. Note that the answers are those of the author, and that the Examination Groups accept no responsibility for the accuracy or method of working. Each answer also contains hints and guidelines to show how the question should be approached and the line of thinking required for a full answer. These are printed in **bold** type.

UNIT 1

(a) **Comprehension** of the text gives: long waiting lists to see specialists; long waiting lists for operations; closure of wards; low wages.
(b) You need to apply your **understanding** of the three basic economic ideas: scarcity of resources; government income is needed for many services; health care is an increasingly more expensive sector. Resources are limited but health wants are expanding.

   A choice has to be made by the Chancellor of the Exchequer whether to allocate extra to the NHS or to other government spending e.g defence, because of scarce resources.

   The opportunity cost of any decision is the alternative foregone. For instance, if more is spent on the NHS then less may have to be spent on something else, assuming a finite budget.
(c) The **arguments** for/against the private provision of services (capitalism and privatization) should be applied here. This question requires knowledge of sections 2.2 and 3.1.

UNIT 2

(a) See 2.3 and **recall knowledge** learned.
(b) The introduction to the question gives some clues and then you should remember 2.3.
(c) See 2.2 and **recall knowledge** learned.
(d) See 2.2 and **recall knowledge** learned.

UNIT 3

(a) **Understanding of term** is needed. It means that the assets of an industry or firm are owned by the country as a whole, rather than by a private organization.
(b) **Interpretation of data** gives:
 (i) The United States.
 (ii) By the individual owners in the pursuit of profit.
(c) **Interpretation of data** gives:
 (i) 50 per cent.
 (ii) Privately.
(d) **Recall of knowledge** or **application of ideas**. Possible reasons are outlined in 3.2.
(e) This requires **judgement** and some **knowledge**. The four reasons might be: Conservative Government committed to privatization; government need for revenue through asset sales; Conservative's desire to widen share ownership; to encourage competition in areas where there is currently a monopoly.

UNIT 4

(a) (i)

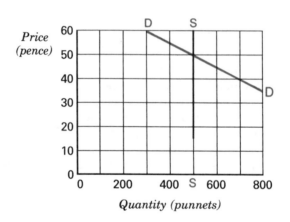

 (ii) 50p if diagram accurately **interpretated**.
 (iii) **Correct application** of demand/supply understanding: a shortage would be created so quantity demanded would fall from 500 to 400 and the price would rise from 50p to 55p. This would create a fall in total revenue (£250 to £220).
 (iv) **Recall of knowledge** and its **application** to strawberries gives: a change in the conditions of supply would affect supply onto the market; bad weather, such as a very wet summer, would lower supply; higher wages for strawberry pickers would raise costs and thus lower supply; a technological advance in strawberry production might raise supply; as would a government subsidy.
(b) (i) **Correct calculations**: £180+£30=£210.
 (ii) **Interpretation** and **application**: cheaper and self-selection could lead to better quality being chosen.
(c) **Application** of basic economic D/S theory: At Wimbledon, there is high demand and a restricted supply, thus causing a high price. Conversely in late July there is a large supply and (possibly) lower demand (as people get fed up of eating them). Diagrams could be drawn to illustrate this. In addition, during Wimbledon the suppliers could make monopoly profits thereby pushing up prices.
 There are also the labour and transport and sales costs of supply at Wimbledon. On the other hand with self-picked strawberries you are not paying these costs directly.
 The idea of price elasticity could also be used to explain the position at Wimbledon.

UNIT 5

(a) Accurate interpretation of diagram gives:
(i) £4.2 million.　　**(ii)** £210 (4.2m ÷ 20,000).
(b) (i) £8m (10−2).
　　(ii) Wages, parts (**recall** of notes, see 5.5).
(c) (i) This question requires **recall of knowledge** and seems to assume that profit is revenue less costs. It does not distinguish between normal and abnormal profit. It is thus the return to the producer for risk taking in the production of Quasar Systems (see 5.5).
　　(ii) £1.5m (7.5-6).
(d) Understanding of idea: total fixed costs are a horizontal line because they are paid whether the firm makes thousands of home computers or none. They do not change with production levels (see 5.5).
(e) (i) This is just **recall of knowledge**: economies of scale are the benefits to a firm of large scale production (see 5.6).
　　(ii) Application of information in 5.6 to the computer industry.
(f) This question requires some simple **judgements** based on your understanding of business growth (5.7).
　　(i) Points to make: lower costs as technical economies of scale and greater efficiency but rate of interest changes could have a detrimental effect.
　　(ii) Points to make: possibly fewer employees needed as capital substituted for labour, although more may be required to build/service the investment. The result might be greater profit and thus higher wages for the existing workforce.

UNIT 6

(a) Application of knowledge regarding location factors: the cost and availability of land (see 6.2).
(b) Application of ideas/selection of relevant information from data: cheaper land; closer to motorway so cut transport costs; new factory could allow re-organization in the firm (see 6.2).
(c) Interpretation of (map) data and **application of ideas**: no direct link to motorway; away from built-up area which makes selling finished product more expensive; loss of experienced workers who do not move.
(d) Application of knowledge on mobility of labour (see 12.4): cost of travel to work; extra time in getting to work; family reasons; no car/no available public transport.

UNIT 7

(a) Understanding of term gives: home sales.
(b) Interpretation of data and **application of concept** gives: 20,000.
(c) Interpretation of data and **application of concept** = 11,000 (12,500 − 23,500).
(d) Interpretation of data and **application of concept** = £233,200 (22,000 × £10.60).
(e) Interpretation of data and **application of concept** = £12.80 (new supply curve).
(f) (i) Application of concept gives: 10 ÷ 6 approx. [i.e. (11,500 ÷ 23,500) ÷ (3 ÷ 10)].
　　(ii) Interpretation of own calculation: elastic.
(g) (i) Understanding of term: allowing for inflation, people are receiving more and thus better off.
　　(ii) Application of knowledge to problem: an increase in real incomes for most goods leads to an increase in demand. Thus price is likely to rise and supply expand.
(h) (i) Application of knowledge: mergers tend to reduce competition and create oligopolies (or a monopoly). This would give the suppliers more control. They might reduce the range of footballs produced and raise prices. However, if the existing remaining firms compete then there might be non-price competition, rather than lower prices (see 7.5).
　　(ii) Application of concepts: this could cause a reduction in supply and thus higher prices, because of the shortage. In the longer term these strikes might cause less efficient production (through reduced skill and poorer industrial relations (see 13.7).

UNIT 8

(a) Recall/application of concepts: cheques, credit cards, charge cards and telephone cards are not 'a store of value' which is usually considered to be a characteristic of money. However, they are all means of exchange which is the other main characteristic of 'what is money' (see 8.3 and 8.6).

(b) Application of ideas and **reasoning** is required for each statement. For instance Statement A could be explained as follows: some supermarkets will not accept credit and payment because the credit card company charge commission to the retailer. This is an extra cost to the supermarket. On the other hand, cheques do not have such a charge. There is an extra administrative cost with credit cards because if spending exceeds a certain limit then the supermarket has to ring the credit card company to check on buyer's credit-worthiness.

(c) (i) Recall of knowledge and **application** gives: the development of alternatives (see 8.5 and 8.6).

(ii) Application of concepts and **reasoned judgement**: the increased use of credit has caused possibly higher inflation via demand pull inflation (or quantity theory of money). It has also led to improved living standards as people have been able to purchase consumer durables on credit. It may have contributed to increased imports, which have been bought on credit, too.

UNIT 9

(a) Recall of knowledge/concept: 'the cost of living' is the amount of money which has to be paid out to obtain necessary goods and services. If the price of goods and services increase, then the 'cost of living' has risen (see 9.2).

(b) Interpretation of data gives:
  (i) Food, transport and vehicles.
  (ii) Food, fuel and light.

(c) Reasoned judgement gives:
  (i) They are more dependent on help from others and work being done for them because of age and infirmity e.g. home care assistants.
(ii) Pensioners on average have lower incomes (and probably less desire to travel) and so fewer can afford to run cars.

(d) Recall of knowledge: weights, basket of goods etc. (see 9.4 and 9.5).

(e) Recall of knowledge: pensions are index linked (see 9.4).

UNIT 10

(a) Interpretation of data gives:
  (i) 90 day building society.
  (ii) 90 day building society.
  (iii) High interest cheque account.

(b) Reasoned explanation/understanding:interest encourages savings which banks can use in order to make profits.

(c) Understanding of data and **reasoned explanation**: the accounts requiring a larger minimum amount pay higher interest, also building society with most days notice pays highest interest.

(d) Recall/understanding: banks compete over the range of services offered (e.g. free gifts with suitable examples); opening hours also differ and can influence customers.

(e) Reasoned arguments/judgement/application of concepts: *yes* or *no* answers could be given but each line of argument must have clear reasoning.

  (i) A choice of services and interest rates is available. Thus households could 'shop around' to get the highest interest rates for deposits and to secure the lowest interest rate on borrowing. The competition might lead to the development of new services and improved quality in those services.

  (ii) Competition could lead to more efficiency and perhaps invisible trade benefits. Help to business, via loans, could stimulate investment, employment and economic growth. As a place for savings, banks and building societies act as a channel for investment.

  A *no* answer might concentrate on duplication of resources, wasteful advertising, increased money supply leading to inflation.

UNIT 11

(a) Interpretation of data.
(b) (i), (ii) Interpretation of data and simple **judgement**.
(c) (i) Understanding of term 'fringe benefit' and **application** of the idea to the data.
  (ii) Recall of knowledge (see 13.4).
(d) Recall of knowledge (see 11.5).

UNIT 12

(a) Interpretation of data: it looks like B, but the data does not show live births (strictly speaking).

(b) Interpretation of data gives: A.

(c) Interpretation of data and **reasoned explanation** gives: A. Possible reasons might be more people over 85; many more over 45 both male and female.

(d) Understanding of term and **application** of it to the data: in country A the dependency ratio will be lower as there will be fewer children but more workers; whereas in country B the dependency ratio will be higher because of the many people beneath working age.

(e) Recall and **application of knowledge**: much public spending and higher taxes to raise the revenue; a large percentage of non-workers in the economy.

(f) Interpretation of data gives: A. Possible reasons might be that advanced industrial countries have higher living standards; smaller population growth; longer life expectations. The latter two are shown by the age structure whilst the former is the probable consequence of a lower dependancy ratio.

UNIT 13

(a) (i) Interpretation of data (or recall): as unemployment increases so there are fewer members of trade unions.

  (ii) Recall of knowledge or **reasoned judgement**: another possible reason might be changes in trade union law which discouraged membership. Other reasons could be the increased employment of part-timers and women, both of whom are generally less likely to be unionized.

(b) (i) Reasoned judgement: firstly you need to recognize the direct effects on employment and secondly the longer term possible benefits through higher pay and perhaps increased production.

(ii) Reasoned judgement: in answering you need to show awareness of the elimination of demarcation disputes; single union deals; reduced trade union influence.

(c) Recall of knowledge and **application**: the functions, advantages and disadvantages are needed here (see 13.7).

UNIT 14

(a) (i) Interpretation of data gives: no!

(ii) Reasoned judgement (or application of knowledge): factors to explain include inflation; population size; distribution of income (see 14.3).

(b) Recall of knowledge (see 14.4).

(c) (i) Recall of knowledge, concepts and **application**: these costs are termed 'social costs'. They are borne by society as a whole – it may be directly through reduced amenities as the countryside is ruined and the atmosphere is less healthy. Also, society may bear the costs indirectly in the form of higher taxes needed to employ people to catch the polluters and make good the damage caused.

  (ii) Application of knowledge (see 19.3).

UNIT 15

(a) Recall of knowledge (see 15.6).

(b) Recall of knowledge (see 15.1).

(c) (i), (ii) Application of knowledge/reasoned judgement: the economic reasons may be general or specific. The general reasons relate to the objectives of economic policy (see 19.1) e.g. unemployment might be reduced by cutting income tax, which enables more consumption and thus raises demand for goods and services. Alternatively, specific reasons might be given (see 15.4) e.g. lower income tax is argued to give greater incentives to work and so increases economic growth to some extent.

(d) Recall of knowledge and **reasoned judgement** (see 15.6).

UNIT 16

(a) Interpretation of data gives:
  (i) Northern Ireland.
  (ii) South East.
  (iii) 11 per cent.

(b) Interpretation of data: most regions are in the same position relative to other regions in

1987, compared to 1982, except Wales, Scotland and West Midlands. Wales did worse than North West in 1985 and 1986 but then declined whilst Scotland's position declined in 1987 so that they suffered the third highest percentage. The West Midlands moved from a position which was worse than Scotland's unemployment 1982–84 but better after 1985. The regions doing better than the national average in 1982 remained so in 1987.

(c) Recall of knowledge (or application) and **reasoned judgement**: (see 16.2 and 16.5).

(d) Recall/application and/or **reasoned judgement** (see 16.7).

UNIT 17

(a) Interpretation of data gives: cheaper and choice.

(b) Reasoned judgement: if people buy foreign imports rather than British goods then demand for British goods will fall; this will mean that there is less need for workers and so they may be made redundant.

(c) Recall of knowledge (see 17.5).

(d) Reasoned judgement: if labour is mobile between occupations and industries, then there will not be labour shortages. Overseas trade will create demand for British goods. Thus, British firms will need to take on workers in order to produce the goods which are exported overseas. The increased sales may have a multiplier effect which further raises employment opportunities.

UNIT 18

(a) Recall of knowledge (see 11.3).

(b) Understanding and **application of knowledge** gives:

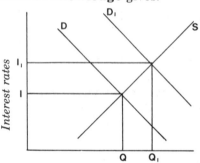

Quantity demanded and supplied

(c) Reasoned argument: the higher interest rates in New York attract investors' funds. These New York rates are higher than those in London and so investors can secure a greater return on their investments.

(d) Reasoned argument: the supply of sterling increases as sterling is sold when people buy dollars instead. This causes the price of sterling to fall.

(e) Reasoned argument: by raising interest rates, the Bank of England makes sterling and halts its fall in value, causing a rise in sterling's value.

UNIT 19

(a) (i), (ii) Recall of knowledge (see 19.5).

(b) Recall of knowledge (see 19.5).

(c) Reasoned argument and **application of knowledge** gives:

(i) We cannot say definitely if the parents lose or gain as it all depends on their previous rates bill. If they paid low rates, or rates were included in their rent, they might lose. However, it is more likely that they would gain, particularly if they were owner/occupiers. However, their children would definitely lose, as they previously did not pay rates but now pay the poll tax.

(ii) This is rather more clear cut, assuming that the people on high incomes are owner/occupiers. Their poll tax bill is likely to be lower than their rates bill, if they lived in a large house. However, rates bills do vary a lot around Britain, even for similar sized properties.

UNIT 20

(a) (i), (ii), (iii) Reasoned argument: some ideas can be found in 20.5 and 20.6.

(b) Recall of knowledge (see 20.5).

(c) Application of knowledge (see 20.5).

(d) (i), (ii) Recall of knowledge (see 20.5).

23 COURSEWORK

INTRODUCTION

As part of your GCSE you will be expected to produce some pieces of coursework. Some of these will count towards your GCSE grade. During the course you will practise coursework skills. Once you have mastered these skills you will produce coursework. Much of this work will be done in class, although you will probably have to get some information from parents, writing off to people, interviews, and possibly work experience.

Your teacher will guide you on how to get information and the general outline of your work. Do not be frightened to ask for help. Teachers cannot do the coursework for you, but they can tell you how to get access to information.

SKILLS

In your coursework you must learn three basic skills.

1 How to gather information

You must learn to collect relevant information and to understand why and how you are collecting it. You will find it easier if you set yourself a problem and gather information to answer a question. The information needs to be relevant to economics and to the question you are trying to answer.

Sources of information include questionnaires, newspaper and magazine articles, reference books, letters from people or firms, visits and interviews, surveys and electronic databases, e.g. Prestel, Ceefax.

2 Analysing information

Having collected information you must then try and use it so that you can make sense of it. In doing this, you must use terms used in economics. You must show a clear understanding of the material you have gathered and how it is relevant.

The following is not an exhaustive list, but illustrates the ideas that you might explore in relation to their study:

    scarcity, choice and opportunity cost
    interdependence
    demand and supply
    private v. public sector
    private costs and benefits
    social costs and benefits
    conflict of economic interests and views
    trends and sequences/changes in the economy
    political factors.

3 Evaluation

Having collected your information and set it out in an understandable way, you must now develop arguments from it. You could then make some recommendations to deal with a problem. Alternatively, if the assignment is posed as a question, then you will have to make judgements such as:

    who should pay?
    who is to blame?
    what should be done?
    how could it change?
    who has gained/lost?

IDEAS

Choosing your own title

You could think of an *issue* in which you are interested. Local ones are usually better for collecting data. Alternatively, you might list your *interests* and consider if they have an economic dimension which could be researched. It is probably best to choose a narrow topic. If you select a wide area you may get buried in mountains of information. Thus examining the causes of local unemployment may be easier than looking at the national position.

When you have chosen an issue, you could examine how the issue affects different people, firms and organizations. Questions such as the following could be posed to stimulate ideas for research:

who is affected?

how are they affected?

what is their economic interest?

what are they doing?

can you contact them?

EXAMPLES: FROM THE MIDLAND EXAMINING GROUP'S SYLLABUS

1 Using local newspapers, do a survey of second-hand cars. What factors do advertisers consider important to stress? What factors do you consider determine the prices of second-hand cars?

2 A local study of part of a town, a village or the area around the school classifying business functions and types and explaining their presence and importance to the community.

3 A diary following an economic issue, using cuttings and with comments, e.g. a wage claim, factory closure.

4 A survey of local house prices. Explanation of the factors which influence supply, demand and price.

5 The Local Authority Budget. Briefly consider how the Authority finances and spends its budget and comment on its priorities. Take a sample of people in your neighbourhood (e.g. wage-earner, unemployed worker, pensioner) and evaluate the effects of the budget on individuals.

6 Study of a local firm/industry following a visit and explaining its locational features, importance to the local/national economy.

7 Shopping basket survey. Take a sample of ten well-known branded items and cost them in a local small shop, a voluntary retail chain and a national supermarket. Record and comment on the results.

8 Work out the costs of running a freezer taking all aspects into consideration.

9 Record, present and comment on the movement in prices of some commodity, e.g. livestock, gold, coffee, over a three-month period.

10 Survey the prices of some fruits, vegetables and fish in a local market over the summer term. Account for the variations in price of similar items.

The Midland Examining Group — An actual example in detail

Study of a local extractive or manufacturing industry: its importance to the local/national economy

In this unit of work, candidates are advised to undertake a study of a local extractive or manufacturing firm/industry and make a reasoned assessment of its importance to the local and national economy.

The following outline is intended to give only general guidance and is not prescriptive. Clearly the emphasis will vary according to the nature of the local industrial environment and candidates should be encouraged to pursue any particularly relevant issue which emerges.

Possible areas to be investigated

(It is not intended that this list should be followed in its entirety and it may vary according to local emphasis.)

1 Locational influences.

2 Numbers of employees/nature of employment/area of recruitment.

3 Organization and ownership of firms.

4 Production methods—division of labour.

5 Interdependence—(a) sources of supply of materials (local, national, international)

(b) sources of supply of services, e.g. transport, banking, advertising (local, national, international).

6 Markets—local, national, international.

7 Incentives to work—recruitment and training

—wage levels, incentives, holidays, etc.

—working conditions

—company provided benefits and facilities

—communications and decision-making within the firm; industrial democracy

—trade union organization.

8 Other costs and benefits to the local community—pollution, relationships with local community.

9 Influence of local and central government.

10 Recent trends in output, employment and prices.

GENERAL GUIDANCE

Coursework projects

The objective of this form of assessment is to provide a means for students to demonstrate the ability to identify (and select in some schemes) an economic issue, collect data of a relevant nature, analyse that data, draw conclusions and present findings in an appropriate form. A little may be given to all candidates or there may be a free choice (see syllabus analysis).

The project may take the form of a **hypothesis** (statement) which needs testing by the collection of evidence, e.g. 'A quiet revolution is occurring in where we shop and how we pay. This trend is one that can only benefit the customer.' The evidence could be assembled by fieldwork, conducting surveys and by examining published sources (i.e. books, newspapers). The time available might be prescribed by the Board.

GCSE projects may be local in emphasis, reflecting the requirement of relevant and practical involvement in the immediate economic environment. This contrasts with a lot of old-fashioned project work which was based on extracting information from secondary sources such as library books.

For example, the Southern Examining Group requires two items of coursework designed to emphasize the research and data-handling skills. A certain amount of teacher guidance in the selection of assignment is to be allowed. In addition, teachers may brief candidates on source material and give advice when problems arise, as long as records of such assistance are kept.

The **presentation** of a project requires a clear and logical format. The exam boards usually provide suitable instructions. An acceptable structure might be, (**a**) title, (**b**) list of contents, (**c**) introduction: explaining the purpose of the project, (**d**) investigation: the collection of data, (**e**) analysis of the data, (**f**) presentation of results and conclusions, (**g**) bibliography. The work usually must be submitted in a written form in a file or folder. Each examination board lays down guidance on word length.

Authentication of a project is also necessary. The project should be the candidate's own work, although teachers can advise on choice of topic and give general guidance on approach and sources of information. In addition, copied material from books, etc., must be acknowledged and failure to do so may lead a candidate to be accused of deliberate deception and thus disqualified. Any candidate who is suspected of unfair practices during the coursework may similarly be disqualified.

The **assessment** of projects will be by teachers in the first instance but subject to external moderation. Within the overall assessment objectives certain levels of performance will need to be identified and marked. These are specified in the following example.

Example of an individual study

Title set: 'The people of South Yorkshire need a subsidized bus service'. Discuss.

Candidates were introduced to the very controversial issue of local transport policy via press cuttings. Having created an awareness of the meaning of rates, subsidies, implications for local people, alternate sources of revenue, alternative areas of spending etc., candidates were then set the above title.

A worksheet was designed to give guidance on how to approach the problem, the method of enquiry, the interpretation/analysis of data and the formation of judgements. In this framework it was hoped to provide structured guidance yet allow for individual initiative.

Buses: it's make your mind up time

UNLESS South Yorkshire councillors can find a last-minute legal loophole, they must increase bus fares by an average of 75 per cent on Tuesday—the first rise for seven years.

If they do not, their legal advisors have told them, they face the risk of huge surcharges and disqualification from public office.

That's bad news for them, and it's bad news for anyone else who uses the buses in South Yorkshire at all regularly.

For, although higher fares could save you between £5 and £30 on your rates, depending on the size of your house, your bus fare bill could increase by anything up to £120 a year.

The people who will gain from a fares rise are industry and commerce, with their savings ranging from around £100 for the city centre shopkeeper to around £10,000 for a big Sheffield steelworks.

Transport officials are insisting on the fares increases after hearing that they must run the buses 'according to business principles' to comply with the law.

This is how the fares package affects you:

ADULTS: An initial fare rise averaging 75 per cent, which would bring in up to £11 million in a year. But South Yorkshire's average fare would still be easily the cheapest in Britain—12p, compared with 20p in West Midlands and 36p in West Yorkshire.

Couple, two children, husband drives to work

Present fares: £32 p.a.
Proposed fares: £58 p.a.

Couple, two children husband uses bus, others travel by car

Present fares: £140 p.a.
Proposed fares: £260 p.a.

Working couple, two children, no car

Present fares: £139 p.a.
Proposed fares: £250 p.a.

RATES: What a 75pc fare rise would save you a year

Your rateable value	Property	How much your rates would subsidise buses		
		No fare rise		75 pc fare rise
£50	Terrace	£15		£10
£130	Semi-det.	£39		£25
£200	Detached	£60		£39
£300	Large detached	£90		£58
£1,000	High St. shop	£301		£195
£12,000	Supermarket	£3,606		£2,336
£75,000	Large office block	£22,553		£14,603
£98,000	Large industry	£28,866		£18,691

CHILDREN: Existing fares doubled to 4p for up to seven miles, 8p for up to 12 miles, 12p up to 22 miles, and 16p above that, bringing in £700,000.

PENSIONERS would still travel free at off-peak times, because this is allowed by law.

SHEFFIELD'S City Clipper and Early Bird services, and Doncaster Inner Circle route, currently free, would have a flat fare of 5p for both adults and children, bringing in £75,000 a year.

TRAIN fares on local lines between Sheffield and Kiveton Park, Thorne and Darton would also go up by 75 per cent, bringing in £500,000.

SERVICES would be cut by $2\frac{1}{2}$ million miles a year because higher fares would mean a loss of passengers, saving £1$\frac{1}{2}$ million.

WHAT NEXT? There would be another increase in fares later in the year; its size would depend on how many passengers were lost by the first increase.

Further fare increases would follow year by year until it reached the stage where further rises would actually reduce the PTE's income, because they would reduce the number of passengers.

Children's fares would be increased progressively to half the adult fare.

Pros and cons of cheap fares

ALTERNATIVELY, the council could plump for an immediate 120 per cent increase bringing in an extra £1 million, but there would be 'a substantial loss of passengers'.

The vast majority of people benefit financially from cheap fares. What they save in fares more than makes up for the extra they pay in rates.

Families in low-income brackets benefit proportionately more than the better-off because they pay lower rates.

But car-owners also benefit because the roads are less congested. And we all benefit because expensive road-building schemes are less necessary. Sheffield is one of the few major cities in Britain without a traffic problem or an urban motorway.

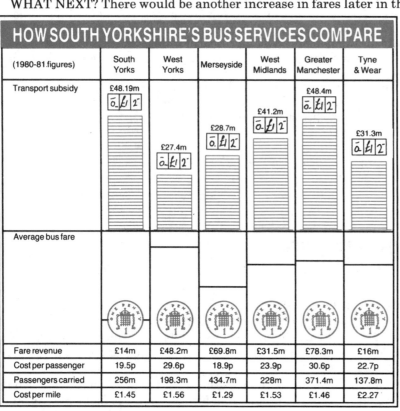

HOW SOUTH YORKSHIRE'S BUS SERVICES COMPARE

(1980-81 figures)	South Yorks	West Yorks	Merseyside	West Midlands	Greater Manchester	Tyne & Wear
Transport subsidy	£48.19m	£27.4m	£28.7m	£41.2m	£48.4m	£31.3m
Average bus fare						
Fare revenue	£14m	£48.2m	£69.8m	£31.5m	£78.3m	£16m
Cost per passenger	19.5p	29.6p	18.9p	23.9p	30.6p	22.7p
Passengers carried	256m	198.3m	434.7m	228m	371.4m	137.8m
Cost per mile	£1.45	£1.56	£1.29	£1.53	£1.46	£2.27

But someone has to foot the bill for cheap fares, and that someone is industry and commerce, who between them pay half the county's rates.

The cost of subsidizing transport can cost a large firm £20,000 a year—money that cannot be spent on wages or investment.

A small shopkeeper can be paying £200 a year towards cheap travel through his rates, and that helps put up the prices of goods in his shop.

Transport officials concede that 'at a time of economic recession most firms are operating at reduced levels. The burden of rate increases are more difficult to absorb than during a period of expansion.

'There is a more direct impact on the profitability and even survival for firms and hence the employment levels in the private sector at large.'

Source: *Morning Telegraph and Star*

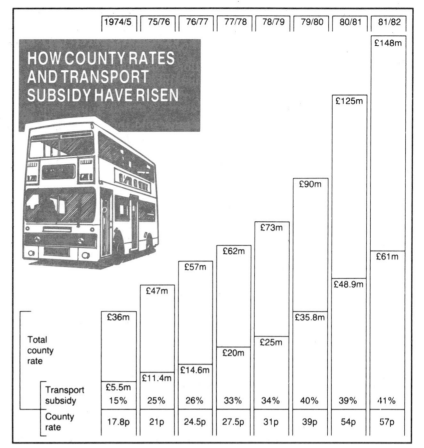

	1974/5	75/76	76/77	77/78	78/79	79/80	80/81	81/82
Total county rate	£36m	£47m	£57m	£62m	£73m	£90m	£125m	£148m
Transport subsidy	£5.5m 15%	£11.4m 25%	£14.6m 26%	£20m 33%	£25m 34%	£35.8m 40%	£48.9m 39%	£61m 41%
County rate	17.8p	21p	24.5p	27.5p	31p	39p	54p	57p

HOW COUNTY RATES AND TRANSPORT SUBSIDY HAVE RISEN

Your first problem is to decide the needs of South Yorkshire by talking to the people of this area.

1 What groups of people will be interested in the bus service in South Yorkshire?

2 Devise a question sheet of no more than 10 questions which you can ask these people. You are trying to find information on how often they use buses, what time of day, how much they pay, what they may expect to pay, the frequency of buses, comfort and convenience, any improvements they would make.

Question Sheet

1 _____

2 _____

3 _____

4 _____

5 _____

6 _____

7 _____

8 _____

9 _____

10 _____

3 Interview three people from each of your groups in question 1.

4 You now have information on what different groups of people believe is needed plus the information from the newspaper article. These are some possibilities:
(a) Buses should be provided free.
(b) Buses should be subsidized as at present.
(c) Buses should be run to make a profit.

5 Write your study drawing conclusions about each of the following.
(a) What people need.
(b) Who has to pay—passengers or ratepayers?
(c) Who gains and loses under each system?
(d) Any effects on employment.
(e) Any effects on road use and traffic levels.
(f) Other effects e.g. on shopping in town.
(g) Other uses of money raised by the rates.

Assessment

For example, if the **objectives** of coursework are:

1 To understand and apply knowledge of economic terminology, concepts and theories in verbal, numerical and graphical form (10 marks).
2 To select, analyse and interpret data (20 marks).
3 To make and communicate reasoned judgements (10).

Then the **detailed marking criteria** might be

OBJECTIVE 1

0–1 marks. Little (or no) evidence of the use of economic knowledge relevant to the research aim. Little (or no) illustration of the knowledge by reference to the data.

2–4 marks. Slight evidence of relevant knowledge with some application to the aim. Some limited use of an appropriate format but not well applied.

5–7 marks. Useful and appropriate application of economic terminology, concepts and theories relevant to the aim. An attempt to apply and convert information into relevant forms of communication where appropriate.

8–10 marks. Considerable evidence of thorough application of terminology, concepts and theories to the research aim. Materials fully and clearly explained with a range of appropriate presentational skills being demonstrated.

OBJECTIVE 2

0–5 marks. Little (or no) relevant data and a tendency to make unsupported generalizations. Little (or no) explanation of data and little (or no) application of the data to the research aim.

6–10 marks. A limited amount of relevant data, with some evidence of selection. A reasonable attempt to break down the material into an order with some planning of the sequences. A spasmodic attempt to apply the data to the research aim.

11–15 marks. Substantial data presented largely relevantly. A well-ordered selection with ideas and techniques applied to the research aim.

16–20 marks. A wide range of data applied relevantly to the aim. Data presented logically with salient features highlighted. A clear analysis of the problem with accurate explanations.

OBJECTIVE 3

0–1 marks. Unsubstantiated (or no) arguments with statements unsupported or generalized. Uncritical use of the work of others and occasional contradictions.

2–4 marks. Simple statements with judgements which are secondhand or invalid. Little use of data to infer conclusions and some use of the opinions of others.

5–7 marks. Some ability to critically examine arguments and evidence. Some valid judgements based on clear reasoning and data. Distinct capability in applying judgements to problems.

8–10 marks. Well-established coherent argument with valid judgement. Data used clearly and often to substantiate judgement. Can differentiate between well-supported argument and a statement of opinion. Some originality in solutions and judgements.

24 LAST MINUTE HELP

The amount of **revision** done on examination day depends on the thoroughness with which you have prepared yourself for the examination and the time of day when the examination is sat. If the examination is in the **morning** there will be little time for revision, anyway. If the examination is in the **afternoon** then some time might be usefully spent revising in the morning. This is particularly necessary if you have done less than six hours in total, because you will not have covered enough of the syllabus adequately. In this case last-minute revision will be useful, although you should probably not do more than two hours. This will give you enough time to have a substantial break before the afternoon session, so that you can start the examination in a fresh state of mind. The message with regard to last-minute revision is therefore—do sufficient to reduce your worries but not too much that you are mentally exhausted.

Half an hour before the examination you should check your equipment to make sure that it is working. Always have a spare pen and pencil available. It is often a good idea to get physically prepared by going to the toilet!

On receiving the paper, **read the questions carefully** and check the **rubric** (instructions on the number of questions to answer). Some examinations allow reading time, usually ten minutes. When you have a choice of questions, **tick** those which you know something about. Then answer the question which you think you know **most** about first. After that, decide the order in which you are going to tackle the other questions.

It is usually advisable to **divide your time** equally between the questions. On a typical GCSE paper there may be 5 questions to answer in $2\frac{1}{2}$ hours. This means 5 essays of roughly 30 minutes each. In general, try to leave 5 minutes at the end for reading through your answers.

If it is possible, start each question, particularly essays, on a **separate sheet of paper**. This enables you to return to a question if you have some spare time at the end and possibly add extra information.

Try to write **legibly**—it helps the examiner and YOU! Markers aim to give credit for information. Thus neat writing enables them to spot the points more easily. You should write down as much as you can in the time available as it will increase your chances of passing. However, in doing so make your information relevant to the question set.

INDEX